A Shot in the Dark

Keepsake DIAMONDS
Shyer's
BULOVA WATCHES
Coca-Cola
WEINSTEIN CO.
TENNESSEE
Jewelers
HAMBURGERS
JEWELRY CO.
LOEWS
TENNESSEE STATE FAIR
SEPT
21 26

A Shot in the Dark

MAKING RECORDS IN NASHVILLE, 1945–1955

Martin Hawkins

Vanderbilt University Press
& Country Music Foundation Press
NASHVILLE

This book is for everyone who thinks,
"That looks interesting";
for Jennifer, who helped me take the time;
and for my own peace of mind.
I hope we all decide it was worthwhile.

First Edition 2006
Published by Vanderbilt University Press
and the Country Music Foundation Press

10 09 08 07 06 1 2 3 4 5

Printed on acid-free paper
Manufactured in the United States of America
Text design by Dariel Mayer

Library of Congress Cataloging-in-Publication Data

Hawkins, Martin.
A shot in the dark : making records in Nashville 1945–1955 /
Martin Hawkins.—1st ed.
p. cm.
Includes bibliographical references and index.
ISBN 0-8265-1532-0 (cloth : alk. paper)
1. Sound recording industry—Tennessee—Nashville—History.
2. Popular music—History and criticism. I. Title.
ML3790.H387 2006
781.6409768'55—dc22
2006003517

Contents

Aerial shot of downtown Nashville, 1940, looking north. Courtesy of Metropolitan Nashville Government Archives.

Introduction

This book has its origins in the Forrest Acres Drive living room of the late Jim Bulleit, where Colin Escott and I visited in Nashville in 1973 to interview Jim for a book about Sun Records of Memphis. Jim was an early investor in Sun and acted as their first promotion man. Sun's subsequent owner, Shelby Singleton, suggested we go see Jim, and he kindly made an employee available to drive us—we were riding the Greyhounds in those days.

Jim looked a little uneasy as two travel-worn Englishmen in their early twenties, slightly long-haired and dressed in black despite the summer heat, stepped out of the beaten-up car of Shelby's black employee. Perhaps Forrest Acres didn't get too many visitors like us.

Once he was satisfied that we were on the level, Jim proceeded to tell us his part in setting up Sun Records. He continually veered off into the Jim Bulleit story, which, looking back, he must have thought we should have found more interesting.

Jim was sixty-five years old then, semi-retired, and long out of the record business. But his sharpness of thought and likable amiability hinted at the pioneer spirit that had fed so many of his endeavors over the years. This was the man who had studied classical music in the Midwest, played drums in variety shows in Germany, sold radio airtime to anyone who would take it, announced radio programs all over the country, and one day in 1945 hit on the idea of making and selling records in Nashville.

By the time Colin's and my book was published in March 1975, Colin had moved into the record business in Canada, and I had a job in health management. We both continued to write about 1940s and 1950s music, compiling LP reissues of the blues, jazz, country, and rock & roll we had been interested in since we started comparing record collections at grammar school in England in the early 1960s. As students of English and history, I guess we both thought the transition to writing about the old records we liked was pretty natural, if not inevitable.

In the spring of 1975, I decided that it would be an interesting spare-time activity to write a book about the pioneering record companies of Nashville. People seemed to write about the north-central Tennessee city only in terms of the promotional hype of the day about country music, or about the stereotypes of the Grand Ole Opry. As a record collector who had scoured the basements and attics of record distributors across the South, I was more interested in knowing about Tennessee and Republic Records, Nashboro, Hickory, Speed, and the other labels that I knew sprang up in Nashville in the decade after World War II. The earliest of these was Bullet Records, partly Jim Bulleit's company, and that was obviously the place to start. Bullet's logo had featured a bullet speeding toward a target above the commendably hopeful, if not always accurate, legend "Always a Smash Hit." Initially, Bullet was more a shot in the dark. Yet, within ten years there was a thriving recording industry in Nashville.

My three further visits to Jim Bulleit, and numerous telephone calls, became part of a concerted program of research with people who had owned or been involved with record labels in Nashville, people such as Reynold and Alan Bubis, who had gone into the liquor and real estate business; Murray Nash, then working with the post office; pressing-plant owners and distributors such as John Dunn and Hutch Carlock; and other even less-sung heroes of the days of 78-rpm. I focused on the research with a fierceness that made me cut short an interview with country legend Lefty Frizzell at the ABC Records office because I had to go meet Howard Allison of Bullet and Tennessee Records, who then ran Ernie's Record Mart in Nashville; and when I went into a Music Row office to meet pianist Roy Hall, I told Waylon Jennings, who directed me down the corridor in a bemused fashion that indicated he expected me to ask him for an interview, that I would really like to talk to him but couldn't right then.

There were stranger diversions still. As I arrived to meet Reynold Bubis, one of the former partners in Tennessee Records, at his liquor store, someone came running out announcing, "He's been shot." In the seconds it took me to consider what part of town I was in, and whether I should run inside or outside, I realized that a woman was talking to me: Reynold would still see me, I gleaned, but Ronald Reagan had been shot and Reynold would be keeping the radio on while I spoke to him.

As the interviews progressed, it became clear that Bill Beasley was an unsung hero of the piece—or a villain, as some people preferred to describe him. Second only to Jim Bulleit among the main recording pioneers, Bill had an innovative idea to match any situation. As recording director of the Tennessee/Jamboree/Republic group of labels and later, he managed to upset the musicians' union, the IRS, and most influential interests in between. Nevertheless he welcomed me openly when we met in 1974 and said he wanted to help; I should contact him anytime. Then he disappeared. When I eventually unearthed him in 1981 at a video business in Florida, he said: "So you tracked me down at last, then. Well, we'd better get on with this; you've wasted enough time." Bill wanted to tell me about how Nashville couldn't recognize a pioneer when it saw one. Years later when I needed to track Bill down again, I found him in Texas, aged seventy-two and in bad health. He spoke again at length about the early days of recording in Nashville, his memory clear and his opinions forceful. The indie recordman's eye for the main chance was still there, too. Bill talked about getting back into the record business—we would be partners; he had a stack of ideas. Within months, he was dead.

Alan Bubis, who spoke to me many times over the years, put me in touch with one of Tennessee Records' employees, Ted Jarrett, the first black record producer and arranger in Nashville. Ted told me his life story twenty years ago, unfolding a fascinating world of gospel and R&B music, recalling the venues, musicians, recordings, hopes, and dreams. He led me to several other colleagues from those days, among them the queen of local blues singers, Christine Kittrell, who told me her story, invited me to stay at her house, sang a beautiful rendition of "Happy Birthday" over the phone when I turned fifty, and put me in touch with many others in the old R&B scene.

My work had started from an interest in collecting blues, folk, hillbilly, and jazz discs, but as it developed I became increasingly aware of Nashville's popular musicians and gospel singers. Contact with some of them, as well as the various proprietors of the record labels, helped me appreciate the wider complexity of the story I had set out, so innocently, to tell.

Nashville is a city of some half million residents, and around ten million annual visitors, many of whom are lured by the trappings associated with the music business. It is one of those towns that has acquired the mantle or myth of being a particular type of place, famous for country music in the way that other places symbolize coal mining or steel products or jazz. Often the tourism and civic promotion industries start to appreciate that key characteristic just when there is no longer any coal or steel or whatever left, and often they simplify history and discard much of it along the way.

I think the standard Nashville music story ignores much

of what went on in the city before the Nashville Sound was born in the late 1950s. The standard version follows the rise of WSM's Grand Ole Opry show and of star performers like Roy Acuff, Eddy Arnold, and Hank Williams, and describes the development of Music Row by the major record companies. It tells of the crafting of the Nashville Sound and country music's successful invasion of the middle ground of U.S. music. But the standard story leaves out the local origins of the Nashville music business in the ten years after World War II, and it neglects a large part of the city's music scene: Country music was far from the only music played in Nashville. In 1945, as the war ended, the town that would become Music City, USA, had no dedicated recording studios, no career session men, no record companies, and only one or two music publishers. As late as 1946, Los Angeles, Atlanta, Cincinnati, and especially Chicago were the hubs of the folk, hillbilly, and western music business. WSM's role in Nashville's musical growth can't be understated, but it tends to obscure the influence of another local high-megawatt station, WLAC, in fostering an altogether different Nashville Sound. At night, WLAC's R&B programming blanketed the eastern United States, laying the groundwork for a thriving black music recording scene in Nashville.

By the mid-1950s, most of the major national recording companies were well represented in Nashville. During the preceding ten years, though, the only locally grounded record firms were a handful of independent labels. While the majors saw Nashville mainly in terms of country music, the independent labels delved into the local wells of the pop and jazz bands, black and white gospel music, blues and R&B as well. In other words, apart from classical music, they reflected the Nashville music scene as it really was.

Nashville's independent labels issued more than 1,500 records between 1946 and 1955. Depending on your definition, some 35 percent of these were folk, hillbilly, or western music—country music, as it was becoming known. About 25 percent were popular, dance-band, or jazz music. Another 25 percent were gospel music, and around 15 percent were blues or R&B.

This book documents that vital decade, which saw the rise of Nashville as a viable recording center. It is the story of Nashville's musical development from the point of view of the Nashvillians and Nashville-based businesses and performers who were in at the beginning—those who helped provide the impetus, the continuity, and the outrageous stories that contributed to Nashville's growth as a music town. Two events that barely rated a mention at the time bracket the story: in December 1945 Bullet Records cut its first session, and in January 1956 Elvis Presley came to Nashville to make his first recordings for RCA, among them, "Heartbreak Hotel."

The focus here is on the local heroes and local labels that laid the groundwork for so much of what would happen in the years ahead. The record labels profiled were all based in Nashville or its immediate vicinity, run by a few influential, optimistic entrepreneurs who shared the freewheeling, outlaw mentality of the independent music business. Some were dreamers, some were realists, and some just aimed to capitalize on the music enterprise's reputation for quick profits. Largely forgotten today, the little labels like Bullet, Nashboro, Tennessee, and Republic helped make "Nashville" synonymous with "music." They gave many big artists their all-important first break, from Chet Atkins to B. B. King to Pat Boone. They built the foundations on which Nashville's fabled music business grew. And they accounted for several national hits—when "Near You" on Bullet Records showed up on every trade chart as the biggest-selling pop record of 1947, anything must have seemed possible.

Martin Hawkins
Maidstone, England
April 2006

Lower Broadway, between Fourth and First Avenues North, 1947. Courtesy of Showtime Archives [Toronto] and Colin Escott.

1

Walking Down Broad Street

It was 1945 and I was a booking agent, working in Nashville. One day I was walking down Broad Street with a feller named Wally Fowler, a gospel singer. Out of the blue, he turned and asked, "Jim, how would you like to go into the record business?" He took me into a store on Broad called Hermitage Music to meet a man named C. V. Hitchcock. He said, "Mr. Hitchcock thinks we can make a go of recording." We talked for about fifteen to twenty minutes, and when I got out of the store I was in the record business.

—Jim Bulleit

When Jim Bulleit met C. V. Hitchcock, he was immediately hooked on the notion of making records, but it was some weeks before he figured out how to go about it: "It had never been done in Nashville. Bullet Records were the first to record the music here in town, to manufacture it with 'Nashville' on the label, to promote it, distribute it, really sell it as a Nashville product."

After two years as a radio announcer for WSM, Bulleit had recently branched out on his own as promotion agent for a number of folk and hillbilly musicians and had an office on Seventh Avenue North downtown. Wally Fowler, with an office in the same building, was a singer, songwriter, and music publisher who straddled the thin line between hillbilly folk music and white gospel song. On the day in November 1945 that Fowler would ask his question, the two men had lunch at George Linebaugh's restaurant on Broadway, which the locals called Broad Street. Fowler was trying to sell Bulleit on the notion of making recordings of his group, the Georgia Clodhoppers, and other WSM radio performers.

Heading back to work, they walked west on Broadway away from the Cumberland River. To the south, at their left, residential streets soon gave way to the city's low-rent commercial area extending out to the feed mills that exuded a heavy odor of cottonseed oil on warm, still nights. To their right, prosperous shopping, business, and government districts stretched to the state capitol that commanded the hilltop. Beyond the capitol in North Nashville, lived most of the city's black population, focused on Jefferson Street and extending into land enclosed by a bend in the Cumberland. To the west, Broadway led out toward a residential section more prestigious than others east of the river.

Bulleit and Fowler walked past Phillips & Quarles Hardware, and Wolf & Company secondhand furniture, H. G. Hill and Company grocers and Southern Automatic Music Company, vending machine suppliers. Ace Music Vendors was opposite at 416 Broadway, close by the Bell Café, later famous as Tootsie's Orchid Lounge, with its back-alley connection to the Ryman Auditorium. The two men stood talking outside Hermitage Music, a purveyor of jukeboxes and coin machines at 423 Broadway, when Fowler asked Bulleit about going into the record business.

Nashville in 1945 had plenty of live music, three radio stations—WSM, WLAC, and WSIX—and seven sheet-music dealers, most of whom also dealt in phonographs, jukeboxes, and other "amusements." The city was home to extensive government, religious, commercial, banking, and insurance enterprises and a radio barn dance broadcast from the Ryman Auditorium, WSM's Grand Ole Opry, less revered

Jim Bulleit, 1944. Courtesy of Robert Ikard.

(Above): Driving up Broad Street, 1948. Courtesy of Metropolitan Nashville Government Archives.

(Right): The Broadway premises of Hermitage Music and Bullet Records, 1950s. Courtesy of the Nashville Public Library, the Nashville Room.

in its hometown than by its listeners across the country. But Nashville had no record companies and no apparent desire for one.

From Nashborough to Nashville

Frenchman Charles Charleville's trading post, established around 1710, drew the first settlers to what would become Fort Nashborough—and later, Nashville—named in honor of Revolutionary War hero General Francis Nash.

The population had mushroomed to 76,000 by 1890 and to 167,000 by 1940, of whom 99 percent were U.S. born and about a quarter of black African origin. By 1945, Nashville had been the permanent capital of Tennessee government for just over a century and had supplied the nation with two presidents: local lawyer, war hero, and politician Andrew Jackson in 1828, and James Polk, another Nashville-based lawyer and congressman, in 1844.

By the mid–twentieth century, the city had more than lived up to its then fifty-year-old reputation as the Athens of the South, with a replica of the Parthenon erected for the Tennessee Centennial in 1897 and eleven higher-education establishments, from Fisk University, formed in 1866, and Vanderbilt University, established in 1873, to Meharry Medical College, founded in 1876, and Lipscomb College, opened in 1891 as the Nashville Bible School.

For a time in the 1920s, Nashville could claim not only to be the Athens of the South but also to include the Wall Street of the South, Union Street. What boosters described as "the advantageous business climate" drew many commercial enterprises to the town at this time. A prototype shopping mall, the Arcade, had opened in 1903, and a year later Nashville had its first "skyscraper," a twelve-story building on the southeast corner of Church Street and Fourth Avenue

Church Street, central downtown Nashville, 1930. Courtesy of the Nashville Public Library, the Nashville Room.

North. Louis Buckley, later a record distributor, arrived in the city during the first decades after the war along with many others who would be in on the ground floor of Nashville's music business. He got "off the train, and a Red Cap tried to take my bag. I told him to get his hands off. I was so raw, I asked a policeman which way to the Arcade, where I was to meet someone. He told me, but the truth is I didn't know what an arcade was." As Jim Denny, a boy from the country who would become a major promoter and music publisher, later told the *Tennessean,* he arrived "alone, broke and scared. Even the streetcars scared me. Four people standing together looked like a mob."

With the onset of World War II, many of Nashville's businesses were converted to the war effort. The Aviation Manufacturing Corporation of California set up the Vultee Aircraft Plant in Nashville, and soon there were seven thousand workers in Nashville making bombers. The Army Air Classification Center at Thompson Lane was busy processing recruits for military service, and the Nashville area became a focal point of military activity, with airfields at Smyrna, Tennessee, Camp Campbell near Clarksville, and Camp Forrest at Tullahoma. It was estimated that around one million servicemen visited Nashville on leave in 1942 alone.

Pianist Johnny Maddox, who in the early 1940s lived thirty miles north of Nashville in Gallatin, told me that during the war:

> All of middle Tennessee was just loaded with thousands of soldiers. Mostly they were northern soldiers, and up to then no one had much love for people from the North. The war was really when attitudes started to change. My mother would send me out to bring soldiers back for dinner, a lot of families did that. The Third Army was there, just up the road from Gallatin, from 1942 to 1945. They did maneuvers and built a pontoon bridge up here across the Cumberland River, where there wasn't one before.

The *Nashville Banner* carried a picture of young Alan Bubis, one of Nashville's earliest record men, off to flying school in Florida. The *Globe* reported in February 1945 that Robert Evans was in the U.S. Navy, stationed "somewhere in the Pacific." He had sung with the Fairfield Four Juniors gospel quartet and "now sings in a group, 'The Five Strings of Harmony' in the South Pacific." A year later, the *Globe* reported that Nashville musician William Ellington, graduate of Pearl High School and sax lead in a "Stateside Swing Band," was playing in a former German government office, "now an entertainment venue for occupying troops."

Maddox's main contact with the army was in the many

New recruits undergoing Air Force Classification take time out at a weekend YMCA dance, July 1942. Courtesy of the *Tennessean.*

clubs that sprang up around the service camps. "I played every night for soldiers, all the wartime music. Sometimes at the camps, and other times at clubs like the Plantation Club out on Murfreesboro Road." A number of new clubs opened in Nashville as the war drew to a close. The *Globe* reported, in November 1944, the "grand opening of the Casa Blanca Club" at 428 Fifth Avenue North. The Five Bars and other radio stars from local radio station WSIX would be there in "the beautiful Egyptian Café." "As Time Goes By," the advertisement recommended, "spend it here."

By 1945, Nashville had six major banks and 180 insurance companies. Some three hundred manufacturers turned out rayon, cellophane, clothing, agricultural goods, and furniture. The city had twenty-seven book publishers, many specialized in religious books, following the lead of the city's first major religious publishing enterprise, the Methodist Publishing House, founded in 1854. Twenty-three denominations now occupied 358 churches; what had once been the Union Gospel Tabernacle, built by Thomas Ryman and opened in 1892, was now the Ryman Auditorium. Two daily papers—the *Tennessean* and the *Nashville Banner*—carried the V-J Day headlines, along with one Sunday paper and four weeklies, including the *Nashville Globe and Independent: The Progressive Journal of the New South.*

Nashville's Early Music and Musicians

Perhaps the earliest account of musical activity in Nashville comes from a shipping statement dated 1780, when an order of Jew's harps was put on a riverboat from St Louis to provide music for a wedding. By the 1820s, writer F. G. Davenport could declare: "There was not a city in the U.S. of equal size that showed as much interest in music as Nashville." Davenport observed that "organ, flute, violin, harp, and piano concerts were well-attended" and that "minstrel melodies" were popular. The same decade saw one of the first music books published in Nashville, *Western Harmony,* a collection of hymns and singing instruction. Sixty years later, the city had thirty music teachers, five piano tuners, and three purveyors of musical instruments. In 1849, Nashville hosted six grand-opera concerts and a recital by Maurice Strakosch, pianist to the emperor of Russia, and Rachmaninoff and Caruso played the Ryman Auditorium many decades before it became the Grand Ole Opry house.

In 1902, eight musicians chartered Local 257 of the American Federation of Musicians, which grew to some 120 members by the early 1920s under Robert Payne, saxophonist and pianist, who ran the union for thirty-five years before bass player George Cooper took over in 1937; Cooper headed the group for the next thirty-six years. He would preside over a dramatic expansion in the early 1950s, when black musicians were first accepted, along with rising numbers of country pickers, and by the end of that decade Local 257 had more than seven hundred members.

In the early part of the twentieth century, Nashville's music venues included the Ryman, along with the Masonic and the Vendome, home to the Nashville Symphony Orchestra beginning in 1904. The expanding number of theaters, all with pit space for decent-sized orchestras, encouraged musicians to come to Nashville. Between 1907 and 1908 a num-

Inside the Club Del Morocco, 1944. Courtesy of Theodore Acklen, Jr.

ber of movie theaters opened on Fifth Avenue North between Church and Union Streets. The Dixie, Crescent, Crystal, and Alhambra were soon followed by the Capitol and the Princess, which by 1917 had its own orchestra for vaudeville shows. The Bijou Theater opened in 1904 on the site of the old Adelphi Theater at 423 Fourth Avenue North, where Jenny Lind, the "Swedish Nightingale," had sung in 1851. The Bijou closed in the face of competition from the movie houses but reopened in 1916 and became a showplace for black performers and black patrons, especially after 1921, when one of its owners, Milton Starr, became the first president of the national Theater Owners Booking Association. The Bijou became a major stop on the black theater circuit, attracting virtually every recording star and touring show, from the "Empress of the Blues," Bessie Smith, on down.

The Rise of Radio

In the 1920s, Nashville joined many other towns in embracing the new entertainment medium of radio. Nearly seven hundred entrepreneurs nationwide applied for licenses to broadcast in the three years after station KDKA was first established in Pittsburgh in 1920.

Nashville's first broadcasts hit the airwaves between 1922 and 1924, but the earliest stations in the town were strictly limited in their scope. The first, WDAA, licensed by the Department of Commerce in May 1922 to Ward-Belmont School, enabled music teacher G. S. deLuca to help sixteen year old boy scout leader and amateur radio enthusiast, Jack DeWitt, to broadcast records by Enrico Caruso from the school to the River and Rail Terminal on Broad Street. In

The Bijou Theater, early 1900s. Courtesy of the Nashville Public Library, the Nashville Room.

November 1923, a license was granted to radio WABV, a more ambitious if short-lived experiment by Jack DeWitt. In March the next year, WCBQ was set up by the First Baptist Church, and in October John Cain launched WEBX to promote the Cain-Sloan store in Nashville. The commercial potential of radio was seen by another store owner, L. N. Smith, in September 1925, and he launched WDAD from a studio in his Dad's Radio Supply Store on Eighth Avenue North. The following year, WBAW was formed by Braid Electrical Services, and WSIX was set up in nearby Springfield before moving into the Andrew Jackson Hotel in downtown Nashville.

The stakes were raised considerably in 1925 when the big guns of Nashville's insurance industry became interested in the idea of using radio to promote their services. On September 11, 1925, the Life and Casualty Insurance Company licensed WLAC, then bought half the shares in WDAD before buying that station out altogether and taking over its frequency in 1927. Just a month after WLAC was licensed, the call letters WSM (an acronym for "We Shield Millions") were licensed in October 1925 by the National Life and Accident Insurance Company. Vice-president Edwin Craig was fascinated with radio and he persuaded the board of National Life to install a studio in the company's new buildings on Seventh Avenue North. WSM went on the air with a thousand-watt signal on October 5, 1925. Among the first to send music over its airwaves were the Al Menah Shrine Band, the Fisk Jubilee Singers, Beasley Smith's band from the Andrew Jackson Hotel, and Francis Craig's from the Hermitage Hotel. The station's wattage rose to 5,000 in 1927, when the station joined the new but rather limited NBC network. In 1928 WSM became a clear-channel station, and after 1932, with 50,000 watts, blanketed much of the eastern United States. The station began originating shows out of Nashville for NBC on a regular basis as early as 1935. The pioneering engineer of WDAA, Jack DeWitt, joined WSM early on, supervised its wattage increases, and eventually became president of the company. Although WSM lost money every year for ten years, it quickly became the preeminent radio station in Nashville.

The first official broadcast of the *WSM Barn Dance* came on November 28, 1925, within two months of the station's founding, and again for economic motives: National Life's management believed that a barn-dance format would help pitch insurance to rural communities—and they were right. The *Tennessean* reported in May 1926: "Recently, an announcement was made putting the question of barn dance programs up to the radio public. So far the replies have been very much in favor of continuance of these programs." As the concept developed, listeners would hear the likes of Dr. Bate's Possum Hunters, the Crook Brothers, Uncle Dave Macon, Uncle Jimmy Thompson, and black harmonica player DeFord Bailey, a phenomenal self-taught musician who could play society pop tunes, the folk music of his youth, or the blues of singers like Bessie Smith he saw performing at the Bijou Theater.

At first, WSM broadcast mostly "serious" music and dance bands. The *WSM Barn Dance*, which had been juggled between days and time slots, did not acquire its own regular Saturday-night slot until 1927, and it was billed in the program schedule for January 3, 1928, under a new name: the Grand Ole Opry. Station manager George D. Hay, who had been an announcer on Chicago's WLS and had assisted with the *WLS Barn Dance*, coined the "Opry" tag when he was explaining the difference between the operatic program that listeners had just heard and what was to follow. For several years, the musicians performed the Opry in their Sunday-best suits, and it was only gradually that it took on a hillbilly image and then a western influence. By 1945, the Opry would be a nationally popular program broadcast from the Ryman Auditorium and a platform for stars such as Roy Acuff, Minnie Pearl, and Ernest Tubb.

Bing Crosby, *center*, guesting at the Belle Meade Club, 1943, with Nashville musicians, *from left*, Jack Shook (holding guitar), Beasley Smith, George Cooper (behind Crosby), Owen Bradley, and Farris Coursey. Courtesy of the American Federation of Musicians and Harold Bradley.

Sweet Bands and Swing

The advent of radio led to steady work for popular music bands, and many musicians later active in the local record industry were veterans of that scene, among them bandleaders Vito Pellettieri, Beasley Smith, and Francis Craig. The Nashville-born Pellettieri, a professional violinist with the Nashville Symphony, formed a society dance band that switched to WSM from WCBQ. Pellettieri became WSM's music librarian and later, stage manager at the Grand Ole Opry. With station manager Harry Stone, he packaged the show in fifteen-minute segments and marketed it to sponsors, laying the foundation for its success.

The musical careers and personal lives of Beasley Smith and Francis Craig crossed and recrossed through the years. For a time Vanderbilt University roommates, each led a hotel orchestra that performed on WSM's initial broadcast. Smith had come to Nashville from his hometown, McEwen, Tennessee, as a teenager, spent some time in the army, and doubled as a pianist and dance-band leader from 1923 on. Craig organized his first band while he was at Vanderbilt and in 1925 took up a residency at Nashville's Hermitage Hotel, where he stayed the better part of twenty-two years. When Smith took over the WSM Orchestra in 1933, he hosted *Mr. Smith Goes to Town;* Craig hosted *Sunday Serenade.* NBC eventually broadcast both shows coast-to-coast.

Between 1927 and 1933 the Beasley Smith orchestra toured the country, grooming such well-known swing-era musicians as clarinetist Matty Matlock (later to organize Bob Crosby's Bob Cats), Ray McKinley (a leading big-band drummer with the Dorsey Brothers and Will Bradley), and saxophonist Charlie Barnet. Sidelined by an operation in 1933, Smith disbanded the group and moved to WSM as musical director and to play piano. He wrote or cowrote several tunes for Opry regulars, including "Tennessee Central Number Nine" and "Night Train to Memphis" for Roy Acuff, and he cowrote the pop standards "That Lucky Old Sun" and "The Old Master Painter."

Jimmy Gallagher's Band at the Andrew Jackson Hotel, 1935. Courtesy of the American Federation of Musicians and Harold Bradley.

Meanwhile, Memphis-born Roy Landman, working under the name Snooky Lanson (from the Irving Berlin tune "Snooky-Ookums"), joined Craig's band as vocalist in 1935. After later stints with the Ray Noble Orchestra and during the war with Ted Weems, Lanson returned to Tennessee, where WSM manager Jack Stapp gave him a job on Beasley Smith's pop music show, *Sunday Down South.* In 1949 Lanson recorded "That Lucky Old Sun" at the Ryman Auditorium, and on the strength of that hit song he replaced Frank Sinatra on NBC's *Your Hit Parade.*

Other local bandleaders included saxophonist Jimmy Gallagher, a native Nashvillian, graduate of Vanderbilt, and contemporary of Francis Craig and Beasley Smith—many said his jazz dance band was "the best band in town" in the 1930s. Part of Gallagher's three-hour set at the Wagon Wheel Club or the Andrew Jackson Hotel went out live over WLAC, as did his program *Theater of the Air.* Bandleaders Karl and Clint Garvin, from Clarksville, Tennessee, learned their trade as trumpeter and saxophonist respectively with Francis Craig. Karl played with Joe Venuti and Jack Teagarden in the 1930s, and Clint worked with Louis Prima in New Orleans before he joined his brother with Teagarden. Returning to Nashville in the later 1940s, the Garvin band went all out to play swing jazz. Drummer Paul Broome said: "That was the band I went to play with most often. Karl Garvin was a fine trumpeter and one of the most respected musicians in town."

Nashville had become a mecca for bandleaders and musicians. Charles Nagy led the WLAC radio orchestra on CBS; bandleader Dave Matthews had been a featured soloist with Harry James; Tommy Knowles, Bill Yandle, Tom Hewgley, and Marge Rainey all headed local bands. (Members of Rainey's Rhythmettes were all women.) As guitarist Harold Bradley claimed, in the 1930s and 1940s, "Nashville was a big-band town. . . . We had Phil Harris, Red Hawn [Goldie's uncle], Red McEwen, who I worked a lot with in the early days, and singers like Kitty Kallen and Dinah Shore."

Dinah Shore, who at one time sang with Beasley Smith's band, was the biggest star to come out of Nashville in the swing era. Born in Winchester, Tennessee, in 1916 (her publicity said 1917), Frances Rose Shore arrived in Nashville at age six and later attended Hume-Fogg High School downtown, then Vanderbilt University, where her singing talent won her a fifteen-minute radio spot on WSM with Owen Bradley's band. She always opened with the song "Dinah," and people so often called her by that name that she eventually adopted it legally. After graduation, Shore went to New York's WNEW radio, singing alongside Frank Sinatra. When she joined the Xavier Cugat band and recorded for RCA, and then joined Eddie Cantor's NBC radio show, she became a national star. Starting with "Yes, My Darling Daughter," she had a colossal number of popular chart successes and jukebox favorites, the biggest being "Buttons and Bows." Moving to the West Coast, Shore starred in the popular movies *Thank Your Lucky Stars* and *Follow the Boys* before making a new career in television.

Shore remained loyal to Nashville and Winchester, though, appearing during the 1940s at the Ryman Auditorium and the Franklin County Fair. As the *Banner* reported in 1950:

WSM's Jack Stapp watching Dinah Shore and Beasley Smith work out the fine detail of a radio broadcast, 1943. Courtesy of the American Federation of Musicians and Harold Bradley.

> On her visit to Nashville last year over 5,000 people were at the airport to greet Dinah. She so appreciated it that she wanted to do something in return. She went home and found a song that had been prepared for a show that was never produced—"Dear Hearts and Gentle People"—and she recorded it and sent it to Nashville DJs to play for her hometown folks.

The Black Band Scene

Drummer Paul Broome described the 1930s in Nashville as

> a time when people danced, when jazz was still focused on the dance halls and clubs. Nashville was a club town in those days, a town of both private and public clubs, a quasi-speakeasy kind of place where people loved to go out and celebrate in a quasi-legal way. The bands thrived in that atmosphere.

Broome was one of many musicians from the big hotel bands who also played after-hours jazz at small clubs like the Palms or Hattie Ray's; he said he used to spend time with two other white musicians, guitarists Red Wortham and Hank Garland, seeking out black music:

> Jazz in Nashville was primarily black. Nashville was loaded with black jazz. That was the music the white musicians sought out to listen to and jam with after the hotel ballrooms were closed. Nashville was famous for its white dance bands, but what they played, mostly, was the sweet-music end of jazz.
>
> There was always a mixture here in Nashville. There was no problem between black and white musicians. Often we would work at the Woodmont Country Club, which was Jewish, but we would have Brenton Banks with us, a fantastic piano player. Red Wortham would just take time out to lean on the piano and watch him. Brenton was that good. He later joined the Nashville Symphony and became professor at Tennessee State.

Many of Nashville's black musicians left town to flourish elsewhere. Some, like Brenton Banks, came back. Fisk University in the early decades of the century boasted Lil Hardin (Armstrong), Jimmie Lunceford, and Willie Smith, all prominent hot-jazz and swing-era musicians. Perhaps the best-known jazz soloist from Nashville was Adolphus "Doc" Cheatham, born in 1905. Learning cornet, sax, and drums in a chapel band tutored by William Meredith, Cheatham worked in the orchestra pit at the Bijou Theater but soon moved on to Chicago, where in 1926 he recorded with Ma Rainey on "Broken Soul Blues" and other classic blues titles. In the 1930s, Cheatham played with Chick Webb, Benny Goodman, and Cab Calloway; in New York during the 1940s, he worked with Billie Holiday and Teddy Wilson; and he performed almost until his death in 1997.

But the road out of Nashville was a two-way street, and Owen Bradley recalls being influenced by black dance bands who came through the city in the 1930s.

> They stayed at a hotel on Fourth across from the streetcar transfer station; Fletcher Henderson's band with Red

Allen on trumpet and Coleman Hawkins on sax, for instance. Visiting bands played shows over WLAC often. I remember one particular show on the radio where Fletcher Henderson couldn't play because the piano was out of tune.

From then on, Bradley always took along for his own shows a small tuned piano on a car trailer.

Billed by the *Globe* as the "Trumpet King of Swing," Louis Armstrong played to a full house at the swing-oriented Cotton Club, formerly the Silver Streak, on February 5, 1939; admission was one dollar. The next year, with a dollar ticket from Price's Pharmacy or the Florsheim Shoe Shop downtown, you could hear at the same venue the Taft Jordan orchestra and "the First Lady of Swing," Ella Fitzgerald.

Nashville's black jazz and blues scene thrived, fed by plenty of local talent along with the out-of-towners. Beady Conner's dance band, which got under way around 1927, included players from Fisk and Tennessee State Universities—trumpeter Chick Chavis, pianist Edwin Wilcox, sax player Willie Smith, and trombonist Henry Wells, who later joined the band of fellow Fisk graduate Jimmie Lunceford in Memphis. The thirties and forties saw the emergence of several groups from local music-school programs, including bands run by Thurman T. Grant, Don Q. Pullen, and Chavis.

In 1949 readers of the influential black *Pittsburgh Courier* voted Chick Chavis's Tennessee State Collegians "Best College Band," for which honor the band was invited to New York to perform at Carnegie Hall. Chavis had come to Nashville in 1912 from Greensboro, North Carolina; his music teachers were William Meredith and, at Pearl High School, bandleader B. R. Murrell. After stints at Walden University in Nashville, Tennessee State, and Fisk, Chavis taught in public schools, then during the war played in a navy band based in Seattle with fellow Nashvillian Don Q. Pullen. Chavis went on to lead the Tennessee State Collegians to national glory—partly the result of the band's lineup, which included trombonist and singer Tommy Brooks, Clifford McCray on bass, Andy Goodrich on alto sax, Doc Kendricks on trumpet, and trombonist Jimmy Cleveland, who went on to work with Lionel Hampton, Dizzy Gillespie, and Quincy Jones.

Don Q. Pullen, Chick Chavis's fellow navy-band member, had moved to Nashville from Starkville, Mississippi, in 1917. He learned piano, saxophone, and musical arrangement at Tennessee State, formed the Black and Gold Orchestra, went on tour with Chavis and then with the Walter Barnes Orchestra, and studied at the Julliard School under Teddy Wilson. Back in Nashville in the 1930s, he arranged songs for the Francis Craig Orchestra—"In those days," he said later, "it was considered quite the thing for a black arranger to write for a white orchestra." In the 1950s, Pullen became one of the first black members of A.F.M. Local 257. For years he assembled a bewildering array of school bands, concert bands, marching bands, and string ensembles, and was generally known around town as the man to see if you wanted a black band in Nashville. Singer Earl Gaines, who worked for Pullen in the early fifties, recalls both Pullen and the Sunday jam sessions at the Elks Club:

Don Q. was a good man to work for, and a fine pianist and musician. A jazz musician, really. He wouldn't mess with anyone who couldn't play well. He ran much of the scene locally. He'd have a blues trio one night, then a bigger band at a white club like the Stardust the next day, then a complete big band on a Sunday, when he gave park concerts organized by the state. Most of the best musicians in town worked for Don Q.; people like Kid King and Big Mac McCray got their start with him.

[The jams at the Elks Club] were the main event in Nashville for many musicians for years through the forties to the sixties. The show went on all day, from one or two past noon through the matinee and on till one in the morning. People would go after church. It gave them an outing. They were already dressed up, so they would buy a bottle and go down there to Fourteenth Avenue. Hugh Rucker was the musical director of the Elks Club, and he packed the club every Sunday for years. All the black bands in town would call in. He'd give them a time slot,

The Tennessee State Collegians, late 1940s: standing, *at right,* leader Chick Chavis; trombonist Tommy Brooks next to Chavis; singer Frank Carruthers; saxophonist Andy Goodrich in the middle of the front row; and Clifford McCray on bass. Courtesy of Tennessee State University Special Collections Unit.

and they'd come back and play. One band, then another, then another, all day long. It was the place to hear and be heard.

More regular venues for black music were the clubs that grew up around Charlotte/Cedar and Gay Streets, on the north edge of downtown, and Jefferson Street, a little farther north across the railroad tracks. Establishments like Maceo's, Pee Wee's, and Behind the Green Door competed with the larger Bijou and Club Baron (later the Elks Club) at 2614 Jefferson. Brown's Dinner Club was famous for its own Sunday jam sessions, but the Del Morocco at 2417 Jefferson had everything: live music, a gambling room in the back, and fine dining upstairs in the Blue Room. (Guitarist Jimi Hendrix would play a residency at the Del Morocco in 1962 in a combo with Billy Cox.)

Postwar redevelopment affected many of the black music venues, as some forty thousand houses went up in the immediate Nashville area in the ten years after 1945. Parts of the red-light district around Vine Street fell to the bulldozer in 1948, and the Capitol Hill redevelopment project that got under way in 1952 disrupted a large number of families and businesses, including the New Era and other clubs along Fourth Avenue. William "Soo" Bridgeforth had started the New Era as a hundred-seat piano bar in 1939, moved it to Fourth Avenue off Charlotte in 1941, and kept it going until 1995, although he regretted having to leave Fourth Avenue: "Downtown was a good location. It was about the only place that blacks could go, and it was a meeting place. When they came into town they would all wind up at the New Era."

Nashville and its musicians, like the rest of the nation, were in transition. According to Paul Broome, Chick Chavis called the city "a pilgrimming place" to which black musicians gravitated. The same year the New Era changed locations, 1952, W. O. Smith joined the faculty of Nashville's Tennessee State University, then known as Tennessee A&I, and later founded the Nashville Community Music School and teamed up with pianist Brenton Banks in both a string quartet and a jazz group that played in Printers Alley. From Bartow, Georgia, Smith had worked with pioneer blues singer Bessie Smith, played in the bands of Lucky Millinder and Dizzy Gillespie, and provided the bass on the famous 1939 recording of "Body and Soul" by saxophonist Coleman Hawkins.

Little Richard and John Coltrane were both active in Nashville in the early 1950s. Richard frequently played the Club Revillot, which local musician Al Garner characterized as a "knock-down, drag-out sort of club, a little dive on the corner of Fourteenth and Jefferson." It was also a center for the black gay scene to which Richard—and more especially the Bernard Hardison Band—contributed. For touring musicians, Nashville offered a convenient stop-over. Fats Domino, Memphis Slim, and Ray Charles, joined Little Richard in making the city their second home in the early fifties, playing resident gigs and one-nighters at popular black venues. Locally, a lot of musicians gathered around Blind Jimmy Osborne and his Knights of Rhythm, who were resident at One Arm George's club.

Live Jazz Venues

Throughout the 1930s, 1940s, and 1950s, then, Nashville's clubs for both black and white patrons resounded with live jazz, blues, and dance music—in north Nashville, Del Morocco and Revillot; downtown, New Era, Doc Mandrel's Road House, Ed Redmond's, and others; in Printers Alley, the Carousel, the Unique, and the Gaslight, magnets for visiting businessfolk and for local musicians looking to play all night.

South of town were the Ridgeway Inn, Charlie Carney's Stork Club, and the Palms in Brentwood. The finest and biggest club in town was the Skyway on Murfreesboro Road, with a band organized by Paul Broome. When the exclusive Plantation Club opened in the 1940s, jazz pianist Earl Hines brought a band in for a three-week residency, with Dizzy Gillespie on trumpet and vocalists Sarah Vaughan and Billy Eckstine; Adrian McDowell led the club's regular band. West Nashville had, on Highway 70, the Biltmore Club (formerly Hattie Ray's Dinner Club) at Nine Mile Hill, owned by Slocky Kelly, and the Pines Club; the Belvedere and the Colonial Club on Harding Road; and on Highway 100 the Wagon Wheel, a premier big-band venue beginning in the 1930s.

In the early 1950s, Frank Duncan opened the Dixieland-oriented Celtic Club in the back of Vaughn's Restaurant on Broadway at the corner of Thirteenth Avenue, the site occupied by the Hermitage Dinner Club in the 1940s and before that by the Trocadero Club. Harold Bradley played guitar there as a teenager and remembers that "the club always had a policeman stationed out front, because it would be full of soldiers and it could get very hectic. That was the club where I first watched James Cleveland, the great black trombone player, in a band with drummer Morris Palmer."

The view south up Capitol Hill, 1950, with the housing area in the foreground scheduled for redevelopment. Courtesy of the *Tennessean*.

Recording and Publishing Pioneers

Music heard live or over the radio remained constant for Nashvillians through the 1920s, 1930s, and 1940s, but that was not the case with music heard on phonograph records. Before the advent of mass radio in the early 1920s, annual record sales topped 100 million nationally. In the main, recordings were made and distributed by national companies operating in the North and East. There is some indication that a commercial cylinder company operated in Nashville around 1900, but the first records made in Nashville were probably a series of seven-inch aluminum discs produced in the Vendome Building on Church Street by Houck Piano, an established Tennessee company active since the 1880s. Between about 1925 and 1930, locals could make a two-minute recording for about a dollar, and musicians probably used these discs to audition for major record companies in New York.

The wider availability of phonographs and the rush to discover niche markets in the face of increasing competition sent record companies scurrying after specialty music. Pioneer recording crews showed up in cities in the South and West to capture on disc a range of white folk music and black musical styles. Almost inevitably, Nashville became a field location, although recording activity there paled beside that in Atlanta, Memphis, Dallas, and New Orleans.

Not willing to wait around for recording crews to find them, some musicians left mid-Tennessee for more likely venues, especially New York City. The Fisk Jubilee Singers had recorded spirituals there in 1909. Folk artists who headed for New York included Uncle Dave Macon and Sid Harkreader in July 1924, to record for the Aeolian Vocalion Company, and Uncle Bunt Stephens and Sam McGee in 1926. Atlanta drew another contingent, eager to record with Columbia: Francis Craig's big band in 1925 (Craig recorded his theme song, "Red Rose," in Atlanta in 1928); Uncle Jimmy Thompson in 1926; and WSM performers DeFord Bailey, Obed Pickard, and the black gospel group the Golden Echo Quartet in March and April 1927. Humphrey Bate and the Possum Hunters traveled to Atlanta to record for Brunswick in May 1928.

The Victor Talking Machine Company's field unit, led by Ralph Peer, visited Nashville between September 28 and October 6, 1928, marking the city's first formal commercial recording sessions. During that week, Victor recorded about seventy songs by hillbilly and gospel performers in the YMCA building on Seventh and Union. Several of the discs identified the performers as being "of Station WSM, Nashville," and it was rumored that the station had invited Peer south to showcase its artists. If so, Peer branched out, also recording performers who worked on WLAC and WBAW.

The musicians Peer recorded included Opry stars like the Crook Brothers, DeFord Bailey, and the Binkley Brothers, who played the very first song recorded at the Nashville sessions, "Watermelon Hanging on de Vine," which was never issued. Instead, the Brothers' "All Go Hungry Hash House," paired with "It'll Never Happen Again," along with the Vaughan Quartet's gospel offerings "Master of the Storm" and "What a Morning That Will Be," seem to have been the first of these Nashville recordings commercially released, both in December 1928. DeFord Bailey's "Ice Water Blues," backed with "Davidson County Blues," was the first disc recorded in Nashville by a black artist. Although the sessions appear to have gone well, only about half the titles recorded were issued, as national record sales slumped during the Depression from 104 million in 1927 to 6 million in 1932.

When recording activity picked up in Nashville in the 40s, it was not a commercial enterprise. Fisk University music professor John Work III, later joined by Alan Lomax, set about documenting several blues, gospel, and string-band styles. Among those Work recorded were Nashville string musicians Nathan (Ned) Frazier and Frank Patterson on fiddle and banjo duets, and the Nashville Washboard Band, a black group led by mandolin player James Kelley, whose repertoire included old-time folk and blues tunes. A black music collector and Yale-educated professor at Fisk and one of the first to see the importance of black string bands, Work traveled unheralded all over Tennessee, Mississippi, Alabama, Georgia, and South Carolina between 1935 and 1942 to preserve the best black folk music. Bruce Nemerov of Middle Tennessee State University wrote that Work

> was really ahead of his time. Other black academics didn't start digging around in this music until the 1950s. He was like a record scout—out to find people who knew the old tunes and old styles. His 1930s and 1940s field recordings stand out from previous field recordings because he was such a good musician. He knew when people could really play.

Alan Lomax arrived in Nashville from the Library of Congress in the spring of 1941, invited by Fisk to the seventy-fifth anniversary of the university's founding. He arranged for the Library to assist Work in maintaining Fisk's recording equipment; in exchange, many of Work's academic recordings went into the Library, including gospel songs by Nashville's Fairfield Four. In a book later published under his own name, Lomax drew extensively on a manuscript Work wrote on black music.

Tom Parker, *left,* overseeing Eddy Arnold, *left of placard,* and Wally Fowler, in dark shirt and hat, promoting their show in Florida in 1946. Courtesy of Country Music Hall of Fame and Museum.

Eddy Arnold

Not only did the Depression decimate record sales, but wartime shortages of labor and of the binding agent, shellac, cut production even further. In a dispute over the increasing use of recordings by radio and the jukebox industry to replace live music, the American Federation of Musicians in August 1942 banned all recording activities. The recording companies settled one by one with the A.F.M. during 1943 and 1944, and soon after RCA Victor's settlement, Eddy Arnold, one of Nashville's rising folk singers, recorded a session at *WSM*, generally reckoned to mark the birth of modern commercial recording in Nashville: December 4, 1944.

That session was hardly a planned affair. Harry Stone of WSM, together with Chicago music publisher Fred Forster, had persuaded Frank Walker at RCA Victor to offer Arnold a recording contract, but his debut was delayed because of the A.F.M. ban. The recordings that record companies had stockpiled to last through the ban had run out by the time RCA settled with the union, and Walker was desperate for new material. RCA booked its own studios solid with sessions for established artists, while untested newcomers like Arnold took second place. So instead of overseeing Arnold's first session, Walker simply wired the singer and told him to get into a studio, make some recordings, and send them to New York.

On December 4, 1944, Arnold and the Tennessee Plowboys went into WSM Studio B with RCA engineer Percy White and WSM engineers Aaron Shelton and Carl Jenkins. They recorded four songs, which were issued on two discs on RCA's Bluebird label. The first was the height of sentimentality: "Mommy Please Stay Home with Me" and "Mother's Prayer." The second, which did not appear until June 1945, was "Each Minute Seems a Million Years" and "Cattle Call."

Richard Edward Arnold, born in 1918 on a farm near Henderson in Chester County, Tennessee, always preferred singing to farmwork and quit school at sixteen to make it his career, first in west Tennessee, then in St. Louis. In 1939 he sent a transcription of some of his best performances to Pee Wee King and in January 1940 joined King's Golden West Cowboys, one of the slickest and best bands around, which married the folk and hillbilly of the East with western swing styles. King's band had made its WSM Opry debut in June 1937 and was among the first Opry groups to join the A.F.M. King insisted that his was "a proper band" in comparison to the many part-time aggregations on WSM.

After working out of Louisville, King and his band returned to WSM in mid-1941. Eddy Arnold married Sally Gayhart later that year and set up house on Dickerson Road at the northern edge of east Nashville. In 1941 and 1942 Arnold further enhanced his reputation with King on the prestigious Camel Caravan show, a troupe of WSM artists who toured U.S. military bases under the sponsorship of the R.J. Reynolds Tobacco Company. By 1943, when Arnold was ready to go it alone again, WSM manager Harry Stone hired him to join the station as a solo artist. That fall, Arnold formed his first Nashville band, the Tennessee Plowboys, who included fiddler Speedy McNatt, bass player Gabe Tucker, steel-guitar stylist Roy Wiggins, and Herbert "Butterball" Paige as lead guitarist.

Around the time Arnold's first Victor discs appeared, the singer came to the attention of "Colonel" Tom Parker, who would later become Elvis Presley's promoter. In a prerun of the Presley story, Parker set out to make maximum capital from Arnold's abilities, first persuading the industry that Arnold was even bigger than he was and then achieving liftoff when Arnold delivered the hit that confirmed his talent in September 1946, "That's How Much I Love You." Cowritten by Jim Bulleit's friend Wally Fowler, the hit presaged a phenomenal string for Arnold that included "I'll Hold You in My Heart" and "Bouquet of Roses." In a run of fifty-three weeks, from November 1947, Arnold held the top-selling folk and hillbilly recording position, and *Cashbox* reported that in 1947 he sold 2.7 million records. Significantly, all his recordings from 1946 through 1949 were made not in Nashville, but in Chicago or New York.

Arnold himself had cowritten a few songs since he left King's band, and Wally Fowler put these together in a songbook that Arnold sold at stage shows. This was common practice. Because of the dominance of live music, especially in the years before 1945, sheet music and song folios were still far more important than records. Many different artists recorded the same song, and there could be ten or more versions of a top seller. The song, not the singer, was the hit.

The Vagabonds and Fred Rose

With the exception of the early twentieth century gospel music publisher, the Benson company, most song publishing in Nashville had been undertaken on a small scale. Several Nashville-based performers self-published their songs during the 1930s, following the example of an Opry group, the Pickard Family, who had pioneered this route the previous decade. A WSM trio, the Vagabonds, for instance, formed the Old Cabin Company. When they came to WSM in 1931 from St. Louis, the Vagabonds were Dean Upson, Herald Goodman, and Curt Poulton, who published several songbooks from addresses in the WSM building and the Hitchcock building. Pop singers who developed a successful

The Vagabonds, *from left* , Dean Upson, Curt Poulton (with guitar), and Herald Goodman. Courtesy of Country Music Hall of Fame and Museum.

line in folksy material such as "When It's Lamp Lightin' Time in the Valley," the Vagabonds also issued three records in 1933 on the Old Cabin label, custom pressed by Gennett Records and recorded at Gennett's studio in Richmond, Indiana, to mail out to radio stations to promote the group's songs and songbooks. In all likelihood, Old Cabin was the first record label with a Nashville address.

New York and Chicago companies affiliated with the American Society of Composers, Authors, and Publishers (ASCAP) dominated the world of music publishing. Set up in 1914 to collect payments on sheet music and live concerts, ASCAP tended to exclude all but the most popular ethnic and folk songwriters. When ASCAP threatened to raise its rates for broadcasting rights, the radio lobby set up a rival collection society, Broadcast Music, Inc. (BMI), in October 1939. By the time ASCAP and radio made peace, BMI had a strong pop, hillbilly, and blues catalog. Among BMI's new affiliates was the first popular music-publishing company to operate as a fulltime business in Nashville, Acuff-Rose Publications, which set out to vigorously acquire and promote copyrights.

Company principal Fred Rose had moved to Nashville from Chicago in 1933 as a songwriter and radio personality. His songs had been recorded by jazzmen and dance bands for almost a decade, and titles like "Red Hot Mama," "Deep Henderson," "Honest and Truly," "Deed I Do," and "Flamin' Mamie" were already standards. Rose was in his midthirties and in an alcohol-induced decline when he arrived in town, but his WSM show, *Freddie Rose's Song Shop,* brought him renewed success and friendships. From that base he moved to the West Coast and launched himself into writing for cowboy movie stars like Gene Autry and Ray Whitley in the late 1930s. Back in Nashville in October 1942, Rose signed a partnership agreement with Mildred Acuff, and Acuff-Rose Publications opened a small office at 220 Capitol Boulevard. Mildred had been active in publishing songbooks for her husband, Roy Acuff, who was the new company's figurehead and supplied $25,000 in reserve capital. One of the biggest country music stars of the day, Roy had a six-year string of hits that included "Great Speckle Bird," "Wabash Cannon Ball," "Fire Ball Mail," and "Night Train to Memphis." Acuff's name attracted writers to the company; Rose's role was to work with them and to develop a strong catalog. In January 1943, Acuff-Rose advertised in *Billboard:* "Look out for folk tunes and popular hits from Nashville."

By October of that year, *Time* magazine reported: "The dominant popular music of the U.S. today is hillbilly; . . . the rage has taken a good part of U.S. song writing out of the hands of Tin Pan Alley's veterans." The article cited Fred Rose as part of "the biggest revolution in U.S. popular musical taste since the 'swing' craze began in the middle 30s," and added that Bing Crosby and Frank Sinatra were making their biggest smashes with hillbilly tunes.

Old Cabin, the first record label with a Nashville address, 1933. Courtesy of Country Music Hall of Fame and Museum.

The Recording Scene of 1945

In the final weeks of 1945, around the time Wally Fowler talked Jim Bulleit into going into the record business in Nashville, the top pop songs were Bing Crosby's "It's Been a Long Time," Peggy Lee's "Waiting for a Train to Come In," and Sammy Kaye's "Clickety Clack." The "*Billboard* Popular Juke Box Hits" for the year included "Sentimental Journey" by Les Brown, "On the Atchison, Topeka, and the Santa Fe" by Johnny Mercer, and "Rum and Coca Cola" by the Andrews Sisters. In black music, the hot tunes were Louis Jordan's "Caldonia," Erskine Hawkins's "Tippin' In," Cecil Gant's "I Wonder," and the gospel tune "Strange Things Happening Every Day" by Sister Rosetta Tharpe. The white gospel hit of 1945 was Albert Brumley's tune "If We Never Meet Again," and the trade papers referred to folk, hillbilly, or western music rather than to country. The "*Billboard* Cavalcade of Folk Juke Box Hits 1945" included "Shame on You" recorded by both Spade Cooley and Red Foley, "Oklahoma Hills" by Jack Guthrie, and "There's a New Moon over My Shoulder" by both Jimmie Davis and Tex Ritter.

Of the three major recording companies active at the close of 1945, the largest was RCA Victor, followed by Decca and an ailing giant, Columbia Records. The quasi-majors were headed by Capitol—the only sizable record company based on the West Coast—and Majestic, a New York–and Chicago-based affiliate of Majestic Radio & Television. Three other companies that would move up by the end of the 1940s were just getting started: Chicago-based Mercury Records, MGM Records in New York (an affiliate of Loews Inc.), and King Records in Cincinnati, which soon had a strong presence in the blues and folk music fields.

More than a hundred new recording companies sprang up in the months after the war. In April 1946, *Billboard* reported an important trend in the article "Indies Are in There Swinging": "Some indies frankly admit that they are going to stay out of fields in which the majors push heavily, and concentrate on items where the majors do more or less of a token job." These neglected areas included R&B, modern jazz, ethnic music, and folk, western, and hillbilly.

The Jukebox Era

Most of what the new indies recorded was for jukebox sales, which by 1946 would account for close to half of all records sold nationally. Even before the war, there were half a million jukeboxes in the United States. Less than 30 percent of households had any kind of record-playback equipment in 1946, a statistic that would change radically in the economic boom of the late 1940s.

But in the decades before World War II, records were distributed to electrical-appliance stores and furniture dealers who sold phonographs; it made sense for them to keep a counter in the corner stocked with records. In 1930 Nashville had only three phonograph-record dealers: the O. K. Houck piano company, the John H. Sloan company, and Freeman Phonograph. Over the next decade, amusement companies dealing in jukeboxes and other coin-operated machines emerged as Nashville's pioneering record distributors. Bullet Records would start as an offshoot of the jukebox business, setting a pattern for several Nashville record labels that followed. Their focus was not the home but the jukebox.

Nashville recordman Murray Nash, who sold records for McClung's department store in Knoxville in the 1930s and 1940s, described the pragmatic strategy of jukebox operators:

> Back at that time, the jukebox business had some very large operators, several in Nashville. Two in particular had hundreds of machines around in various places. But there were many others who either just owned their own machine in their café or maybe owned, say, five machines. There was a counter on each machine. The operator could tell how many times each record had been played. If they didn't play well, they would pull that one off and put another one on. At that time, all the operators came to the wholesale places to buy records.

RCA's southern regional sales manager in that period, Brad McCuen, notes the importance of jukebox owners:

“They didn’t get a returns privilege because they used all the records, and they didn’t get an advertising allowance. So you worked with them to the extent of maybe paying for some of the equipment they used. They were especially important if they weren’t linked to a dealer.”

Jukebox dealer Louis Samuel Buckley, born in Allensville, Kentucky, arrived in Nashville at the age of eighteen in 1928 after an abortive stab at playing pro baseball in Chattanooga. While working at Burk & Company, a clothing store on Church Street, he got his start in the amusement-machine business with an $800 loan from his boss to buy ten used jukeboxes. His first rounds as a supplier included mainly black restaurants, like the Cotton Brothers Restaurant at Twelfth and Edgehill and places in the red-light district:

> Before I had a record shop, I owned and serviced jukeboxes. That was back when nobody wanted the jukes in their place of business. It was considered undignified. It was hard to find a white place that would have them. Back in those days, Negro places had jukeboxes, white places didn’t. I had boxes in places like Clarksville and Bowling Green, and I would have to ride the bus to service them out of my regular working hours. I got into the record business by accident. Jukeboxes were my business, but the boxes carry records, and we kept the used records in a place on Second Avenue we used to store the jukeboxes. I made no effort to sell the records. But people started asking for them, and so we sold our first used records when we moved into proper premises.

Hank Williams, Ernest Tubb, and Red Foley broadcasting over WSM at the opening of Hank and Audrey’s Corral, a western clothing store on Commerce Street. Courtesy of Showtime Archives [Toronto] and Colin Escott.

Buckley established his first record store in 1939, at 141 Eighth Avenue North. He was the first to have a primary focus on records and he developed further stores on Church Street and Broadway over the next two decades. But he came up against some stiff competition when Opry star Ernest Tubb opened the first Ernest Tubb Record Shop, on Commerce Street, in the spring of 1947. On the strength of Texas honky-tonk hits like “Walkin’ the Floor over You,” Tubb arrived in Nashville in January 1943 to join the Opry. By 1946, he was a major star and looking for investment opportunities. Tens of thousands of fans flocked to Nashville every year to go to the Opry, and Tubb saw the chance to sell them some records, at first only by mail. Then he opened his store and began plugging it and his mail-order operation on a show that went out every Saturday night on WSM after the Opry. By 1948, Tubb was broadcasting his *Midnite Jamboree* from his store, which in August 1951 moved to 417 Broadway to accommodate the crowds it attracted. The new store became almost as much a country music icon as the Ryman Auditorium, and the *Midnite Jamboree* almost as much a fixture as the Opry.

C. V. Hitchcock and Eugene Cashion

When Ernest Tubb opened his record store, he had trouble keeping it stocked, because, he said, “there was only one place in Nashville you could buy country music records, and this was a jukebox operator with Hermitage Music.” That man was Conrad Vertre “C. V.” Hitchcock, one of the city’s earliest

C. V. Hitchcock, c. 1940. Courtesy of Richard Cashion.

Linebaugh's, where Jim Bulleit and Wally Fowler lunched in 1945, with George and Gus Linebaugh behind the counter, *first and fourth from left,* and Eugene Cashion, *third patron from right,* late 1940s. Courtesy of Richard Cashion.

jukebox operators and wholesale record salesmen, who would remain vital to the town's business infrastructure for forty years. He ran Nashville's first proper recording label, he had publishing interests, and he started the record-pressing business in town. C. V.'s cousin John Moore recalled:

> Conrad was making a pretty good living during the 1930s despite the Depression. He had several restaurants. Then in 1938 he started up Hermitage Music and Novelty Company. He had become interested in jukeboxes and pinball machines when he was running his restaurants, and I guess he could see that there was money to be made in that. He set up in that business, and in no time he had a lot of jukeboxes and novelty machines out there. He operated hundreds of jukeboxes in this area, literally hundreds.

Born in Spencer, in Van Buren County, Tennessee, in 1896, Hitchcock came to Nashville in the early years of the twentieth century with his parents, Herman and Rosie, who were in the catering business. By 1928, the tall, red-headed Conrad was running his own restaurant on the southeast

Alice and Eugene Cashion with lunch guest, c. 1940. Courtesy of Richard Cashion.

corner of Milsom and Ninth Avenue North. By 1933, he had opened another restaurant and lunchroom, at 615 Twelfth Avenue North, and he continued to run this business until 1938. When he started Hermitage Music, it was located at 616 Twelfth Avenue North. Around 1943, Hitchcock took a lease on new premises downtown at 416A Broadway. Then the company diversified and Lewis Moore, a relative of Hitchcock's, opened another downtown outlet for phonographs and new and used records. This was Hermitage Amusements, operating from 210 Printers Alley. In 1945, Hitchcock moved Hermitage Music again, to larger space at 421 and 423 Broadway. Just nearby, at 405 Broadway, was George Linebaugh's little meat and three restaurant, known as "George and Gus," where Hitchcock and his partners could feel right at home every lunchtime.

Hitchcock's main partner for many years was Eugene Hilton Cashion. The two men met as restaurateurs in the 1930s, went separately into music sales, and finally joined forces in 1944. Cashion was born in Fayetteville, Tennessee, in 1898 and he came to Nashville in his late twenties to work at Crawford Tire Company. He had worked as an electrician in Kentucky coal mines and had built roads in Chattanooga with the WPA. He and his wife, the former Alice Parks of Wartrace, Tennessee, opened a little restaurant at 1501 Broadway in 1932 and three years later ran the J&K Café at 823 Broadway. "Mother always called it the 'Squeeze Inn' " remembered their son, Richard Cashion, "because it was only a small place and that was what you had to do—squeeze in." When Eugene Cashion deduced that there might be money in the amusements business, he began to rent peanut vending machines and gumball stands. In 1937, on becoming a salesman for the G&S Amusement Company, Cashion discovered that one of the more lucrative lines in the amusements business was jukebox sales. He often described his earlier work as that of "a jack of all trades, but good at none"; now he discovered his true niche.

By 1943, Cashion had moved on to co-ownership of Ace Music and the Ace Music Shop at 112 Shelby Avenue with Al Engeln and Paul Morrison, which sold automatic and Wurlitzer phonographs. In February 1946, Ace advertised "hard-to-get" used records in the *Globe* at fifteen cents each, mostly black jazz and blues by the likes of Duke Ellington, Lena Horne, Pinetop Smith, and Sonny Boy Williamson. In 1946, Cashion sold his interest in Ace and formed Automatic

PAGE EIGHT

HARD TO GET RECORDS

Free 1946 Sonora Radio. Be Sure and Register, You May Be The Lucky One

USED RECORDS 15c EACH, 7 FOR $1.00

Permo Point Needles Over 4,000 Plays. We Use Permo Point Exclusively On All Our Juke Boxes

LIST PRICE $1.00 — ONLY 75c AT ACE

ACE MUSIC COMPANY

416-A BROAD ST. — 5-3320

Nashville, Tenn.

AULD HAWKINS—
Porgy
Pick Up Boys
IVORY JOE HUNTER—
Blues at Sunrise
You Taught Me To Love
SEVENTH STREET BOOGIE—
Reconversion Blues
COOTIE WILLIAMS—

Jam Jam Blues
I Feel It
Lost Baby Blues
Sooner or Later
Watch That Stuff
Make Believeable Girl
ERNIE ANDREWS—
Green Gin
Dream Awhile
Wrap It Up and Put It Away

Headline from *Nashville Globe* advertisement, February 22, 1946. Courtesy of National Baptist Publishing Board.

Hermitage Music on the south side of Broadway, opposite the Ryman Auditorium, late 1940s. Courtesy of the *Tennessean*.

Sales Vending Company, which he operated from 421 Broadway, next door to Hitchcock's Hermitage Music, of which Cashion was now vice-president.

"Dad was a very easy-going person," said Richard Cashion.

> He was friendly and not really a hard businessman. He went out and collected the money from the jukeboxes and kept relationships going with the customers. Mr. Hitchcock did the desk work more, keeping the books straight and lining up the deals. That way, it seemed to work out perfectly between them.

Local musician Red Wortham agreed:

> Mr. Hitchcock was a jukebox man, first and foremost, a huge distributor of juke sales. He was one of the most pleasant people I ever met, a heavyset man, slow moving, quiet and easy-going. Red was one of the biggest juke operators in the area. Sold them, leased them, placed them in every restaurant and beer tavern and grocery store and every little sandwich shop. He sold them records in return for half the proceeds. He operated a wholesale record business and a retail store. He really knew his business, but he was not a recording man or a publisher. You had

to get around to handle that kind of business, and he didn't do the running around. He had people to do that.

By the end of 1945, Hitchcock and Cashion were contemplating going into the record business, but the city offered only a skeleton to build on. They and Buckley had the local jukeboxes covered, there were radio stations to draw upon for recording artists, and there was Castle Recording Laboratories, a fledgling recording operation developed by WSM engineers in the aftermath of Eddy Arnold's first recording session at WSM. But the business organization, the publicity, the goodwill—all would have to be built from nothing. It helped that the key ingredient in record manufacture, shellac, was no longer the restricted commodity it had been during the war. New record-pressing plants were opening to cater to the independent labels. Quite often, the quality was abominable, but the major record companies' stranglehold on pressing was no longer in effect.

Still, as Jim Bulleit told me:

Nashville in 1945 was really not geared up to the music business at all. There was the networked Opry show from WSM, but I was practically the only booking agent in town, the only studios were the ones owned by the radio stations, and the only publisher in town was Fred Rose. It seems obvious now that the logical step was to form a record company dealing in the music that was promoted by the Opry. But I didn't see that straightaway, not until 1945.

Eugene Cashion, *left*, with C. V. Hitchcock, and Cashion's son, Rick, early 1950s. Courtesy of Richard Cashion

2

The Beginning: Bullet Records

Bullet Records was the beginning of the record business in Nashville, though we didn't know it at the time. We had no idea of how big it would all become.

—Jim Bulleit

When Jim Bulleit used the term "we" throughout our interviews at his home in the 1970s, "we" clearly meant "I." This pioneer of the postwar music business, approaching his seventies, lived in the same south Nashville home he had bought in 1947 on the proceeds of one of the biggest hit records of the 1940s, or indeed of any other era—"Near You." As he spoke of the record business, some of the enthusiasm that fired him in the 1940s began to spark his narrative. This was the Jim Bulleit one of his colleagues recalled as "a rumbustious kind of man, a real entrepreneur."

Jim Bulleit

"Nothing worth mentioning happened in my life until graduation," he once said, but "from the moment I selected Bloomington's Illinois Wesleyan University, I seemed not to miss a single item in the business of living." Bulleit was an Indiana native, born on November 4, 1908, in Corydon, a town of some two thousand people in the southern part of the state. When he entered Wesleyan in 1928, he joined an offshoot band from the university's orchestra as a drummer, singer, and occasional tap dancer. This triple talent got him onto the French ocean liner *Rochambeau* when the band toured Europe that summer as a vaudeville troupe, playing cabarets in Paris, Hamburg, and Berlin.

The next summer, Bulleit traveled across eleven states with the Lyceum Company, working in theater management. On one midnight trip through Brownsville, Texas, he tried his hand at radio announcing on KWWG. Another trip took him into Mexico, where he found himself with no money, "a frequent experience in those days." In the summer of 1931, Bulleit sold magazines in Louisville, Kentucky, drove a sightseeing bus in Yosemite Valley, California, and wound up in Pinedale, Wyoming, working with a well digger who claimed he had discovered the site of a lost gold mine.

Bulleit graduated from Illinois Wesleyan in 1932 with a bachelor of music degree, specializing in voice rather than the drums, clarinet, and trumpet he played proficiently. That summer, he taught school in Idaho and sold musical instruments to his pupils for a department store in Boise. His combined weekly income, three hundred dollars, was "the most I had ever drawn for any kind of labor until I went into the record business." His explanation for leaving such rich pickings was that "the urge to keep on a constant go still dominated my soul," and he tried salmon fishing in Idaho and worked with an engineer in Salt Lake City before "blazing a trail into Dixie, destined to try my hand with an advertising agency; but as usual, I derived nothing but bad luck."

Still restless, Bulleit decided nevertheless to try teaching again, first at Troy State College in Alabama and then at

Auburn University, where he and two piano teachers started the music school. "I didn't have the patience to teach," he explained when recounting his almost immediate decision to move on again. In the Depression years, he found it increasingly difficult to get well-paid work and spent much of 1934 in the Atlanta area,

> looking for work and doing the best I could. Ultimately I found my calling—the radio world. I had fooled with radio in Texas and had briefly served as announcer at KTFI in Twin Falls and at KIDO in Boise during my summertimes in Idaho. Eventually I found some employment at WGST radio in Atlanta, doing relief work when the regular announcers were away. Next, I saw duty at WSFA in Montgomery, Alabama, and WKEU in Griffin, Georgia. My chores consisted of practically everything—directing the programs, procuring the commercials, and doing the announcing.

At WAIM in Anderson, South Carolina, in 1935, Bulleit discovered his forte: announcing. He read the news, linked variety programs, and commentated "live" on baseball games, describing the plays as they came over the telegraph machine. He became one of the best radio announcers around, as well as the station's program director. His advice to aspiring announcers, published in the local paper:

> A college education is necessary, particularly in music or English. Reading aloud is good practice. Never fall into the mistake of reciting poetry, don't mumble, let the world hear you clearly and distinctly. Be sure a large dictionary is within your reach, study the meaning of words and . . . good luck!

Tent showman and musician "Ramblin'" Tommy Scott worked with Bulleit in Anderson:

> Jim put me on the air down there. I had a little radio show, and we used it to advertise shows that Jim booked. He would hire the National Guard Armory and put on a show. And he would buy a block of time on WAIM and sell it to the sponsors of square dances that we would put on. He charged a dime to get in, and we both made a little money together. He was always full of ideas that way.

Jimmie Bulleit, Manager Station WAIM, Is Quite A Globe Trotter

Wesleyan University and Then His Adventures Began.—Has Made Music in Paris and Starved in Mexico.

—BY FRANK DICKSON, JR.—

Part One

"Your announcer is Jimmie Bulleit."

Day in and day out such an explanatory statement flies throughout the Piedmont Section from radio station WAIM, known as the "Voice of the Electric City," with studios at Anderson College. Yet none of the multitudinous listeners are in the least aware that this particular "man behind the mike," still in his twenties, boasts a young but comprehensive history replete with thrills from mingling with aristocracy in Europe to starving in Mexico to rising to the position of program director at the local broadcasting institution.

Southern Indiana—to be exact, the town of Corydon, populated with 2,000 people—claims the youthful adventurer as a native son. When only four years of age, a severe

JIMMY BULLEIT

Jim Bulleit makes headlines in South Carolina, 1936. Courtesy of Gayle Moses.

In a roundabout way, one of those square-dance sponsors introduced Bulleit to the folk, or hillbilly, music that would later bring him such success. Vim Herb, a patent medicine, bodybuilding tonic, and laxative produced by A. C. Durham was promoted by Scotty the Drifter, a folk musician. That kind of music "was big in that area at that time," Bulleit recalled. "It wasn't my music, I was used to big bands and orchestral music, but I got accustomed to it and I could see the potential."

Bulleit met Rachel Chapman, former captain of the Anderson High School girls' basketball team, in October

1935, not long after he arrived in town. According to their daughter, Gayle, "they both had beautiful voices and they met through singing. They got engaged at Christmas after meeting for three months and they were married on April 15, 1936." The Bulleits moved into a house on Carolina Circle and Jim was elected to the board of the Junior Chamber of Commerce. The family moved in 1941 to Spartanburg, South Carolina, where on WSPA Jim sold advertising by day and announced the news and music programs in the evenings.

To make the leap to big-city radio, Bulleit said, "I applied first to KIBA radio in San Francisco, and they gave me a job. That was an influential CBS station. This was in the early forties." Bulleit produced Ted Weems's orchestra in the *Coast Guard Show,* with Snooky Lanson as vocalist. He was now set fair, professionally. But San Francisco was too close to the war in the Pacific.

> Frisco was blacked out during the war, and that sort of thing. My wife didn't like it out there. In 1943, we decided to move away from the West Coast. Things were tough, and we were living with my mother and sister, so it was crowded, and we never did find a place that was our own. I looked around for a while and then picked Nashville because it was in between San Francisco and South Carolina. How's that for a compromise?
>
> I wrote off to radio WLAC, sent them an audition tape, and they sent me an offer of a job for a four-week trial period. I left my wife in Anderson for that month and headed for Nashville. The next day I went for the interview at WLAC, and my probationary job was confirmed. The very next day the people at WLAC said that I was too experienced for them and they kindly offered to get me a higher-paid job with a bigger station. Two days after arriving in town I found myself in my second job, having passed an interview at WSM. I had been given an appointment with Ott Devine, the program director, and Harry Stone, the station manager. The day I was given the job at WSM was December 7, 1943. I remember the date clearly, because it was the second anniversary of Pearl Harbor.

The man who took the spot reserved for Bulleit at WLAC was Sam Phillips, who later founded Sun Records in Memphis. Phillips recalled that he was living in Decatur, Alabama, but

> happened to be in Nashville auditioning for WSM. Jim was due to report at WLAC but he didn't show up as he had gotten a job at WSM. I heard about this and went right over to WLAC to see the program director, Paul Oliphant. He gave me Jim's job, which was to take the place of John Richbourg while he went into the service, and I worked at WLAC for nearly two years before I moved to Memphis.

Bulleit worked the early-morning shift at WSM, alternating news, records, and live singing acts in fifteen-minute segments. Francis Craig had a morning record show, Jim told John Rumble of the Country Music Foundation,

> but normally it was live talent. We had Eddy Arnold early in the morning selling pecan trees or something down in Mississippi. We had Paul Howard and Clyde Moody and Lew Childre. John Daniel's Quartet would come on. They would all want to announce their show dates and what they were doing.

Bulleit got to know most of the musicians in Nashville and became friendly with Eddy Arnold and J. L. Frank, the manager of Pee Wee King's group. In his first nationally networked spot on WSM, Jim worked with Beasley Smith's band, broadcasting to the nation from the Maxwell House Hotel on New Year's Eve, 1943. At about the same time, he worked the *Dr. IQ Show* broadcast from the Paramount Theater, on Church Street between Seventh and Eighth Avenues North, scattered through the audience with other *Dr. IQ* announcers to ask people questions as they vied for a silver-dollar prize.

> During that time I gained tremendous experience of radio, and also of the record business, particularly folk music and hillbilly. In fact, after being in Nashville only one month I was given an additional job. I had been

A typical Saturday-night crowd outside the Ryman waiting to get into the Grand Ole Opry, 1950s. Gordan Gillingham photograph courtesy of Grand Ole Opry Archives.

> away for a few days when my son was born back there in Anderson. When I walked back in, Harry Stone asked me if I would schedule all the hillbilly acts out on the road. Effectively, I was put in charge of the Artist Service Bureau. That was the organization that found bookings for the country singers [who were] on the Grand Ole Opry. That was how I really got my start in the music business. I was lucky to work with some of the country old-timers. Uncle Dave Macon, he was still one of the kings in Nashville at that time. He never could recall my name; he just called me "boy." "I killed them tonight, boy," he'd say, and he'd slap me on the back as he walked out to face the autograph hunters.

The rest of the Bulleit family moved to 1900 Riverside Drive in Nashville in early 1944, soon after son Jack's birth, and in 1946 relocated to 1705 Nineteenth Avenue South.

Jim Bulleit's picture appeared on a Certificate of Merit issued by WSM in connection with *Rhythm, Rations, and Recipes,* a morning program "dedicated to housewives whose food conservation efforts are such an important contribution to the war effort." But the early-morning shows were not his preference, and as soon as a slot opened up, he moved to the six-to-midnight shift, again announcing a mix of news, musical programs, and variety shows. He fed into the Francis Craig program that started at eleven P.M. and his became a familiar Saturday-night voice to listeners who tuned in to the NBC network. But it was time to move on.

> After I had been at WSM for nearly two years, I decided that I was happier in the Artist Service Bureau than I was doing my original job as an announcer. So I left WSM in the late fall of 1945, in October, and formed my own booking business. I made the move because I figured that there was a lot of potential in Nashville. Apart from real stars like Uncle Dave and Roy Acuff, the other musicians on WSM mainly played at little schoolhouses and the like. I knew that they could do better, so I started getting them booked into better venues and had them touring further. After a year of selling the hillbilly acts wider afield, we found that WSM had taken over $55,000 in the 15 percent booking fees that they took off the artist's fee. That was a lot of money.
>
> When Eddy Arnold realized how successful we were being, he wanted me to handle him exclusively, for bookings, but I told him that I couldn't do that. What a mistake that was! Instead, I handled [him along with] Paul Howard, Clyde Moody, and Curley Williams—a whole range of them. That was the beginning of the expansion of the promotion of hillbilly music out of Nashville, other than the jamborees organized by Joe Frank. And Nashville was by no means solely a hillbilly town. There were gospel singers, popular bands and singers, and some blues men. I was equally familiar with the Fairfield Four, a black gospel group led by Sam McCrary, and with John

Daniel, who sang gospel. Of course I knew Francis Craig and other bandleaders. I did not know but was aware of some of the blues groups, people like Rudy Green.

The story of Bulleit's departure from WSM to become an independent booker comes in several versions. Some, like Irving Waugh, suggest that Bulleit occasionally blurred the line between his employer's interests and his own. Waugh, who came to WSM in 1941 and worked alongside Bulleit for a time, said that "Jim was a nice enough chap, but a so-so announcer, and it was unusual for an announcer to get involved in promoting." Others, like singer Sheb Wooley, go further:

> WSM charged 15 percent for booking shows by anybody who was on the Opry, took 15 percent whether they booked it themselves or not. And Jim was doing that when I met him. Shortly after that he got caught where he'd booked something at one price and reported it at another price. He was raking some off the top for himself, so they let him go.

Bulleit told Douglas B. Green later that he "got greedy about that booking business, and away I went," which may simply have been an allusion to his desire to strike out on his own as a show promoter. Wherever the truth lies, Bulleit left WSM; Jim Denny took his place at the Artist Service Bureau. Bulleit remained a fixture in the building when he set up his own agency; many contemporaries remember that he used the lobby at WSM as his virtual office.

Typically for Jim Bulleit, the booking business that had seemed so lucrative, and attractive enough to lure him away from radio, lasted no more than a few months. "Then we got this bug to do the records," he said.

That bug may have been incubating for some time. Columbia Records' Art Satherley had visited WSM in the winter of 1944/45 to line up a number of Grand Ole Opry musicians for sessions to be recorded in Chicago—Bill Monroe and his Blue Grass Boys, the Old Hickory Singers, publisher Fred Rose (recording under his hillbilly nom de disc, the Rambling Rogue), Curley Williams and the Georgia Peach Pickers, and Clyde Moody. Williams and Moody were on Bulleit's books as WSM Artist Service director, and their Columbia and RCA sessions may have catalyzed Bulleit's thoughts about going into the recording business almost a year before he actually did so. He spoke of being present in WSM's Studio C when Clyde Moody recorded "Two Timin' Blues," and the recording appears in Satherley's logbook as having been made on March 7, 1945, but it is likely that the master disc was made in Chicago and that Bulleit witnessed an audition or practice session.

As the war ended, along with its restrictions on raw materials and consumer expectations, the demand for Nashville's music grew. Despite his personal preference for pop dance bands, Bulleit would have seen the opportunity for someone to step in and record all the up-and-coming acts on the Grand Ole Opry, as well as the untapped blues and gospel singers in Nashville. When Wally Fowler introduced him to C. V. Hitchcock, Bulleit became convinced about the recording business, and the deal was quickly struck.

> After we talked briefly, Mr. Hitchcock went to the back of the store and got me a check for $1,500. So I put up $1,500. Mr. Hitchcock and Mr. Cashion had pinball machines and the whole bit, but particularly they had jukeboxes out on lease to operators. They were selling records to jukebox operators and they could not get enough country music. That was why C. V. Hitchcock started out recording.

Early Bullet: Trial and Error

"Our record label was called Bullet, but Wally Fowler had thought up that name before he ever found me," Jim told me. "My name is Bulleit, properly pronounced 'Bulay' because my name originated in Belgium." Having put the Bullet Records deal together, Fowler either couldn't come up with the money he needed to join the company or decided it was too risky and that he would stay with his performing, publishing, and songwriting interests.

Hitchcock and Bulleit went ahead anyway. In the background was Orville Zickler, assistant cashier of the First American National Bank. Bulleit remembered:

I was just in there one day at the bank—First American on Church Street—trying to see if we could get some money to do something or other with records, and Mr. Zickler asked me if he could get in on it. He apparently thought it was a good idea too. So we let him put in his share.

Like Hitchcock, Eugene Cashion needed a steady supply of records to feed his jukebox business and he too was integrally involved in Bullet, but not as a formal partner.

The Bullet Recording and Transcription Company incorporated on April 25, 1946, and issued five thousand ten-dollar shares. The incorporation certificate sworn out by Jim Bulleit, Rachel C. Bulleit, and C. V. Hitchcock in front of H. A. Van Trease, Notary Public, and sealed by Secretary of State Joe Carter enabled Bullet to "carry on the business of manufacturing or causing phonograph records and transcriptions to be manufactured and to distribute the same," to acquire other similar businesses, to enter into contracts, to borrow money, and to do everything necessary for the purposes of the corporation, "provided that it is not forbidden by the laws of the State of Tennessee." A small office Bulleit shared with Fowler became the company's principal address, 703 Medical Arts Building at 119 Seventh Avenue North, opposite the James Robertson Hotel. People remember Bulleit doing at least as much business in the hotel coffee shop or in the lobby at WSM, three blocks away.

Bulleit described the first of the label's false starts before it was fully launched in May 1946:

Bullet Records did their first recording in 1945, the week after Christmas. The very first pressing we had was on a feller named Sheb Wooley. It was just a market test. Nothing happened, it was just a beginning. We took him and his wife down to Studio B at WSM and did our first record session. We used WSM engineers and WSM transcription discs to put the things on.

Later known for his acting roles in films such as *High Noon* and *Giant* and on the television series *Rawhide,* Sheb Wooley was born in Oklahoma in 1921 and had met Bulleit during a brief stay in Nashville in 1945, when Bulleit was at WSM and Wooley was singing on WLAC. Bulleit recalled that Wooley came into town in an old, broken-down bus and needed to earn some money to cover the cost of repairs. A few months later, after Bulleit left WSM, he remembered Wooley and recruited him to take a hillbilly troupe, the Mountain Scandals, on a tour of southeastern states. Wooley made far less than he expected from the trip and recalled: "I guess Bulleit thought he owed me something. So he said, 'I'm gonna put you on record.' So we did. I made the first Bullet record."

At that session, Wooley recorded covers of current hits by Eddy Arnold and Ernest Tubb, apparently unissued, and two original songs, a lively "Oklahoma Honky Tonk Girl" and a ballad, "I Can't Live On Without You." He was backed by Wally Fowler's Georgia Clodhoppers, including Zeb Turner on guitar, fiddler Joe Carroll, Charlie Bares on steel, rhythm guitarist Curley Kinsey, and bassist Johnny New. Western

Jim Bulleit in his office on Twelfth Avenue South, 1947. Courtesy of the *Tennessean.*

Owen Bradley, second from left, playing vibes with Jack Shook's Missouri Mountaineers, mid-1940s. Shook is in the center and AFM president George Cooper is playing the bass. Some of these players made up "Brad Brady's Tennesseans" on Bullet. Courtesy Country Music Hall of Fame and Museum.

swing—a marriage of folk and blues instrumentation and songs with big-band styles—was at the peak of its popularity, particularly on the West Coast, and Wooley was one of the pioneers who brought it to Nashville; the session reflected its influence. That sound would be surprisingly prevalent on Bullet's Nashville-recorded output of this period, and it had more commercial currency east of the Mississippi than we might imagine today.

Though Wooley was the first artist Bullet recorded, his only known Bullet record did not appear until late spring 1946. By then, the label had made another start and even scored something of a hit, Bulleit said.

> The first commercial disc that was out was "Wave to Me, My Lady." This was when we were at the very beginnings of setting up a distribution system. We only had two outlets, Nashville, through Hermitage Music, and Birmingham, Alabama, through the Monarch Sales Corporation. We started with a pressing run of one thousand discs. Of those thousand, we gradually found that the juke operators were reordering the other side, "Zeb's Mountain Boogie."

Released on the canary-yellow Bullet label as Bullet 600 and credited to Brad Brady and his Tennesseans, an effective mix of accomplished pop and folk musicians put together by bandleader Owen Bradley, "Wave to Me My Lady" featured a vocal by Joe Carroll, a member of Wally Fowler's singing group, who had played fiddle on the Wooley session. Bulleit had good reason to think this was the side to watch. It had been written by top pop tunesmiths William Stein and Frank Loesser and introduced by Guy Lombardo in 1945. Country cover versions proliferated in 1946, including a best-seller by Elton Britt. Like many other recordmen before and since, Bulleit was dumbfounded when his throwaway B-side became the hit.

On "Zeb's Mountain Boogie," Owen Bradley and some of his dance band set up an infectious swing-band rhythm closer to Benny Goodman than to what we now think of as country music. Out of the mix leaped a number of instrumental soloists—fiddle, clarinet, and trumpet—but the guitar soloist, "Zeb Turner," stood out. Turner was in fact William Grishaw from Lynchburg, Virginia, a self-taught musician who came to Nashville in the early 1940s with Wally Fowler's Georgia Clodhoppers. By 1946 he was working with his own band on WSM and WLAC, and in September, Eddy Arnold recorded a song that Turner and Fred Rose had written, "It's a Sin," which became a #1 hit in 1947.

At first, Bradley wanted his name kept off "Zeb's Mountain Boogie." But when Bullet Records' original estimate of a thousand sales escalated to nine thousand, Bulleit said:

> Owen came to me to say, "Jim, I think you might have something with this hillbilly thing. If it would be all right with you, I just might like to put my real name on the record after all." So I called up American Label Works in Nashville, and we relaunched the record by Owen Bradley, not Brad Brady.

In September 1946, pioneering country music journalist Floy Case reported in *Mountain Broadcast & Prairie Recorder* that the record was "running close to the top of jukeboxes and programs throughout the country."

As Bradley told me later:

> I really came into record production by mistake. I had a pop orchestra and was approached by Jim Bulleit to record a song for his new label in 1945 in something more of a country style. Because of that first record selling, despite my reservations, I was able to become involved in a lot of the pop music sessions on Bullet, and that led on to other labels. When I started playing music professionally it was always in a variety of styles. I had my own pop orchestra, but we also played jazz and then again I often worked with a hillbilly outfit, Jack Shook's Missouri Mountaineers.

"Announcing Bullet Records"

After the false starts with Wooley and Bradley, Bullet advertised in *Billboard* at the end of April 1946: "Announcing Bullet Records—Hillbilly records from the home of Grand Ole Opry—Release date May 1st." The advertisements went on to list not only Bullet 600, but also Bullet 100, the first in a series of white gospel records, and Bullet 251, the second in the "Sepia Series—blues recorded in the South as only the South can." The hillbilly and white gospel series listed for seventy-nine cents and the sepia series for a dollar, although by July the prices had evened out to seventy-five cents for all series.

With no experience in the business, Bulleit was prone to error on any front.

> Labels caused me to make the first of many mistakes. When I went to the American Label Works, they had never had a call to make a record label before. In fact the first four hundred dollars' worth of labels had the hole punched one-thirty-second of an inch too big, so we had to throw them all away because they would not fit onto the pressing equipment when they were shipped out to Los Angeles. That was 10 percent of our capital gone right there.

Before long, Bulleit transferred his source of both label and disc manufacture to Ivin Ballen, who had set up the 20th Century label in Philadelphia in February 1946 and had spare

The first known Bullet Records release, early 1946.

Billboard June 1946.
Courtesy of Showtime Archives [Toronto] and Colin Escott.

capacity at his plant. The arrangement lasted at least until 1948, when Ballen began to devote more of his time to his successful Gotham label.

The April 20, 1946, edition of *Billboard* mentioned the new board of Bullet Records: Hitchcock, Bulleit, and Zickler, who brought economic realism to the project and quickly had Hitchcock set up a corporate child, the Volunteer Music Company, as the distribution arm for Bullet Records. Hitchcock ran his jukebox operation, Hermitage Music, from 423 Broadway, while Volunteer started out as a desk on a balcony above the main floor. Hitchcock soon took over the lease on the adjacent building, formerly John Veatch's secondhand-furniture store, and he ran Volunteer Music and Bullet Records from 421 Broadway. He rented a building at 1710 Portland Avenue in south Nashville near Ward Belmont School to serve as a warehouse and shipping address for Volunteer Music. Briefly, Jim Bulleit moved his office there, too. He wrote on May 28 to a prospective recording artist, Bill Bolick of the Blue Sky Boys, "We're in the process of moving. We are now at our new location, 1710 Portland." He offered Bolick a royalty deal of 2.5 percent, pointing out that it was more than anyone else got, "but we will go this far in your case."

Volunteer Music made deals for the wider wholesale distribution of Bullet discs with Eastern Music in New York, Associated in Chicago, Trilon in Los Angeles, and smaller concerns in Charlotte, Oklahoma City, Oakland, and Philadelphia. Bullet placed advertisements in the trade papers in June 1946, which noted: "Some territories still available." The company's cast of distributors would change rapidly over the next few years as many new companies started in business to handle the plethora of new labels and older ones fell away. As Bulleit explained:

> There was no record wholesale distributor in Nashville until we set up Volunteer Music Sales. And beyond Nashville, we just used the few independent record distributors that were set up in the South. The major labels had their own distribution networks. First we had Birmingham, and the reason for that was that C. V. Hitchcock had a friend down there, and he persuaded this friend to take the first records we ever sold. Then we got Memphis next. After a while we started to work through Ed Levi in New York. He had a record distributing company on Eighth or Ninth Avenue down here and we hooked in with them.

Sometime in the early winter of 1946, Hitchcock and Bulleit decided to give up the Portland Avenue premises, and they took a lease on an old warehouse at 2320 Twelfth Avenue South, at the intersection with Elmwood near Linden, which served as a makeshift office as well as a distribution hub. "It wasn't heated, and so you had to wear an overcoat inside in the winter," Bulleit remembered. He moved in with a secretary; bookkeeper Howard Allison; and two salesmen: Jimmy Green, who had been a salesman for King Records before joining Bullet, and Hutch Carlock. This was Bullet's day-to-day headquarters for a couple of years, although trade ads often listed the label's address as in care of Hitchcock's buildings on Broadway.

Of the recording in those very early days, Bulleit recalls:

> There was so much to be done, and it was all a "first"—trial and error. I recorded Zeb Turner, Chet Atkins, Bradley Kincaid, Minnie Pearl, all artists from the Opry, and I did it almost alone. I had a young man named Howard Allison, and two salesmen. Other than that, I relied on Owen Bradley for musical advice. We paid him a flat fee per session. He furnished me with WSM house-band musicians for my sessions, and I engineered the sessions myself at Studio C at WSM on Seventh Avenue. The songs were recorded directly onto sixteen-inch acetate discs, the same as WSM engineer Aaron Shelton used for transcribing radio shows. You could get four songs on a disc. There was no tape in those days, and the acetates tended to dry out or splinter or warp, but that was all we had, and we got by all right.

Opry Artists on Bullet

Most of the early Bullet 600 series hillbilly discs showcased Grand Ole Opry artists who weren't under contract elsewhere. In the summer of 1946, Bullet issued one disc each by Opry artists Bradley Kincaid, Minnie Pearl, and Pee Wee King, all backed by King's band, the Golden West Cowboys. The recordings had been made that April at WSM by King and his manager, J. L. Frank, and were apparently intended for a different label (to be called either Nash or King Records). Frank sold the recordings to Bulleit in return for a few copies to sell at live shows.

The vocal on Pee Wee King's cautionary tale "That Cheap Look in Your Eye" was taken by Jimmie Wilson. Cowboy Copas played rhythm guitar; Redd Stewart and Shorty Boyd played the fiddles; Chuck Wiggins was on bass; and Don Davis was on steel guitar. Davis recalled, "This was my first recording session. It was in the spring of 1946 in the WSM studio. The session was piped via telephone line to the transmitter some twenty miles away, where it was recorded on disc." Julius Frank Anthony Kuczynski had reinvented himself as Pee Wee King by the time he brought his blend of cowboy music, western swing, hot jazz, and polka to the Grand Ole Opry in 1937. He was a good accordionist, but an even better talent spotter, recruiting Eddy Arnold, Cowboy Copas, and Redd Stewart, and was a star on WSM radio and in cowboy movies by the time he began recording.

Courtesy of Showtime Archives [Toronto].

Cousin Minnie Pearl, 1940s. Courtesy of American Federation of Musicians and Harold Bradley.

WSM star Minnie Pearl's "Jealous Hearted Me," her first single, was a Carter Family song and a radio favorite from the 1930s, when the Deason Sisters (Kitty Wells and Bessie Choate) sang it regularly on WSIX radio. Born Sarah Colley in Centerville, Tennessee, in 1912, Pearl worked as a teacher after graduating from Ward-Belmont School, bringing her comedic talents in 1940 to the Opry as the gal from Grinder's Switch, Minnie Pearl.

Smooth-voiced Bradley Kincaid recorded the amusing novelty "Ain't We Crazy" when he was fifty-one. From Lancaster, Kentucky, he was a longtime favorite with fans for his old ballads and folksy story songs, for years appearing on Midwestern and Northeastern radio stations and as the "Kentucky mountain boy" on Chicago's *WLS Barn Dance.* Other Opry stars to record for Bullet Records during the first half of 1946 included Clyde Moody and Ford Rush, Bulleit's predecessor in the Artist Service Bureau. On "Remember Sweetheart" Rush was billed as the "Singin' High Sheriff," a nickname bestowed by George Hay when Rush joined the Opry.

Pete Pyle debuted on Bullet with "Living in Sorrow" and "Talking the Blues." Born in Burnsville, Mississippi, in 1920, he picked up the fiddle and worked professionally from 1940 in Sheffield, Alabama, then in Memphis. He first recorded for RCA Victor in Atlanta and came to WSM in 1940. "Bullet gave me a pretty good advance to sign a contract with them," Pyle said in 1974. "So, like a fool, I quit Victor and signed with them. I had just recorded for Bullet, and J. L. Frank got in touch with me and said he had a contract for me to do the singing on Pee Wee King's records." Pyle also covered Wayne Raney's hit, "Why Don't You Haul Off and Love Me," and recalled: "Bullet wanted that. I had to learn it and record it in one day. They got a lot of sales on it."

WSM and the Opry seemed to offer Bullet Records a supply of talent that would never run dry. As guitar-legend Chet Atkins confirmed, Bullet made the first records to feature him as a leader: Wally Fowler had alerted Bulleit to this new musical phenomenon after Atkins played the fiddle as sideman with Fowler's Georgia Clodhoppers in 1945—Atkins's first recording—and Bulleit signed him up as soon as the guitarist hit Nashville. He arrived in April 1946 with Red Foley, although Atkins left Foley after six months when Red's WSM sponsors cut his featured jazzy solo performances.

For the Bullet recording, Atkins said: "We took a pick-up band to Studio B at WSM Radio. We made four sides and they issued two." Atkins was never a great vocalist, and it was Jack Shook, one of Nashville's premier rhythm guitarists, who took the vocal on "Brown Eyes Crying in the Rain." But Atkins's dampened four-note bass-string intro to "Guitar Blues," played with dexterity and verve, started a recording career that lasted more than fifty years. Atkins was fond of

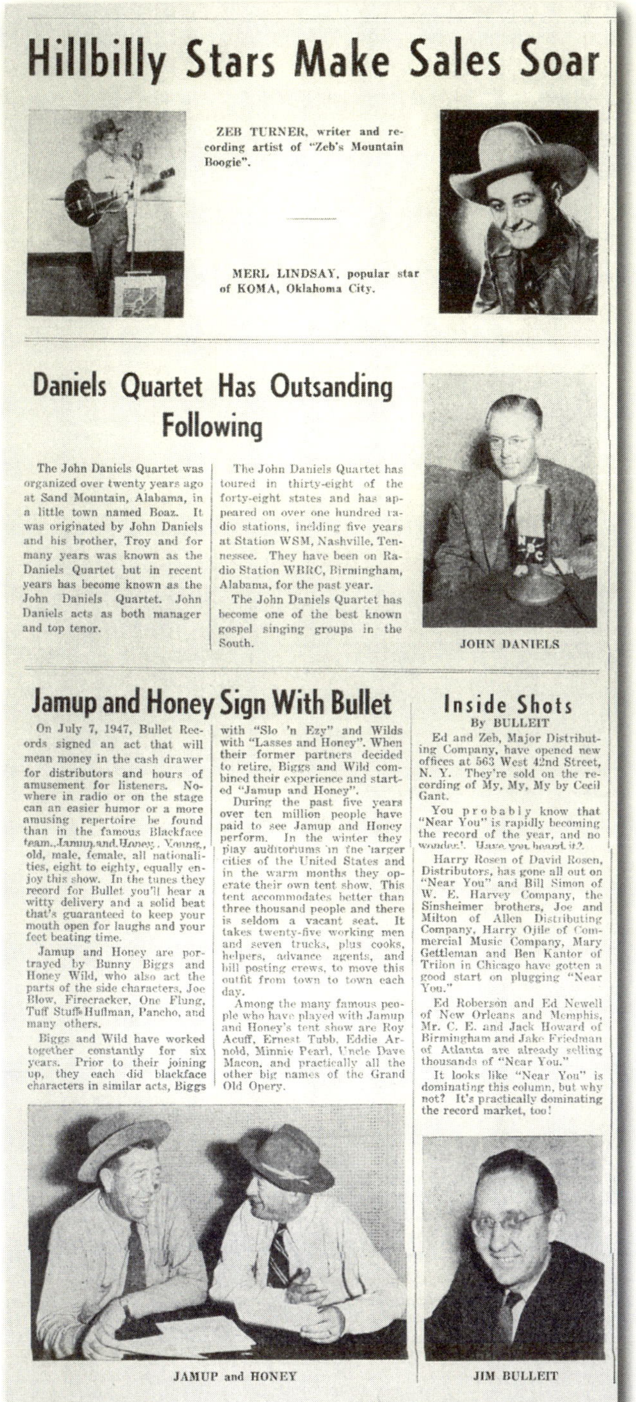

Hillbilly Stars Make Sales Soar

ZEB TURNER, writer and recording artist of "Zeb's Mountain Boogie".

MERL LINDSAY, popular star of KOMA, Oklahoma City.

Daniels Quartet Has Outsanding Following

The John Daniels Quartet was organized over twenty years ago at Sand Mountain, Alabama, in a little town named Boaz. It was originated by John Daniels and his brother, Troy and for many years was known as the Daniels Quartet but in recent years has become known as the John Daniels Quartet. John Daniels acts as both manager and top tenor.

The John Daniels Quartet has toured in thirty-eight of the forty-eight states and has appeared on over one hundred radio stations, inclding five years at Station WSM, Nashville, Tennessee. They have been on Radio Station WBRC, Birmingham, Alabama, for the past year.

The John Daniels Quartet has become one of the best known gospel singing groups in the South.

JOHN DANIELS

Jamup and Honey Sign With Bullet

On July 7, 1947, Bullet Records signed an act that will mean money in the cash drawer for distributors and hours of amusement for listeners. Nowhere in radio or on the stage can an easier humor or a more amusing repertoire be found than in the famous Blackface team, Jamup and Honey. Young, old, male, female, all nationalities, eight to eighty, equally enjoy this show. In the tunes they record for Bullet you'll hear a witty delivery and a solid beat that's guaranteed to keep your mouth open for laughs and your feet beating time.

Jamup and Honey are portrayed by Bunny Biggs and Honey Wild, who also act the parts of the side characters, Joe Blow, Firecracker, One Flung, Tuff Stuff Huflman, Pancho, and many others.

Biggs and Wild have worked together constantly for six years. Prior to their joining up, they each did blackface characters in similar acts, Biggs with "Slo 'n Ezy" and Wilds with "Lasses and Honey". When their former partners decided to retire, Biggs and Wild combined their experience and started "Jamup and Honey".

During the past five years over ten million people have paid to see Jamup and Honey perform. In the winter they play auditoriums in the larger cities of the United States and in the warm months they operate their own tent show. This tent accommodates better than three thousand people and there is seldom a vacant seat. It takes twenty-five working men and seven trucks, plus cooks, helpers, advance agents, and bill posting crews, to move this outfit from town to town each day.

Among the many famous people who have played with Jamup and Honey's tent show are Roy Acuff, Ernest Tubb, Eddie Arnold, Minnie Pearl, Uncle Dave Macon, and practically all the other big names of the Grand Old Opery.

Inside Shots

By BULLEIT

Ed and Zeb, Major Distributing Company, have opened new offices at 563 West 42nd Street, N. Y. They're sold on the recording of My, My, My by Cecil Gant.

You probably know that "Near You" is rapidly becoming the record of the year, and no wonder!. Have you heard it?

Harry Rosen of David Rosen, Distributors, has gone all out on "Near You" and Bill Simon of W. E. Harvey Company, the Sinsheimer brothers, Joe and Milton of Allen Distributing Company, Harry Ojile of Commercial Music Company, Mary Gettleman and Ben Kantor of Trilon in Chicago have gotten a good start on plugging "Near You."

Ed Roberson and Ed Newell of New Orleans and Memphis, Mr. C. E. and Jack Howard of Birmingham and Jake Friedman of Atlanta are already selling thousands of "Near You."

It looks like "Near You" is dominating this column, but why not? It's practically dominating the record market, too!

JAMUP and HONEY

JIM BULLEIT

recalling that he received twenty-two dollars in royalties from Bullet for the record. It would be another year before Atkins recorded again as the leader of his own group, this time with RCA Victor.

One of the best of the popular brother duets, the York Brothers from Louisa, Kentucky—George and Leslie—joined WSM after the war. Their Bullet material ranged from "Blue Ridge Mountain Blues" to the spirited "Hop Skip and Jump," but the first and best of their five recordings for Bullet was a reprise of their song about the sexual appetite of the title character of "Hamtramck Mama," which had outraged the predominantly Catholic and Polish Hamtramck area of Detroit when they had recorded it on Universal five years earlier.

When Bulleit signed another brother duo, the Turner Brothers, their first session marked the recording debut of Zeb Turner's brother and fellow guitarist Zeke, born James Grishaw in Lynchburg, Virginia, in 1923, eight years after Zeb. Zeke Turner remembered that

> the first recordings I did after I got out of the navy were with Zeb for Bullet Records. We'd known Jim Bulleit when he was in Anderson [South Carolina]. I played with Zeb on "Guitar Reel." I used his guitar, an old Epiphone that he got out of a pawnshop in South Carolina. I had a Gibson, but I liked the tone of the Epiphone better and traded him.

But it was Zeb, not Zeke, who pursued a solo career with Bullet and later with King Records. On "Ain't Had No Lovin'," "Chattanooga Boogie," and "Coal Miner's Blues," he sang in the bemused, detached style that Merle Travis was popularizing, although Zeb never gained the recognition due him for his achievements in integrating jazz and blues influences into hillbilly music.

Bulleit seemed well tuned to unrecognized potential. The Texas Troubadours were kept on a pretty strict diet of honky-tonk ballads as the road band for Decca artist Ernest Tubb, but on "That's All She Wrote" for Bullet they cut loose, showing what a fine, jazzy little unit they were. Tubb had emerged as a major star, and Bullet obviously also hoped for spin-off sales. The Bullet record would give the Troubadours

Ramblin' Tommy Scott, the last of the tent showmen, 1940s. Courtesy of Country Music Hall of Fame and Museum.

(Left): Page from Bullet Records' promotional *Bullet-In*, 1947. Courtesy of Country Music Hall of Fame and Museum.

Bill Nettles, Loyce Nettles, and the Dixie Blue Boys, late 1940s. Courtesy of the author and Mary Edwards.

something to sell during intermissions at Tubb's live shows, where they had their own spot. For the Bullet recording, Jack Drake took lead vocals and played bass; Jimmie Short was on electric guitar; his brother, Leon, was on rhythm; Ray "Kemo" Head played steel; and Johnny Sapp played fiddle.

When he could, Bulleit brought in artists he knew personally. Tent showman Tommy Scott, who had worked with him at WAIM in Anderson, South Carolina, told me:

> When Jim wound up in Nashville, he called and asked would I like to go on the Opry show. But that was every Saturday night, and I had good paying jobs on Saturday nights. Eventually, I did join him in Nashville. I worked for WSM and the Opry for nearly a year, but for very little pay. The money came in outside appearances. Then Jim told me he had bought into this record company owned by a man named C.V. Hitchcock, and he wanted me to record for them. So I went in there to the little office that Hitchcock had on Broadway. He told me that people could not get enough really good folk music and that they were able to sell anything they could get that was halfway decent. I signed up with them, and Mr. Hitchcock sent me over to WSM studios to meet up with Owen Bradley, the bandleader, who worked for Bullet and produced my first session for Bullet. We used my own band led by Gaines Blevins.

Another tent showman, Bunny Biggs, recorded with Lee Davis "Honey" Wilds as the blackface comedy duo Jamup and Honey, playing auditoriums in the winter and tent shows in the summer, with an entourage of twenty-five. For Bullet, the duo recorded the blackface routines "Feudin' and Fightin'" and "Used Car Blues." When Jamup and Honey signed with the label in July 1947, the publicity material promised:

> This will mean money in the cash drawer for distributors and hours of amusement for listeners. Nowhere in radio is there a more amusing repertoire, with the duo playing all their other characters like Tuff Stuff, Joe Blow, One Flung and others.

Drawing Talent from beyond Nashville

Despite their primary aim to record WSM artists, it soon became obvious to Bullet Records executives that they could not keep Opry stars under contract in the face of better offers from the major labels; many WSM acts made only one record for Bullet. Jim Bulleit had to extend his search for country talent beyond Nashville, and at the end of 1946 he acquired three folksy items from Pappy Howard and the Connecticut Kernels, including a version of the hit song "Cool Water," earlier recorded by the Sons of the Pioneers. Then he recorded Johnnie Barfield, born in 1909 in Tifton, Georgia, who had scored a huge hit with "Boogie Woogie" on Bluebird in 1939 before joining the army in 1942. After the war, Barfield's only record for Bullet, "Doin' the Boogie Woogie," became an underground hit and a jukebox favorite, though the musician never reaped the rewards of the country boogie music he had helped create.

Bulleit headed for the Southwest looking for unsigned talent, stopping in Louisiana to sign Bill Nettles and Owen Perry, then further west, where he found recordings by Tex Justus and his Texas Cowboys. His main Southwest contact was distributor Bob Dunbar in Dallas, who, Bulleit recalled, "also owned distribution companies in New Orleans and Houston. He always treated us well because his three distribution points grew up from an initial stake of five hundred records that I advanced him. That was how he got started in the record business."

It might have been the approaching A.F.M. recording ban of 1948 that sent Bulleit scouting the area, and a considerable amount of the label's output emanated from Texas and Oklahoma after mid-1947. Some sides were recorded during the ban itself, using either nonunion musicians or union musicians recording on the sly, a practice that seems to have been fairly widespread in Texas, especially.

West of the Mississippi, Bullet Records boosted the careers of some musicians, gave others their start, and, with Bill Nettles's "High Falutin' Mama," revived the career of a prewar recording artist. Bulleit recorded Nettles's minor hit "Too Many Blues" in Dallas in 1947, two years before he had the only charted hit of his career with the original version of "Hadacol Boogie" on Mercury. He is reckoned to have written the standard "Nobody's Darlin' but Mine," which he turned over to Jimmie Davis in return for getting Nettles out of jail more than once. From Natchitoches, Louisiana, Nettles served in World War I and began singing on KWKH, Shreveport, in 1935 when he was a brakeman on the Missouri Pacific Railroad; he began recording for Vocalion in 1937.

For Leon Payne, one of the great songwriters, recording for Bullet Records looked like a big career boost. Born in Alba, Texas, in 1917 and legally blind, Payne had been active professionally since the mid-1930s and had recorded for Bluebird in 1941. At his first Bullet session in November 1947 in Dallas, the *Houston Press* reported, Payne "sat in while some friends made some test records for a small recording concern. The agent asked Leon to sing a few songs and he recorded them." Payne had been singing for some time with these "friends," Jack Rhodes and the Lone Star Buddies. (Rhodes, getting established locally as a bandleader and songwriter, later wrote several successful country songs and an early rock & roll hit for Gene Vincent, "Woman Love.")

Payne's first Bullet record, "Lifetime to Regret," marked the beginning of a string of fine songs and performances. Payne is best known for writing "I Love You Because" in 1949, and he later claimed to have written—and sold—the major 1940s hits "Sioux City Sue" and "Detour." It is a shame that his classic Bullet recordings of "Lost Highway" and his autobiographical "They'll Never Take Her Love (from Me)" were soon upstaged by Hank Williams's MGM versions. "Lost Highway" was pure Texas honky-tonk with uncharacteristically few swing overtones, but even Payne was impressed. "Oh, that just flattens me out, Red Hayes!" he calls out during Hayes's fiddle solo. "Greatest thing in the world! I mean, that's great!"

Bulleit had set up Payne's 1947 session for Bullet in the Dallas studio of Jim Beck, who had his own label, Dude Records. Bulleit first met Beck when he was setting up distribution arrangements in Texas. With a background in radio and in record and appliance sales, Beck worked with Bulleit on various schemes, including recording machinery development. Along with the new recordings Bulleit arranged on his western forays, in 1948 he leased for reissue a number of Dude Records' western music items by Art Davis, Bob Manning, and "Cowboy Pal" Loyd Weaver.

But not all recording sessions happened in studios. Bulleit remembered going "to record Merl Lindsay out in Oklahoma City, right there in the dance hall they were playing." One of the better-known western swing artists, fiddler Merl Lindsay Salathiel and his band had four releases on Bullet in 1947 and 1948. The swing instrumental "Safety Pin Rag" featured Benny Garcia, one of the greats of western swing guitar, who owed a stylistic debt to former Oklahoma City resident and electric guitar legend Charlie Christian.

Leon Payne, master songwriter, c. 1950. Courtesy of Showtime Archives [Toronto].

Zeke Clements and Liberty Records

When talent from even farther west—Hollywood—showed up in Nashville, Bulleit often got it into the recording studio. Smiley Burnette's "Swamp Woman Blues" should have been a California recording, but Bulleit remembered recording Gene Autry's famous movie sidekick in Nashville along with other western acts, such as movie singer Ken Curtis, later associated with the Sons of the Pioneers and best known as Festus in television's *Gunsmoke.*

In 1948, Bullet issued "Brown's Ferry Boogie" by Zeke Clements, whose voice was familiar to millions as that of another favorite movie character—Bashful in Disney's 1937 *Snow White and the Seven Dwarfs.* The Warrior, Alabama, native was no stranger to Nashville, where he arrived at WSM in 1931 from stints on Chicago radio and with Otto Gray's Oklahomans. In Nashville, he worked on the Opry, played the theater circuit, and wrote songs, among them a wartime hit for Red Foley ("Smoke on the Water") and postwar hillbilly classics for Eddy Arnold ("Just a Little Lovin'" and "Why Should I Cry"). Clements first appeared on the Opry in 1933, working with his brother as Zeke and Curley and debuting Minnie Pearl on his show. On the theater circuit, Clement remembered

> playing at the Princess Theater in Nashville for the first time. We were supposed to do our show at 2:30 in the afternoon but the manager called us at 9:30 in the morn-

ing to say there were enough people standing on Church Street to fill the theater now. So we played two shows.

It seems likely that Wally Fowler, Jim Bulleit, or both were responsible for brokering the deal that would take recordings of the music of WSM via Clements to the West Coast; certainly Bulleit was in Los Angeles early in 1946 making contacts for Bullet. Clements had left WSM in June 1945 to work on Venice Pier in Los Angeles. By November he was running Liberty Records from an address in Santa Monica. Most of the nine records on Liberty were by Clements and his Western Swing Gang, starting with a sequel, "New Smoke on the Water," but around February 1946 he issued three discs by Nashville-based groups—two by the white gospel quartet of John Daniel, and one by the hillbilly band Paul Howard and his Arkansaw Cotton Pickers. The three discs were almost certainly made in Nashville, because John Daniel and Paul Howard were on WSM at the time, and the Howard disc features local musicians Owen Bradley, Billy Byrd, and Jabbo Arrington among the "Cotton Pickers."

Liberty Records did not thrive and, faced with legal action from Liberty Music in New York, Zeke Clements changed the name of his label to Blazon. He and his Western Swing Gang made their way back to Nashville and in 1948, Bullet issued Clements's "Brown's Ferry Boogie," a follow-up to the Delmore Brothers' big song "Brown's Ferry Blues."

A Broader Vision

Few of the early Bullet hillbilly recordings made any of the national sales charts, but many sold well regionally. By 1948, Bullet Records had a lengthy and well-established catalog of folk and hillbilly material. Jim Bulleit had been responsible for raising the stakes for musicians working out of Nashville. The major recording companies now knew that if they were interested in a singer but didn't record that singer quickly, then Bullet Records would. After the first year, though, Bullet was no longer reliant on Nashville's musicians. The label, and particularly Jim Bulleit, had a broader vision, which extended well beyond country music.

3

Standing in the Safety Zone: Gospel on Bullet

Back then, the crowds would be great. There were only a few major groups traveling then. You told people the Fairfield Four was coming, and that was it.
—Isaac Freeman

Bullet and all the early Nashville labels that followed relied heavily on gospel music, and with good reason. Gospel music was everywhere in Nashville and the southern record markets, both black and white, in the 1940s and 1950s. Although there were no sales charts for this music, a gospel record would occasionally make the folk listings or the "sepia" R&B charts, and the postwar independent record labels saw the genre as a growth opportunity. In the 1940s, Nashville, "the buckle of the Bible Belt," with its 358 churches of twenty-three denominations, numerous local church choirs, and several high-quality singing quartets, was as good a place as any to be recording and issuing religious music.

Nashville's eminent history in religious music stretched back at least to the nineteenth century, in both the black and white communities. In 1825, the presses of the *Nashville Republican* produced the influential songbook "Western Harmony," helping spread religious songs throughout the country and especially the South. The spirit of European Christian music had been fused with black African traditions almost as soon as the two cultures arrived in America, and in Nashville there developed an especially strong tradition of black spiritual singing that was carried to an international audience by the singers of Fisk University.

Jubilee and Gospel Traditions

A year before Bullet records got off the ground, the *Nashville Globe* reported on February 16, 1945: "Fisk Jubilee Singers Will Give Concert before State Legislature." The Fisk University singers were to perform for the governor and other state officials at the capitol, reviving a tradition that went back to the 1870s, when the Jubilee Singers of Fisk University, under director George White, became the first black group to perform spirituals in public.

According to the *Globe:* "The original band of singers went forth from Nashville after liberation from slavery, eleven simple, brave, and devout men and women, to sing their songs to an uninterested world in an effort to raise money that their institution might survive." The proceeds of an international tour by the original Fisk Jubilee Singers built the university's Jubilee Hall in 1876, and it was from the Fisk campus that the university's choir of "a hundred voices" broadcast live on CBS on March 9, 1946 in a radio program of Negro spirituals, "Wings over Jordan."

In the 1870s, inspired by public interest in the first Fisk group, the Tennesseans of Central Tennessee College formed, followed in the 1880s by the Tennessee Warblers and others. Doug Seroff, the noted authority on Nashville's gospel music

The original Fisk Jubilee Singers, 1871. Courtesy of Fisk University, Franklin Library Special Collections.

tradition, wrote in "Nashville: Historic Capital of Gospel Singing":

> For decades, jubilee companies took names which implied connections with Nashville or Tennessee that did not actually exist because the names had become so synonymous with quality jubilee singing the world over. . . . The Fisk Jubilee Singers added a new dimension to American popular music. The troupe from Fisk established a relationship between traditional plantation spirituals and the business of public performance.

Northern groups who adopted names that implied Tennessee connections included Brooklyn's Tennessee Jubilee Singers, formed in 1888, and the Nashville Students, from Chicago. Jubilee music took its name from the spirituals that one of the Fisk singers, Ella Sheppard, described as "associated with slavery and the dark past, sacred to our parents." The songs referenced shared hardship, freedom, and future joy, and "jubilee" became a standard term for several decades until it was overshadowed during the 1920s, in style and in name, by gospel music—bringing the good news of the gospels. Nashville itself experienced a golden age of jubilee singing, with the Meharry Quartet, the Monitor Chorus, and the Nightingale Quartette, a female group from Shelbyville, Tennessee.

In the early 1900s, Professor John Wesley Work II led the Fisk Jubilee Quartette, one of the earliest black groups to make commercial phonograph records—ten 78-rpms for Victor in New Jersey in 1909, followed by others for Victor, Edison, and Columbia by 1916. Work, who trained the choir at the First Baptist Church in Nashville, became a pioneer folklorist and musician, gathering three collections of Negro folk songs that were produced by the Work Brothers Publishing Company.

When Bullet Records formed forty years later, their catalog would also include music emanating from Fisk and the spiritual tradition, but in the main, Bullet recorded the newer gospel style of religious music.

The roots of the modern gospel music, black and white, that Bullet Records and others would record developed in rural churches and neighborhood communities after the Civil War. Some churches—principally black Baptist churches and white Holiness-Pentecostal groups—forged a more fervent style than their more traditional Christian neighbors and developed their own songs. The modern concept of "gospel music" emerged with these newly written songs, often of a more popular nature.

During the nineteenth century, revivalists like Dwight Moody, based in Chicago, inspired a new wave of religious songwriting. Ira Sankey's book "Gospel Hymns and Sacred Songs" linked the word "gospel" to religious song in 1875. As late as 1944, Nashville music scholar and professor of German at Peabody, George Pullen Jackson, observed that, "aside from the Bible, the book found oftenest in the homes of rural Southern people is without doubt the big oblong volume of song called 'The Sacred Harp.'" This collection of hymns, published a century earlier by Benjamin White, built upon earlier volumes still, and earlier singing styles that had sought to make learning hymns easier for the masses through the use of songbooks with "shaped" notes.

The late nineteenth century saw religious teachers

criss-crossing rural areas across the United States, setting up temporary schools and teaching music. Professional evangelists organized singing conventions for those who wanted to learn the new songs. In Giles County, in middle Tennessee, James David Vaughan studied Moody's book before forming a singing group in 1882. He moved to nearby Lawrenceburg in 1902 and continued to publish a popular series of songbooks called *The Gospel Chimes,* bringing out a new book every year for four decades. In 1910, Vaughan began to sponsor a touring quartet to publicize his songbooks. The group contributed enthusiastically to summer "singing schools" and singing conventions, and branched out as one of the first professional white gospel quartets.

A change that increased the popularity of gospel singing in the 1920s and 1930s was radio's early-morning live music programming. By 1922, Vaughan had a license to set up WOAN radio in Lawrenceburg, Tennessee, to promote his music and the gospel message, selling songbooks and the Vaughan name. WOAN used the same channel that the fledgling radio WSM was later allocated in Nashville, and it was partly through Vaughan's good offices that WSM was able to continue and expand. As WSM developed—and obtained its own radio frequency—the Vaughan Quartet appeared regularly on Nashville radio for many years.

Listeners across the South regularly tuned in to the Vaughan group, and by the later 1940s other white groups such as the Blackwood Brothers and the Statesmen Quartet had developed huge followings, laying the groundwork for the Jordanaires, who would move from their gospel roots into lucrative recording-studio work behind Elvis Presley and others.

The Rise of Popular Gospel

In the 1920s and 1930s, as gospel singing groups increasingly eclipsed larger choirs, the word "quartet" came to describe not the number of a group's members but its four-part harmony, with one or more members singing alto, tenor, bass, and baritone. Within the black communities especially, the singing quartets formed among working people sang very differently from the university-based jubilee groups. Rhythms grew less straightforward and expanded to include "blue notes," syncopation, and popular harmonies. Gospel scholar Tony Heilbut wrote in "The Gospel Sound": "Modern gospel style continues a tradition of singing, preaching, and shouting familiar to generations of black people. . . . The basis of gospel repertoire remains hymns but gospel music has also embraced other songs, spirituals, and anonymously composed tabernacle songs often common to rural Southerners of both races."

The blues, though often characterized as "the devil's music," often held a fascination for gospel singers and vice versa. The most famous link between gospel and the blues came in the person of Thomas Dorsey, born in Georgia in 1899 to a Baptist Minister and a church organist, who moved to Chicago and played with jazz and blues singers in the 1920s. He recorded blues under the name "Georgia Tom" and other aliases, but he also formed a gospel-music publishing company in 1930 and devoted most of his life to religious songwriting. The term "gospel" has been much associated with Dorsey, who once claimed that, in the early 1920s, he "coined the words 'gospel songs' after listening to a group of five people one Sunday morning on the far south side of Chicago. There were no gospel songs then, we called them evangelistic songs." Although the term in fact predates Dorsey, songs like "Just a Little Talk with Jesus," "Peace in the Valley," "Precious Lord, Take My Hand," and "Wings over Jordan" have cemented his place in gospel-music history.

Southern white gospel quartets continued to promote sheet music and songbooks, and while Otis McCoy's Tennessee Music and Printing Company in Cleveland, Tennessee, founded in 1931, remained important in selling shape-note music, new avenues opened up and widened the market for gospel music. With the radio era, gospel songwriting improved, and the songs' melodies and sentiments caught the public's ear. Arguably the best at fusing gospel fervor with easy-to-sing ballads and up-tempo, rousing rhythms was Albert Brumley, who between 1932 and 1945 wrote "I'll Fly Away," "I'll Meet You in the Morning," "Turn Your Radio On," and "If We Never Meet Again." An Oklahoman born in 1905, Brumley was a singing teacher in Missouri in the 1930s and, as the "Gershwin of the rural route," was important in connecting professional gospel song and professional country singers.

Country gospel pioneer Wally Fowler, mid-1940s. Courtesy of Country Music Hall of Fame and Museum.

Commercial recordings of white Southern gospel groups went as far back as the Vaughan Quartet in 1921, Frank Smith's Sacred Singers in 1926, and the Stamps Quartet in 1927; in Nashville, at the 1928 Victor field sessions, Ralph Peer recorded the Vaughan Quartet, the Gentry Quartet, and others. Nashville's Golden Echo Quartet from WSM, a black religious group, traveled to Atlanta for recording sessions with Columbia at this time.

After the war, the new independent labels were hungry to sign up talent. Bibletone Records of New York and White Church in Kansas City were among the labels set up specifically to record gospel music. Songwriter Lee Roy Abernathy's Homeland Harmony Quartet recorded his song "Gonna Have a Wonderful Time up There," backed by a spirited, rolling piano rhythm. The record sold more than 200,000 copies for White Church and became known as "The Gospel Boogie," spawning many cover versions, black and white.

Bullet Records, of course, issued Nashville's first postwar gospel records. In April 1946, Bullet announced the label's dedicated 100 series of discs by white gospel groups, and issued recordings by Nashville's premier black gospel singers in the company's black music series.

By the 1940s, black gospel music had become increasingly saleable nationally. Three smooth-sounding quartets, the Golden Gate, the Deep River Boys, and the Charioteers, broadcast every Sunday over national radio networks, inspiring many local groups to promote themselves, exposing a wider range of gospel styles. By 1950, every black neighborhood was aware of the latest hits by the likes of the Trumpeteers, the Georgia Peach, the Angelic Gospel Singers, Sister Rosetta Tharpe, or Mahalia Jackson. Male quartet singing flourished on records by the Dixie Hummingbirds, the Pilgrim Travelers, the Chosen Gospel Singers, the Swan Silvertones, and the Spirit of Memphis.

Cross-fertilization of white and black gospel music was commonplace, and more prevalent in the years before the U.S. Supreme Court's 1954 decision in *Brown v. Board of Education* than after. The main difference between the sounds lay perhaps in the intensity of the rhythms of the black quartets; each singer sang one of the four harmonic parts—as in white quartets—but each also developed his own rhythms that together created a more complex sound. White singers were quite familiar with black groups like the Golden Gate Quartet or Nashville's Fairfield Four in the 1940s. Blacks and whites heard each other's styles and songs on the radio or the jukebox, and when the *Nashville Globe* of February 15, 1946, advertised a performance by the popular Southern Echo Quartette, stars of radio WATL in Atlanta, the ad noted: "Special seats for white people."

The Ubiquitous Wally Fowler

One who drew from both black and white gospel traditions, as well as from hillbilly music, was Nashville's ubiquitous country-gospel singer, songwriter, publisher, and idea man Wally Fowler—the same Wally Fowler who declined to, or was financially unable to, become a partner in the infant Bullet Records and who gave the label its name. Born in Adairsville, in Bartow County, Georgia, in February 1917, Wallace Fowler was singing at age six and won an amateur contest at fourteen. He joined the Harmony Quartet and later the John Daniel Quartet when they began appearing on the Opry in April 1940, then moved to Knoxville.

By 1943, Fowler's Georgia Clodhoppers were firmly established on radio in east Tennessee, with a solid following for their mixture of folk tunes and religious music. When a nuclear weapons plant was set up at Oak Ridge, Tennessee, in 1943, the Clodhoppers regularly performed for the defense workers, and in 1945, Fowler cashed in on a hot topic by renaming his group the Oak Ridge Quartet and going on to record a number of songs about atomic power. He was not the only one to attempt to cash in on the making of the atomic bomb in Tennessee. In December 1946, the *Tennessean* reported that a company in Nashville was marketing a board game devised by four chemical engineers from Oak Ridge and titled "Up-an-Atom." Wally Fowler recorded for New York's Asch label in 1944 and joined Capitol in 1945 with the Atlanta session that marked Chet Atkins's recording debut as a sideman. Fowler's record of "Propaganda Papa" was a big seller on Capitol, reflecting the change in public and political

WSM announcer Grant Turner, left of microphone, introduces Wally Fowler, right of microphone, and his secular group, the Georgia Clodhoppers: *left to right*, Zeke Turner, Red Bennett, Joe Carrol, Curley Kinsey, Lon "Deacon" Freeman, and Johnny New, mid-1940s. Courtesy of Country Music Hall of Fame and Museum.

emphasis from the hot war to the cold. He had written the song with J. Graydon Hall from Birmingham, a frequent songwriting partner.

In 1945 Fowler moved back to Nashville, where he and his wife, Evelyn, and their two daughters, Faith and Hope, lived at 220 Woodland. He returned to the Opry in September and organized Wallace Fowler Publications, a Broadcast Music, Inc., affiliate, and an ASCAP-affiliated company, F&M, administered by a top publisher, Edwin Morris. In November, Fowler recorded another session for Capitol, this time in Los Angeles, and things looked promising for him when he returned to Nashville and helped pitch to Jim Bulleit the idea of starting up a new record label.

Bulleit recalled the scene of his very first meeting with Fowler:

> It was early in 1944, during the time I was announcing at WSM. It was a day when Fred Rose, the local publisher, and Syd Nathan, of King Records in Cincinnati, were in the office. I had just been for an army physical in connection with being called up, and failed it when they found I had bad eyesight. It so happened that Fred Rose was long-sighted, and Syd Nathan was extremely short-sighted. It was quite a thing to see those two together in my office checking a contract or the details of a lead sheet. One of them would have the page at arm's length, and the other

The John Daniel Quartet, 1942: *from left*, John Daniel, Troy Daniel, Percy White, Wally Fowler, and Jess McCurdy, with Gordon Stoker at the piano. Courtesy of Bear Family Records.

one would have it stuck right in front of his face. That same day, Wally Fowler was there. He was pitching songs to Fred and Syd. Wally was working out of Knoxville at that time, but he had several publishing and performing interests connected with WSM.

From his office in the Medical Arts Building at 119 Seventh Avenue North, Fowler promoted songbooks and song copyrights for himself, Eddy Arnold, and others. (He wrote part of "That's How Much I Love You," Arnold's first top-selling hit.) With Eugene Cashion, a copartner of Bullet Records, he set up a company called Tennessee Music Sales, operating from 145 Lafayette Street, then forged a sales link with Mercury, for whom he started recording in 1946. Ruth Bradley, sister of musicians Owen and Harold, assisted Fowler in these various enterprises.

The *Tennessean* was soon reporting that Fowler had written three hundred songs and appeared over 237 radio stations via the Purina-sponsored *Opry House Matinee,* broadcast over WSM at noon on Saturdays, and starring Eddy Arnold and Ernest Tubb. "I'm just a Georgia country boy at heart," Fowler told the press. "We try to put on a good clean show full of homespun humor and songs. That's what the folks like." One song they liked was "Faith Is the Grain of a Mustard Seed," and Fowler marketed "Wally Fowler's Mustard Seed" on the back of that song's popularity. He told the *Tennessean,* "Gospel music is what I prefer. It's the sort of music that never dies and I figured it would be better to stick with it rather than fool around with the stuff that is here today and gone tomorrow." The *Tennessean* called Fowler "one of the few really sincere exponents of gospel music."

Bullet's White Gospel Series

When Jim Bulleit made a deal with the Stamps-Baxter organization in Dallas to launch Bullet's white gospel series, Wally Fowler brokered the deal. Stamps-Baxter had been the top gospel-song publisher in the country for ten years or so, and a number of professional and amateur singing groups bore its name. The company had been established by Virgil Stamps and Jesse Baxter in 1926 to promote the Methodist message. Virgil's brother, Frank, led the Stamps Quartet, and Jesse Baxter made the deal with Bullet. The first disc, Bullet 100, "They Have Gone Away," was a traditional quartet item, accompanied by piano and delivered straightforwardly by a mixed quartet with an unidentified female voice in the lead. A second disc, "Who Is That," credited to the Stamps-Baxter Mixed Quartet, and with organ replacing the piano, followed it immediately. Jim Bulleit remembered the discs thirty years later: "The Stamps-Baxter people recorded their group and sent it to me for release. We paid royalties from the first copy sold, but they had covered the cost of recording."

The connection with Stamps-Baxter was short-lived, perhaps because Bulleit found a number of professional and family-based groups available nearer home. John Daniel, the Goodman Family, the Speer Family, the Crusaders, the

Wally Fowler opens the mailbag of fan mail for his "All Night Singing" shows. Courtesy of Country Music Hall of Fame and Museum.

Rangers—all were ready and willing to record, and all had heavyweight reputations among the community that bought gospel records.

Born in Boaz, Alabama, in 1903, John Tyra Daniel formed the Daniel Quartet with younger brothers Troy and Luther and sisters Mary and Orell, working for the Vaughan company as one of many unofficial pioneers and boosters of commercial gospel song. The group traveled through thirty-eight states, promoting their songs at singing conventions, before switching allegiance to Stamps-Baxter in 1940. At that point the quartet consisted of John and Troy Daniel, along with nonfamily members Wally Fowler, Jim Waits, and Carl Rains.

By 1942, the Daniel Quartet played WSM on a regular basis, and they became one of the best-known gospel groups in the country. Daniel recorded five discs for Bullet over six years, starting in late 1946 with "Careless Driver" and "Heading for the Pearly Gates," the first in a body of work that repeatedly mined the theme of the religious journey. With songs such as "Crossing over Jordan," "On the Glory Road," "Looking Beyond," and "Get Aboard This Train," Daniel specialized in exhorting his listener to travel with him. The group had a professional sound, with a clear separation of voices and a rather traditional gospel style, perhaps slightly restrained. Two of their Bullet discs from late 1947 had been issued the year before by Zeke Clements on Liberty, underlining the probability that they had been recorded by Jim Bulleit in the first place, and leased to Liberty.

Bullet recorded the Rangers Quartet on "Just a Little Talk with Jesus" in 1948, Bulleit said.

> The Rangers Quartet came in to record one time when they were on a Wally Fowler all-night singing program. They were out of Georgia and had been on WBT in Charlotte, North Carolina. They were popular, so we took a chance to record them.

Their Bullet recordings were classily delivered with a trademark high-pitched lead voice and hurrying, piano-supported rhythms. Formed in 1936 for the Texas Centennial, the group had soon dropped the "singing Texas Rangers" theme and worked as the Rangers all through Kentucky, the Carolinas, Virginia, and Kansas, reaching Shreveport around 1950. Marion Snyder had joined mainstays Vernon and Albert Hyles in 1941, adding a distinctive piano style.

The all-night sing Bulleit mentioned was a concept introduced by Virgil Stamps of Stamps-Baxter. In 1938, Stamps held a singing school in Dallas that inspired a follower to say, "Mr. Stamps, I could listen to you sing all night." Stamps went on to broadcast a late-night "All Night Singing" program over KRLD, Dallas, before a live audience. The Dallas event was promoted by Wilmer Nowlin, sometime Methodist preacher and Stamps Quartet singer who turned concert promoter and took the idea to various venues in the following years. In 1948, Nowlin explained to Wally Fowler how to bring the concept of all-night singing to Nashville. The first of Fowler's many "All Night Sings" took place on Friday, November 5, 1948, at the Ryman Auditorium, broadcast live for two hours by WSM.

The Fairfield Four, c. 1947: *from left, back row,* Rufus Carrethers, Willie Frank Lewis, and Rev. Edward "Preacher" Thomas; *front row,* Sam McCrary, James S. Hill, and George Gracie. Courtesy of Jerry Zolten.

Black Gospel and The Fairfield Four

Fowler's "Sings" included several black gospel quartets, principally Nashville's own Fairfield Four, a group of national stature who had been the first black gospel artists on Bullet. Formed at the Fairfield Baptist Church on Hermitage Avenue, the original trio became the Fairfield Four in 1925 under the leadership of Rufus and Harold Carrethers. By the late 1930s the Four were broadcasting regularly on WSIX, led by tenor Sam McCrary, recognized as the most outstanding gospel singer to come out of Nashville.

The Fairfield Four first recorded in 1941, singing "Don't Let Nobody Turn You Round" for Fisk professor John Work III, son of John Wesley Work II, who recorded them in their church for the Library of Congress. In 1942, they won an early-morning slot on WLAC, sponsored by the Sunway Vitamin Company and hosted by announcer Herman Grizzard. Soon, they moved to a Colonial Coffee–sponsored evening show for the CBS network, where they broadcast to a large national audience. "We were on WLAC for twelve years," member James Hill recalled. "Every morning at 6:45 you heard the Fairfield Four, either in person or on transcriptions. Sam McCrary had a unique voice, a full sound. People liked it because it had a lot of feeling in it." McCrary confirmed the strong following the group generated, and the wide coverage of the WLAC signal, remembering: "When we used to sing every morning, we had people [at our live shows] say, 'Well, we used to get up by you.' They waited. They wouldn't go to work until we got off the air."

McCrary reminisced of the 1940s: "We traveled a lot by train. We had to, as they were rationing tires then. We were not a professional group. I worked for the railroad for sixteen years. Other members of the group had jobs too." And Isaac Freeman remembered:

> Back then, we would travel maybe six hundred miles a show, and the crowds would be great. There were only a few major groups traveling then. You told people the Fairfield Four was coming, and that was it. You couldn't get in the place.

When the group first recorded for Bullet Records, the Fairfield Four comprised McCrary, Willie Lewis, John Battle, the Carrethers brothers, and possibly George Gracy. They were a tight-run organization and developed their own joint business—a funeral parlor on Lafayette Street in south Nashville—and their own written rules of operation, or "by-laws" as they called them; these included a business meeting and rehearsal twice weekly, arrival at the studio thirty minutes before airtime, no arguing in public, no chewing gum in church, and "any member found drinking within 8 hours of program be fined $5." Jim Bulleit promoted the group widely and remembered that he sold large numbers of copies of "Don't You Want to Join That Number" in 1946 and of "Standing in the Safety Zone" in 1947. He remembered what he called their "fervent, insistent singing style," and their refusal to sing anything other than gospel songs, noting in 1947: "The Fairfield Four have appeared in some of the largest auditoriums and some of the smallest churches in the country, and have turned down many offers to sing popular and classic numbers, preferring to stick with their gospel music."

Then the group split up, having argued over remuneration from a show at the Ryman. Sam McCrary and Harold Carrethers each organized his own version of the Fairfield Four until McCrary prevailed. On later Bullet recordings, McCrary and Lewis were joined by experienced singers from other quartets: Preston York from the Reliable Jubilee Singers, Edward Thomas from the Famous Blue Jays, Isaac Freeman from the Kings of Harmony, and Alabaman James Hill, who said their secret was simplicity—"Start slow, raise it up high, catch on fire, then stop."

The Fairfield Four made nine discs in all for Bullet over a number of years before recording for Jim Bulleit's Delta Records in 1949 and moving on to Dot Records in the early 1950s. Isaac Freeman and James Hill left at this time to form the Skylarks, after the group's funeral business failed. The Fairfield Four have continued intermittently as leading players on the Nashville scene through a number of different line-ups, and the group enjoyed an international renaissance at the turn of the twenty-first century, appearing on discs and videos with Lyle Lovett and on the traditional music soundtrack of *O Brother, Where Art Thou?*

In 1948, Jim Bulleit recorded the Famous Jubilee Singers, an offshoot of the Fisk Jubilee Singers. They were directed by Mrs. James Myers (wife of the tenor who had recorded with the Fisk Jubilee Quartette for Victor forty years earlier), who placed several Fisk groups with recording companies over the years. This incarnation featured vocalists Starling Hatchett, Norton Evans, Brooks Alexander, and Samuel Floyd. "This lady came to us and wanted to have a record to take with them to sell as they went touring around," Bulleit said. "It helped them promote what they were trying to do." Bulleit also recorded the Evangelist Singers of Detroit in 1948, a male quartet led by Oliver Green—probably in Nashville, as they made several high-profile personal appearances at the Ryman Auditorium with Sister Rosetta Tharpe in the late 1940s.

Jim Bulleit, who was involved in church activities and singing himself, liked gospel music. The Bullet 100 series sold well and was recycled steadily over a number of years. It eventually included a virtual who's who of white southern gospel groups. There is no doubt that the music made by white vocal groups was as important to the development of secular forms of Southern music as was the emergence of black singing groups to the development of rock & roll and soul music. Surprisingly, given the success of the Fairfield Four and the receptive market for gospel music generally, Bullet Records recorded less black gospel music than white. Possibly this was because the company found greater than expected success with their recordings of more worldly black music.

4

Nashville Jumps: Bullet and the Blues

Seen you goin' up Cedar Street hill,
I know you got your whiskey from Jack Daniel's still,
Nashville really jumps, really jumps all night long,
I'd rather be in Nashville, than be way back at home.

—"Nashville Jumps" by Cecil Gant

Successful as Bullet was with hillbilly and gospel music, the market that gave the label a kick start in the summer of 1946 was the one Jim Bulleit knew least about—"race" music, the term the industry applied to blues and to black music generally.

Bulleit had the good judgment to forge a link with booking agent Harold Oxley, as *Billboard* reported on April 27 of that year:

> Oxley Acts to Disk on Bullet . . . Booker Harold Oxley has closed a deal to represent Bullet Record Company, of Nashville, in Hollywood and New York, and has already cut Wynonie Harris, blues singer, and Cecil Gant, of *I Wonder* repute, for the label. Oxley will concentrate on the race and Latin field for Bullet, using a goodly portion of his stable of talent for waxings. Jim Bulleit, prexy of the Bullet plattery, continues his personal supervision in recording hillbilly talent. Tie-up works both ways in that Oxley will book some of the corn country talent Bullet puts on platters.

In fact, Harold Oxley did not record Cecil Gant or Wynonie Harris. Jim Bulleit recorded both in Nashville, but they were working on the West Coast in the mid-1940s and Oxley had tipped Bulleit off to their availability. Gant's first recordings had caused a sensation in 1944 and 1945. His "I Wonder" was a #1 R&B record in the cocktail-combo style that Nat "King" Cole had perfected. The liaison with Oxley gave Bullet an entrée into the growing R&B market.

"Through my time in selling," Bulleit told me, "I knew that you had to get in first, with the most. And when I decided to start releasing blues records—the 'sepia series' we called it back then—I wanted something that would stand out and be identified with Bullet Records." Bullet's first advertisements touted its country and gospel songs as emanating from the home of the Grand Ole Opry. Later, the label opened its pop music series with a signature tune, "The Bullet Bounce." It was, then, part of a grand plan when the 250 sepia series opened with a song called "Nashville Jumps."

Cecil Gant

The voice and piano behind "Nashville Jumps" belonged to Cecil Gant, a West Coast–based Tennessean who was one of the stars of black music early in 1946. "I Wonder" had boosted the developing boom in independent record businesses in and around Los Angeles in 1944 and 1945. As Jim Bulleit recalled:

I had not been in the record business when I lived on the coast, but I did know most of the agents and promoters. When I started Bullet Records, I would travel around—to L.A., to Chicago, to Philadelphia, to Dallas—to set up my networks. I had a main contact in every town. In Chicago it was Lester Melrose, but my first contact was Harold Oxley in Los Angeles. Oxley met me one day when I was setting up distribution on the coast for my country records. He said he was managing some of the big names, Wynonie Harris, Cecil Gant, and others. I said he should send Cecil Gant to see me, and I set up a recording session at WSM in Nashville. Cecil then moved back home to Nashville. He came in, and I asked him if he was under contract to anybody, and he said no, so I said, "Well, how about working with me?" and he said that would be all right. I gave him some money—it wasn't much because we didn't have much. We put him under a contract to pay so much a record. But he always kept ahead of us by needing advances all the time.

Bulleit summed up Gant as "a small black feller who never did record a thing that didn't sell and make money." He described how Gant would sit at the piano with a bottle of booze and make up songs on the spot, but this was a misreading that sprang from Bulleit's lack of exposure to black music and Gant's two decades of learning and playing blues, boogies, and ballads. Bulleit didn't realize that Gant was often simply reworking his already substantial repertoire rather than composing new tunes.

Bulleit asked Gant to come up with a celebration of his hometown for his first Bullet disc. "Nashville Jumps" was just what Bulleit had ordered, though whether Gant had already written the song to play when he was in town is unknown. The recorded song was a tour de force by Gant himself, with only minimal rhythm support, underlining what a clear vocalist and clever two-handed pianist Gant was. In his lyrics, Gant paints a picture of the joys of drink and the joys of Nashville, and he probably ranked them in that order.

Cecil Gant was born in Davidson County, near Nashville, in April 1913. He played music around the local area in the 1930s and appeared on Nashville radio before spending some time in Cleveland and winding up in the army on the West Coast. Actress Bette Davis presented him with a citation for his service in a special unit in World War II, playing music on a hospital ship that plied between the West Coast and Hawaii. Gant's musical influences ranged wide. Among them was another Nashvillian, Leroy Carr, who had recorded "How Long, How Long Blues" on Vocalion in 1928 and whose fresh piano style and relaxed blues vocalizing made him one of the blues superstars of the prewar era; one of the first male blues singers to come from the city rather than the cotton patch, Carr's trademark was thoughtful and literate lyricism. Gant was also influenced by the boogie piano of Albert Ammons,

Cecil Gant at the piano, late 1940s. Courtesy of Showtime Archives [Toronto] and Colin Escott.

Bullet recording session at Castle Studio: Cecil Gant at piano, with Charley Grant, sax; Farris Coursey, drums; Jack Charamella, guitar; and Ted Swinney, bass. Courtesy of Country Music Hall of Fame and Museum.

who toured the South in the thirties and appeared frequently in Nashville. Finally, upon hitting the coast, Gant was as keen on the popular vocal styles of band singers like Frank Sinatra as he was on the hip black sound of Nat Cole's Trio, which permeated the intimate supper-club venues across the country.

Gant's original recording of "I Wonder" was made around June 1944 by Leroy Hurte for his Bronze Records label. Around September that year, Gant recorded the song again, this time in Cliff McDonald's garage studio. Issued by Bill McCall and Richard Nelson on their Gilt-Edge label, the McDonald recording became such a hit that it was dubbed "the song that launched the independent record business." "I Wonder" entered the charts in October 1944 and made #1 best-seller in what the trade papers called "sepia music," crossing over to reach #20 on the popular music charts. The following year, Gant made the sepia Top Ten with "Cecil's Boogie," "The Grass Is Getting Greener," and "I'm Tired."

Jim Bulleit maintained that Gant's discs were all cut in Nashville, and he clearly remembered his first session at a WSM studio, assisted by Aaron Shelton and Carl Jenkins, WSM engineers who also ran the Castle Recording Laboratory there. Sometimes Gant came alone, sometimes with his own supporting musicians, but usually Bulleit organized a rhythm section for him. Most often these were white musicians who loved to play late-night jazz, particularly guitarist Jack Charamella, tenor-sax player Charles Grant, bassist Ted Swinney, and drummer Farris Coursey. They all played with popular WSM bands by day and also made country music sessions in the days when the Nashville studio system was in its infancy. Bulleit told me:

> Cecil Gant would say, "I want to do a session" whenever he ran out of money. We would get a bass player and a drummer, and he would sit at the piano and tinkle around on it sorting out a song. I'd go in the control room, and he'd rehearse with a bottle of booze on top of the piano. When he was ready, he'd tap that bottle, and if you didn't get it the first time you didn't get it at all, because he could never remember exactly what he'd done.

The ballad "I'm All Alone Now," issued in the fall of 1946, was a deserved, if minor, hit for Gant and Bullet that helped put the company in the black for the first time. For the next Gant disc, "Ninth Street Jive," the band and the engineer created the atmosphere of a north Nashville Ninth Street drinking club. This was a storming piano boogie, complete with audience participation and spoken asides from Cecil such as, "Bring me another drink and I'll be all right." Next, released around March 1947, "Boozie Boogie" was the subject of a trade advertisement proclaiming that Randy's Record Shop in Gallatin had sold thirty thousand copies in thirty days. Harold Bradley remembered:

> My brother Owen played sessions with Cecil Gant, who always turned up with a woman and a drink, and he would often make up the words. If the recording went wrong, they would ask him to do it again, but he couldn't do it the same. So he'd turn to the woman and say, "Hey, pour me some more words."

A lot of stories circulated about Gant, and many were even true. Some, though, stem from a patronizing *Tennessean* feature on Bullet Records in 1947: "Bullet Recording's most prolific recorder and top individual artist, by all rules, is a short, stocky Negro named Cecil Gant, a slightly sensational Los Angeles pianist and singer." According to the newspaper,

Billboard May 17, 1947. Courtesy of Showtime Archives [Toronto] and Colin Escott.

all Gant's records had made money, and his bluesy recording of "I'm All Alone Now" had sold a highly respectable hundred thousand copies. The article went on to claim:

> Bulleit and Gant never discuss what tunes he is to record. Gant, whose formal musical education doesn't go much further than an ability to distinguish the white keys from the black, just sits down at the piano, messes around a little, and comes up with a tune. After he has run through it a time or two for the benefit of his accompanists and for timing, it is recorded, and that's that. "Nashville Jumps" was born in such a fashion, as was "Anna Mae," which was inspired by the presence of one of Gant's personal admirers. For Bullet, Gant has composed and recorded five tunes in 50 minutes, and at a session not so long ago he started composing a tune called "Boozie Boogie" at 8:50 and by 8:58 it had been rehearsed and recorded.

Around April 1947, Cecil Gant made his third recording in three years of "I Wonder," his most famous tune. When the song had first come out, it had tapped into the era of uncertainty just before the end of the war, when a lot of people were wondering what had happened to their loved ones. The song had been a hit for Gant in 1944. It was covered by Roosevelt Sykes and was again a hit. It was covered by Louis Armstrong and became a #3 R&B hit. Woody Herman recorded it, saying "it was bluesy even though it wasn't really the blues." At the height of the song's success, in 1945, Gilt-Edge had apologized in the trade papers for being unable to press enough copies to keep up with demand. At one time, black-market copies were selling for $2.50, and distributors were paying just a cent short of the theoretical retail price of 75 cents. In 1947, at the tail end of the era when a song was the hit more than any specific version of it, Jim Bulleit wanted a copy of the song in his catalog.

Gant took the Bullet version at the same laconic pace as the hit version, though the real talking point was the relegation of his piano to the role of chording in the background. Jim Bulleit genuinely thought he could bring the song back to the charts if it was a little different: "I brought in Owen Bradley to play on that record, as I thought it needed some new life." Bradley seems to be playing a celeste or possibly a vibraphone, but instead of taking on new life, the song lost some of Gant's expressiveness. It sold well as a catalog item, though Bullet Records couldn't put the song back on the sales charts.

But Gant had plenty of hits in him. "Another Day Another Dollar" sold steadily in 1948 and eventually entered the *Billboard* R&B Juke Box Hits chart in October 1948, reaching #6—Gant's fifth national chart hit, his first on Bullet. A strong song with cleverly constructed lyrics and real commercial potential, "Another Day" was written by country singers Wally Fowler, Curly Kinsey, and Jimmie Short, and Gant took it at his slow, pop-ballad pace—explaining his lot, working every day for his baby's benefit, another day, another dollar.

By 1948, Gant was working for his dollar mainly in the Nashville area. He often played in Louisville, and from September to December 1948 he was at the Manhattan Club in Newport, Kentucky. "I'm a Good Man but a Poor Man," released in October 1948, became a #12 R&B hit the following spring, but by the end of 1949 Gant had made his last session for Bullet.

Gant "did everything from his heart and soul, as if he was pining for something or reminiscing some sad occasion," blues shouter Roy Brown told researcher John Broven. "He had something catchy in his voice that made you feel what he was trying to convey to you." Gant was equally capable of ferocious boogie pounding and hipster patter. Full of humorous asides or insightful commentaries, his recordings ran a gamut of styles from Leroy Carr's Depression-era blues to Slim Gaillard's 1940s "slanguage."

In New Orleans in February 1950 Gant recorded for Imperial, then made the first of nine discs over several sessions for Decca under the name Gunter Lee Carr, perhaps in recognition that he was still under contract to Bullet. Decca's producer in Nashville was Owen Bradley, who recorded Gant on blues sessions and also with country star Red Foley. Bullet issued two more Gant discs, the last, in mid-1951, a version of the Andy Kirk hit "Take It and Get." In terminal decline physically, Gant made his last recording early in 1951. When publisher Arnold Shaw met him around this time, "He was a much troubled man. His failure to recreate his hits gnawed at him. I have seen this frustration and puzzlement through the years and it is a painful and unforgettable sight."

Gant continued to play music locally right to the end, and singer Billy Wright has recalled being with him on the Saturday before he died. They were scheduled to do a show on the next day. Instead, Gant ended up in Hubbard Hospital.

Billboard reported in February 1951: "Cecil Gant died last week, February 4 in Nashville. He was a prolific tune writer and recording artist. His discs appeared on as many as a dozen labels at the time of his death." Jim Bulleit maintained that Gant had died of syphilis, and the official verdict was pneumonia, but the general feeling is that the main contributing factor was those bottles of booze that stood on the piano while Gant played.

Wynonie Harris

Not long after Cecil Gant's first session for Bullet, agent Harold Oxley scheduled singer Wynonie Harris for a spring tour that took in Omaha, St. Louis, Cleveland, San Antonio, Miami, and Nashville's Club Zanzibar. An experienced agent and manager when he became Harris's representative in 1945, Oxley had guided the Jimmie Lunceford Orchestra to success, and in Harris he added the rising star of blues big-band vocalizing to his client list. No wonder Oxley divided his full-page ad in the *Billboard Encyclopedia of Music 1946/47* between Gant and Harris.

Bullet artists riding high, 1947. Courtesy of Colin Escott.

The uniquely named Wynonie Harris was born in August 1913 in Omaha to a fifteen-year-old mother and an Indian father named Blue Jay. He grew up to be a precocious dancer and an engaging—if opinionated and rather uncontrollable—human being. He graduated to emceeing local shows and taking the occasional turn at belting out blues vocals in the declamatory style of his Kansas City idol, Joe Turner, moved to the Los Angeles area in the forties and spent some time as featured singer at the Club Alabam, and first recorded in 1944, when he became featured vocalist with the successful Lucky Millinder band. He had recorded for Philo, Apollo, and Hamp-Tone in Los Angeles before he arrived in Nashville around March 1946 to record for Bullet. Harris's musical resume included a flashy stage act, a belting vocal style, and a string of impressive small-band, jazz-based blues discs, often with risqué lyrics. He was used to performing in front of impressive players like Millinder's sidemen, the Johnny Otis band, or sax stylist Illinois Jacquet. Bullet issued two Harris discs simultaneously, "Lightning Struck the Poor House" and "My Baby's Barrel House."

Bulleit described the recording sessions:

When Wynonie Harris made the deal for these records, he had just finished a residency at a club here in Nashville. He did not have a contract, so I asked him how much he would charge to record. He said, "Three hundred dollars, and you pay the studio and the musicians and I'll give you the songs." So that's what we did. We took him up to WSM Studio B, and we made four sides. He had a pianist with him, and we added a band.

The band was the Club Zanzibar house band led by Chicago alto-sax player Jimmie Jackson. On piano was Herman "Sonny" Blount, who had just joined the band from his base in Alabama, on his way to a blossoming career as Sun Ra. On "Barrel House," Harris's raucous exclamations sound as

Wynonie Harris swings into town, 1946. Courtesy of Nashville Public Library, the Nashville Room.

though he is trying to make himself heard above the noise of a party, which makes the disc entertaining if unfocused.

Bulleit's experience as a music producer was limited, particularly in R&B. "The first Wynonie Harris record sold three hundred thousand copies, and I couldn't even understand the words of it," he said. "It was just a bunch of screaming as far as we were concerned." He revised his opinion a little when Jake Friedman of Southland Distributing Company in Atlanta called him about the disc, saying, "Bulleit, we can't get enough of these Wynonie Harris things." Bulleit said later: "We made a killing on his records because we just paid him and the sidemen and the studio costs. We didn't have a royalty deal. We went crazy on his records."

That summer, Wynonie Harris returned to Nashville to headline the Swing Parade of 1946 package that played to a full house at the Ryman on July 11. Tickets were on sale at Hermitage Music and other downtown venues, and Harris's Bullet discs sold briskly. But despite good sales over time, neither of Harris's Bullet discs made the charts. By the end of the year, Harris had moved to New York, and in 1948 he recorded on King Records of Cincinnati, where he made a #1 hit with the proto–rock & roller "Good Rockin' Tonight," which Elvis Presley would later record for Sun Records.

Still, Harris and Gant helped put Bullet Records' bank balance into the black, Bulleit confirmed.

We did much the best in R&B. See, three hundred thousand was a big record in both country and blues, but it was far more easily attainable for us in blues. We sold our R&B in the big cities, nearest to the pressing plants—easier for the distributors—and to a market concentrated in a small area. Even based in Nashville, we ultimately found hillbilly harder to sell.

But Jim Bulleit never developed an affinity for R&B music. Talking to the *Corydon (Ind.) Democrat* in September 1947, he remarked that he was recording "Negroes who had neither the talent nor initiative to take their wares to the big recording firms on the east or Pacific coasts." Despite this attitude, Bulleit had the sense to realize that the future was in urban and cocktail blues rather than in cotton-patch blues.

Bullet's R&B Roster

Jim Bulleit took an opportunistic approach to selecting artists: By simply being in the right place with a fistful of money, he made and bought some good R&B records. He was dismissive of Wynonie Harris's records, yet Harris registered hits in the uptown styles, as did two other Bullet acts, Red Miller and the Big Three Trio. Sherman Williams and Rudy Green were local Nashville R&B artists who racked up steady sales for Bullet, which also cultivated a roster of R&B musicians who had made their names in the prewar era, such as St. Louis Jimmy and Walter Davis.

Over three decades, Rudolph Spencer Green recorded for labels in Nashville, Chicago, and New York, but his origins are a mystery. He recorded for Bullet in 1946 and was still on a Nashville label, Poncello, in 1961, and several contemporaries remember him as a local artist. Rudy Green had three discs on Bullet, performed in a tight, jazzy blues-trio style with Green on guitar and Cecil Gant on piano. Green's "Buzzard Pie," a kind of reply to Nat Cole's 1944 hit "Straighten Up and Fly Right," has the overall feel of the jivey tradition of the Nat Cole Trio, with instrumental riffs translated into vocal ones. Although it was common practice for record labels to take a share of composer credits on their releases, this disc was one of the few purportedly written by Jim Bulleit. Perhaps it actually was.

At about the same time, alto saxophonist Sherman Williams made "Sherman's Boogie" for Bullet, which seems to have been his first recording. Released around July 1947, the disc was accompanied by a brief note in an issue of the *Bullet-In,* a promotional newspaper put out by the label: "Sherman Williams and band have made great progress since being formed October 1940. Williams plays alto sax and writes many of his own numbers. He has been studying music since age nine." Williams's vocalist and pianist, a native of Birmingham, Alabama, who had settled in Nashville, was Edward Brooks, known as "Skippy" because of his limp. Charles Gillum played trumpet, William Jones the tenor sax alongside Sherman's alto, James Brown the bass, and Alvin Woods the drums. Together, they made a tight, booting combo of some quality and jazz influence. The band's vocalist, Iona Wade, on the Bullet recording "Keep Your Man at Home" written by Wade with Williams, sang a warning to some bad, evil woman, and Williams's fluid alto sax break and two-bar fills around her vocals underscored what a polished act this was.

Sherman Williams made four Bullet discs, which brought him to the attention of Foto Records in Los Angeles. Williams's band recorded next in Houston, and then in Los Angeles. Their style was modeled on that of West Coast bandleader and recording entrepreneur Roy Milton, and the two men seem to have made a deal whereby Williams helped run the Foto, Ace, and Miltone labels for Milton and supplied musicians for Milton's bands. In 1951, Williams was resident at the Barrel House on Central Avenue in Los Angeles, and he recorded there on Unique and Flip until 1956. Back in Nashville in the mid-1950s, Williams was last heard of playing downtown nightclubs like the Basement Bar in Printers Alley in a band with baritone-sax player Tot Randolph, jazz pianist Jimmy Osborne, and Bobby Hebb on guitar.

Bullet Records released one of the country's best-known blues songs, St. Louis Jimmy's "Goin' Down Slow," but its version was not the first, even though the artist was a Nashvillian. Born James Oden in 1903, by 1917 he was working in a barbershop in St. Louis. He moved to Chicago in 1933 and was an established blues recording artist with Champion and Bluebird by the time Chicago recording agent Lester Melrose connected with Jim Bulleit and put Jimmy onto his hometown label in 1947. Jimmy had learned his music in the joints and house parties around the St. Louis area in the twenties and thirties, traveling often with pianist Roosevelt Sykes and guitarist Big Joe Williams. His three Bullet discs may be Chicago recordings, but Roosevelt Sykes has recalled traveling to Nashville to record with Jimmy. Bullet also recorded Jimmy's wife, Rose Oden.

In another Chicago connection, the Four Clefs' "Am I Still Your Baby" appeared on Bullet in April 1947. The Clefs were a popular, sophisticated, jive-styled combo led by guitarist Johnny Green and vocalist Willie Chapman. Their "Dig the Blues" had been a big hit on Bluebird in 1940. Guitarist Harold Bradley remembers being in their session when the Clefs traveled to Nashville to make their sole Bullet disc.

BULLET HAS GREAT SEPIA STARS

**Gant, Williams, St. Louis Jimmy, Four Clefts
Big Three Trio and Fairfield Four
Among Sepia Stars**

Bullet Records is justly proud of its sepia artists. More progress has probably been made in the race department than in any other division of their operations.

Cecil Gant heads the list of Bullet's great sepia stars, being a well-known singer all over the country. Gant composes most of his own numbers, among which is "I Wonder," made popular by Woody Herman.

St. Louis Jimmie, a native of Nashville, Tennessee, is well known in the night spots of St. Louis and surrounding territory.

Sherman Williams and his band have made great progress since they were first formed in October, 1940. Williams plays the alto sax and also composes many of his own numbers. He has been studying music since the age of nine.

The Fairfield Four are a religious group who have been in operation since 1921. They have appeared in some of the largest auditoriums and some of the smallest churches in the country and have turned down many offers to sing popular and classic numbers, preferring to stick with their gospel music.

Among the other sepia stars of whom Bullet Records is justly proud are: The Four Clefts, the Big Three Trio, and Rudy Greene.

Top portion of page from Bullet Records' *Bullet-In*, 1947. Courtesy of Country Music Hall of Fame and Museum.

The Big Three Trio

None of the talent Jim Bulleit's contacts in the major cities brought in could have delighted him more than the Big Three Trio. Firmly rooted in black culture, the group had a crossover sound that Bulleit could relate to. They could play boogie blues, sweet blues, popular novelties, and ballads. And Leonard "Baby Doo" Caston, Willie Dixon, and Bernardo Dennis had a unique selling point: They sang the blues in three-part harmony.

"You Sure Look Good to Me" was the song Baby Doo Caston associated most with the genesis of the Trio. He told researcher Jeff Titon:

> I created the style of singing the blues in harmony. All the stars were singing single. So me and Bernardo Dennis and Willie Dixon, we all got together and I arranged this song. It was done first by Big Joe Turner and Art Tatum, but I rearranged the melody and harmonized it. It was the first time the blues was played like that and it was all over everywhere.

The Big Three took their name from well-publicized 1945 performances by Caston and fellow soldiers Ollie Crawford and Alfred Elkins as Negro USO Troup 56 in front of the big three Allied commanders, Eisenhower, Montgomery, and Zhukov. Caston, who organized the group after the war, was from Sumrall, Mississippi, learned piano in the Natchez area in the 1930s, and moved to Chicago in 1937, aged thirty, where he worked as a guitarist and pianist and hung around bluesmen like Tampa Red and Caston's hero, Leroy Carr. Late in the decade, Caston met a fellow southerner, Willie Dixon, who would later become famous as Chess Records' bass player and songwriter supreme. From Vicksburg, Mississippi, Dixon was a gospel singer and a songwriter of all kinds of music who in 1936, at age twenty-one, had hoboed to Chicago. Caston and Dixon put together the Five Breezes in 1940, and Caston then formed the Rhythm Rascals and switched from guitar to piano on a regular basis.

Home from the war, Caston sought out Dixon and, with guitarist Bernardo Dennis, formed the Big Three. The trio started at the Sky Club on Chicago's west side and developed a flashy act—brightly colored suits and Dixon doing tricks with his double bass—continually refining their harmonies, singing the tune and all the riffs together. They were approached by Chicago blues kingmaker Lester Melrose, who had opened a music store in the city in 1922 and soon became a song publisher and agent for musicians. During the thirties and forties, he had the city's recording scene tied up. As Dixon recalled: "Lester Melrose was the go-between man between the blues artists and the recording companies. Very few artists had their own contract with the label, they had to have their contract with the go-between man." Melrose signed the trio early in 1946 and, according to Caston, "got in touch with Jim Bulleit, who came in from Nashville and heard us." Melrose cut the Bullet sessions at the World Studio in the Wrigley Building on Chicago's Michigan Street. "His way was to tap his feet and enjoy the music and say, 'Let the guys sing and play it the way they feel,'" Dixon said, "and if it gave him goose pimples then he felt he had him a hit."

The trio's first disc on Bullet, issued in May 1947, illustrated their range of material. "Get Up Those Stairs, Mademoiselle" was funny, friendly, easygoing, and laden with hooks, jazzy phrases, French phrases, and quiet little bombs dropped by the unknown drummer; Caston had spent some time in France toward the end of the war and wrote the song about a soldier meeting a girl while on leave and needing to get on with the action. The other side of this disc was "Lonely Roamin'," a mellow minor-key blues ballad that was something of a hit in the South.

"Signifying Monkey," the Big Three's first big hit, was an update of two traditions—"signifying," or bragging, and the "dirty dozens," or rude rhyming couplets. The dozens started out as a means of teaching twelve religious facts by rhyming them for children, but parodies developed immediately, and in adult hands the dozens became an insult routine aimed at friends or neighbors. Mixed with signifying, the dirty dozens became a natural for recordings. Leroy Carr and Speckled Red were just two bluesmen who became associated with hit versions of the signifying dozens, and gradually one of the popular couplets about a monkey became a song title. Jim Bulleit came to Chicago in an agitated state shortly after its release, when he had been plugging the disc's other side, "You Sure Look Good To Me," and suddenly found himself with a lot of orders for a title he didn't realize he had.

Caston recalled the ending of the Big Three's time with Bullet:

> Well, naturally, when you get things going with a little company, the big companies want to get you then. So Mr. Melrose was the go-between—the scout for Bullet Records—and he told us, "We're going to get you on Columbia."

"Bewildered"

The biggest-selling record of the Bullet sepia series was not by Cecil Gant, Wynonie Harris, the Big Three, or anyone else contracted to the label. It was "Bewildered" by the Red Miller Trio, first recorded in Detroit and issued there on the Staff label. C. V. Hitchcock liked the song and decided to pick it

Billboard December 11, 1948. Courtesy of Showtime Archives [Toronto].

up for reissue on Bullet just as it started to sell in October 1948.

"Bewildered" made the *Billboard* charts in November 1948 and hit #1 on both the R&B Best Seller list and the R&B Juke Box chart that winter. Written as a pop jazz song in 1938 by Leonard Whitcup and Teddy Powell, the song was a hit for the Tommy Dorsey Orchestra. Miller's version was covered by Amos Milburn on Aladdin, whose disc entered the charts a month after Miller's, in December 1948, and also made #1. "Bewildered" could have been black, white, or crossover, and that is its appeal, along with its lyric about a man's uncertainty over parting from a woman. Miller's piano triplets and little runs occur throughout to add some interest, but they don't explain the song's popularity. Maybe male record buyers recognized "Bewildered" as a state they got into with women, and maybe women bought it to celebrate the phenomenon.

Something of a surprise hit in 1948, "Bewildered" was a cocktail-time ballad, and although he sang strongly, in an appealing, pleading light tenor, Red Miller was not exactly a household name. He was born John Miller in Fort Wayne, Indiana, and first took to music when he joined a spiritual quartet in church, from which he graduated to singing in Detroit's Twelve Horseman nightclub. "They waited for me one Sunday till church was over. They liked my style of singing," was his explanation. By then he was following the styles of Billy Eckstine and Perry Como, and he cited Duke Ellington as a big influence. From the nightclub he connected with United Records in Detroit and recorded "Bewildered" on December 31, 1947. His musical philosophy was simple:

> I like swing and blues and bop, but I believe you reach more people with sentimental music than any other. You get the feeling inside when you hear a vocalist put the expression in a song.

5

The Musical Miracle: Bullet Goes Pop

> *To my way of thinking, this is the story of a miracle. It started back in March 1947. I had contemplated giving up my band, so I wanted to record a little number that I had written and arranged. "Near You" was my swansong, something I could show my children and say, "That's what your pappy did."*
>
> —Francis Craig, radio interview, 1948

Most independent-label R&B or folk-hillbilly discs sold at best twenty-five thousand copies, and sales of a few hundred thousand counted as real success. In those terms, Bullet Records was a solid label through its first three years of operation. But the big money lay in popular music, and Jim Bulleit had always eyed that market. It was, after all, what he knew best. For most of 1946, Bulleit's partners, Hitchcock and Zickler, had parried his expansionist schemes. He became difficult to resist, however, when Francis Craig offered to record for the label, and in 1947, Craig's catchy if unexceptional big-band pop recording, "Near You," sold over two million copies, rocketing Bullet Records into the big leagues.

That Francis Craig recording almost didn't happen, because Bullet was short on funds. It was November 1946, and the label was still finding its feet, despite some promising sales in the folk and black music worlds. Bulleit was sitting in his Twelfth Avenue warehouse-cum-office when,

> Francis Craig came to me and wanted to record his theme song, called "Red Rose." It had been networked on his NBC radio spot and was a well-known tune. I saw it as an opportunity for our company. But I had to tell him that we couldn't afford to pay for a full orchestral session. I owed the bank $13,000. Craig said that Fred Harvey in the big department store in town could sell enough records to pay for a session, as there were a lot of middle-aged people in Nashville who could remember dancing to his music at their high school graduation dances. Then we started to collect on a song called "I'm All Alone Now" by Cecil Gant, and that paid off the bank note.

Bulleit had wanted to record popular music since Bullet went into business, but session costs were much higher for the full orchestras needed on popular songs. Bulleit had started the label's pop series with a compromise, a six-piece group rather than a full orchestra—"what we hoped would be a signature or identifying tune, 'The Bullet Bounce' by the Eddie Wiggins Sextet."

How Eddie Wiggins, a jazz alto-sax player based in Chicago, came to make Bullet 1000 with a song titled especially for the label is not clear. Bulleit evidently saw the band in New York or Chicago and arranged either to record them there or to purchase sides already recorded. The A side, "The Bullet Bounce," was an instrumental workout featuring Wiggins on alto and Red Cody on vibes, and the B side was a vocal by the guitarist Frank Glassi. *Metronome* asked its readers: "Have you caught the Wiggins Sextet at the Brass Rail on Chicago's Randolph Street since they added Red Cody? The band jumped before, and now it jumps even more." Jim Bulleit obviously felt it played more with a bounce.

Born in Tacoma, Washington, in 1917, Wiggins had played in jazz violinist Stuff Smith's band and in Billie Holiday's orchestra. Around 1943, he settled in Chicago to lead his own hot jazz group. His sextette recorded two sides for Detroit's Sultan Records early in 1946 and played New York's Aquarium Club that October. So Bulleit had good reason to believe in Wiggins, who continued to get rave reviews in the black jazz press. His Bullet record, however, issued in January 1947, disappeared almost without trace. Enter Francis Craig.

Francis Craig

A native Tennessean, Francis Jackson Craig was born in September 1900 in Dickson, the ninth of ten children of a Methodist minister. He was related to the Craig family who soon would help build the National Life and Accident insurance business into one of the major enterprises in Nashville, and cousin to Edwin Craig, who developed radio WSM. Francis was brought up in a reasonably affluent family, but his prudent father taught him the value of saving money where he could, a lesson he carried forward when managing and booking his dance bands. The story goes that when he was eight years old he heard a ragtime pianist in a pool hall in Clarksville, Tennessee, and went home and copied the style from what he remembered. His mother encouraged his talent, while keeping from her husband the source of Francis's inspiration.

By 1914, the family had moved to Gallatin, just north of Nashville, and there Francis's father caught his teenage son illicitly listening to Emory's Saxophone Orchestra from Memphis, a black jazz band. Craig formed his first band as a student at Vanderbilt University in 1921 to play at a fraternity dance. For most of 1923 and 1924, he and his orchestra toured the South, perhaps inspired by ragtime and hot jazz but for the most part developing a calmer big-band jazz acceptable to society audiences. He first performed on radio in 1923 on radio pioneer Jack DeWitt's short-lived station WABV. The broadcast was made from DeWitt's living room.

In 1924, Craig married Elizabeth Gewin in Birmingham, Alabama, but the couple's stay there was short; by 1925, Craig was back in Nashville with a regular engagement at the most posh hotel in town, the ten-story, 250-room Hermitage, built in 1910. His band played the Grill Room for lunch and dinner, continuing to develop the soft jazz style that suited the hotel's diners, and for WSM's historic debut broadcast in October. In January and September, Craig and his band had traveled to Atlanta to make records for Columbia. The first session was not issued, but by the end of the year "Marble Halls" and other tunes marketed as "ballads or novelties with a regional flavor" were extending Craig's reputation. At his last Columbia recording session in 1928, the band played "Red Rose," a song Craig wrote for his wife, Elizabeth. The number became Craig's theme song and was well known all through the South for many years; the Delmore Brothers, a country duo, recalled playing it regularly on WSM in the 1930s.

For many years, Craig's was *the* society orchestra for Nashville's upper crust. (Trombonist Bradford Smith led the band when Craig was sidelined with tuberculosis in 1930 and 1931.) Several fine singers traveled with the group in the 1930s, including James Melton, Snooky Lanson, and Dinah Shore. Kitty Kallen, whom many remember as Craig's sole female vocalist, was with the band only in 1940. In Nashville, Kallen was briefly married to Craig's saxophonist Clint Garvin, the two having also worked together in Jack Teagarden's band in 1939. She went on to top the charts with Jimmy Dorsey's band, among others, and to have a solo #1 with "Little Things Mean a Lot."

After twenty-five years on the road, Craig was ready to retire the band. The war was over, and WSM offered him a job running the music library, playing records on the radio, and advising on other aspects of music. But first he wanted to record "Red Rose" in a newer version, for posterity, and Bullet Records was the only game in town. With Bullet's accounts barely in the black, and on the strength of Bullet's market test with "The Bullet Bounce," Jim Bulleit eventually got the green light from his partners: "I was able to call Craig and say that we had decided to go ahead with some popular band recordings. We went into WSM to Studio C."

There, on January 20, 1947, Bulleit assembled Francis Craig and his orchestra, with singer Bob Lamm, a blind trumpeter from Newcastle, Pennsylvania, who had been with Craig since September 1943; session "producer" Owen Bradley; and recording engineer Aaron Shelton, who sent the audio signal three miles to WSM's back-up transmitter on Fifteenth and Weston, where the music was cut onto a sixteen-inch acetate disc. Craig recorded "Red Rose," then "Hot Biscuits" and "Sometimes I Wonder." This left just about enough time for the one more song Bulleit needed to get two records out of the evening's work. Owen Bradley had to leave around 9:30 to get to his dance-band job at the Andrew Jackson Hotel, so it was Bulleit and Craig who decided on "Near You" as the fourth tune.

"Near You"

When Francis Craig recorded "Near You," the song was less than a year old. In April 1946, Craig had met a New York songwriter, Kermit Goell, at Nashville's Hermitage Grill Room. He played Goell some new music he had written called "Near You" and asked whether Goell might have an idea for some lyrics. Goell, who thought the music a little trite, quickly dashed down some words on a Grill menu and took them back to California with him, promising to finish the song. When Craig later got in touch with Goell and asked for the lyrics, Goell decided the song was not worth more attention and sent the words almost exactly as he had first drafted them.

Craig's arranger, Jim Hall, told him the song was too corny, but as Craig told the *Kingsport Times* in 1947: "In order to satisfy my personal vanity I decided to work up the song and build it around myself"; he had in mind an extended piano solo. Bullet agreed to record it after Rachel Bulleit picked it out when Craig "auditioned" songs for the Bulleits on his NBC radio program, *Francis Craig's Sunday Serenade.* Craig had worked out a complicated ending for the song, but when he jumped from the podium to the piano stool during the broadcast, he ended "Near You" simply with three chords—he was rusty on piano and had forgotten his original ending. The Bullet recording session ended by ten the next night, but the Craig band was due on the air half an hour later and apparently stayed behind in the studio, broadcasting, among other things, "Near You" with Craig's more complex ending. The Bullet recording had retained the simpler version.

The Francis Craig Orchestra with singer Dinah Shore; *rear,* featured mascot Pee Wee Marquette. Courtesy of Vanderbilt University Special Collections and University Archives.

"We issued the disc of 'Red Rose' / 'Near You' [Bullet 1001] in April 1947," Bulleit remembered.

> It was the second in our popular series, and when "The Bounce" failed to take off, I put all my promotional activities behind "Red Rose." We were still not what you would call established or successful. In fact, we were back in debt on the day "Red Rose" came out. I took a chance on that song. I gave it everything. I hired several planes to fly promotional runs dropping red roses as they flew over the city. Most of them fell on roofs. For a time, "Red Rose" sold slowly. Then a disc jockey down in Griffin, Georgia, [by the] name of Cal Young, started

Courtesy of American Federation of Musicians and Harold Bradley.

to play "Near You" on his program instead. It was the B side but he didn't know that, and we gained ourselves an international hit that was started out in Griffin, Georgia, unlikely as that may seem.

Cal Young, the nephew of a Nashville record dealer named Ernie Young, was in the habit of visiting his family in Nashville regularly and taking records back to Griffin to play. He told me:

> I would go to my uncle's record store downtown to pick up records, because at that time it was not so easy just to obtain product. Well, I picked up this disc and started to play "Near You" from it. Then a local store in Griffin started receiving requests for it, so they ordered a hundred copies, and then they wanted more. That alerted Bullet to something strange going on.

Jim and Rachel Bulleit were driving through South Carolina on vacation when "Near You" began playing on every radio station they tuned in. Bulleit soon received a frantic telephone call from Eugene Cashion asking him to get back to take care of business—"Near You" had started to hit.

In June and July 1947, Bullet Records started promoting "Near You" as the top side of the disc. The company sold 80,000 copies in June, Jim Bulleit said,

> then 185,000 in July, then in August over 425,000. By October, total sales were over one million, and Bullet Records was on top of the charts and making $25,000 a day. We got paid in all for 2.5 million copies. It stayed at the top of the jukebox charts for over six months. What I was most proud of was that we were the first little record company to ever not let the majors catch us on a sale. We outsold them. When I saw the record start to take off, we only had four distributors. We had Nashville, Atlanta, Birmingham, and Memphis. So I called up every major distributor all over the country that had a name. I offered them 500 copies on a guaranteed-sale basis. That way we blanketed the country and by the time the others got their discs out we were in every record store in America. The one problem we did have was pressing the records fast enough.

In New York that summer to secure additional record-pressing capacity, Jim Bulleit had an unforgettable experience.

> I registered at my hotel—the Paramount, just off Times Square—and I walked down Forty-eighth Street to Forty-seventh. They had record shops and novelty shops down there, and I was walking along—wasn't anyone knew who I was—and all down those streets I kept hearing "Near You" playing. It was coming out of speakers onto the sidewalk. I went up and down to Fifty-first Street, and I couldn't stop hearing "Near You." I thought, Boy, you've done it, you've conquered the big city.

"Near You" entered the *Billboard* Most Played on Air chart at #9 on August 9, moved to #3 two weeks later, and on August 30 hit #1. Major-label artists—the Andrews Sisters (Decca), Elliott Lawrence (Columbia), Alvino Rey (Capitol), and Larry Green (RCA)—had already covered it. By September 20, "Near You" was the best-selling record on the *Billboard* sales charts, and by October 4 it was #1 for Sheet Music Sales and for Jukebox Plays. The press called the song "the musical miracle of 1947."

In July Bullet had issued a second Craig disc of the other two songs recorded at the "Near You" session back in January, but "Sometimes I Wonder" and "Hot Biscuits," good dance-band tunes, got lost in the rush of "Near You" sales. Instead, the "follow-up" Craig hit the trade papers touted around Christmas 1947 was another Bullet recording, "Beg Your Pardon," written by Beasley Smith with Craig and delivered by Craig and Lamm to the formula of "Near You." When Craig's "Near You" left the *Billboard* Honor Roll of Hits chart in January 1948 for the first time in many months, the swinging, contagious "Beg Your Pardon" replaced it. The new hit, featured for eleven weeks on NBC's *Your Hit Parade,* reached #3 and sold well over a million copies.

Craig retired as an orchestra leader, according to his plan, and signed on with the William Morris Agency as a single act.

On a six-month national tour that netted him $50,000, he took along singer Bob Lamm to help him recreate the magic of "Near You." Convivial and relaxed, free of the responsibility of running a band, Craig indulged himself onstage by doing his piano party trick: playing "Dixie" with one hand and "Yankee Doodle Dandy" with the other. Back home, when he played a special concert at the Ryman Auditorium, the announcer said: "Everywhere you go, 'Near You' is either sung, played, or fried in deep fat." The WSM band then proceeded to play the tune in pop, Hawaiian, country, and operatic versions.

On the strength of his share of the profits from "Near You," Jim Bulleit moved in 1948 to a house he had specially built on Forrest Acres Drive in the richer part of southwest Nashville. "There was nothing there but us," he reminisced. "There were woods on all sides then." Lauded from New York to Nashville, where he was invited to speak to the Men's Civic Club and the Chamber of Commerce, he learned something about fame: "When you're hot, everybody is your friend. I couldn't buy a meal in New York—everybody wanted to buy my dinner."

Given the old saying that a writ isn't far behind a hit, a surprising four years passed before "Near You" saw its day in court. In 1951, the U.S. District Court of New York heard a case brought against Supreme Music, the song's publisher, by Thelma Jones, who contended that her 1934 song "Just an Old Fashioned Mother and Dad" was the basis for the chorus of "Near You." Jones's song was published in 1936 by Metropolitan Music of Los Angeles and two thousand copies of the sheet music made, but no recordings other than radio performances. The court determined in 1953 that absent proof that Francis Craig had received or copied the sheet music, there was "no cause for action." The judge cited *Dorrell v. J. Morris Music,* insulting both Craig and the public in the process:

> Such simple trite themes are likely to recur spontaneously. While there are an enormous number of possible permutations of the musical notes of the scale, only a few are pleasing and fewer still suit the infantile demands of the popular ear. Recurrence is not an inevitable badge of plagiarism.

Recurrence was certainly the theme as far as Bulleit and Craig were concerned, as three more discs from Bullet Records in 1948 and 1949 followed the "Near You" and "Beg Your Pardon" formula of catchy dance-band ballad and swing number. But when "Foolin'," "Disallusioned" (as spelled on the label), and "It Hurts Me More Than It Does You" all failed to chart, Craig gradually settled into semi-retirement. He wrote a few songs and held court at the National Life cafeteria and the WSM library, recorded intermittently for other labels, and in 1960 moved to Sewanee, Tennessee, some ninety miles southeast of the city he decided was now too big and too busy for him, and died there in 1966.

Bullet Plastics

The success of "Near You" brought into sharp focus the problem of obtaining sufficient record-pressing capacity. Bullet had started out when a few companies in the northern cities and in Los Angeles controlled all the business that the limited supply of raw materials would allow. As late as the end of 1946, companies such as Nelson Milling, which supplied Four Star Records, were advertising in *Billboard*: "Wanted—Record scrap. We will pay 7¢ a pound for worn out or broken shellac records. We will buy any quantity." Jim Bulleit remembered that Bullet's experience with "Near You" marked

> the origins of the record-manufacturing business in Nashville. At the height of the success of "Near You," we had forty pressing plants around the country working for us. It was then that we found that some of the pressing plants were selling records direct to distributors without accounting to us for them. We never did know what the true sales figure on "Near You" was. Because of these difficulties, I saw that we needed greater control of the manufacturing process. I contacted Jimmy Beard in Los Angeles and with his help I bought ten thousand dollars' worth of distressed stock-pressing equipment. I had it

A press at Bullet Plastics, 1947. Courtesy of the *Tennessean.*

> shipped to Nashville, and we bought a site out on Bogle Road, near the airport, and called our new company Bullet Plastics.

Bulleit's recollection was somewhat inaccurate. Bulleit, Hitchcock, and Zickler in fact incorporated Bullet Plastics on September 25, 1946, a year before "Near You" reached its zenith. Their certificate noted one thousand shares of common stock and a capital holding of twenty-five thousand dollars. The new company could transact business in the form of "extruding, pressing, coating, or otherwise forming, processing or shaping, any and all substances now known as 'plastics' into articles or products." Their registered office was 2320 Twelfth Street South, and the pressing plant at Lot T-314, Berry Field. The plant was set up by Jimmy Beard's colleague, Leonard Matson, who showed Bullet employee John Dunn how to run the business. A local lawyer, Jordan Stokes, who had the Nashville musician's union as a client and took a particular interest in the music industry, handled the legalities.

Stokes's son, Nashville lawyer Ogden Stokes, remembers his dad taking him out to the wartime Quonset hut where the records were made.

> The squares of plastic were cooked on a grill, like a short-order cook's, until soft. Then they were transferred on a spatula to one of the vertical presses, which had a stamper from the master recording. I remember the female machine operators using a foot switch, and the steam, which was used to operate the press, would come out, then down would come the press. While it was down she would take a knife and trim the plastic off that had squeezed out at the sides. The yellow labels were put on the press first. The whole place was very dimly lit, it was hot, regardless of the outside temperature, the cut-off plastic was all over the floor, and steam was leaking everywhere. It seemed to me then that this was what hell must look like. I always compared it to Dante's Inferno.

The *Tennessean* reported on November 2, 1947:

> Bullet Records has set up the first record pressing plant in the South in a surplus building at Berry Field, and is gearing up to turn out 45,000 records a week. Bullet Records are also being pressed in Los Angeles, St. Louis, Richmond, Philadelphia, and New York. The Bullet Recording and Transcription Co. is the only thing of its kind in the South, and the only independent company

in the U.S. to break into the chain stores and the Sears Roebuck catalog.

By March 1948, the *Tennessean* could report that Bullet was "doing $2 million a year, and has run its capitalization up to $220,000."

Bullet's records now appeared in dust jackets emblazoned, "The Fastest Growing Independent Record Company in America."

Capitalizing on Craig

If Bullet was going to capitalize on the success of Francis Craig, Bulleit realized, he needed to scout out some untapped popular music sources.

> I had the idea to pick up songs and recordings while I was traveling. All the remote recording we did was on leased equipment. I didn't carry any with me. There was no need. All the radio stations had an acetate recorder back then, because they would record things straight off the network. We would record the people straight off the bandstand where they were playing, [like] Danny Cassella . . . from Cleveland. His "Cruel Love" was recorded there in a club. My wife went with me usually on those trips, and she would help with the business end of it all.
>
> I would go to Chicago and New York and all the big cities and look for acts. In New York, [music publisher] Dave Dreyer and I would go around all the nightclubs and the big bands—Guy Lombardo and so on—and try to find a band or a singer that wasn't under contract or that had a radio show or some way of promoting themselves.
>
> In New York, we met Les Elgart. He was very famous back then. His band was too far ahead of its time though, and they had a great sound like Stan Kenton later developed. Les had recorded his own masters, and we picked them up on a royalty basis from him.

Elgart had played trumpet with Harry James and others and went on to enjoy strong record sales with his sophisticated swing music, but, despite Elgart's name, the Bullet release "I Lost My Heart in Hartford" sold poorly beyond Connecticut.

Even better known than Elgart was radio personality Milton Berle. On Berle's disc for Bullet, Bulleit said:

> We left the *e* off his name on the label. That was the greatest catastrophe that happened to me. He always had a bunch of people with him, and they came up to see me when I was at Dave Dreyer's office in New York, and they really gave me a hard time.

Despite Bulleit's clear memory, no records by Berle were listed in Bullet catalogs and none have turned up on the Bullet label. It may be that Bulleit confused this episode with promotional work he undertook some years later for a package tour Berle was on, or materials related to Berle's adoption of "Near You" as one of the theme songs for his radio and television shows.

Undaunted, Bulleit continued his search.

> In Chicago, I found Vi and Jerry Wagner at a nightclub, the Glass House. They were stars of ABC radio, and I went to hear them and liked what I heard. They were pretty good, played the vibes and organ and so on. Ray Pearl was a star. Russ Carlyle was a famous orchestra leader and we recorded him in Chicago too. We recorded him again in Memphis, where Sam Phillips was working on a radio show at a hotel, and we took the sound straight off the broadcast. Sam recorded Denny Beckner with me in Memphis, too. Beckner was something of a name in those days.

Beckner, who had recorded on Savoy in New York in 1942, recorded for Bullet the amusing "Seven Days a Week," which recounted some of the things that could come round to haunt people in a tight, jazzy swing band on the road. On the flipside was an homage, "Texas," by Beckner's female vocalist, Dale Belmont, who also appeared in Bullet's country series with the appealing western swing novelty "Gonna Go back to Texas." Belmont sang at the Sky-Vue Club in Dallas owned by her husband, Joe Bonds, and was renowned for her risqué versions of pop songs. Bullet's Dallas distributor, Bob Dunbar, linked the label with Belmont, as well as with smooth R&B bandleader Red Calhoun and fine western swing musicians Dick Dyson and Paul Blunt.

Jim Bulleit cultivated Dunbar and a number of other key distributors, but in addition he spent a lot of time on telephone selling, an activity he felt he pioneered in the record business. He explained:

> There was the guaranteed-sale deals I did with distributors that made "Near You" take off. Another thing I introduced was playing records to distributors over the telephone, which worked too, as it was cheaper than going to New York all the time. But one time I was trying to make myself heard long distance, over a bad line, introducing myself to someone. I repeated my name and clarified it by explaining, "It's what you put in a gun." The guy replied, "Hello, Mr. Shell."

Although Bullet scored a small hit with Russ Carlyle's "Chapel in the Moonlight," much of Bulleit's pop selection was only average, for two reasons. First, the sessions were made in a hurry, sometimes using less than prime song material, because they were recorded just before or leased during the musician's union ban on new recording sessions, called early in 1948 and lasting most of that year. Second, Bulleit did better at selling than at scouting out talent. As the *Tennessean* noted:

> Bulleit admits that his taste in recorded music does not conform to the popular taste—his biggest flops have been records he thought would go over and some of his biggest hits have been records he was almost ashamed to release.

Still, Bullet Records had high hopes for bandleader Bob Crosby from Spokane, Washington, who recorded for them in Los Angeles. Bing's brother Bob had a hot act in his own right, was a veteran of several big-name swing bands, and was the leader of a Dixieland swing revival movement, popularizing tunes such as "Dixieland Shuffle," "March of the Bob Cats," and "Call Me a Taxi." He had a fifteen-minute daily show on CBS on which "he couldn't promote any of his records by label," Jim Bulleit said, "so he would say something like, 'Mr Bulleit let me record this the other day,' to get the point over. But we never did do anything with him saleswise."

Jim Bulleit seemed willing to try anything once.

> One time, in the spring of 1947, I was visiting our distributor in Houston, Texas, and from what I heard down there I had the idea to create a series of Mexican recordings on Bullet. The distributor was heavily involved in Mexican and conjunto music, and he had bought up several items which I put out on Bullet.

The Mexican series came and went in May 1947 with two discs by the Cinco Troubadores, who performed "Las Altenas" and "El Mescal" to little acclaim beyond Bullet's Texas and Los Angeles distributors.

In another detour from mainstream pop, Bulleit's Chicago connections led to a series of children's albums by "Uncle Al" Trace, who recorded party-piece stories and whose regular Bullet discs included "I Can't Spell Schenectady."

A detour Bulleit himself rated "stupid" resulted from Bullet's concept to provide relief for all the cafeteria and barroom patrons who couldn't stand the blast of the jukebox. For the Country Music Foundation's oral history project, Bulleit told Douglas B. Green:

> We cut the first silent record that ever was on the market, called "Three Minutes of Silence." We thought it might have value; it turned out to be a lot of fun, but stupid. They put it on the jukeboxes and if a guy would go in somewhere and the music was just blaring, why then he put his nickel in and the needle would go around the platter for three minutes and not a sound came out. We had a lot of luck with it. A good many jukeboxes used it, and we had no royalties to pay or anything.

No copies of this disc have been found, unfortunately, but its sound is not difficult to reproduce.

Bullet recorded some popular music made in Nashville, including the Owen Bradley orchestra's "I'd Love to Live in Loveland," and Owen and Harold Bradley contributed

BULLET-IN

NASHVILLE, TENN. AUGUST, 1947

BULLET SIGNS SENSATIONAL STARS

FRANCIS CRAIG

NBC Star Clicks With "Near You"

If you like music that's sweet but solid, Francis Craig's "Near You" is just your dish. Craig wrote the melody last summer, but did little to develop it until Kermit Goell, writer of "Huggin' and a-Chalkin'" heard it and asked to do the lyrics. Craig gave his permission and thought little more of it until three months later he received a sweet, simple little ditty called "Near You". Craig tried it out at local dances and pretty soon the new tune was being requested wherever his orchestra played.

Ever since Bullet recorded it last spring, its popularity has been rising until now "Near You" can be heard on almost any disc jockey's show. Evidently the big wax cutters know a good thing when they hear it, too, for several of the larger companies will soon be releasing their versions of "Near You".

Francis organized his first orchestra while still a student at Vanderbilt and recorded for sveral other companies prior to becoming a Bullet star.

He has been with Radio Station WSM for twenty-two years and for fourteen has carried an NBC Network show. He has also appeared on the "Spotlight Band" program and on the Mutual and Blue Networks.

Francis Craig recently completed the longest engagement on record for any orchestra—twenty years at Nashville's Hermitage Hotel.

Along with his many other activities, Francis Craig has recently been appointed Musical Director for Radio Station WSM.

Send Names To Us For Free Copies Of BULLET-IN

Popular ABC Stars Record For Bullet

In response to many requests from fans all over the country Vi and Jerry Wagner of "The Wagners And Their Music," popular Chicago night club and radio stars, have signed a recording contract. Their first four sides were cut by the Bullet Recording Company of Nashville, Tennessee on June 24, 1947.

The numbers the Wagners cut are "Hold Me" backed by "Ja-Da," Bullet No. 1003, and "I Do Do Do Like You" backed by "Honey," Bullet No. 1004. Baritone Jack Lester does the vocals.

"The Wagners And Their Music," featuring the Hammond organ, piano, solovox and drums, are completing their first year as musical stars over facilities of the American Broadcasting Company and their second year in the Glass House of Chicago's Graemere Hotel.

VI and JERRY WAGNER

Russ Carlyle And Ray Pearl Are Now Recording For Bullet

RUSS CARLYLE, well-known orchestra leader from coast to coast, has just recorded "Why Don't You Answer the Phone?" and "In the Chapel in the Moonlight," Bullet No. 1005, and "It's All My Fault" and "Hanging On the Garden Gate," Bullet No. 1006.

RAY PEARL, popular Mutual Network star, recently recorded "Flaming Mamie" and "Dear Old Donnegal," Bullet No. 1007, and "Pick-In-icking (In the Park)" and "Please Don't Tell." These have not yet been released.

Courtesy of Country Music Hall of Fame and Museum.

a good arrangement to a pop song that had real potential, "Let's Drive out to Joe's Drive-In," cashing in on the resurgent movie business in its outdoor guise. The vocalist, Seger Ellis, Bulleit remembered, "lived in Houston, and he was the manager of the Mills Brothers. He could sing and he wanted to make records. We recorded him right here in Nashville at the Castle Studio together with Alcyone Beasley and the Dixie Dons singing group."

Joe "Red" McEwen, another stalwart of the local Nashville scene, recorded his signature hot Dixieland jazz for Bullet late in 1948. McEwen was musical director of the Tennessee State Fair for several decades, beginning in 1938, was bandleader at the Princess Theater vaudeville shows in the 1930s, and played in the WSM radio orchestra on and off during the 1940s. He gave a string of good female singers their starts, including Nashville-based Joyce Paul and Joan Hager; Kitty Kallen was the vocalist with his band in the late 1940s.

Although white dance-band music dominated Bullet's pop series, black groups on Bullet Records included Pepper Neely and the Ace Trio, who recorded "Rendezvous with a Rose," and the Five Bars, with lead vocals by Jimmy Sweeney. The Bars' "I'm All Dressed Up with a Broken Heart" was too late to cash in on the popular success of groups like the Mills Brothers and possibly too pop for the emerging R&B market, but it represented a significant desire for sophisticated nightlife in some segments of Nashville's black population. Newspapers such as the *Globe* and the *Nashville Commentator* peddled a developing line of racial and personal improvement. The *Commentator* reported on nightclub activities in 1949:

> Reviloting at the Revilot: Socializing in a modern manner. During the past few weeks, Reviloting has become one of the most enjoyed pastimes in the city of Nashville. Many noteworthy personalities are reflected by the mirrors which cover the walls of this new establishment. The crowd went wild when the Five Bars sang "Write Me a Letter." Eddie Cox and his Be-Boppers will play this coming weekend. Please come at any hour for socializing in the modern manner, or Reviloting if you choose to say.

Bulleit's Exit from Bullet

An event whose effect on Bullet the *Tennessean* shrugged off in late 1948 would in fact weigh heavily in Bulleit's downfall. As the *Tennessean* continued to feature Bullet Records, emphasizing the novelty of having a record label in town, a November 1948 article, "Bullet Hits the Bull's Eye," noted:

> It is already a little over a year since Francis Craig's Cinderella recording of "Near You" was released. By now almost everybody in town knows that the top song in the nation was issued under the bright yellow label of a local concern. . . . The Petrillo strike, by the way, will not affect Bullet in the predictable future: it has enough unreleased records to last over two years.

In fact, Jim Bulleit's reaction to the Petrillo strike—the ban that A.F.M. leader James C. Petrillo called on recording activity between January and December 1948—triggered his exit from Bullet Records.

As the strike loomed, record companies scrambled to stockpile recordings. Brad McCuen, who then worked in Chicago for Majestic Records, explained:

> Every company knew that in order to exist they had to have masters to release. RCA did a series called "Issued by Request." Well the request was from the sales department! The majors could reissue their catalog, but for the others the steady flow of product was not forthcoming.

Jim Bulleit persuaded his partners to issue a large number of discs in late 1947 and the first part of 1948 and in the process "overstretched himself," explained Bill Beasley, a later Bulleit associate. "He bought a lot of pop masters and went in for several lengthy hillbilly recording sessions just before the ban came, and then the records didn't sell, and the strike didn't last long enough to justify the expense Bullet had incurred." Bulleit's own take was that the label

> had significant problems with distribution at the end of 1948. Around that time there was a large increase in the

number of wholesale distribution companies. It was a time of an expanding economy. Many of those companies were unstable and went by the wayside. We had around fifty thousand dollars due to us from bankrupt distributors all within a six-month period. Allowing that to happen contributed greatly to my downfall at Bullet.

Bulleit's apparent frittering away of the profits from 1947 annoyed Orville Zickler. Meanwhile, Cashion and Hitchcock discovered that many of the distributors who were in financial trouble were longtime contacts Bulleit had persuaded into taking discs they couldn't sell. C. V. Hitchcock did not take kindly to being blamed for colleagues' going out of business.

Bulleit "recorded too much bad music," was the succinct diagnosis of Reynold Bubis, who with his cousin Alan, was a canny newcomer to the jukebox business back then. "Jim and I were friends. We went through the Shriners together. He was a real nice man, but he wasted all his money, and his partners didn't like that." Alan Bubis said bluntly: "Jim Bulleit spent a fortune on recording popular bands, and he spent all the money Bullet made on 'Near You' doing that stuff. So Mr. Hitchcock and Mr. Cashion ran him off, basically." More diplomatically, Bullet's bookkeeper, Howard Allison, told me that "Bullet Records folded up in its original form because Jim thought he could do anything. He really believed that he was up there with the major labels. He recorded at random, and his partners disagreed with his policies."

A glance at the Bullet catalog at the end of 1948 reflects the label's attempt to cover all the bases. This small independent aped the approach of the major recording companies and larger independents rather than that of the more circumspect new independents, who stuck to recording regionally available music for targeted black, western, hillbilly, or gospel markets.

Jim Bulleit later gave me his view of the problems that caused him to leave the Bullet Records operation:

> Other than "Near You" and "Beg Your Pardon," we were not very successful with pop music at all. Country was better, steadier, but our most profitable catalog, as a group, was R&B by far. During the three years or so that I ran the Bullet label, I was responsible for doing all the deals, making all the sales and promotional initiatives, and generally running the label. But I didn't do those jobs because I was particularly good at them, it just worked out that way.
>
> After "Near You" we recorded a lot of big names. I thought at the time that if you recorded big-name artists, that was all you had to do. But it isn't so. That was what took us down the drain. I thought Bob Crosby and Milton Berle, those names would carry the weight, but they didn't. We had several good sellers, but we were inexperienced and we also took a lot of advice from people who knew no more about it than we did. I can't blame anybody. We just thought wrong in some cases. Of course, you can't prepick a hit.
>
> In 1948, late in the year, was the time when things started to go wrong at Bullet, and I left the label in the new year. I was happy with promotion, that was the best job I did, but I wasn't, I now realize, the best businessman in the world.

Many who knew Bulleit professionally took the same tack. For example, Red Wortham:

> Jim was a salesman. I've seen Jim sell leftover records that were lying on the floor. He was a master at it. But he invested his money in pop orchestras and those cost a fortune to record. Those things by Red McEwen and Bob Crosby, they didn't even get out of the shop.

And Sam Phillips:

> Jim was a real good promotion man. He was a hustler, good on the road, but he did not have an ear for music or production. Like so many, when he came upon that big hit he didn't know how best to handle it. If he had known, I think Bullet Records could have stayed out front and led the music scene in Nashville for decades.

Bulleit, in a way, agreed: "We really had no business to go out of business. We were making money despite our mistakes." But later he told Douglas B. Green: "They had the musicians union strike in 1948, and we couldn't make any records. So we decided to go our different ways. Mr. Hitchcock and Mr. Zickler bought me out."

The February 5, 1949, edition of *Billboard* carried the story, filed from its Chicago office—"Bulleit Peddles Share in Bullet Disks to Execs":

> Jim Bulleit, general manager of Bullet Records this week sold out his entire interest in that label to C.V. Hitchcock, prexy of the label; Orville Zickler, treasurer, and Jordan Stokes, attorney for the waxery. Bulleit, who would not disclose reasons for severing his connections with the Nashville diskery, said that Hitchcock will replace him as general manager. Bulleit said that the deal called for the trio to take over complete ownership of the firm's masters, artists' contracts, the Nashville pressing plant and Volunteer Music Sales, Nashville distribution point which handles national sales for Collegiate label and regional sales for about six independents. Bulleit told *Billboard* that his present plans are indefinite, but that he will make a definite decision soon.

6

Music for the World: Bullet's Nashville Competition

We'll confederate the whole darn forty-eight,
the way it should have been
Save that Confederate money boys,
the South shall rise again.

—Eleanor "Hank" Fort,
"Save That Confederate Money Boys," Select Records

Inspired at least in part by Bullet Records' success with "Near You," four new recording ventures challenged the label for shelf space in Nashville's record outlets in 1948 and 1949. Though varied in their operations and musical philosophies, the Cheker, World, Collegiate, and Select record labels shared a belief that the way was open for Nashville to take the lead in bringing a unique blend of popular musicianship and down-south folksiness to the attention of the wider world.

The first was the strangely spelled Cheker Records, which had probably got going sometime in 1947. Next, World Records decided in the summer of 1948 to dive into the folk and "race" music markets. Bill Beasley, who had spent some time working alongside C. V. Hitchcock and Jim Bulleit and knew firsthand just what a hit "Near You" had been, set up Collegiate Records that fall to record popular and dance-band music. Select Records entered the field in 1948, a small but fascinating label that put an unashamedly southern slant on popular music.

Cheker Records: Maurice Likens

Cheker was the part-time plaything of Maurice Likens, an electrical engineer from Kentucky, and for a time his casual activity developed into a real flirtation with the commercial record business. Born in 1918 near Paris, Kentucky, Likens attended Lexington's Transylvania College, where he recorded voice students and college choral groups. But his future lay in Nashville, where he moved in 1938, spent time in the navy, then worked as an electrician with John Bouchard and Sons. By 1946 he was married with two sons and living at 726 Benton Avenue in south Nashville.

Likens continued to dabble in sound recording and had bought equipment to record either on location or at home. He chose an enterprise in which, he later told the *Tennessean,* he could both "serve the public and do something for myself, without too much competition." He traveled to schools, colleges, and clubs, recording high school bands, vocal groups, and family events and, at home, turned his den into a recording studio. To his wife's stoic dismay and his sons' delight, when he needed more space, he extended the studio into the living room, where he balanced guitar amplifiers or other equipment on the baby chair and allowed his sons, Donald and Jere, to sit in on recording events as long as they kept quiet.

On his travels for the Bouchard company, Likens let it be known that he was available to make recordings, and in time, he told the *Tennessean,* he was "beset on all sides by hillbillies who told me over and over that they knew they could sell records, if only there were somebody to make the

records." After about the twentieth request from "hillbilly singers, minor-league guitar pickers and yodelers, some of whom had spots on small-town radio stations," Likens went into business, had discs pressed for him by Bullet Plastics, and let the performers promote their discs at personal appearances and over the radio. He apparently had some records pressed on labels customized to the artists' desires, but he also set up his own Cheker Records imprint and issued up to six or seven records on that label. At least one disc, Richard Armstrong's boogie and blues piano tributes to WLAC deejay Gene Nobles, had a checkerboard-patterned label, although it is unlikely that Cheker was connected with the *Checkerboard Jamboree* radio show broadcast from Nashville.

All the surviving Cheker discs are associated with performers who played on radio WLAC in Nashville. Jack Henderson, who ran a country band on the station, may have been Likens's partner when his custom recording adventure gave way to a full-fledged commercial approach. Henderson himself appears to have made Cheker's first commercial disc, "The Tramp on the Street," backed by Big Jeff Bess's band. Probably recorded soon after Molly O'Day's popular 1947 version, it mined a sentimental seam stretching back to the roots of folk and hillbilly music and that Hank Williams was starting to pursue successfully. Henderson's disc saw little action, having limited distribution other than the emerging WLAC link to the mail-order operation of Randy Wood's record shop in Gallatin, Tennessee.

Jack Henderson, from Hundred, West Virginia, had worked with his brother, Ted, as the Sunshine Brothers on WBLK, Clarksburg, West Virginia, in 1936. Ted had started the WLAC act Ted and Wanda in 1945, and Jack joined them there the following year. Two other WLAC announcers and singers, Bob Jennings and Big Jeff Bess, soon joined Henderson as artists on Cheker. Bess's wife, Hattie Louise, sang with Bess's band and also with Henderson on the Jack and Lou show. Bob Jennings's "That Old Moon Seems to Know" was styled in the popular mold of Eddy Arnold. "Poppin' Bubble Gum" by Big Jeff was a novelty ditty often performed on the Opry by Lonzo and Oscar; it was backed by a sincere hillbilly song, "A Kiss and a Memory."

Jeff Bess, *left*, Lou Tatum, and Jack Henderson around the time of Cheker and World Records, 1948. Courtesy of Bear Family Records.

Cheker's other releases remain shrouded in mystery. There is some evidence that the smooth-sounding novelty Mississippi vocal group, Dusty Brooks and His Tones, recorded for Cheker. And although Likens didn't mention the name of the performer when he told the *Tennessean* in December 1948 that a Cheker disc that "has had some renown" was called "Shut Up and Drink Your Beer," the title fits Big Jeff Bess's uncompromising style and image; no trace of the Cheker record has surfaced, but the song, written by singer Bob Newman, was recorded by several others in 1947, including Doye O'dell and Luke Wills.

World Records: Jordan Stokes III

It wasn't long before Cheker had new competition. The *Cashbox* of August 28, 1948, reported:

> From the hillbilly capital comes word that Jordan Stokes who heads International Records Inc. is entering the race and hillbilly field. World Records will be the trading name and the following will be featured artists. Don Q., race; Red Gilliam, western; Buck Buchanon, hillbilly. Distribution will be handled nationally by Volunteer Music Sales.

For a label with aspirations to cover the globe with Nashville music, World was at something of a disadvantage in the fall of 1948. The label's national distributor, Volunteer Music, comprised five people: C. V. Hitchcock and Eugene Cashion; their two salesmen, Hutch Carlock and Jimmy Green; and Jim Bulleit, who was in the process of falling out with his partners. The industry was in the middle of a national musician's union ban on recording sessions, and World's principal, Jordan Stokes, was a lawyer, not a music businessman. As it turned out, few World discs got much farther beyond Tennessee than Cheker discs did.

Nevertheless, the long-lost story of World Records reveals the important part played by Jordan Stokes III in the rise of Nashville's music business. The lawyer for the Nashville Local of the A.F.M. since 1933, Stokes knew the town's music scene, acted for many of the small record labels, and brokered lease deals and buy-outs well into the 1950s.

World was based at Stokes's law-office address, 315 Warner Building, on the northeast corner of Church Street and Sixth Avenue North. Setting their sights high, and proclaiming on their label, "Music for the World," World Records had launched some twenty hillbilly and western records by December 1949, and at least eighteen releases in an R&B and gospel series.

Details of the label's beginnings remain murky, but Stokes advised the Nashville A.F.M. branch to vote against the recording ban proposed at the end of 1947 by national president James Petrillo, and when the ban was enforced anyway through most of 1948, Stokes may have been persuaded to announce the formation of World Records as a test case.

Jordan Stokes III was the youngest law practitioner in Nashville's history, having gained a special license from the chancery court to practice before reaching the age of twenty-one—he had qualified as a lawyer in June 1925 at the age of nineteen, a distinguished addition to a distinguished family. Stokes's great-grandfather was a state senator and speaker of the house in the 1850s, and by 1930 five Stokeses were practicing law in Nashville: Jordan Stokes Sr., Jordan Stokes Jr., his brother James Stokes, and Jordan Stokes III, along with his brother Whitworth Stokes. Jordan Stokes III was born on December 6, 1905, and attended Vanderbilt University, where he "studied academics in the morning and law in the afternoon. I wasn't quite through school when I took the bar examinations and passed."

Jordan Stokes III, 1940s. Courtesy of Ogden and MacNeill Stokes.

At first young Jordan worked at criminal law, but he found being responsible for a person's life or liberty too great. After a spell traveling in Texas, he returned to Nashville to run the state Finance Department's gas taxes division. In January 1931, he married Mabel Ogden of Louisville, a graduate of Peabody College, who worked in the state school system for many years. Stokes returned to the law in 1933 in offices at 311 Church Street; by the late 1930s, the Stokeses were living on Ashwood Avenue in a prestigious part of southwest Nashville.

Stokes soon became involved in a series of human rights and freedom issues. "I came to my liberal attitude early, lawfully, and ethically," he said later. In this, he was following family tradition. His great-grandfather had been involved in a controversy in 1859, defending the rights of free Negroes to remain free. Eighty years later, Jordan Stokes III came to prominence when he defended the workers at a meatpacking firm in Nashville. "That was in 1938. The firm was studying what each worker could do, and as soon as they saw how fast a worker could produce, they raised his quota. It was like Charlie Chaplin's film *Modern Times.*"

In the early 1930s, Stokes had helped set up the Highlander Folk School in Monteagle, Tennessee, an innovative venture aimed at providing holistic education, preserving dignity and confidence, and helping minority groups become

NASHVILLE GLOBE

★PROGRESSIVE★ ★JOURNAL★ AND INDEPENDENT OF THE ★ NEW ★ ★SOUTH★

VOLUME XLI.—No. 50. NASHVILLE, TENN., NOVEMBER 17, 1944 PRICE FIVE CENTS

On Furlough

INCREASE IN AUTO DEATHS SHOWN CAUSED BY SPEED OF FAULTY CARS

Seek Public Support of Legislation for Better Checkup of All Vehicles Using Highways; Bar All "Jalopies"

SCRANTON, Pa., Nov. 16—Public ... be safely driven at speeds over 30 miles an hour. But the public has

In Service

Civil Liberties Union Takes Controversy To Supreme Court

Jordan Stokes of Nashville and other Southerners Join Legal Fight on Behalf of Two Negro Firemen, Discriminated Against

NEW YORK—The right of trade unions to discriminate against Negroes in collective bargaining contracts with employers is challenged in a brief just filed in the U. S. Supreme Court by the American Civil Liberties Union in a case to be heard in November. The brief, signed by prominent Southern lawyers as well as counsel for the Union, supports the suit of two

Passes Away

Globe report from 1944 of one of Jordan Stokes's legal battles. Courtesy of National Baptist Publishing Board.

organized in a peaceful and meaningful way. "I had a friend called Myles Horton," Stokes remembered.

> Myles had been in Germany and had seen how the endemic racial prejudice was undermining the country. He saw prejudice amongst the mountain people in east Tennessee, too, and he said he was going to set up a school there that taught against prejudice of all kinds. He had union members, white people and black, all studying and living together there. When I went up there, it was the first time I had ever sat down to eat dinner with black people. It worked well; everybody was treated equal.

Highlander focused at first on folk traditions and the rights of white working people but soon embraced the cause of racial equality. In the spring of 1955, NAACP organizers visited the school, among them Martin Luther King Jr. and Rosa Parks, whose refusal to give up her bus seat to a white passenger in Montgomery, Alabama, was a catalyst in the civil rights movement in December that year. According to Stokes: "She had been treated just like anybody else up there [in Monteagle], you know, and she couldn't see why it should be any different back in Alabama." Highlander closed in 1959 under anti–civil rights pressure, despite, the *Tennessean* reported, "the best efforts of Highlander attorney Jordan Stokes."

In 1942, Stokes took on Memphis "Boss" Ed Crump, standing against Crump's candidate for the U. S. Senate. "A political monopoly is just as sinister as an economic monopoly," Stokes said. Two years later he was among the lawyers who defended two black locomotive firemen from Alabama who had filed suit against the Louisville & Nashville Railroad's Jim Crow collective-bargaining contracts. The *Knoxville Sentinel* wrote that Stokes had been

> fighting monopolies all his life. He is a lawyer by profession, but a crusader by preference. He wrote the bill that brought the TVA power to Nashville. He is in a battle to keep gasoline prices down. He has led a fight against sales

> taxes. At the moment he is waging a war on the Nashville Bus Company, which he says is being milked dry by the owners.

Later on, Stokes commented: "I was for the Tennessee Valley Authority and against segregation. It's nice to know that so many of the things I was for, people are now doing."

In 1948, when Stokes founded World Records, he was local chair of Henry Wallace's Progressive Party, the organization touted as taking up the battles of Jefferson, Jackson, Wilson, and Roosevelt against entrenched powers of money, military rule, and political bossism. "We are for social justice for all, against all racial and class prejudices, for the common man against all special privilege," the party declared. It is not recorded whether this extended to setting up a record label to put the national musician's union's nose out of joint.

Jordan Stokes became involved in representing the Nashville musician's union in 1933, when the Stokeses lived in a duplex at 1221 Sixteenth Avenue South owned by George Cooper, the business agent of the Nashville local of the American Federation of Musicians.

> George and I used to talk about union matters and things of that sort in the evenings, out on the front porch. He finally came to me one day and said, "I really need some help. Would you represent the union?" and that's how we got started.

Over the years, Stokes fought hard in defense of the union and was instrumental in the widening of its membership. In the 1930s, few folk or hillbilly musicians, and no black musicians, belonged to the union. Stokes argued with George Cooper, who had become president of the local, that country musicians should be admitted. "George . . . said they couldn't read music. I said, 'Well, they sure can play it,' and I also pointed out that it could mean increased membership. He began to let them in but he insisted that they show up on time for performances and not be drinking." The admission of black musicians took a lot longer, but Stokes felt it was overdue. "After people got used to seeing the black man

Sometime pianist and recent president, President Harry Truman strikes a chord with national musician's union boss James Petrillo in 1954. Courtesy of American Federation of Musicians and Harold Bradley.

performing up there next to white folks, it wasn't any shock to see them join the musician's union."

Of Stokes's attitude toward the Petrillo strike, his son, McNeill Stokes, said:

> Dad's view was that aiding the growth and prosperity of the music business in Nashville aided the prosperity of the musicians. He was adverse to James Petrillo and the national federation in thinking that. Nashville did not toe the party line, because of dad's leadership and his advice on what was best overall for the music business in Nashville.

In Nashville's best interest, Stokes represented not only local music businesses but also individual musicians and even

songs. Among his early music clients was Wally Fowler, with whom Stokes worked to set up Tennessee Music Publishing and to clear the legalities associated with Fowler's "All Night Sing" concerts at the Ryman. Fowler was one of the first songwriters in Nashville to work with Broadcast Music, Inc. (BMI) and to try to cultivate a business in music publishing. Stokes arranged to work out the legalities of a deal whereby Fowler had arranged for Eddy Arnold to record a song Fowler had cowritten with J. Graydon Hall, "That's How Much I Love You," on the understanding that all three men would figure as writers. The song was a hit for Arnold and for Red Foley, Bing Crosby, and Frank Sinatra, as Stokes remembered:

> The song did well, and Wally needed some money, so I went to see P. D. Houston at First American National Bank, and we got him to lend five thousand dollars on the BMI payments due. That was the first time a Nashville bank had ever lent money on a song. Soon, other banks were loaning money. It used to be that a songwriter had to put up the car, farm, or house to get a loan.

Once Stokes was established as a man who had the interests of the music community at heart, C. V. Hitchcock approached him about becoming Bullet Records' lawyer. As McNeill Stokes remembered:

> Bullet was the first record company that Dad was involved with. He owned an interest in the company and was involved in advising on their strategy. All the start-up businesses would come to him to handle their initial incorporations. Dad was drawn magnetically to such problem-solving opportunities and he would take a real interest in his clients' businesses. He was a true mechanic and could easily have worked as an engineer, and he was very involved in the engineering of the record-pressing machines Bullet Plastics put in at the war surplus building in the Vultee part of the airport. The clients loved him being interested too. He would often go to recording sessions, but I don't think he had much of a musical acumen.

Nevertheless, on June 21, 1948, Jordan Stokes incorporated International Records with one hundred shares and one thousand dollars in capital for "the production, distribution, and sale of phonograph records and the power to engage in the business of publishing songs and music." Swearing out the incorporation certificate with him were his partners, Jewel Elizabeth Nesbit and Robert Hamby. "Miss Jewel" was Stokes's longtime legal secretary; Hamby was a draftsman with the John Parmelee architectural firm next door to Stokes's office in the Warner Building. There is no indication that International Records ran anything other than the World label, and Stokes's corporate partners were, apparently, not involved in the day-to-day business of World Records either. This was left to others, including C. V. Hitchcock and Bill Beasley, who attended to distribution, and Maurice Likens, who turned Cheker's living-room studio over to making records for World.

There were only two recording games in town. Jim Bulleit was preoccupied with a large and increasingly out-of-control roster of union-registered recording talent, but Maurice Likens dealt mainly in nonunion musicians, just what Stokes needed in the middle of a national recording ban. According to Likens, "the World outfit was looking for somebody to do recording work for them, and they let me try it." It is unclear whether Likens was a formal partner or the provider of master recordings for World to lease, thus keeping the label another step removed from the recording ban.

World's Artists: "No Masks, Either"

As soon as World struck a deal with Maurice Likens, word was passed to Bill Holder at the *Tennessean* that there was a story here for their weekly magazine supplement. Holder had heard about the goings-on across the country to defeat the recording ban and was pleased to report that an outfit in Nashville had gotten around it. He knew that union officials had discovered union musicians, wearing masks to hide their identities, making records in New York studios. The *Tennessean* carried photographs of Likens recording Buck Buchanon's hillbilly group in his living room and experiment-

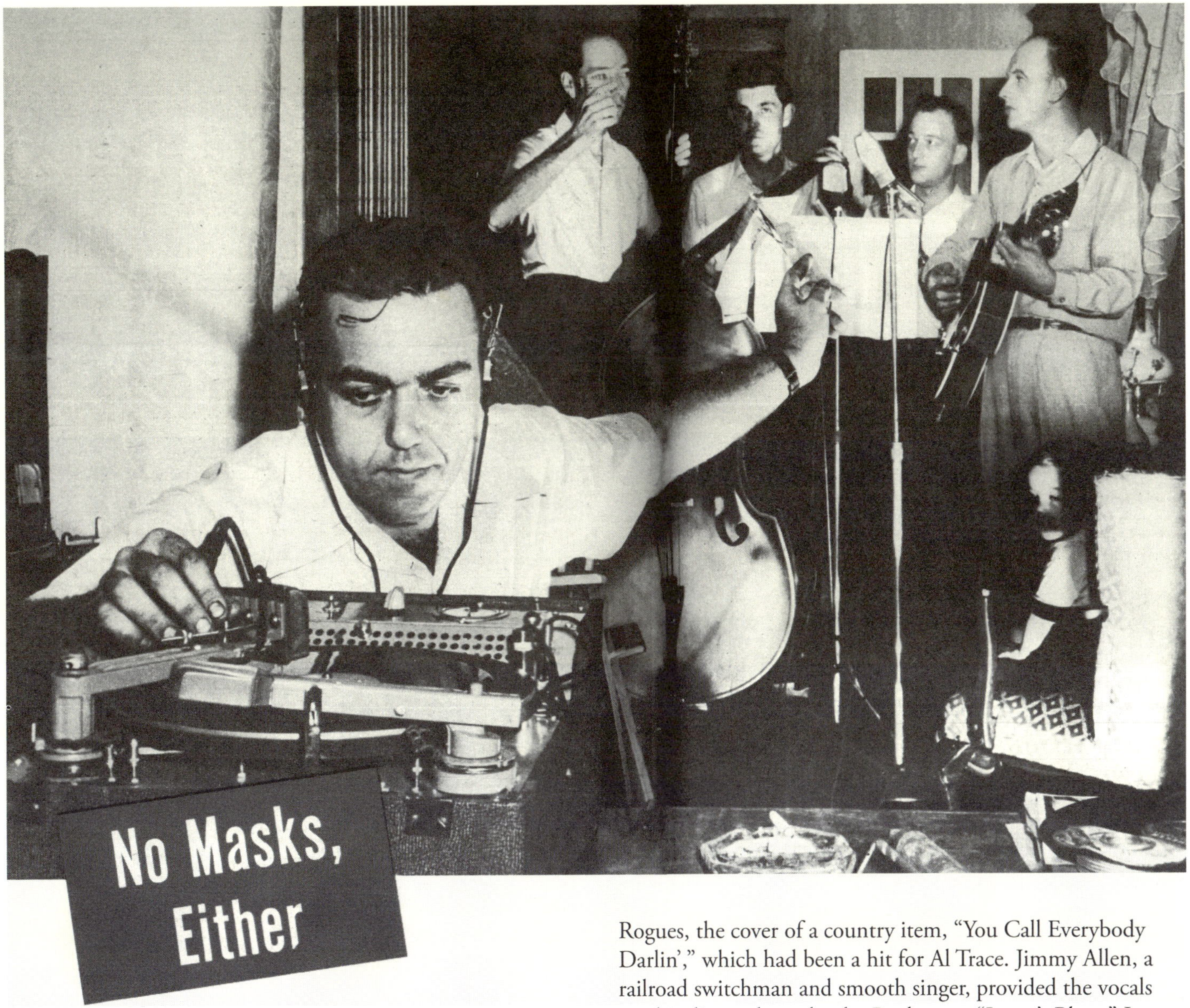

Maurice Likens engineering an at-home Cheker session with Buck Buchanon's Rhythm Rogues, late 1948. Courtesy of the *Tennessean.*

ing with the acoustics in his bathroom. "No Masks, Either," read the headline.

Billboard reviewed World's first releases on August 28, 1948. World 1501 was by Buck Buchanon and the Rhythm Rogues, the cover of a country item, "You Call Everybody Darlin'," which had been a hit for Al Trace. Jimmy Allen, a railroad switchman and smooth singer, provided the vocals on this disc and another by Buchanon, "Lover's Blues." It was reported in the *Tennessean* that Allen's songs were "by local Nashville housewives," but if so they were all named Allen, according to the record labels. The second group to appear on World, Red Gilliam and His Texas Pals, specialized in corny western numbers like "Hair of Gold." Gilliam was an accordionist from Denison, Texas, who had been involved with several top western swing bands and who appeared from 1947 on the influential *Big D Jamboree* on KRLD in Dallas.

Bob Jennings, WLAC disc jockey and local smooth hillbilly vocal stylist, recorded four discs for World with the Eagle Rangers, later known as the Farm Hands. The band also backed up Harry Blair on a cover of the popular western song "Dear Okie," as well as Buddy Pelham, known as "the Tall Texan," and other World acts. Jennings's record of "That Old Moon Seems to Know" and "Be My Darling," reissued from Cheker, became the best-known World disc. One of the top-rated deejays in Nashville, Jennings had made several attempts at a recording career. Born in Cannon County, Tennessee, in September 1924, he grew up in the Auburntown area and got his first radio job on WGNS in Murfreesboro in 1947, fronting the Eagle Rangers band that included Billy and Floyd Robinson, Jerry Rivers, and Bob Moore. Jennings joined WLAC in 1948 as a performer, but program director Paul Oliphant quickly recruited him as a deejay, and he became a fixture on the daybreak shift, dubbing himself "the Old Farm Hand."

The Eagle Rangers' Bob Moore told me that he had

> known Billy and Floyd Robinson since I was three years old. We went to school together and were first known as the East High Eagles. We started playing as the Eagle Rangers when we gained some radio work on WGNS, and that was when Bob Jennings joined us.

The band made a connection with Maurice Likens and recorded "That Old Moon Seems to Know" for Cheker, which Moore thought "was very good for a group of teenagers." Jerry Rivers went on to make his name playing behind Hank Williams, and Bob Moore became one of Nashville's best-known session musicians.

World then turned to Rusty Gilbert and the Louisiana Swing Boys, who carried the country series through to June 1949. Their repertoire included swinging items such as "New Orleans Stomp," as well as an optimistic cover of Hank Williams's "Lovesick Blues." John Horace "Rusty" Gilbert was not a singer or musician, but the figurehead, manager, and promoter of his group, which came from Minden, Louisiana, and played over KRUS in Ruston for many years, promoting a hardware store. The featured vocalists with the band, and on their World records, were Jim Dunningham and Roy Heflin.

The series ended on a high note, a disc by one of the

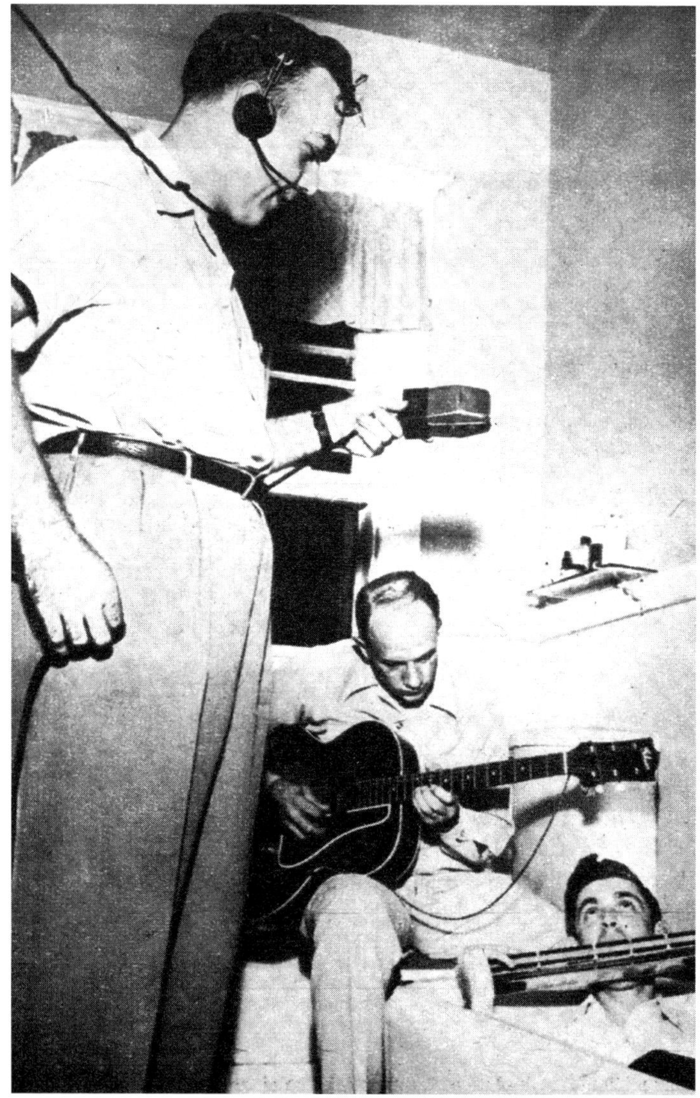

Maurice Likens, Buck Buchanon, and a Rhythm Rogue testing the acoustics of Likens's bathroom. Courtesy of the *Tennessean*.

kingpins of the Nashville music scene, Big Jeff Bess. The A side of his World record was a reissue from Cheker, "Poppin' Bubble Gum." The flip side, "After We Are Through," newly recorded, was an accomplished midtempo ballad that stands comparison with almost anything the major labels were producing.

Big Jeff coined his professional name from his initials, "G. F."—the "Big" came naturally to a man who was six feet two. "He has," the *Tennessean* remarked dryly, "been known to stand up well in an argument."

Born Grover Franklin Bess in 1920 on a sixty-acre, sharecropped farm near Ashland City, Tennessee, Bess moved to Nashville around 1940 and worked for a wholesale grocery business and a bomb manufacturer before playing his guitar with Goober and Dixie Belle Buchanan on WSIX in 1942. He moved to WLAC and quickly became a fixture of the Nashville music scene, both as a bandleader and radio announcer, early mornings for the Morris Furniture Company and in the evenings for Hadacol and other sponsors; he also hosted a Saturday-afternoon jamboree on the station. His band, the Radio Playboys, became known as Big Jeff's Finishing School because so many ace Nashville pickers graduated from it. Among those who worked with Bess were Grady Martin, Jerry Rivers, Ike Inman, Floyd Robinson, Hillous Butrum, Tommy Vaden, and George McCormick. "I used to tell 'em," Bess told Colin Escott, "if you got somethin' better, take it."

Within a month or so of the first World releases, the label came out with a 2500 series, apparently designed for blues and black gospel music. The first disc was by the leading black bandleader of Nashville, Don Q. Pullen, and his orchestra. "I Ain't Looking" and "Tom, Tom the Piper's Son" were Pullen's first recordings, predating his two Bullet outings by one and two years respectively. Each is a fine, jazzy mix of swing and blues styles featuring singer Tommy Brown. With a band that included another important black musician from Nashville, Louis Brooks, Pullen also backed bluesy jazz singer Olive Brown on "Just a Drag." Brown, who had worked in Detroit with the big R&B bands of Todd Rhodes and Tiny Bradshaw, was in Nashville en route to Texas when she connected with Pullen and World. It is a shame that the numerical gaps between the Pullen and Brown discs in the 2500 series probably mean we have lost two other important early Nashville R&B recordings.

Big Jeff Bess and the Radio Playboys. Courtesy of Bear Family Records.

Musician Al Garner is among many who recall Pullen's role in Nashville music with awe.

> Don Q. was the esquire back then. He had a schooled band and he would get all the affluent gigs, high-society gigs. You knew you were going to get paid that night if you got a booking with Don Q. He would play anything, anyplace. Whatever the show was, he would play it, from white society to the black clubs. He would play popular tunes, whatever was on the jukebox. Even in the nightclubs, you had to have variety. Even name artists had to do the popular items; you had to please the crowd.

Pullen and his wife, Wilma, lived at 1215 Villa Place in south Nashville, near the Peabody and Vanderbilt campuses,

To Present Fascination

DON Q. PULLEN

Washington Jr. High School is presenting again, by public demand, its new musical, "Fascination."

Don Q. Pullen, popular Band Master and Producer, has added a new touch to this year's extravaganza, attracting a turn-away crowd to its first performance.

"Fascination," by command performance will be presented Monday night, March 27th, at Washington Jr. Hign School, in the new auditorium, and from all reports

Don Q. Pullen featured in the *Nashville Globe,* March 1950. Courtesy of National Baptist Publishing Board.

and Pullen taught at Washington Junior High School, where in 1946 he arranged a music program titled "4000 Years of Music," the *Nashville Globe* reported on February 15.

After the Pullen discs, World's 2500 discs consisted of gospel music—the Four Gabriels' "Recess in Heaven" and "How Many More Times," and in June 1949 the Reverend W. M. Anderson's version of the popular theme "Jesus on the Mainline," which ended the series.

Eventually, Jordan Stokes dropped World in favor of Bullet Plastics, in which his interest had increased when Jim Bulleit sold out in the spring of 1949. As his son McNeill Stokes remembered, he continued to represent all manner of music business clients:

> many local music companies, including the record sales operations and the like. He represented Randy's Record Shop, Ernie's Record Mart, and C. V. Hitchcock's Hermitage Distributing Company. As far as record companies, he helped set up Bullet, Nashboro, Dot, Republic, and some others. Every record company wanted Dad to be their lawyer and adviser.

Harold Bradley first knew Stokes, he said, when "he was doing Ernest Tubb's books. He had a great overview of the music business. . . . He was a wonderful old southern gentleman, a scholar, a most interesting man."

Stokes never slowed down. The same love of machines that drew him to dabble with the Bullet presses took him in 1996, at age ninety, to an auto-parts store to get a fuse for his car. He fell on some steps and with a broken leg drove eleven miles to his son Ogden's house. Ogden Stokes

> heard a car horn blowing intermittently. Dad couldn't walk in, but he was sitting outside in his car quietly reading the evening newspaper and listening to the radio and occasionally blowing his horn. He had to have his leg pinned and was recovering in hospital when I last saw him. He was dictating letters to his secretary of forty years from his hospital bed. After I left, a blood clot came loose and killed him, still dictating to his secretary.

Select Records: Hank Fort

Jordan Stokes's World Records had recorded folk music for the world; Select Records leaned toward a sound born of the dance band and the musical theater. The label was the brainchild of a west Nashville society woman, Eleanor Hankins Fort, known to all as "Hank." She started Select with Owen Bradley and singer Dottie Dillard, who explained that

> the label had three equal partners, but it was Hank's obsession. Owen led the recording sessions, I sang and did the paperwork, and Hank wrote the songs and rushed around promoting the label. She loved it—and about drove Owen crazy, always writing new things and having ideas.

Hank, born Eleanor Louise Middleton Hankins in June 1914, the daughter of well-known portrait painter Cornelius Hankins and writer Maude McGehee, played piano from the age of three and at ten composed songs. She attended Peabody and Ward-Belmont Colleges, then met and married Walter Fort, joining one of Nashville's blue-blood families. (The most famous family member was Nashville-born Cornelia Fort, a pioneering flight instructor in Tennessee who clocked up 1,100 flying hours during World War II and died in a midair collision during a ferrying mission from California to Texas in 1943.) Eleanor Fort enjoyed the combination of circumstances that allowed her to blend her artistic background with Nashville's old money; she ran theatrical events and operated a children's ballroom-dance class for many years, on a "Fort-nightly" basis. She also started to dabble in radio as a writer and performer. She told Edwin Dunham,

> I started in radio in the 1930s at WSM. My friend Ed Kirby had written a show and my first part was to come on and say "Fire away." Well, the director stopped and said that I wasn't saying it right, so I said—I was only getting two dollars fifty—"can't you pay me one dollar and a quarter and I'll say 'shoot' instead?" They had Dinah Shore singing on WSM then, a show called *Rhythm and Romance*, and my job was to write up

little four-line couplets and I'd introduce each song in rhyme. Then I went up to Harry Stone, the manager at WSM, and I said 'please let me rhyme some of the commercials. They are so dull.' So I made these rhymes for Shyer's jewelry that Snooky Lanson sang for years and years on the radio. That led me into writing the links for shows like *Sunday Down South* with Snooky and Dottie Dillard.

It was at this time, around 1947, that Hank started writing songs and taking a real interest in the music business. By now, she was divorced and living on Hillsboro Road, thinking seriously about a career in entertainment. She soon had six of her songs recorded, including "Pic-a-nic-in' in the Park" (recorded in 1947 by Ray Pearl on Bullet Records and then by the Lawrence Welk Orchestra on Decca), "Protocol," "Sure'n I Do," and "Zingarella" (recorded in mid-1949 by Bob Lockwood and Nina Claire with the Hawes Coleman Orchestra on Nashville's Collegiate label). Then came her biggest hit song, "I Didn't Know the Gun Was Loaded," and her pièce de résistance, "Save That Confederate Money Boys (the South Shall Rise Again)," featuring the line, "if at first we don't secede, I say let's try it again." The composer of many musical scripts and commercials, as well as pop songs, Hank Fort was fascinated by people, lifestyles, and places, an interest she registered in songs like "Southern Cookin'," "Tall Tales of Texas," and "I Love Connecticut."

The recordings of Fort's songs that wound up on Select were initially made with other labels in mind; Fort persuaded Owen Bradley to cut them in the WSM studios in the winter of 1948 for her to take to New York in the spring of 1949—the idea was to sell them to a major label. As Fort told the press, explaining the genesis of Select Records:

> I took the master recordings up there with me, only to find that the songs had been recorded by other labels with their own artists. They didn't want my versions. So I just called Owen and Dottie in Nashville and told them we were going into the record business ourselves. Their arrangements were so good, I knew they would sell. So we started Select Records, and by Select we mean just that. We are going to cut only a few records and they are all going to be good.

Hank Fort not only wrote some good pop songs but also succeeded as a self-publicist. In August 1948, the *Tennessean* reported that she was booked to play the Flamingo Club in Las Vegas and had just returned from a visit to producers of Hollywood musicals, for whom she demonstrated songs like "My Favorite Friend" and "Put Your Shoes On, Lucy" (based on the tendency of her friend Lucy Stokes, sister-in-law of lawyer Jordan Stokes, to get comfortable by taking her shoes off in company). That year, when Fort appeared on ABC-TV's *Hollywood Screen Test* show in New York, she said, she "was introduced as an unknown southern gal who wrote songs and broke into Tin Pan Alley." In 1949, she appeared singing "Lucy" in the movie *Feudin' Rhythm* with Eddy Arnold, but largely she was humored by the movie industry, and later that year she was back in New York pitching songs.

In March, the *Tennessean* reported that she was writing songs for a New York musical show. She had signed with Saul Bourne, a well-known New York publisher, whom the article quoted: "It looks like 'Put Your Shoes On, Lucy' is going to be one of the biggest hits in a long time. It has been issued as sheet music and recorded by every record maker." Bourne was also enthusiastic about "Have a Heart," cowritten by Fort and Lucy Stokes, and a calypso, "Due to Circumstances Beyond My Control." Hank Fort premiered some of her songs for the musical on WSM.

Most of all, Fort wanted to be a successful performer, but she was at best an adequate one. Saul Bourne explained diplomatically that "she could go far professionally in singing and playing if she desired, but I'm sure she's headed for real fame as a songwriter." Hank herself confirmed his implication: "Owen and Dottie would only let me do the rebel yell on our discs." When she made an LP of her best songs a decade later, it featured the comical, "I Never Took a Lesson in My Life." In 1950 Hank appeared on the *Arthur Godfrey & His Friends* TV show made on the West Coast and with western swing bandleader Spade Cooley on CBS. She wrote a feature for the *Tennessean* that year titled "What It Is Like to Be a TV Star":

Eleanor "Hank" Fort at the piano in 1949. Courtesy of the *Tennessean*.

"Great, except for having to wear the thick make-up and black lipstick" that early TV demanded; she also described the dismay of black baseball star Jackie Robinson, who balked when the TV people started putting white powder on his face.

Hank genuinely loved both songwriting and Nashville. In 1949, she entered the "Know Nashville" campaign and won the Chamber of Commerce contest for the "Best Expression of Nashville's Friendliness." Her entry, "Nashville's Such a Friendly Place," was performed by local trio Joanne Polk, Eve Weatherford, and Jackie Joslin, calling themselves the Pepperettes. Joslin later became Jackie Gershwin, singing in the Skylarks vocal group on prime time television with Dinah Shore. She told me:

> We Pepperettes were in our senior year at Hume-Fogg High School and we had an early-morning and late-afternoon radio show on WLAC with bandleader Fred Murff. We would be running all day, from our homes in the old Victorian houses on Sixth Avenue South down Broadway to WLAC and to the school, then back to WLAC. It was hectic, but Hank Fort rehearsed us and got us ready. She was a wonderful, sweet person, and she got us an audition with bandleader Horace Heidt, who ran talent shows nationally. We sang at the Ryman, and we won. Horace took us on tour to Louisville and on to the West Coast. He put us on records, too, in Hollywood. That was funny because I never attended shows at the Ryman as a child. We lived three blocks away, but we never had money for things like that. I used to sit at the front steps at night, gaze at the stars, and dream of going to Hollywood.

The Pepperettes made six records for the Magnolia label as part of a series, "Horace Heidt presents . . .," including a successful version of Fort's "I Didn't Know the Gun Was Loaded," for which the Pepperettes were pictured on the sheet music, and other Fort songs, not least "Nashville's Such a Friendly Place."

On the strength of this success, Select Records put out Owen Bradley's version of the song, one side featuring Dottie Dillard and the other side Bob Johnstone singing the same lyrics:

> It's just the garden spot of Tennessee,
> with true southern hospitality.
> Once you're there you won't regret it,
> if you leave you won't forget it,
> The town with all the charm and grace,
> yes Nashville's such a friendly place.

"The Mayor received the first recording of Hank Fort's popular song from the composer's own hands," reported the *Tennessean* in September 1950. "Nashville got a '100 percent Nashville' song from a group of Nashvillians yesterday, and the name of the song had Nashville in it." Mayor Thomas Cummings remarked, with some restraint: "It's a nice song for a nice town." Hank Fort left Nashville in 1952 for Washington, D.C., where she became a well-known society host for the great and near great in public life, the theater, and music. Her bubbling personality and ingratiating style was focused equally on the Speaker of the House, for whom she wrote "Mr. Sam" (Rayburn), as on the latest unknown performer to whom Hank had taken a liking. She died in Washington in 1973.

The Bradley Connection

Owen Bradley was the natural first port of call for Hank Fort when she wanted to make recordings of her songs. The bandleader had known her since their earliest days in radio at WSM and he was now the leading orchestral arranger in town, working with Hank on WSM shows including *Sunday Down South*. He had developed a recording pedigree with Bullet and Decca, and he had access to the WSM engineers who ran the Castle studio and who were happy to help him record Hank's songs.

Bradley came by his musical talent genetically. His father, Vernie, raised his family with his wife, Letha Mai Owens, gave Owen guitar lessons, and led singing sessions out in the farming community of his birthplace, Westmoreland, Tennessee, just south of the state line; Owen's grandmother, Samantha

Crowder, musical herself, came from a family of schoolteachers and musicians. When bad rains washed out Vernie Bradley's crops a few years after the birth of his son William Owen Bradley in October 1915, the Bradleys moved to Nashville. Vernie took a job as a salesman for the Cumberland Tobacco Works. They lived on North Second Street and Cleveland when Owen's brother Harold was born in January 1926, the third of five surviving children, including Owen, Ruby Audine, Charles, and Bobby. The family was reasonably comfortable if not exactly well off, and when Owen's uncle left them some money, they invested in such luxuries as an electric radio, a piano, and a player piano.

Harold Bradley told me:

> My dad came home one day and said to my mother that he liked the new piano roll she had bought. She said, "No, that's William Owen." He had learned a tune by watching the keys on the player piano. He was gifted as a pianist and he never did have lessons until much later on.

At seventeen, in 1932, Owen talked himself into a pianist's spot with singer Eddie Snyder. Later that year, Owen formed his own band, the Blue Diamond Melody Boys, with trumpeter Ben Brasselle. They played at the Ridgeway Inn, and Owen doubled on trombone and piano. He sat in with the Jimmy Gallagher band too. Gallagher's granddaughter, Michael Sayles, remembered her grandfather, "with a twinkle in his eye and a grin on his chin, saying that he gave Owen Bradley his start in the industry. Owen wrote arrangements for the Gallagher band when Owen was starting out. He was paid $3.50 for each song."

From nightclubs, Bradley expanded to radio. Harold Bradley said:

> Owen played his first radio dates up in Bowling Green, Kentucky, where he knew people. He had played piano in clubs and gambling places up there. He'd drive up there just to be on radio, just for the experience and very little money. Often, they would give him complimentary sheet music, and he stored all that at our house at 120 Lucille Street in Nashville.

Owen Bradley at piano with, *from left*, AFM president George Cooper, WSM announcer David Cobb, drummer Farris Coursey, guitarist Harold Bradley, singer Dottie Dillard, and guitarist Jack Shook (on this occasion, singing). Courtesy of Michael Bevington Sayles.

Graduating to Nashville radio, Owen at first played "spots" on WSM between 1935 and 1936—filling in "on the spot" for musicians who were unavailable. He sometimes played with the WSM orchestra and led the band at a show that starred up-and-coming singer Dinah Shore. Bradley took various WSM players with him when nightclub owner Charlie Carney asked him to put together a band to play at Carney's new Stork Club. The band included Malcolm Crain, Charlie Grant, and singer Kitty Kallen.

In 1935, Owen married Mary Katherine Franklin, and in 1937 he switched to a more secure radio job at WLAC, then back to WSM in 1940 as an arranger and musician. He formed another dance band, the Owen Bradley Orchestra, which soon rivaled the Francis Craig and Beasley Smith bands. In 1944 and 1945, in the army and based at San Mateo, California, Bradley worked in Special Services with the Ted Weems Orchestra. Returning to WSM, he played mainly trombone, vibes, and organ, since WSM already had a number of good pianists, including Marvin Hughes, John Gordy, and Kathryn Pellettieri.

Owen Bradley's younger brother Harold, who would later play guitar in Owen's dance band and on all the Select label's recordings, grew up in the family musical tradition. (Their sister Ruby played piano behind several gospel quartets and worked as a secretary for Wally Fowler, and later for Owen.) In 1931, when the Bradley family moved to Lucille Street, Harold Bradley said, a carpenter building a house next door, Truman Clayborne, "was the first person who taught me anything on the guitar. He taught me to play 'Steel Guitar Rag.'" Harold already played the banjo because he liked the sound of it on the radio, "but my brother Owen said, 'No, you need to learn the guitar. That's the coming thing.'" At Isaac Litton High School, Harold started on the mandolin, and he continued to be surrounded by musicians at home.

> Farris Coursey was my next-door neighbor—he was Owen's drummer. Owen was a pop musician. Our attic was full of old sheet music when I was growing up. And when I started trying to learn the guitar I used those pop sheets, trying to figure out how to play. And I also started listening to Charlie Christian, because Billy Byrd, the guitar player with Ernest Tubb, was trying to play jazz. He started dating a girl living down the street from me, and he would come to our street with his guitar and a little old amplifier, and I would join in. He really got me started, when I was a little over twelve years old, I guess. He would play electric and I would play rhythm, and then we'd swap, you know. I've still got my Gibson S150 that I used on the first session I ever played. It is a jazz guitar that I bought from Billy Byrd, with a Charlie Christian bar pickup.

In the late 1930s Harold's guitar gurus were Charlie Christian and Django Reinhardt, but he also liked the Stamps-Baxter gospel quartet on radio, Gene Autry's records, and Bob Crosby's jazzy music on songs like "Little Rock Getaway." Another radio influence was hillbilly singer Zeke Clements, who "played minor keys and stuff that not many hillbillies played. I also listened to the Opry religiously. But that is what the family did—everyone in those days."

In 1941, at fifteen, Harold got his first music job. His cousin, pianist Fred Shoemake, who had a band engagement at the White Horse Bar, told Harold's mother: "Everybody in the union is working tonight. I need Harold to come play with me. I promise to look after him and only let him have Cokes, and he'll be fine." Harold's first experience as a road musician came in 1943, when his brother Owen

> called me on the phone and said why didn't I go on the road with Ernest Tubb in the summer while I was off from high school. And I said, "What, you mean playing old corny country music?" And he said, "It'll be good for you," so I did. And I found out that I really couldn't play what I thought I could. I was trying to be a jazz/pop guitar player and I had all those Charlie Christian licks in my head. Ernest gave me a bunch of his records to listen to, and I figured out what to play. I also played the early-morning radio show with him while I was in school. We played in Birmingham with Tex Ritter, and in Dallas, and I remember we went to New Orleans by train because of the wartime gas problem, and that was really something for me then. We had to be back in Nashville every Saturday night for the Grand Ole Opry show though.
>
> [When Bradley played radio shows with Tubb,] Ernest was living in Madison, and it was no trouble to pick me up on the way into town. He and I would play the morning radio shows and then we would go to eat at the Pie Wagon afterwards—half a block down Seventh Avenue, right below and across from the YMCA, which was on the corner of Seventh. We would eat with Eddy Arnold, who was also on the radio, and afterwards me and Eddy would ride the streetcar home to the end of North First. Then I would walk two blocks to Lucille Street.
>
> Eddy would carry on walking another five or six blocks. I remember watching him disappear in the distance in his wrinkled old suit. Then, a few years later when I was in the navy, my sister wrote to me telling me what a big star Eddy was, and it was hard for me to conceive because of remembering that wrinkled suit.

A week after he left Isaac Litton High School, Harold was in the navy as a radioman. He served from 1944 to 1946 and inevitably formed a little band at Wahiawa Naval Station in Hawaii. In the summer of 1946, Harold started his music career proper.

> Vito Pellettieri booked me on spots with Eddy Arnold on the Opry show, and with Bradley Kincaid and others. He would put you on right on the spot, say, "Go out there and play behind that square-dance thing, so-and-so's not here to do it." I got six dollars a spot.

In the fall of 1946, Harold enrolled at Peabody College. "I took music, and I majored on the string bass. They had no guitar teacher available at the time." His fellow students included Opry star Bradley Kincaid's twin daughters.

Harold worked on and off with his brother Owen's dance band from 1946 to 1958, backing up singers Snooky Lanson, Dottie Dillard, and Bob Johnstone—"The recording industry in Nashville was growing, but we still depended on the dance band for the main part of our income."

Bradley's memory of those days is sharp, because making a record was a novelty then, for him and even for Owen.

> People today come into Nashville and they can't imagine the town like it was when I grew up, that there was not a recording studio here at all. There were four or five radio stations, and we played the clubs, but there were no records before Bullet and very little else apart from Bullet for several years. I remember making those Select records. I don't remember any action happening on them. Hank Fort was a wonderful lady, great friends with Owen and Dottie Dillard. I think Owen did those records just to please Hank, and I don't think they would have had much distribution. It was a vanity label that they did for Hank.

Dottie Dillard and the Select Eight

Singer and Select Records partner Dottie Dillard recalled that the label may have issued its first discs in 1947, but the only ones found date from 1949 and 1950. Judging by the release numbers, Select may have produced up to eight discs, but only three are known today, all by Owen Bradley's Orchestra and featuring his lead singers, Dottie Dillard and Bob Johnstone. The first was "Save That Confederate Money Boys" backed with "Put Your Shoes On, Lucy." Next was "I Didn't Know the Gun Was Loaded" and "Let the Good Things Happen." Both records had Dottie up front of the band. "Nashville's Such a Friendly Place," the last known Select disc, became the theme song of Bob Johnstone, who had joined WSM in 1940 and had just returned there from singing with the Paul Whiteman Orchestra for five years. The flip side was the same song, sung by Dottie Dillard.

"Dottie was the best pop singer we had here in town when she was here," declared Harold Bradley. "We were around her so much, you know, it was like being brothers and sisters." Select Records survived in a largely dormant state at least until 1952, when it was still listed in trade papers care of Dorothy Dillard at Nashville's Memorial Hotel. Dillard recalled that

> the Memorial was an apartment hotel, just at the opposite end of the block WSM was on. I had come to Nashville in 1947 from Springfield, Missouri, to be the girl singer on *Sunday Down South.* I had been in an all-girls trio and sung in nightclubs in Springfield when my friend, Charlie

The Select crew, advertising a concert at Centennial Park: Courtesy of the *Tennessean.*

Owen Bradley, left, Snooky Lanson, and Dottie Dillard rehearsing for *Sunday Down South*. Courtesy of American Federation of Musicians and Harold Bradley.

> Brown, the producer of *Sunday Down South,* asked me to Nashville. Snooky Lanson was the boy singer and I was the girl. Later, Don Estes was the boy singer, then Buddy Hall. I did an evening WSM show with Owen Bradley on organ, Cecil Bailey on alto sax, and Jack Shook, the wonderful left-handed guitarist. At the same time, I did the *Waking Crew* show on WSM in the early evening, so I really needed that apartment near to the studios. Often, I wouldn't get to sleep at all between shows.

Aside from Select, Dillard pursued a varied career in Nashville music. She was on the *Arthur Godfrey Show* for ten years; worked with the Dixie Dons, the vocal group from *Sunday Down South* who often backed Alcyone Beasley in the act Betty and the Dixie Dons; and occasionally did a sister act with Minnie Pearl. Dottie would appear on stage with Minnie as "Sister" Dottie Dillard from Grinder's Switch, a shy, man-fearing, struck-dumb-by-the-big-city sort of character. "It's the funniest act in Nashville," said the *Banner* in 1951. Dillard added country songs to her pop repertoire, a necessity, she said, when she began working with Eddy Arnold on the Purina shows on WLAC. "Owen Bradley was the musical arranger, and he had to teach me a new country song every day before the show at the Andrew Jackson Hotel, because at the start I didn't know any country songs."

Dottie Dillard remembered the Select days with affection:

> Hank was involved in community theater and she was wanting to promote Nashville, but her ideas were not often new ones or forward-looking. That song about Confederate money had a limited market, I guess you could say. The Select label was really a bomb, so we just did a few discs, that was all.

As the year 1950 approached, the visions Select, World, and the other new labels had for Nashville and its place in the recording business were not so far off the mark. The city had grown in musical stature during the 1940s, as the wartime mixing of people and cultures revealed a national readiness to embrace southern music. The postwar search for the good times and the good songs brought Nashville and Nashville-based music to the fore. People knew that Dinah Shore was the "Nashville nightingale," that WSM radio meant good popular dance-band music as well as the Grand Ole Opry, that Hank Williams was the emerging hillbilly star, and that the best gospel and blues came out of Nashville via WLAC. The problem for Select, World, and the others was distribution, and the only Nashville-owned recording company with anything like a national profile remained the original, Bullet Records.

7

Bullet Reloaded: 1949–1952

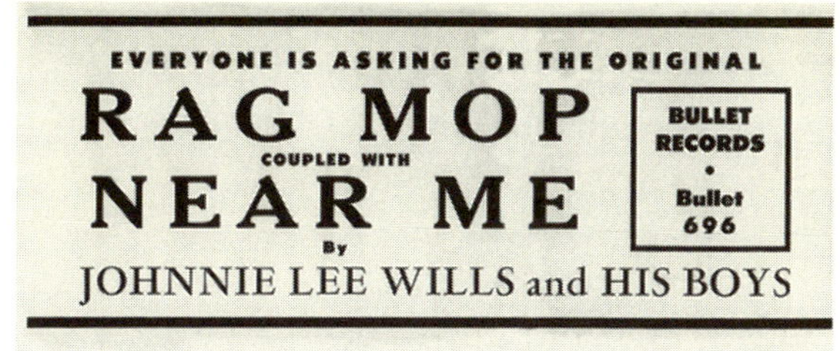

> *Dad brought "Rag Mop" home on a transcription. Mom said, "Overton, that's the stupidest song I ever heard." Well, she was wrong and Dad was right. It was a big hit.*
>
> —Tony Ganong

Bullet Records was synonymous with Jim Bulleit, but Bulleit was with the label for barely three years. After the breakup of the original partnership, C. V. Hitchcock kept the label going for another four years. He had guidance from Orville Zickler, supported by a former teller from First National Bank, John Weber, who came in as company secretary, but Hitchcock directed operations at Bullet Records personally, although he relied on others to head up the distribution and recording ends of the business. He kept on Jimmy Green and Hutch Carlock as head salesmen and promoted the recently hired Overton Ganong to handle artist and repertoire (A&R) duties in Bulleit's stead.

Overton Ganong and Bullet's New Look

Overton Ganong, an optimistic, can-do person, played a short but significant part in the Nashville music business. He was in Memphis, he recalled, when

> Red Hitchcock got in touch with me and asked me to come to work for Bullet Records. I had called on Red's Hermitage Music as a salesman and I evidently impressed him with my knowledge of the music business. I started with Bullet in 1947 and soon moved to Franklin, Tennessee, and then to Nashville, in 1948. My job at Bullet initially was to run the business office, call on disc jockeys and give them acetates of new songs we were plugging, serve as a talent scout wherever I would travel, and organize and direct some recording sessions.

Born in Leland, Mississippi, on April 24, 1909, Ganong had learned to play guitar and banjo and worked as a big-band musician in the 1930s. He was a member of Maurice Haste and the Memphonians, traveling Arkansas, Tennessee,

Overton Ganong, *left,* and Mel Delot at Capitol Records' office in New Orleans, 1946. Courtesy of Tony Ganong.

A Bullet promotional postcard for John Gordy, 1952. Courtesy of Country Music Hall of Fame and Museum.

and the Carolinas before working the Arkansas and west Tennessee fraternity- and sorority-house circuit as the leader of Overton Ganong and His Band. In 1938, Ganong married Myra Pride Smith, a strikingly attractive, petite woman with dark hair and blue eyes, and persuaded her to sing with the band. Before long, Myra advised her husband on his return from driving through a hailstorm from a dance in West Helena: "If you think we're going to lead a life like this, you're crazy. You're going to find a job and go to work." Ganong's day jobs included selling life insurance, driving an ambulance, and working as a field salesman with Columbia Records. After serving in the navy from October 1942 to September 1945, he went to work in Capitol Records' New Orleans sales office, then transferred to Memphis as branch manager for Capitol.

In asking Ganong to relocate to Bullet's head office in the fall of 1948, Hitchcock might have had in mind grooming him to take over from Bulleit. It had become increasingly clear to Hitchcock, Cashion, and Zickler that Bulleit was spending the proceeds of hits like "Near You" as quickly as he had made them. Certainly, Hitchcock retrenched the Bullet operation late in 1948; he had John Dunn move Bullet Plastics' pressing plant from Berry Field to Hitchcock's basement on Broadway, where just ten presses produced two thousand discs a day, and put a recording studio in the back of his premises. As Ganong remembered it:

> I was made more responsible for the sessions after Jim Bulleit left, and Red Hitchcock started to run some sessions also. He had a little studio at the back of Hermitage Music on Broad Street that we both used for country and gospel sessions. We used the Castle Studio for bigger bands and popular music sessions.

The Bullet Records catalog Hitchcock and Ganong inherited from Jim Bulleit in 1949 included a country line split between minor Nashville-based singers and an assortment of recordings bought from Dude Records of Dallas and other small labels; a black music roster based around Cecil Gant, who floated in and out of Nashville, and the Fairfield Four; a white country gospel line built around Wally Fowler, John Daniel, and other local quartet leaders; and a pop label dominated by Francis Craig, supplemented by light dance-band music by Les Elgart, Bob Crosby, and others. (The Mexican series had folded.)

Ganong and Hitchcock had to rethink the roster and the distribution setup. Ganong could tap into new, more stable distribution agreements through his Capitol contacts, but using fewer, bigger outlets put Bullet forever in the middle of someone else's priorities when it came to publicizing and selling. Another matter to evaluate was the debate within the record industry about size and speed that had arisen from the battle between Columbia and RCA to promote new formats to carry sound recordings: With the new 45-rpm discs, companies could minimize shipping costs. The largest single outlet for Bullet Records was now the mail-order division of Randy's Record Shop in nearby Gallatin; an advertisement for Bullet Records in Randy's mid-1950 record catalog emphasized that discs were "now available on 45s as well as 78 rpm."

As 1949 progressed, Bullet replaced the national and international names Jim Bulleit had courted with Nashville artists, including two dance-band musicians—guitarist Jack Shook, who could sing a laid-back, pop-country vocal as well as anyone, and clarinetist Cecil Bailey, who came out front for a version of "Sunday Down South," one of WSM's anthems. The pop series borrowed the Smith Brothers and the Jack Caldwell Trio from Bullet's country lineup, and Pepper Neely from R&B. The aim was to cash in on the increasing number of pop singers who were coming to Nashville to record or who were recording Nashville songs; the approach was to sand down the rough edges, an effort reflected in a couple of releases by the Smoothies, who covered Eddy Arnold's "Bouquet of Roses."

Caught up in the craze for ragtime-based piano instrumentals, Bullet in 1950 issued some Jim Beck recordings of Madge Suttee, a session pianist from Wichita Falls, Texas, who had played on singer Lefty Frizzell's first hit records. Suttee recorded the popular tune "Avalon" with a swing quartet. The following year, Bullet recorded pianists Daryl Harper and John Gordy, whose version of "Salty Dog Rag" sold well.

Before it expired, Bullet's pop series relied on "Papa" John Gordy, who played a mix of ragtime piano and small-combo dance music. Born in New Orleans in October 1904, Gordy had a legitimate pedigree in this kind of Dixieland sound. He studied music in Pine Bluff, Arkansas, and played with the Louisiana Ramblers in and around New Orleans, as well as with Harry James and Francis Craig. In the 1940s he joined the WSM radio orchestra in Nashville, where he was the top pianist for some years despite a misshapen right arm that caused him to play at an odd angle to the piano.

In the 1950s, Gordy formed a loose aggregation of musicians who played Monday nights at the Celtic Room in Nashville. The band, which often included Karl and Clint Garvin, and guitarist Harold Bradley, who played banjo, developed a cult following among white jazz fans in town, which perhaps explains why they made several records for Bullet.

Papa John Gordy's Dixieland band: *from left*, Walt Summers, Jack Shook, Otto Bash, Gordy, Dutch Gorton, Bob Lamm (who sang "Near You"), and Jack Gregory. Courtesy of American Federation of Musicians and Harold Bradley.

Wally Fowler and Bullet Gospel

To balance the decline of popular music in Bullet's second incarnation, the label's country gospel flourished. When Bulleit left, Hitchcock asked Wally Fowler to take the helm of the gospel series. Fowler agreed to oversee an increase in the label's gospel output, in spite of his ongoing involvement in publishing, show promoting, and songwriting, as well as his day job singing gospel music over the radio and in live performance. The popularity of Bullet's gospel series was far greater than we might imagine today, mostly records well within the mainstream of gospel sentiments with the occasional topical song, such as Jack Rogers's "Christ over Korea" recorded early in 1952.

The success of Fowler's first "All Night Sing" in Nashville in 1948 had kicked off a series of irregular—and then weekly—Friday night "Sings" at the Ryman in 1949. A typical show, covered by the *Tennessean* on August 30, 1950, featured Fowler and his Oak Ridge Quartet—the Clodhoppers had ceased to exist as Fowler minimized his country content—along with the Happy Goodman Family, the Speer Family, and the Rangers Quartet.

In 1949, Fowler's group comprised Deacon Freeman, Johnny New, and Curley Blalock along with Neal Matthews on guitar and Boyce Hawkins on piano. Promotional materials proclaimed the act "New, Different, Versatile!"—it was certainly different. "We did a lot of spirituals, always traditional types," recalled Neal Matthews, comparing Fowler's Oak Ridge Quartet to other groups. "The John Daniel Quartet was a gospel quartet, not a spiritual quartet." A later member, Joe Allred, said: "Wally was a good singer and he could really sing a spiritual and do a lot of chanting the way colored people used to."

Putting on a show was a vital part of the Fowler philosophy. *Collier's* magazine in 1955 likened that philosophy to the "formula well known to most secular showmen: make 'em laugh, make 'em cry, make 'em laugh again. That way he [Fowler] says, 'you entertain 'em as well as make 'em feel a spiritual blessing.'" The live audience for commercial white country gospel music did not come just for the religious expe-

The Goodman Family onstage, late 1940s: *from left,* Sam, Eloise, Stella, Gussie Mae, Ruth, Rusty, and Howard. The accordionist is unidentified. Courtesy of *Singing News* Magazine, Boone, N.C.

rience, although Fowler's Oak Ridge Quartet typically opened the show with some classic spirituals, such as "Swing Down, Sweet Chariot." Then they would move into current gospel hits like "Peace in the Valley" and some instrumental duets for piano and guitar. Next would come comedy routines based on Fowler's own tunes, such as "I'm a Bible Lovin' Man," and finally some good old Baptist hymns.

Fowler was famously difficult to work with, demanding and inconsistent. To keep up with his publishing interests, he often bailed out of his group's weekday shows, and Freeman, New, and Blalock had joined the Oak Ridge Quartet to fill the places of earlier members who had quit Fowler to form their own group, the Stone Mountain Quartet.

It was probably the newer Oak Ridge lineup that assembled at WSM radio studios early in 1949 to record for Bullet Records. Their first disc was "Lead Me to That Rock" backed with "Just a Closer Walk with Thee," two country gospel offerings with solid appeal. Fowler and the varying personnel of his quartet made another twenty discs for Bullet over the next four years, of which "I'm a Bible Lovin' Man" and "Dig a Little Deeper" were strong sellers. His records were devout but reflected much of the family-based sentimentalism of hillbilly folk music and some of the commercial craft of the emerging country style. Fowler's Bullet versions of "Peace in the Valley" and Stuart Hamblen's "It Is No Secret" appear to be the models for Elvis Presley's million-selling treatment of the songs for RCA in 1957. But as Fowler experienced mounting financial problems, including $8,750 damages owed to former group member Johnny New for a 1951 auto accident and an unpaid-taxes judgment of $25,000, he sold the Oak Ridge Quartet name in 1958 to Smitty Gatlin, who took the group to new generations as perhaps the most famous of all country gospel quartets, the Oak Ridge Boys.

From the family gospel groups who sang the early-morning shift on local radio, often through several generations and station changes, Bullet chose from WSIX Tom and Lena Speer from Double Springs, Alabama, working with their children Mary, Rosa, Ben, and Brock. George Thomas Speer, known as "Dad," started singing in 1908 but stayed on the farm until 1923, when he took up singing at conventions and putting on shows for the Vaughan company. The Speers moved to Nashville in the 1950s, working early-morning radio for eight years before becoming a staple of WLAC-TV. Another well-known family group, the Goodman Family, first appeared on Bullet at the end of 1950 with a popular version of "Mansion over the Hilltop."

Between 1946 and 1948 Bullet had issued just eleven country gospel records. Between 1949 and 1952 they issued another fifty-three, including the twenty by Fowler's Oak Ridge Quartet, ten by the Speer Family, and seven by the John Daniel Quartet.

After Jim Bulleit left Bullet, C. V. Hitchcock took little interest in black gospel. Margaret Barnes recorded one gospel disc in 1949, "Saviour Don't Pass Me By," and in 1950 Bullet recorded one disc of the Ebenezer A.M.E. Church Gospel Choir, "He Knows My Heart." The Fairfield Four were still appearing on Bullet as late as June 1951 with "Moving up the King's Highway," which along with "John the Revelator" sounds completely different from their previous releases, probably reflecting personnel changes. The original group members apparently fell out in 1950 over a show at the Ryman. Sam McCrary and Willie Lewis formed a new Fairfield Four, which continued the WLAC radio spot and recorded until 1954.

These few black gospel discs continued to appear as part of Bullet's general "race" series, and Cecil Gant saw another six releases in that series after Bulleit left the label.

B. B. King and Early 1950s R&B

Under Hitchcock's stewardship, Bullet's output of blues and R&B releases continued to grow. A prewar blues star, Walter Davis, signed with the label, and "You've Gotta Reap What You Sow" from May 1949 was the first of seven Bullet discs he apparently recorded in Chicago in one or two sessions that year. A basic but recognizable pianist and a moving vocalist, Davis rode his well-constructed and meaningful lyrics to fame. Born in March 1912 in Grenada, Mississippi, he lived in the St. Louis area after about 1925, where he often worked and recorded with Roosevelt Sykes on piano and Henry Townsend on guitar. *Billboard* magazine welcomed Davis's Bullet discs as "high grade blues chanting, should do lively business in the South."

Walter Davis helped carry the label through 1950 and 1951, as did the recordings of another northern-based singer, Roosevelt Sykes. When Sykes recorded "Low Land Blues" in 1948 under the name Boogie Evans, and "Candy Man Blues" late in 1949 under his own name, he was coming off three major postwar blues hits for other labels: his big-selling cover of Gant's "I Wonder," "The Honeydripper," and "Sunny Road." The Bullet sessions were apparently made in Chicago with the Jump Jackson band.

In October 1950 Bullet released "Jivin' Woman" by a third heavyweight prewar bluesman, Joe Williams. Known for his lived-in vocals, a classic mark of the old-time country blues, and a full-bodied guitar sound, Williams often played a nine-string guitar. His "Crawlin' King Snake" and "Baby Please Don't Go" had sold well between 1935 and 1941 on Bluebird. Born in Crawford, Mississippi, in October 1903 of a Cherokee father, Williams learned guitar at fish fries and dances, graduated to playing with touring medicine shows and working the lumber camps and brothel circuit with pianist Little Brother Montgomery, and wound up around 1934 in St. Louis, where his Bullet titles may have been recorded and pitched to Lester Melrose in Chicago before they made it down to Nashville.

Once Hitchcock had exhausted Bullet's connections in the north, Overton Ganong turned to R&B artists closer to home, recording bands led by Tommy Brooks, Joe Costa, Wee Willie Kirk, and Chuck Merrill, who all contributed jumping blues and boogies to the Bullet mix in the early 1950s. Don Q. Pullen, who first recorded for World in 1948, made two instrumental sides, "Major Alteration" and a timely "Thanksgiving" for a Bullet release in November 1949. In his band was saxophonist Louis Brooks, who said Pullen's World and Bullet discs were his own first recordings.

A second record from Pullen and his Q Tones on Bullet, issued around September 1950, was "Private Property Blues," written with band member George White and of the smooth genre popularized by the Ink Spots, Delta Rhythm Boys, and maybe the Big Three Trio. (George White later worked as an announcer on radio station WSOK and went on to become a popular disc jockey in Detroit.) The lyrics of "Private Property Blues" complain that "every time I see something fine for me, it turns out to be private property"; whether this was a deep social message we can only guess. The *Globe* reported in March 1950 that it was a song from *Fascination,* one of the musical shows Pullen produced at Washington Junior High School.

Overton Ganong's connections at Memphis radio station WDIA led to Bullet's release of fledgling radio star B. B. King's first two records, marking with "Miss Martha King" in July 1949 the start of possibly the greatest recording career in postwar blues. King has described the song, a tribute to his wife, as "the best of the four sides. The song reflected some of the stress of our marriage, but I loved that good-hearted lady and I wanted her to hear it in a song." Recorded with Memphis's Tuff Green Band when King was still looking for a style, the disc lacks King's trademark finger vibrato and continual bending or sustaining of notes, like speech patterns. King told Colin Escott: "The funny thing was, when they played back the recordings, I didn't know who it was. I had never heard myself. I asked one of the guys, 'Who's that?' They said, 'That's you, fool.' "

Riley "B. B." King, born on a plantation in Itta Bena, Mississippi, went to Memphis in 1945 to live with his cousin, blues singer Bukka White, went back to the farming life for two years, and returned to Memphis and West Memphis in 1948. He played on KWEM and then WDIA, where he became popular with the *Sepia Swing Show* and others.

B. B. King in the Memphis radio studio (where he recorded for Bullet) in 1949. Courtesy of Showtime Archives [Toronto], Colin Escott, and Ernest C. Withers.

When King approached a DJ at radio station WDIA, Nat D. Williams, about getting into radio, Williams asked station manager Bert Ferguson to listen to the guitarist, and King won a short spot to play the blues. In the spring of 1949, King asked Ferguson if he could help him get onto records. With no record companies based in Memphis, Ferguson contacted his former Memphis acquaintance Overton Ganong. Both were familiar with Memphis bandleader Tuff Green, and it was decided that Ferguson would record King backed by Green's band at Studio A at WDIA with the station's technical manager, Don Kern, at the controls.

B. B. King's second and last Bullet disc was "Take a Swing with Me." For the session, Richard "Tuff" Green's band featured Green on bass, Ben Branch on tenor sax, Thomas Branch on trumpet, Sammie Jett on trombone, Phineas Newborn on drums, and Newborn's sons Calvin and Phineas Jr. on guitar and piano. Phineas Newborn Jr. was at the heart of this boogie-woogie-based item, from its strong opening into a riffing boogie and surprisingly complex harmonies. There is also a pleasing, laid-back solo from female trombonist Sammie Jett and a sax solo with shades of Lester Young. King himself sounds more at ease, and his vocal is better balanced on this track, too, although the thinness is still there and his timing is not impeccable. As King recognized in his autobiography:

> Tuff Green's [band] was one of the best . . . [with] Phineas Jr. on piano and Calvin on guitar. . . . They were both great. Junior, though, was more than great. He was a genius. . . . Folks were calling him the new Art Tatum. . . .
>
> When I hear those [Bullet] tracks today, I barely recognize the high-pitched vocalist and stumbling guitarist, but a baby's got to crawl before he walks. But I was so thrilled I would have paid the man for the privilege of making real records.

By September 1950, "the man" was no longer Overton Ganong. As King said of his experience with the label: "At first I thought I was big stuff, but we didn't sell no records, and I was hearing everyone's records 'cept mine. I thought if you made a record, that was it. I found out that was not it." The West Coast label RPM Records arranged for King to record in Memphis at Sam Phillips's new studio and other locations, and by early 1952, King's "Three O'Clock Blues" hit #1 on the R&B charts. King had seven more R&B chart hits in the next three years, and more than seventy over the next four decades, many of which also appeared on the pop charts, among them King's signatures "Everyday I Have the Blues" and "The Thrill Is Gone."

Part of the deal that took King to Bullet included Tuff Green's own Bullet record, "Let's Go to the Liquor Store," with J. P. Luper on vocals, and Ganong continued to mine his Memphis connections. On "Gonna Bring My Baby Back" and "Beer Bottle Boogie," Bullet showcased "Mr. Swing" with Bobby Plater's Orchestra—in fact, "Mr. Swing" was Rufus Thomas and the band was Lionel Hampton's. Bobby Plater, one of a new wave of alto-sax players who joined the big bands after the war, played on all Hampton's big hits of the day, including "Hey Ba Ba Re Bop" and "Beulah's Boogie," until joining the Count Basie band in the early 1960s. The composer of the big-band classic "Jersey Bounce," Plater made at least four sides for Bullet in 1950, probably while the Hampton band was touring. Singer Rufus Thomas recorded on various other labels before finding his recording niche on Stax in the 1960s with international hits like "Walking the Dog." He was not aware the Bullet disc had been issued until I sent him a copy in 1999. On the telephone, he sounded incredulous:

> That *is* me. I had forgotten all about those songs, but you know, that really is me. I do remember that "Beer Bottle" song, and that is a good band, a quality band on there. And, you know, I sound good on those songs, I think so.

Bullet recorded "Phillips Sent Me" by Plater with vocalist Jerome Richardson at the same time as Mr. Swing's disc, sometime between June and September 1950. The tune had been made for Memphis disc jockey Dewey Phillips, whose catchphrase was "tell 'em Phillips sent 'cha." Something of an alto-sax prodigy, Richardson was from Texas but lived in Oakland, California, playing gigs around the city in his early teens. He joined the Jimmie Lunceford band and then, in 1948, the Lionel Hampton band, in San Francisco, recording with that group from 1949 to 1951.

Another Overton Ganong connection led to recordings in 1952 by smooth-voiced Dusty Brooks from Jackson, Mississippi. Among them, "Chili Dogs" was a slickly performed vocal novelty, an entertaining period piece employing the sweet, mellow, deep-harmony sound of the 1940s. At Lane College in the mid-1930s, Brooks had organized a group called the Four Tones, which found its way to Dallas in 1936 and then to Hollywood to make black musical western shorts like *Harlem Rides the Range.* They recorded for Exclusive Records in a smooth, small-combo style and bounced around a dozen small labels before they ended up on Bullet.

Joining the ranks of labels mining a seam of Crescent City music, Bullet took advantage of Ganong's connections in New Orleans to record the little-known pianist Tucker Coles at around the time his orchestra was booked into Frank Painia's Dew Drop Café in September and October 1951. Coles made good records, full of clever lyrics and tight band work. On "Don't Get Excited" he gave a laid-back piece of health advice as he delivered the late-1951 version of "chill out": "All you cats take my advice / It'll add twenty years to your life." Coles's "House Rockers Jamboree" was issued early in 1952 in a proto–rock & roll style that invoked the Deacon Jones and Elder Brown crowd who populated the lyrics of Wynonie Harris, Roy Brown, and other R&B shouters. The good-time, stop-rhythm instrumental sound is pure New Orleans, particularly the guitar and the extended tenor-sax solo that takes up the exhortation to "Blow, Joe."

New Orleans saxophonists David Lastie and Joe Tillman had formed a band called the Houserockers around this time with Jessie Hill on drums. Touring with Lastie and Guitar Slim, taking in Nashville's Grady's Club, was Little Eddie Langlois, who recorded "My Baby Left Me" for Bullet. J. D. Horton also came to Nashville in 1952 with Eddie Langlois and Guitar Slim. Issued around May 1952, Horton's "Cadillac Blues" was the last record on Bullet's blues series.

Country Hits and Johnnie Lee Wills

The country music series was Bullet's longest-lasting and best-selling line through the early 1950s. Overton Ganong recalled with satisfaction:

> I was quite successful in finding talent, especially in Texas and Memphis. I recorded Leon Payne, who was a really good hillbilly singer, and Ray Price, who was kind of a fixture with me. . . . I was the one who arranged for Johnnie Lee Wills to join Bullet, and I ran the recording sessions.

Bullet Records' third and fourth best-sellers, after "Near You" and "Beg Your Pardon," both came from the Tulsa-based western swing combo Johnnie Lee Wills and His Boys: "Rag Mop," which entered the *Billboard* chart in February 1950, and "Peter Cottontail," which followed it into the charts that spring.

Overton Ganong's son Tony remembered the impact of the first Wills session.

> Even though I was only seven years old, I remember distinctly Dad coming home with an acetate of "Rag Mop" and putting it on the record player, all excited, telling my mother that he thought he had a hit. When she heard it, she said something like, "Overton, that's the stupidest song I ever heard. That thing will never sell." Well, she was wrong and Dad was right. It became a big hit. I remember that I liked it and played it a lot on our record player, driving my mom crazy.

Johnnie Lee Wills, born in 1912, had led one of the top southwestern dance bands since leaving his brother's band, Bob Wills's Texas Playboys, in 1940. Bob and a few others had essentially created the western swing style, and Johnnie Lee's earliest band, one of the toughest and bluesiest western swing bands ever, recorded for Decca in 1941. By the time he followed fellow Oklahomans Merl Lindsay and Al Clauser onto Bullet in the fall of 1949, Johnnie Lee had begun to streamline his band—Curly Lewis and Henry Boatman, fiddles; Buster Magness, steel; Don Harlan, clarinet; Clarence Cagle, piano; Eb Gray, guitar; Chuck Adams, bass; Howard Davis, drums; and longtime Wills vocalist Leon Huff. Perhaps the band's most important asset from 1942 to 1952, Huff had been a member of Bob Wills's band and was one of the great vocalists in western swing history, a honey-voiced singer comfortable in any setting and with any material.

With its simple call-and-response spelling out of its title words—"R-A-G-G M-O-P-P"—the song that became one of the best-selling country releases of 1950 had a complicated history. Its credited composer, western swing steel guitarist Deacon Anderson, claimed to have written the song during the Second World War and played it in various bands, including Richard Prine's All-Stars in Beaumont, Texas. Johnnie Lee heard an acetate of Prine doing "Rag Mop" and later told *Time* magazine: "At first I thought it was crazy. Then it kinda irritated me. We played it again, and darn it, everybody kept asking for it."

C. V. Hitchcock had "Rag Mop" playing in his Hermitage Music offices for years. Figuring that it could be a cross-style hit for Bullet, he had Chuck Merrill record it in Bullet's R&B series, and the song did cross into the pop market. Texas-music authority Kevin Coffey has documented how the song became the rage in the wake of Johnnie Lee's hit, inspiring more than twenty covers, several of which eclipsed the original in sales—notably the Ames Brothers' Coral version. Lionel Hampton recorded it while Jerome Richardson was with his band, and both Hampton and Joe Liggins took the song into the R&B charts. Within a few months, Anderson, Wills, and the song's publisher, Hill and Range, were sued by International Music Company; its song, "Get the Mop," first recorded by jazz trumpeter Red Allen in 1944, bore more than a passing resemblance to "Rag Mop." International won the case and, as Anderson later admitted, the song was just based "on an old Negro blues progression."

Bullet's next Wills release proved to be another charted money-spinner with a long life, and another vivid memory for Tony Ganong:

Johnnie Lee Wills and His Boys ready to ride their success with "Rag Mop." Courtesy of Showtime Archives [Toronto] and Colin Escott.

My dad recorded "Peter Cottontail"—that was a hit for Johnnie Lee Wills. He said he did that one in Tulsa, Oklahoma, at a radio station and that he went out there several times. Mom apparently didn't have an ear for the public taste because she remarked again that "Cottontail" can't possibly be a hit, but it was, and there was a version by Gene Autry, and the song still comes around again every Easter.

By the end of 1952 Bullet had released nine more Wills discs. Among these, "I Needed You" featured vocalist Leon Huff, and "Coyote Blues" was a consistently strong seller during the last days of Bullet Records. A strong piano and drum "stomp" that gave the band solid appeal for dancers and jukeboxes characterized all Wills's recordings, and the group's small-combo drive stood it in good stead as western swing music changed during the early 1950s.

Apart from Johnnie Lee Wills, country music artists who recorded for Bullet between 1949 and 1952 either hovered on the edge of popular acclaim, or they and their songs fed the local jukebox market while they waited for their big break. "Jealous Lies" on Bullet marked the start of Ray Price's phenomenal country career, although there was no hint that Price would one day record the most perfect hillbilly shuffles and it would be several years before he found his own sound. Price, who had been singing professionally for only a couple of years, clearly had Eddy Arnold on his mind in Texas in January 1950 when he recorded for Bullet, backed by accordionist Hy Busse and his trio, the Frontiersmen. A few years later, he sounded like Hank Williams, but his #1 recording of "Crazy Arms" on Columbia in 1956, as complete a country record as has ever been made, cemented his own new direction.

Some of the later Bullet discs worked the honky-tonk end of country music. Herbert "Butterball" Paige recorded a couple of self-explanatory titles around the fall of 1949: "Girl at the End of the Bar" and "Honky Tonk Pete," whose barroom humor almost demanded jukebox play. Two of his soloists, Dale Potter on fiddle and Hal Smith on bass, were Nashville session stalwarts. Paige, who had worked with Eddy Arnold, had just quit Ernest Tubb's employment when the June 23, 1949, issue of *Billboard* noted that Bullet had signed him. Hal Smith helped write and produce Paige's other honky-tonk anthems on Bullet, including "I'm Too Old to Boogie Anymore."

Another part-time record producer at Bullet was Ed Crowe, from the farm country north of Memphis. A former musician with Pete Pyle, Crowe wrote "Salty Dog Rag" for John Gordy, which became a hit for Red Foley, and produced Gordy's Bullet recordings and several others, including Si Jenkins's "One Dollar Boogie."

When Jimmy Work recorded "Hospitality" for Bullet in 1949, he had just written the smash hit "Tennessee Border" and was hoping it would spark his own recording career. Like the York Brothers, Work had left the rural mid-South for Detroit and recorded for some local labels there. The composer of Kitty Wells's smash "Making Believe," Work became one of the most influential and successful songwriters of the 1950s in the wake of his later recordings for the Dot label.

Paul Blunt, an East Texan singer and multi-instrumentalist and a fixture on the Dallas–Ft. Worth music scene, had recorded among his earliest sides as a vocalist a hit cover of the notorious "Cocaine Blues" with Dyson's Musical Texans, released on Tri-State. He made his first release on Bullet in April 1949, and by the time he made "Walking up Stairs" in 1950, he was backed by the western trio the Frontiersmen, who had relocated to Dallas and become studio regulars at Jim Beck's. Young country singer Eddie Cochran heard this song, which later became the model for Cochran's rock & roll hit "20 Flight Rock."

Born in September 1925, Nashville native Ray Batts, who claims on the Bullet release "Bear Cat Daddy" to be from Louisville, had a show on WMAK for a hundred dollars a week and was playing the beer joints around Nashville when he brought four songs to Bullet. For USO shows during the war, he told Colin Escott: "They'd send us to areas Bob Hope wouldn't go. They'd take all us wannabes and has-beens and ship us in. All those GIs thought we were great, so I said, 'Hell, I'm gonna make a go of this.'" Guitarist Gerald Hadley from Ramer, Tennessee, described Bullet's sessions with the Ray Batts Band:

> We recorded at the old Bullet Recording Studio on Broad Street in Nashville. We recorded also with singer Bob Williams. The man who engineered the sessions was Bill Beasley, and I think that he had an arrangement where he kept some of the masters for himself and gave some to Mr. Hitchcock at Bullet. That band included Hal Scott, Andy Johnson, Jerry Mullican, and myself.

Overton Ganong told another bandleader who came to Bullet, steel guitarist Tani Allen, that he liked the band but not their singer. So Allen called a different singer, Houston "Buck" Turner, from Chattanooga, who brought to the session the first song he'd ever written, "Tennessee Jive." The disc begins with vibes and electric guitar, played by Keller Merc and Billy Byrd—like a Benny Goodman record featuring Lionel Hampton and Charlie Christian. "Tennessee Jive" went on to attract a lot of attention, not least from a strug-

(Opposite): Butterball Paige on bass with Ernest Tubb's band at a traffic-stopping promotional occasion in Nashville. Courtesy of Country Music Hall of Fame and Museum.

INSURANCE
THEATRE
FRANK

The wholesale counter at Hermitage Music on Broadway in 1952; *left,* Bullet/Hermitage secretary Betty Lawson; *fourth from left,* Hermitage finance director Jack Tureman; *second from right,* C. V. Hitchcock. On the other side of the wall is Bullet Records. Courtesy of Richard Cashion.

gling Pennsylvania hillbilly swing band led by Bill Haley. In January 1953, when Haley rewrote the song as "Real Rock Drive," Hitchcock sued, despite Turner's advice to wait and see if Haley's disc became a hit. With the suit, Essex Records stopped working Haley's record and promptly issued instead "Crazy, Man, Crazy," which became a Top Ten pop hit.

Other country artists to get a release or two at the tail end of the Bullet operation included Chuck Bridges, Shorty Ashburn, Ray Melton, Dick Dyson, and the popular radio duo of Annie Lou and Danny Dill. Bullet issued material leased from Dude and other Southwest labels by Smiling Ed Gregory, Joe St. Clair ("the Cowboy of the Air"), and Art Davis's Rhythm Riders. In contrast, Charley and Bonnie Barley's two recordings for Bullet early in 1950 were not standard hillbilly or western fare. The first carried two religious tunes, and the second coupled the intriguing "Miner's Welfare Song" with "John L's Contract Tune," celebrating United Mineworkers of America president John L. Lewis and the contract he had signed with coal operators on March 5 that year.

Selling jukeboxes at Hermitage Music, mid-1950s. *Far right corner,* C. V. Hitchcock; *third back on the right,* Marvin Parkes; *front left,* Eugene Cashion, next to the three engineers who maintained the equipment. Courtesy of Richard Cashion.

Bullet's Finale: "I'll Put My Dreams Away"

Overton Ganong left Bullet at the end of 1951, a move Tony Ganong takes the blame for:

> I had asthma and respiratory problems and the doctor advised we move to a warmer climate. So my dad rejoined Capitol in Jacksonville and then moved to Miami. He ran a record store, too, in Miami and then sold stereos and TVs in Tampa. In retirement, he set up a company running nature tours that he kept going until he was eighty-nine years old.

When Ganong left, Hitchcock began scaling back the recording end of the business, and he kept Bullet active for only another six months. He had Wally Fowler on hand to help keep the gospel series going, his connections in New Orleans fed the R&B series until the summer of 1952, and a stockpile of pop recordings and some local jazz contacts took the 1000 series well into that year. But the country discs flowed longest.

After Buck Turner did six singles with Tani Allen, Bullet asked Turner to go solo, and Allen talked him into it. Turner's "I'll Put My Dreams Away" was the last disc ever issued on the original Bullet label.

Toward the end of 1952, Hitchcock and Cashion closed up, moved buildings, and threw most of the Bullet master discs out with the trash. In an appropriate postscript, as the *Tennessean* reported in June 1954, the New York publishing agent Harry Fox had filed suit in chancery court seeking "not less than $9,000" from the now-defunct Bullet company or its partners for nonpayment of fees associated with handling songs on its behalf, and one song in particular: "Shattered Dreams."

Hitchcock continued to operate his wholesale record-distribution network and took an increasing interest in his record-pressing business with John Dunn. They sold the Broadway premises and moved Hermitage Music to 74 Lafayette Street and Bullet Plastics to Franklin Road. Eugene Cashion continued to take care of Hermitage Music day to day with the help of his son-in-law Jack Tureman and Betty Lawson, a relative who came to Nashville as a student from Van Buren County and who became the last secretary of Bullet Records, taking over from John Weber.

When Eugene Cashion died in 1958, his jukebox business was taken up by Alice Cashion, her daughter Mary Sue Tureman, and her nephew Marvin Parks. They did not retain any role in Hitchcock's businesses and according to Cashion's son Richard:

> His partners said that his partnership interest was not worth anything, and they cut us off from the business. There was a lot of animosity between mother and C. V. Hitchcock. There always remained some hard feeling, and it was not talked about at home.

On May 25, 1963, Hitchcock announced to the *Tennessean* that Southern Plastics, formerly Bullet Plastics Inc., had moved to new premises at Chestnut Street: "This expansion triples our floor space, and to celebrate fifteen years of business in pressing records we are holding open house today for manufacturers, distributors, and associates of the music industry." He had just returned from Europe and was proud that "our plant includes all new Belgian-made equipment." At the opening, Hitchcock made a speech recalling the early days, telling his visitors that he was the first man to press records in town and still one of the largest manufacturers in the South.

Hitchcock's cousin John Moore had only good words to say about C. V.

> He was a kind, gentle, accommodating person. He did a lot for the church and for various local organizations. He helped so many people down through the years. He would help put you in business at the drop of a hat—people like John Dunn, Jim Bulleit, Bill Beasley. But I think he had varying returns on his kindness. He trusted people a lot. He stayed close to John Dunn all his life. He also trusted Jim Bulleit and was a good friend to him.

C. V. Hitchcock died on May 21, 1976, aged seventy-six, still the owner of Bulk Vendors Manufacturing. Asked about Hitchcock's retirement years, John Moore laughed and said, "He retired the day he died."

8

Bulleit Enterprises, Inc.

> *I had been in selling long enough to know that you've got to get in there first, with the most.*
>
> —Jim Bulleit

In February 1949, *Billboard* reported that Jim Bulleit, operating as Bulleit Enterprises, Inc., would go into music publishing with a New York partner and continue record production and distribution from a Nashville base.

> He will also produce his own label, as yet unnamed, to specialize in race material, and also previously unwaxed pop tunes cut with small combos. Bulleit Enterprises' first indie client is Collegiate whose distribution was formerly linked with that of Bullet disks.

Bulleit had forged a link with his new company's first client in 1948, when Peabody student Bill Beasley pitched him some pop tunes he had written while a trombonist in college dance bands. Bulleit had been so busy recording and leasing master recordings in advance of the union ban, he already had more music than he could issue on Bullet. So Bill Beasley, at twenty-one years old, decided in October 1948 that the answer was to form his own label, Collegiate, buying spare masters and pressing and distribution capacity from Bullet.

"I started Collegiate with my song 'Cheri,' performed by Rufus Long," Beasley told me. "That sold quite well, so then I went through all Jim Bulleit's masters and took what I wanted for my label." Recorded in the WKDA studio in Nashville, "Cheri" was the title song from a musical show by Beasley and Elwin Erby produced at Peabody College. Later prominent in the Nashville Symphony Orchestra, saxophonist Rufus Long, a music major at Peabody, had led the Nashville Youth Orchestra and been involved with dance band music for several years.

When Bulleit left Bullet, Beasley and his label went with him, and Bulleit promoted at least one Collegiate disc to semi-hit status. "Heart of My Heart" by Danny Cassella, a recording Bulleit bought in Chicago and leased to Beasley, sold a hundred thousand copies. The two men formed a distribution company, Coastline, late in 1948, for which Beasley had primary responsibility, he said.

> I had seen what happened at Hermitage Music, and I knew we could distribute too. Red Hitchcock had tables with discs piled high ready to be shipped out. The higher the pile, the better that disc was selling. I soon got to know what sold, and where.

A half-page advertisement in the April 2, 1949, *Billboard* announced Bulleit's new direction: "Here's Jim Bulleit—he's back keeping company with the hits. See what we mean." A list of new records followed, on labels Bulleit had freshly formed, recently bought, or arranged to distribute. The whole package was wrapped up in a new company Bulleit had

Bill Beasley, *center,* and Jim Bulleit, *right,* promoting Collegiate's "Heart of My Heart" by Danny Cassella to Birmingham distributor Jack Howard, early 1949. Courtesy of the author and Bill Beasley.

worked up in the three months since leaving Bullet: Bulleit Enterprises, Inc., working out of 417 Ash Street, eight blocks south of Broadway. The board comprised Jim Bulleit, Rachel Bulleit, and treasurer Howard Allison, who had also left Bullet Records. Ruth Kilbrew, formerly Bulleit's secretary at Bullet, held the whole act together, while also working for Beasley, Red Wortham, and other associates Bulleit gathered around him.

Bulleit's New Labels: Delta and Village

Early in 1949, Bulleit formed the Delta and Village labels to issue R&B, gospel, and country music. He became involved with Harlem Records, formed in New York in 1946 by a pioneering black record executive, J. Mayo Williams; arranged through Coastline to be a distributor for the Select and World labels in Nashville; and negotiated distribution deals for

Collegiate and Harlem as far afield as Pasadena and Ontario. His own new labels were mainly for southern consumption, a lesson learned in his split with Bullet:

> During the time I ran my own record labels, I ran an altogether smaller operation. I formed two main labels, Village for white spirituals and Delta for R&B. They were only put out in the southern markets and in specially chosen likely markets such as Chicago. They were not pop music, they were for special markets, and I knew where those markets stopped. There was no point in overstretching myself.

Both the Delta and Village labels continued to bear the traditional warning that the discs were for personal use, implying that Bulleit had not yet embraced the new record-industry practice of promoting, rather than discouraging, airplay. He was still keeping an eye out for the main chance, though, as he made clear:

> What I did do at that time, around 1949 to 1950, was to get involved in extensive traveling to visit distributors and to make other contacts and to check out recording artists that had been recommended. On these journeys I sometimes made recordings. Other times I bought up masters from other labels, and if I was lucky I sold them a few of my own.

Out of his traveling and wheeling and dealing, Bulleit picked up several labels for distribution only. The first was Dude Records, a primarily country label owned by Jim Beck in Dallas. Bulleit had made the Beck connection when he was still with Bullet Records in September 1948 and had helped persuade Beck to set up in the recording business.

Though Bulleit described it as an R&B label, Delta Records started in March 1949 with releases in three series. The hillbilly series comprised just one record, “Talkin’ ’bout Susie” by Slim Lay and the Crossroads Follies Gang, fixtures on Alabama radio before they moved to WSIX in Nashville. A second series, devoted to white gospel music, lasted for two releases only—by the Stone Mountain Quartet, comprising

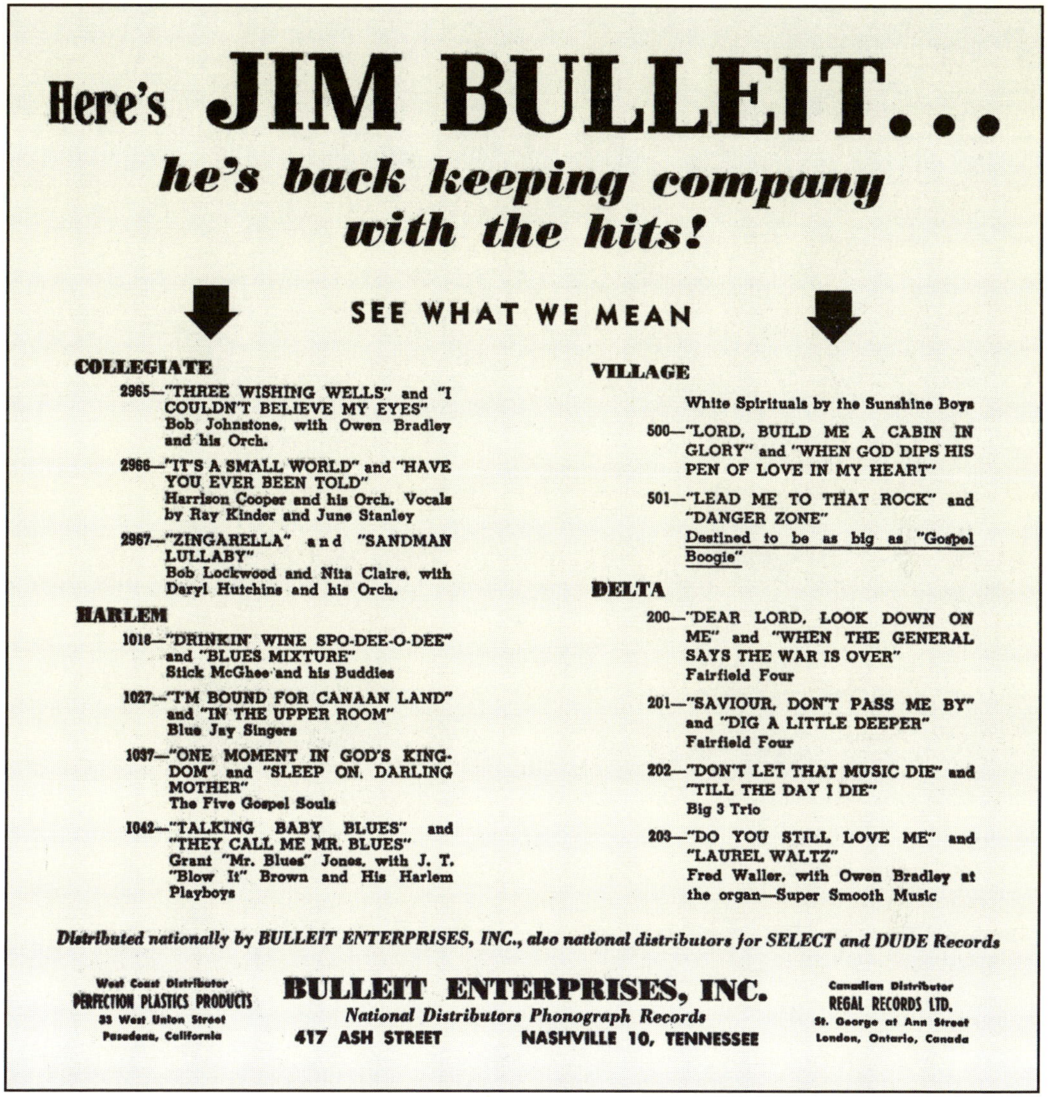

Courtesy of Bear Family Records.

singers who had just left Wally Fowler’s Oak Ridge Quartet, and by the Golden West Quartet, members of Pee Wee King’s country band the Golden West Cowboys. Jim Bulleit persuaded Redd Stewart, Gene Stewart, Shorty Boyd, and Chuck Wiggins that an example of their well-received gospel spot in King’s show could be committed to disc without upsetting King’s label, RCA.

Delta’s main series, R&B, in fact started with gospel music. Bulleit had four unissued masters by the Fairfield

The Big Three Trio: *from left,* Bernardo Dennis, Leonard Caston, and Willie Dixon. Courtesy of Bear Family Records.

Four, which he quickly released as he busied himself making arrangements to record the Big Three Trio again. "In R&B, one of my favorite artists was Willie Dixon, who had the Big Three Trio out of Chicago," Bulleit said. "Songs like 'Appetite Blues' and others on Delta were cut by me on portable equipment in a Chicago nightclub." Since leaving Bullet Records, the Big Three Trio had seen ten discs issued on Columbia with some success. Nevertheless, they were persuaded to work for Bulleit again and recorded all their Delta sides at the Chicago session early in 1949; Delta issued three of their discs around April. The Trio that recorded for Delta was not the original Bullet group: Ollie Crawford had replaced Bernardo Dennis, and a drummer, Alphonse Walker, had been added on some recordings. Otherwise, the discs reflected much the same approach, a mix of blues and novelties sung in harmony. Dixon stands out on "Don't Let That Music Die" with a fine, understated bass vocal lead. "Appetite Blues" was good commercial stuff, with a solid, piano-led boogie sound and a clever novelty lyric, whose other side, "Cigareets, Whuskey, and Wild Women," was a cover of a 1947 novelty western song recorded by the Sons of the Pioneers as "Cigareetes, Whuskey, and Wild, Wild Women."

The main Delta series also comprised a mix of popular styles, including music by three very different local artists. The one Bulleit remembered best had the least chance of success—"Fred Waller, the local tenor. It was a beautiful record." The disc sank without a trace, even though Waller had a regular spot on WSM radio. Waller's dulcet tones were accompanied on "Laurel Waltz" by Owen Bradley on organ, fronting his orchestra. Bulleit also recorded blues singer Ernestine Woodard with Frank Innocenti's white jazz band, Frank and the Four Beats; and a black pop quartet that evolved from the Five Bars, the Rhythm Rockers, with lead vocalist Raymond Scott.

When *Billboard* reported on October 8, 1949, that Bulleit "had an auto accident last week," Jim grabbed the opportunity for some free publicity and told the reporter he had "signed the Sacred Four and was looking to reactivate the Delta and Village labels." That the accident was quite serious, according to Howard Allison, and sidelined Bulleit for many weeks may account for Bulleit's mistake: It was not the Sacred Four but the Fairfield Four who appeared on Delta, and they had already seen several releases.

The temptation to put in his own recording studio never got the better of Bulleit. He often made recordings out of town on portable equipment, as with the Big Three Trio session in Chicago; in Nashville, he used the Castle Studio at the Tulane Hotel, on Church Street between Seventh and Eighth Avenue North, and studios run by his associate Red Wortham, a guitarist, first on Broadway for Bullet Records and then on Fourth Avenue for various labels. Wortham, who credits C. V. Hitchcock for getting him started in recording, explained that

> after Jim Bulleit left, C. V. Hitchcock really didn't know how to record or search for talent. I recorded several artists for him, mainly R&B, but some country and pop.

> Muscular dystrophy affected the muscles in my hands and feet. I couldn't play music anymore but I learned how to operate a recording studio. I was self-taught at that.

In 1949, Red Wortham took an office with Bulleit Enterprises on Ash Street and produced sessions on the side for Delta if the artist or material did not justify use of the better Castle facilities. It was in the Bullet studio on Broadway, late in 1949, that Wortham learned

> how valuable knowing about race music could be. This is what R&B was called then. Shy Guy Douglas had been recording, and we became good friends. As a singer, he visited all the black clubs, and the word got out that I was working with the black artists. In a short time, I had talent running out my ears. Bullet's was a small studio but the artists felt at home there.

Tom "Shy Guy" Douglas, one of the key players in Nashville's black music scene for many years, made his recording debut with "Raid on Cedar Street," which Wortham recorded in the Bullet studio. "Raid" was a jumping combo item taken almost note for note from Louis Jordan's hit "Saturday Night Fish Fry," riding high in the early winter of 1949. Replacing Jordan's refrain, "They was rockin,' they was rockin,' rollin' till the break of dawn" with "They was raidin,' they was raidin,' down on Cedar Street," Douglas tackles the song enthusiastically, explaining the good times they were having after hours until the police raid on Cedar Street, which was at the junction between the old downtown area and the black club district—famous, among other things, for being raided. There is a piano solo by Richard Armstrong, a long-time friend of the singer and an employee at WLAC radio.

Wortham recalled Bulleit hawking a Delta acetate of "Raid" to MGM in February 1950 via Fred Rose (who had strong connections with MGM as producer of Hank Williams and many other MGM artists), along with gospel sides by the Fairfield Four and some blues Wortham had recorded by Beulah Bryant. Intended to be the last disc on the Delta label, "Raid" may not have gone past the test-pressing stage before it appeared instead on MGM. Shy Guy made a little money off "Raid on Cedar Street," but his wife, Johnnie, was disappointed: "My husband was stupid. That song was bought up by a movie company for eight hundred dollars. It must have been worth a lot more." If this is how much Douglas earned from MGM for the record, it was actually not so bad a deal, given the rather unoriginal nature of the song.

From Franklin, Tennessee, Tom "Shy Guy" Douglas worked as a cook on the railroads before and after a stint in the service during World War II, worked in the stockyards for a while, and later catered at several local restaurants. He played harmonica during quiet moments on the railroad and apparently spent a lot of time with DeFord Bailey Jr., son of the harmonica player from the Grand Ole Opry. Douglas took part in local "jigs," where musicians from many different bands got together for impromptu jam sessions, and often both generations of Baileys would play. Described as a small, neat man, he was primarily a singer during the Delta/MGM period, working at the New Era and the Revillot clubs. Wortham spotted him at the Bijou Theater and took him out to play clubs all through the surrounding area; the two became what Douglas's wife described as "best buddies." Douglas also traveled with the Bijou-based Jerrie Jackson Revue, which operated as a kind of tent show with music, dancers, comedians, and a carnival, in residence six weeks a year in Hot Springs, Arkansas, during horse-racing season.

The "Shy Guy" moniker that appeared on many of Douglas's discs was well earned, Wortham explained: "That is what he was. He was a shy guy." In fact, Douglas had taken the name after he started to play Nat Cole's hit record of 1945, "I'm a Shy Guy." His wife agreed that he was quiet, but also noted that his home became a stopping-off point for almost any musician coming through town. "If a player was in Nashville and he needed a place to stay or if he was down on his luck, then they had a place to stay with us." Johnnie Douglas was a hairdresser, and the bonus of a stay at the Douglases was getting your hair fixed.

> I met them all. I did Billy Eckstine's hair, Big Joe Turner, B. B. King, who wasn't nothing in those days. I remember

Thomas "Shy Guy" Douglas, early 1960s. Courtesy of the author.

Little Richard would stay often. He was a regular guy and never became too self-important like some. He would sleep in my beauty parlor and had to have his hair just so.

Village Records, which Bulleit started in March 1949 around the same time he launched Delta, was exclusively a white gospel label that featured the Sunshine Boys, a popular country gospel group that worked out of Atlanta. They had started in Macon, Georgia, in 1939 as a hillbilly group led by A. L. Smith, John O. Smith, Milton Richman, and Pat Patterson, and were known to Bulleit from their days with WAGA in Atlanta in 1941. From 1942 to 1951, they appeared in a number of western movies and recorded for Decca, although A. L. and John Smith left in 1949 to set up the Smith Brothers, and Pat Patterson joined Wally Fowler.

For their Village discs, Milton Richman added Eddie Wallace, Fred Daniel, and J. D. Sumner to form a new group of Sunshine Boys. Their four discs on the label included the fairly successful "Danger Zone" along with "Glory Train" and "Sinner's Prayer," and they backed Red Foley on his 1951 hit recording of "There'll Be Peace in the Valley for Me." In 1954, J. D. Sumner left to join the Blackwood Brothers, then took over the Stamps Quartet, and perhaps remains best known for leading them in the vocal backup to Elvis Presley's Las Vegas stage show in the 1970s.

Village Records was relatively short-lived. Apart from the Sunshine Boys, the label issued only a few sides by the Goodwill Carter Family and the John Daniel Quartet, during 1950.

The Sunshine Boys, early 1950s. Courtesy of Country Music Hall of Fame and Museum.

Publishing and Other Misadventures

When Jim Bulleit founded Bulleit Enterprises in 1949, he seriously intended to make a go of publishing. He had seen the money publishers could make on the back of his Bullet hits and "realized that I had made a mistake by not having some of the songs that were so big on Bullet," he said. Tommy Scott recalled going to Jim Beck's studio in Dallas to record for Bullet; when Jim Bulleit was delayed due to bad weather in Memphis: "Beck and I went ahead and cut four songs anyway. When Jim got there, he said, 'Throw them in the trash. I don't want anything that I didn't authorize the song publishing on.'"

He became involved in two publishing ventures, one an ongoing concern, one new. The history of the first, Jim Bulleit (J-B) Music, dates to April 1948, when Bulleit and Jordan Stokes bought into partnerships in a relaunch of Wallace Fowler Publications. Although the company had a good catalog, with hits like Eddy Arnold's "That's How Much I Love You" and a lot of modern-day gospel items, Fowler within a year was facing foreclosure. In September 1949 Bulleit's attorneys, Farris and Evans, argued on his behalf as a minor partner in the company that Fowler had sold $5,000 in shares to Alice Cashion without offering them to existing stockholders and, worse, had withdrawn "large sums of money from the corporation disguised as alleged salary for the purpose of paying his delinquent income taxes." Eventually Bulleit emerged with 80 percent of the company, Alice Cashion with 20 percent.

Bulleit's second publishing venture grew from his friendship with Dave Dreyer, a former partner of Irving Berlin who, Bulleit thought, "had a pretty fabulous BMI contract" with a monthly cash advance that impressed him enough to go into partnership in Jay-Dee Music. Dreyer ran the Jay-Dee enterprise from New York, but Bulleit lost interest in the venture within two years.

Bulleit became involved in 1950 in one of the strangest, if most indicative episodes in the tangled history of southern music recording and publishing. In a 1976 interview for the Country Music Foundation, he told Douglas Green:

> A fellow from Dallas brought a song in here and asked me to have Jimmy Dickens record it. So I took it to Don Law at Columbia Records. Don said, "I like the song but I like the boy [on the demo disc] also." The singer was Lefty Frizzell. The only thing I knew was that the boy lived in Texas, so I kept calling around till somebody said he was in Big Spring somewhere. So I got the wife and the kids in the car and we drove to Texas. I found Lefty and signed the boy to a record contract and signed up two songs. I wanted to give his record contract to Don Law and keep the songs for my publishing company.

Bulleit told me a slightly different version:

> One of the artists I recorded was Lefty Frizzell, and I had the publishing on his song "If You've Got the Money I've Got the Time," but I mistakenly sold out to Columbia, and Frizzell went on to be a superstar. If I had known what I was at, I could have had a tremendous publishing catalog in the early fifties.

By other accounts, Columbia Records was already interested in Lefty when Bulleit signed up his best songs. Columbia then brokered a deal in which Bulleit sold half his Lefty copyrights to Peer-Southern. What remains constant in every version of the tale is that Frizzell went on to become the top-selling country singer of 1950 and one of the most influential vocal stylists that music genre would ever know.

By the latter part of 1950, Bulleit and his bank manager came to the same conclusion: Bulleit was going nowhere in the recording and publishing business. He was forced to sell many of his Delta master recordings, along with others he had acquired from the Bullet label in his severance deal; the Fairfield Four recordings went to Dot, MGM, and Tennessee; some Cecil Gant tracks went to Dot; and Bulleit's Delta masters of the Big Three Trio went to Columbia, the Trio's new home.

Bulleit now turned to his forte, selling and promotion, which kept him on the road. He went to Florida on several occasions, promoting the Sunshine Boys and other gospel acts, and in the fall of 1951 he helped line up publicity for the Hadacol Caravan, a traveling variety show of epic proportions. Promoting Dudley LeBlanc's Happy Day Company and its patent medicine, this major tour of the South featured an array of popular and country talent that included Bob Hope, Milton Berle, and Hank Williams.

In January 1951, Bulleit took a job with radio KWKH in Shreveport, Louisiana.

> They had wanted Joe L. Frank to manage their artists, but he was too busy, and so I was offered the task of managing and booking the talent for the *Louisiana Hayride* in Shreveport. This suited me well, and I went down there to see Henry Clay. We made an arrangement where I lived in Nashville but worked with them down there. I saw that it was a job I could do well, having done it at WSM in 1945, and I saw it as a chance to get myself some country music copyrights.
>
> The *Hayride* was known as "the Cradle of the Stars" because all their best artists went on to join the Opry in Nashville—people like Hank Williams. Well, the owners of KWKH were wanting to take Hank back from the Opry, because they could use this to build up the show generally as a proper rival to the Opry. I was part of that plan. I promoted and sold the Wilburn Brothers, Slim

Courtesy of
Bear Family Records.

Whitman, Mac Wiseman, and Lefty Frizzell. Now some of those were giants at that time. Eventually, though, the *Hayride* people decided that WSM was too powerful, and they settled for second place, and I went back to Nashville.

Home only briefly from Shreveport, Bulleit next spent some months setting up a radio barn dance in Spruce Pine, North Carolina.

Red Robin and J-B Records

By the first of 1952, Bulleit was back in Nashville working for Liberty Broadcasting and nursing plans for yet another new label, Red Robin, for which he pressed three discs in association with two men identified on the record labels only as "Riley-Winton." There must have been a problem with recordman Bobby Robinson in New York, who had just launched another Red Robin label, and there might have been a falling out between Bulleit, Riley, and Winton, because in September Bulleit changed his label name to J-B, rented space back at 421 Broadway from Conrad Hitchcock, and without partners, reissued the Red Robin discs on the J-B label.

The first to appear on Bulleit's Red Robin was a former Bullet R&B artist, Red Calhoun, whom Bulleit had recorded in Fort Worth. *Billboard* reported that the veteran country singer Bill Nettles, who had recorded for Bullet, had now recorded on Red Robin, but no discs by him are known to have survived. Red Robin did have a short-lived country series, for which Hank and Slim's Georgia Crackers declared "I Love My Neighbor" and Uncle Si recorded "Country Boy." Uncle Si is unknown today, but Hank and Slim had recorded before the war and were regular performers with their brother, Bob Newman, then under contract to King Records. These country discs, with a different look from Bulleit's usual records, may have been pressed not in Nashville but in North Carolina.

When he changed his label's name from Red Robin to J-B Records, Bulleit took the long view and tried to recreate the successful Bullet formula by setting up numerical series for a range of musical styles—a pop series, a blues series, a country series, and two gospel series—although he in the end made only a few discs in each. The R&B series featured Texas-made masters by Red Calhoun and Jimmy Smith as well as Nashville-produced discs by Eddie "Guitar Slim" Jones, Tasso Zachary, and the Propheteers; Sam Phillips in Memphis produced Walter "Tang" Smith.

Calhoun made three recordings for J-B, one featuring mainly the band, one credited largely to singer Jack Dixon, and a third featuring the band's female singer, Vivian Verson—"Payday Lover," the J-B disc that came closest to a hit. *Billboard* carried a big advertisement on October 4, 1952, for the song, along with the first in J-B's country series, "Contented" by Johnny Mathis (not the pop singer of the same name). In a separate article, the paper announced: "Jim Bulleit forms J-B label . . . he now feels the time is ripe. . . . First releases out this week. Bulleit is currently on a national trip lining up distributors."

Red Calhoun's connection with Nashville recording companies and with Jim Bulleit started in 1946, when his "Here Comes the Man with the Gin" appeared on Bullet, a variant on "Here Comes the Man with the Jive" recorded in 1936 on Vocalion by Stuff Smith. Credited to Calhoun with his Dallas Swingsters, there should have been little doubt where Calhoun's group came from, although Bulleit claimed that "Red came from Nashville originally, and I heard him playing in a club in Nashville. That was how he got to be on Bullet, and I kept in touch with him later on."

J-B's most important disc was "Feelin' Sad"/"Certainly All" by one of the stars of 1950s R&B, Guitar Slim, recorded under his real name, Eddie Jones. Born in December 1926 in Greenwood, Mississippi, Jones largely grew up with his grandparents on a cotton plantation in Hollandale. He worked as a dancer at clubs and joints whenever he could, and earned a reputation as a flashy dancer and a ladies' man. In 1948, he left town as a dancer with the Willie Warren band, filled in playing guitar and singing, and developed into a fine guitarist. His style had a Texan fluidity from the influence of T-Bone Walker and Gatemouth Brown, but Jones's guitar and voice had a unique gospel introspection.

In New Orleans by 1950, Eddie Jones worked frequently with pianist Huey Smith. He polished his exciting bar-walking act to include taking his guitar, attached to a long cord, right out onto the street. In August 1950, the first local newspaper reviews of Jones and Smith's act mentioned that Jones was doing good business at the Dew Drop and the Tijuana Club. Sometime in the middle of 1952, Jim Bulleit visited New Orleans and struck a deal with promoter Percy Stovall to record Jones. In December, Bulleit took out an ad that claimed: " 'Feelin' Sad' broke in New Orleans for a National Race Hit." In fact, the record was popular only regionally, but it was a spectacularly good recording at the very roots of soul. Jones's wordless moaning over four bars, harmonized with alto sax, opens and closes the disc, on which Huey Smith plays rolling, bluesy piano; the disc was made at the Castle Studio in Nashville while the band was touring there.

On "Certainly All," the sax section, led by David Lastie, also turns to a vocal refrain. Huey Smith sets up a relentless, loping beat and walking piano figure, and there is a catchy call-and-response hook based on the prewar jubilee spiritual song "Certainly Lord." Jones takes an unusual guitar solo that is exciting, if not as wildly abstract as some he would later develop.

When producer Johnny Vincent heard this disc, he signed Jones to Specialty Records, for whom he recorded next in October 1953 in New Orleans as Guitar Slim. The resultant hit, "The Things That I Used to Do" featured Jones's crying, gospel-style vocal and jazzy blues guitar solos as well as piano by Ray Charles and a solid beat from Oscar Moore. Charles made his own versions of "Feelin' Sad" and "Certainly All," and his later adaptations of gospel songs to secular ones may have been inspired by Eddie Jones's J-B session in Nashville.

While Jim Bulleit was in Shreveport working with KWKH, he had formed a brief alliance with the successful local promoter, publisher, and record producer Stan Lewis. Bulleit was instrumental in obtaining recordings from Lewis for his own use, in return for helping Lewis place other recordings with some of the bigger independent companies like Imperial and Chess. When he returned to Nashville, Bulleit forged a similar arrangement with Sam Phillips in Memphis. In exchange for distribution advice from Bulleit, Phillips fed some recordings to J-B Records. One of these was "High Tone Mama" by Walter "Tang" Smith, a Memphis-based trombonist who had appeared on Bullet with Tuff Green's band in 1949; James Luper, who sang on the Bullet disc, is here on tenor sax. A note in Phillips's files records that the masters of this disc were "sent to Shaw (Manufacturing) for J-B Records" on November 15, 1952, and that an acetate disc dub had been handed to Bulleit on the day of recording. Intriguingly, Phillips's files also record that Bulleit was handed dubs on November 17 of itinerant bluesman Charles Thomas performing "Cold Hands" and "4th and Broad," copies of which, destined for J-B, have never turned up. Thomas later surfaced in Chicago, where he became well-known as Maxwell Street Jimmy.

Eddie Jones, aka "Guitar Slim." Courtesy of Showtime Archives [Toronto] and Colin Escott.

The J-B imprint had a country series along lines similar to its R&B discs: a few local items by Monte Floyd, Bob West, Rocky Kirkland, and others, and some leased masters from Memphis by Buddy Cunningham. Country singer Johnny

The Rebels Quartet, early 1950s: *from left*, Horace Parrish, Lee Kitchens, John Mathews, and Jim Waits. Courtesy of Southern Gospel Music Hall of Fame.

Mathis recorded "Contented" and "Dream World" on J-B as part of a deal between Jim Bulleit and Texas musician-producer Jack Rhodes, who supplied a stream of masters cut in Fort Worth and Dallas to both Bulleit and to his old partners at Bullet Records.

J-B's short-lived pop series featured Carole Wilson on another version of "Contented," and the label released two white gospel discs by the Rebels Quartet, "If You Believe" and "Gospel Boogie." The Rebels were originally from Tampa, Florida, established there by J. D. Sumner before he joined the Sunshine Boys. Their discs on J-B were also issued on a label called Webb City, based in St.Petersburg, Florida; the labels indicate, however, that the company was part of Jim Bulleit Enterprises, and from the pressings and label print it is clear that the discs were made in Nashville. The likelihood is that Bulleit made the recordings in Florida through a deal with "Doc" Webb, a pharmacist, whose picture features on the record labels.

Sun Records and the Prisonaires

After he was back in Nashville full-time around 1952, said Bulleit, Sam Phillips asked him to arrange distribution for his new Sun label.

> So I went in as a partner with him and arranged all the initial distribution for him. Our affiliation was that he would record and I would do the selling, sending him a few masters or artists if I could. By that time, there was some semblance of order in the record-distributing business, as most of the postwar operators who couldn't handle the business had fallen by the wayside. Sam approached me because I was the only person in Tennessee who had enough experience of the business nationally. I had the know-how he needed. What he did was to send his brother, Jud, to join me on trips to New York and other cities and to be taught the business. Jud was a fine guy, and after I got out of Sun he came more into things.
>
> At that time Sun was primarily recording R&B. Sam recorded several Nashville people that I sent down to Memphis, but the biggest act was the Prisonaires, a vocal group from the penitentiary. A man named Red Wortham was working with me on my labels. He was a publisher and booking agent, and he persuaded the prison authorities to let Johnny Bragg, the lead singer, and his pals sing in churches around town. He told me about this, and how good they were, so I had the idea to pitch the Prisonaires to Sam Phillips as a recording act. This led to a big record called "Just Walkin' in the Rain" that later crossed to a pop hit for Johnnie Ray.

Arrested at seventeen on a charge of rape that he always denied, Johnny Bragg in 1943 joined four thousand others inside the Tennessee State Penitentiary, from which he could almost see the house where he was born, one of the bleak north Nashville frame homes that housed much of the black community in the years either side of World War I. He had found inspiration in blues and gospel artists on the radio, and had seen Cab Calloway and Billie Holiday at the Cotton

The Prisonaires on Radio WSOK in 1953, with lead tenor Johnny Bragg left of the microphone. Courtesy of Showtime Archives [Toronto] and Colin Escott.

Club on Heiman Street; when he had the temerity to sing for Holiday, she pronounced him a good singer.

At the penitentiary, Bragg joined bass singer Ed Thurman's singing group, along with Marcel Sanders and William Stewart. John Drue joined in 1952, when Bragg was effectively the leader of the quartet that would become the Prisonaires. Bragg wrote songs and gained quite a reputation, visited occasionally, as were other cons, by singers and agents looking for good songs at bargain rates. Cecil Gant may have acquired some material from Bragg, who also insisted that Hank Williams bought from him the bones of the song that became "Your Cheatin' Heart."

Frank Clement's election as governor of Tennessee in 1953 opened the next chapter in the Prisonaires' success story. From a working class background in Dickson, Tennessee, Clement had been through law school at Vanderbilt and had a reformer's drive to improve things, including the prison system. Also, he liked music and had a record collection. When his friend James Edwards became warden of the penitentiary, both men encouraged entertainment by and for the inmates in an attempt to reduce boredom and violence. That year, Red Wortham visited the prison in search of songwriters, having expanded his activities beyond studio work to publishing. He and Joe Calloway of radio WSIX persuaded Warden Edwards to let the Prisonaires, as Wortham dubbed them, appear on local radio and make appearances at charity shows in the Nashville area.

Red Wortham was impressed by a song that Bragg had written with fellow inmate Robert Riley after they joked about being outside in the yard in the rain. "Just Walkin' in the Rain" (which Wortham copyrighted as "I'm Walking in the Rain") was a haunting ballad whose quality Wortham recognized. He recorded the song at the WSIX studios and pitched the Prisonaires' demo recording to Paul Cohen at Decca and also contacted Jim Bulleit. While Cohen considered the deal, Bulleit placed the group with Sam Phillips at Sun as part of a package that included Shy Guy Douglas and other blues singers Wortham had recorded for J-B. According to Sam Phillips:

> Red was first and foremost a publisher and promoter. He was the one who set up the Prisonaires deal. He had a cousin working as a senior guard at the penitentiary, who alerted him to the group. He called Governor Frank Clement, and then I set up a recording session in Memphis for "Just Walking in the Rain." Governor Clement received some criticism for allowing their rehabilitation program to go so far as a trip to Memphis, so for some other sessions we had to go into the penitentiary to record.

But according to Bulleit, it was he who paid a visit to Warden Edwards and, eventually, to Governor Clement, and secured their agreement to take the Prisonaires to Memphis on June 1, 1953, to make records. Here, the story gets even more strange: Bragg always insisted that Elvis Presley was hanging out in the studio with them, a year before his own recording debut at Sun Records, and that when Bragg had an attack of studio nerves, Presley helped him rehearse his diction and delivery. This event very probably took place, but possibly at a later Prisonaires session in 1954.

Issued on Sun as a B side, "Rain" sold enough to enter the R&B charts that summer. On the strength of this, the Prisonaires appeared more and more on local shows and radio in Nashville, their engagements organized by Wortham, and Sun released five Prisonaires discs before some group members were paroled and the group split up.

Bragg learned that Columbia record producer Don Law had liked "Rain," which he heard via Gene Autry, who had bought the copyright for his Golden West Melodies. Law suggested to Columbia's Mitch Miller in New York that he produce a pop version with Johnnie Ray, who recorded the song in June 1956 at the tail end of a session with the Ray Conniff Orchestra. Ray's "Rain" became a #2 hit and stayed on the pop charts for half a year.

Jim Bulleit's mutually beneficial connection with Sun Records lasted less than a year, during which Bulleit did set up some distribution deals. However, Sam Phillips was careful with a dollar, and Bulleit tended to speculate to accumulate.

Phillips did not find it helpful to have both his brother, Jud Phillips, and Bulleit on the road speculating. Then too, although Bulleit was the pioneer indie record man of the South, he was not able to deliver all the contacts he told Phillips he could. There seem to have been no recriminations on either side. As Bulleit explained the breakup:

> Around the fall of 1953, after the Prisonaires deal and after there was a lawsuit on a Sun recording by Rufus Thomas [unrelated to the Prisonaires deal], I got out of Sun. I had some publishing deals through Delta with Sam, and we had a little difficulty about them. Sam was a frugal man, unlike Jud. But I don't hold any grudges. I liked Sam and I eventually sold my share in Sun for $1,200. At the time—this was a year before Elvis Presley came along—it really wasn't worth any more than that.

Phillips underlined their mutual appreciation, and the mutual recognition of their weaknesses. "Jim was very helpful in visiting all the distributors for me, making deals for Sun Records. But we had it arranged so that I had to approve all the deals."

Jukebox operator Al Bubis has recalled that Bulleit did his Sun deals on the back of a 1952 tour of distributors Bubis set up:

> The last time I saw Jim was in 1952, when I drove him around the country. It was a funny experience because the distributors didn't like him, yet they loved him. They said, "He screwed us up pretty good, but we still owe him a lot." I heard that from so many of them. He had taken advantage of people after he had "Near You," but at the same time they told me that "Near You" kept a lot of independent distributors in business and got them established in their communities. The independent labels and distributors were in bad shape in 1947, really, and Jim Bulleit, almost alone, helped to keep it all going at one time.

"A Fascinating Business"

By 1954, Bulleit was effectively out of the record business; it was that or bankruptcy. He had already sold the catalog he acquired from Wallace Fowler Publications to 4 Star Music, and now he sold his publishing firm Jim Bulleit Music to the Wilburn Brothers, country singers, who renamed it Sure Fire Music. Bulleit went into other ventures, notably plastic bankcard machines. "We sold some of them, but it was too far ahead of what the banks were ready to accept back then," he said. In 1958, Bulleit launched a new firm that specialized in selling local unlisted securities, announcing with his partners that they would soon have thirty salesmen across the state. There is no evidence that the thirty salesmen ever materialized, but Bulleit continued to have big ideas, moving from cemetery developments to insurance, cosmetics, and candy sales. When someone came to him in 1971 with an idea for a new brand of ice cream, he told the *Tennessean:* "The kids will love it. It's been tested on my grandchildren and they love it. I'm sure of a ready market for this. If it were not for men like me, things wouldn't happen."

Bulleit's daughter, Gayle Bulleit Moses, remembers the ice cream episode, as well as many of Jim's other schemes:

> From 1971, he was in business packing and supplying candy to Opryland Park, several of the Six Flag Parks, and so on. The business—Jim Bulleit Sales—did quite well, and he and Mother enjoyed working it pretty much as a retirement activity.

In the late 1950s Bulleit considered going into the LP record business, but he was hampered by the little matter of having sold or otherwise lost the rights to practically all the music he had been involved with. Unable to let go of the music business entirely, he bought up the Bullet Records name and logo. In the early 1960s, with support from Red Wortham, he reactivated Bullet and launched a subsidiary label called Sur-Speed. The new Bullet 11000 series lasted for a dozen or so issues, which still featured the old logo—a bullet speeding toward a target—but the records missed the target by a wider margin than ever. The 1962 Bullet release of "Near You" by Johnny Dee came and went with none of the acclaim Francis Craig's version had inspired fifteen years earlier. Bulleit ruminated in later years over the failure of Bullet's reincarnation: "It's better to start a new label than to try to revive an older one. I found that out the hard way."

Jim Bulleit lived long enough to receive a little late recognition for his role in getting the Nashville music business on its feet, died in his adopted hometown of Nashville on December 12, 1988, and was buried back in his wife's hometown, Anderson, South Carolina. In his later years he turned philosophical:

> Eventually, I heard so much music that I couldn't tell what was good and what was bad. I went to that many clubs on my travels. When the boogie-woogie was in, all you had to do was cut a record with "boogie" in the title and you had a hit. And you could record a session for $250—artists, studio, and pressing costs. It got more difficult as time went on. But even in the fifties, you could set up a session in no time. It was all very flexible and a fascinating business to be in.

9

Tennessee Jamboree

> *I started out distributing silver polish. Then records. Then we formed a company to record our own records. But the independents had a tough time. You had to shell out all the time, and never be sure when or if you'd get paid.*
>
> —Bill Beasley

While Bullet Records and Jim Bulleit were declining in influence during the early 1950s, the mantle of the leading local independent recording company passed to Tennessee Records, organized by Bulleit's protégés, Bill Beasley and Howard Allison. As Nashville's music-related infrastructure grew, Tennessee for a time had the opportunity to wield real influence in the record business.

The Principals at Tennessee Records

Tennessee Records, launched just after Christmas 1949, was an offshoot of Coastline Distribution and was based alongside Jim Bulleit at 415–417 Ash Street, on the corner with Fifth Avenue South. The Tennessee Recording Company had four principals: Bill Beasley and Howard Allison, who had been associated in a series of recording ventures for several years, and cousins Reynold and Alan Bubis, whose background was in sales and marketing.

In 1948, when Bill Beasley had set up Collegiate Records, Danny Cassella's "Heart of My Heart" sold well but Collegiate releases by the Dream Dusters, Ken Carroll, Alan Foster, and Harrison Cooper all failed. Issued in January 1949, "Rockefeller Center" by Les Elgart, Collegiate's best-known artist, fared no better, although Beasley gained some local sales on "Three Wishing Wells," a release by Owen Bradley and his singer Bob Johnstone. Later in 1949, Collegiate issued a recording of a Hank Fort song, "Zingarella," by an orchestra led by trombonist Hawes Coleman with vocalists Nina Claire and Bill Lockwood. Coleman had been working with jazz bassist Charlie Mingus in Los Angeles when Fort was performing the song on West Coast television. It was to be the last record on Collegiate; the label was phased out around October 1949. "After a while," Beasley said, "I realized that recording pop orchestras really had to be done on a union label and could be expensive, and that anyway there was a lot more available talent in Nashville in country, gospel, or blues."

This young entrepreneur, William Donald Beasley, was born in Greenwood, Mississippi, on December 5, 1927, raised in Nashville by his mother and stepfather, went to East Nashville High School, and was training as a navy pilot just after World War II ended. In 1946, Beasley enrolled at Peabody College, living in rented rooms on Twenty-First Avenue South. He became reacquainted with a high school friend, Dorothy Jean Norris, originally from Dawson Springs, Kentucky, a fellow popular music lover and a fine singer and songwriter. Norris sang with the Adrian McDowell Orchestra in her student days and appeared on McDowell's two daily shows on WSIX in the late 1940s, a western music program

Bill Beasley in the navy, early 1946. Courtesy of Kirk Beasley.

Wally Hopper and His Orchestra at the Colemore Club with Hopper on guitar, Adelaide Hendricks (later Del Wood) on piano, and Jean Norris as vocalist, late 1940s. Courtesy of Kirk Beasley.

and the *Housewives Serenade*. Norris also worked with the Wallace Hopper Orchestra at several venues, including the private Colemore Club in an ante bellum mansion east of the city. Guitarist Billy Byrd worked with the band at times, as did pianist Owen Bradley when the schedule of his own orchestra allowed. In later years, Bradley was known to describe himself to mutual friends as "Jean's former accompanist."

It was at this time that Bill Beasley started to take an interest in Bradley's fledgling work in record production, as well as a deeper interest in Jean Norris. Beasley and Norris were married in a ceremony at the Norris home in Nashville in 1951, with Howard Allison, Beasley's business partner, as best man.

Along with Collegiate Records, Bill Beasley in 1948 had

also set up Coastline to distribute a silver polish that Jim Bulleit was selling, according to Howard Allison, who had joined Bullet Records in the fall of 1947 as bookkeeper and clerk. Through Coastline and Volunteer Music Sales, Beasley and Allison got involved in distributing the World Records label as well as Collegiate and Jim Bulleit's labels, Allison said:

> Coastline Distribution was extended to records because there were very few wholesale distributors in Nashville. . . . Coastline was formed just before the Tennessee label. With Coastline, we mainly sold black music through radio outlets. We had a deejay show on radio WLAC that was particularly good for selling blues and gospel, but we were one of the first to try it with country music also. We had a country disc-jockey show on WLAC, and we also sponsored a show on WLW in Cincinnati. We advertised records, and they were sold cash-on-delivery. It was then that we realized we would do better making our own records to sell.

Beasley, a musician, would handle record production, and Allison would run the office. The only drawbacks were finance and distribution. This was where the Bubis cousins came in. Their family owned American Ace Coffee, a successful enterprise based on Charlotte Avenue. Beasley in September 1949 arranged for Jim Bulleit to sell his share of Coastline Distribution to jukebox dealer Reynold Bubis. Alan Bubis remembered it this way:

> Reynold and I had one of our coin machine locations over on Ash Street, and we went by there to check on our jukeboxes from time to time. One day in 1949 we met Howard Allison and Bill Beasley there. They had a partnership with Jim Bulleit in a record distributing company called Coastline. They weren't doing very well and Jim Bulleit wanted to get out. He was somebody Reynold knew previously. So we bought his part out for very little money, mainly to help them out a little and also to see what this distributing business could be as far as we were concerned. Howard had a very good knowledge of the record business and did a really good job on the bookkeeping end of it. He was up on all the details. He hated musicians, though! He said he had had too many dealings with them, and they were unreliable. Bill liked musicians, and he liked to make recordings, so they fitted well together. They were real easy to get along with too.

Wedding of Bill Beasley and Jean Norris, 1951, with Howard Allison as best man. Courtesy of Kirk Beasley.

The Bubis cousins were part of an enterprising family who arrived in Nashville in the early part of the twentieth century. David Bubis and his wife, Hattie, formed the American Tea and Coffee Company in 1917 along with David's brothers, Israel and Kolman, and their wives, Sadie and Minnie, and set up operations at 2424 Charlotte Avenue on the north edge of the downtown business district. Theirs was one of a considerable number of coffee-roasting compa-

Alan Bubis Receives Ensign's Commission

Alan Bubis, 21, son of Mr. and Mrs. Israel Bubis, 104 Lauderdale Road,, was commissioned an ensign in the U. S. Naval Reserve this week, following completion of his flight training course at the Naval Air Training Center, Pensacola, Fla.

Ensign Bubis, a graduate of West End High School, attended Vanderbilt University and entered the service during the school term in 1942. He was recently at home for a brief visit to his parents, returning to Melbourne, Fla., for active duty.

Courtesy of the author.

nies, competing with Hermitage, Colonial, Fletcher Wilsons' Bubbling Over brand, and the market leader in Nashville, Maxwell House, developed from a blend by Joel Owsley Cheek at the prestigious Maxwell House Hotel at Church and Fourth in the 1880s. American Ace Coffee did well throughout the 1920s and 1930s, despite the competition, and the Bubises became established in the local business community.

Kolman and Minnie's son Reynold and Israel and Sadie's son Alan both served in World War II, Reynold flying bombers over Europe and Alan in the U.S. Naval Reserve and commissioned to begin flight training in Pensacola, Florida. Alan said he had never taken much notice of music:

> It was only when I was in the service in 1942 that I realized how big radio WSM—and particularly the Grand Ole Opry show—was in those days. I would tell people I was from Nashville, and they would want to know about the Opry. I was so surprised at this—I really didn't know it was a national institution. Then I realized why it was that my folks used to advertise American Ace coffee on the Opry. They had Roy Acuff and Minnie Pearl, Cowboy Copas and others, all advertising American Ace.

In the 1940s, the American Ace segment of the Opry opened with Minnie Pearl nagging, "Elmer, don't forget the American Ace coffee!"

After the war, Alan and Reynold Bubis moved into the coin-machine world, having seen the success of companies like Hermitage Amusements and Ace Amusements, which supplied jukeboxes and vending machines to the Nashville establishments that took their coffee supplies. Alan described those days:

> When we went into the coin-machine business, we went along to see Red Hitchcock and Eugene Cashion on a regular basis. I would deal with Mr. Cashion two or three times a week, talking about what was going to go over well, either machines or records. At that time, "Near You" was a huge, huge hit, and I'm sure it was the biggest independent label record ever up until then—we used so many of them on our jukeboxes. We went to their one-stop record distributing company that they set up for jukebox operators there.

In 1981 Reynold Bubis, in his sixties and retired, sat in the office of his son's liquor store on Franklin Road and talked about the beginnings of Tennessee Records.

Reynold Bubis, 1950s.
Courtesy of Bear Family Records.

> First of all, we re-formed the Coastline Distribution Company, which was a wholesale business dealing mainly

in R&B records. I went into this with Bill Beasley purely as a business venture and brought my cousin Alan in with me. Soon afterward, we formed the Tennessee Recording Company and then Jamboree Records. . . . The partners in all these ventures were Bill Beasley, Howard Allison, Alan Bubis, and myself. Bill did most of the technical work on recordings, because he was a musician. Howard was particularly involved in distribution. We also owned the Tennessee Music Publishing Company and BABB Music, which you can see was taken from the first letter of all our last names. I was mainly involved in the publishing aspect of the business.

Alan Bubis offered a little more detail:

The Coastline distributing business was soon our main business. We just thought we'd put out some records to add to our product, so we started off with country. Bill looked after A&R. I looked after sales and operations. The record business was interesting back then—I didn't know much about it, so I was just trying to learn and figure out how to sell the stuff, you know. I would attend some recording sessions, and also go to the radio stations at night and listen while they played our records, just to understand the reaction and work out how best to market the things.

The Tennessee Label

Cashbox reported on Nashville's new label on January 21, 1950: "Tennessee Records, a new label specializing in hillbilly material, has been formed in Nashville by Alan Bubis and Bill Beasley, local distributors of the London label and other disk lines." New York–based London Records, initially a subsidiary of the Decca label that had originated in England, had a large catalog containing a range of musical styles. London had been one of Coastline's clients for over a year when the label started a dedicated country music series in October 1949, which encouraged Beasley to consider trying one of his own: If London could run a country line out of New York, then he could certainly do the same out of Nashville.

Tennessee Records started out recording at the Castle studio in the Tulane Hotel or occasionally in the Bullet studio on Broadway, but the new company also used radio studios after hours, first at WKDA and then at WMAK. When Coastline and Tennessee moved their office around the corner from Ash Street and into 824 Fifth Avenue South, between Ash and Mulberry, at the end of 1950, they set up their own Tennessee Records studio nearby at 901 Fourth Avenue South, on the floors above a store, where they often recorded at night to spare the businesses below.

Unlike Bullet, Tennessee Records had no grand ideas, made little attempt to sign star names from WSM, and took no splashy full-page advertisements in *Billboard.* When Bullet had started up, the big names in folk and western music were still mainly radio and movie stars such as Roy Acuff and Tex Ritter, who had emerged before World War II. Five years later, the phenomenal success of Eddy Arnold and Hank Williams, both with a string of hits, had started to change the picture. The focus was now on developing an artist as a recording star. With the market for hillbilly growing, Beasley intended to build up local or regional artists, he explained.

I learned the business traveling with Jim Bulleit. Bulleit went all over to the distributors, and I went along. Then I would pick up artists to record along the way, and tell them to come see me in Nashville.

Harold Bradley, who had been at college with Bill Beasley, remembers the early days of of Tennessee Records clearly.

I was attending Peabody, and one day I was also working a dance job at Peabody College, and in the intermission I went across the street to get a Krystal hamburger or something, still in my tuxedo, and this guy walks up to me and introduces himself. He said "I'm Bill Beasley and I want to start a record label and I want to talk to you about it." So he called me a little later, said he needed a leader for his recording band. I said, "Sure," though he was just young like me, and I didn't think he would have the money to come through, but he did. So I got a band together, and we recorded.

> I would get Farris Coursey on drums and Ernie Newton on bass, people like that. We would record at the Castle Studio or the old Brown Brothers transcription studio, and soon Bill put in his own studio. I recorded country for him with Randy Hughes, I remember, and later some popular tunes with Pat Boone and Snooky Lanson. In those days, every studio had to call in to the union on a Monday morning with their planned schedule of recording for the week. And the business then was still small enough that the union could monitor the business, go check on what was happening.

As Bill Beasley explained it:

> Collegiate had been a nonunion label, mainly issuing leased masters or otherwise recordings I had made at WKDA radio studios with Jim McKinney engineering. When I started Tennessee, it was a union-registered label, and the benefit was that we could use much better musicians.

"When Tennessee Records was formed, it was basically a country label," Howard Allison said.

> We named it Tennessee to identify with the local audience and also because country music was just starting to break out nationally, and Nashville was at the very beginnings of gaining some kind of prominence. Back at that time, a 100,000 sale meant a big hit in country. In blues, you would go up to 125,000 or even 200,000 on a really good sale. The average though, was 25,000 for either type of music. At our company, we were looking for regular sales of 25,000 anyway. Between 1948 and 1953, country and blues were just coming into big business. They were easier to promote and sell since the major companies had pop tied up and they concentrated there almost exclusively. We knew there was a niche we could fit into, and we hoped to expand from there.

Country on Tennessee

The blue Tennessee label debuted with "Second Hand Heart" by Ricky Riddle with Hal Bradley and his band, numbered 711 to signify the luck it took to succeed in the record business. The company soon dropped the label's curly script logo in favor of a typeface dealers could read more easily. Bill Johnson and the Casanova Boys covered the song almost immediately for the London label, underlining the close link between Coastline and London.

Songwriter Ricky Riddle made three of the first seven discs in Tennessee's country series. After "Second Hand Heart," he had a cover version of "Smoke Comes out My Chimney." Then came "Boogie Woogie Tennessee," for which Harold Bradley assembled a slick backing group of musicians whose suave assurance seems almost at odds with the song. The composer was Nashville's first career session bass man, Ernie Newton, who played with the Les Paul Trio before the war and came to Nashville with Red Foley to work on the Opry. Ricky Riddle himself remains more of a mystery. For a while he managed Tennessee Records' music publishing subsidiary, Tennessee Music, a joint venture with New York music publisher Dave Dreyer, who had worked with Jim Bulleit. Tennessee Music was soon succeeded by BABB Music, in which Riddle had no role. All told, Riddle made eight records for Tennessee before moving on to MGM and Decca.

Apart from the Riddle discs, Harold "Hal" Bradley led Tennessee Records' studio band on many occasions, leaving his mark on Jimmy Sweeney's "Boogie Woogie Jockey" and "Tennessee Waltz" (the artist was credited mistakenly as Bob Sweeney), Randy Hughes's "I'd Rather Be a Rooster," and Wes Holly's "Teardrops from My Eyes." In most cases, Bradley was cutting his teeth as a record producer working alongside Beasley, and both men hoped for some of the success Harold's brother Owen was achieving with "Chattanoogie Shoe Shine Boy" and other national hits on Decca.

"Tennessee Waltz," one of the biggest-selling songs of the day, was first a hit for Pee Wee King in 1948 and then sold more than two million copies in Patti Page's chart-topping pop version in 1950. One of the more curious of its many covers came when Bill Beasley recorded a version by Tennessee governor Gordon Browning, a scene Alan Bubis described:

> It was after the Grand Ole Opry one night, and we were with D Kilpatrick of Mercury Records and Governor Browning. The governor started to sing "Tennessee Waltz," and D wanted to record it on the spur of the moment. So Bill opened up our studio on Fourth and called Dick Stratton and his band to come on over, and the governor went in and made the record.

Though produced by the Tennessee partners, this version came out on Mercury in 1951.

Apart from the major record companies, Beasley's was soon the biggest game in town for country musicians, and it attracted some name artists as well as unknowns. Names didn't come much bigger than the Carter Family. "I'm All Broke Out with Love" was a breezy semi-novelty that marked the solo recording debut of the oldest Carter sister, Helen. Born in Maces Spring, Virginia, in 1927 to Ezra and Maybelle Carter, Helen had been appearing with the family act since she was ten and had followed her mother across the eastern half of the United States. Since 1943, her mother had been leading Mother Maybelle and the Carter Sisters. Helen Carter had three duet partners on Tennessee: her brother-in-law Don Davis (married to Anita Carter), WSM announcer Grant Turner, and Bob Eaton, a regular performer in and around his hometown of Nashville.

In the later part of 1951, a separate and short-lived Tennessee 1000 series included a record by the Carter Sisters, June, Anita, and Helen, the new generation of the first family of country music, along with a rare secular disc by the John Daniel Quartet, "Just a Rose Will Do." Despite the success of the Carter Sisters' recording of "Sweet Talking Man," the series was discontinued the following year.

Tennessee Records placed very few discs on the national sales charts, but Alan Bubis said that Helen Carter's "I'm All Broke Out with Love" sold almost as well as anything on the charts at the time. He paid little credence to chart positionings, relying instead on the sums taken from the jukeboxes and the speed with which product left the warehouse.

Helen Carter on accordion, with her sisters, Anita and June, and their mother, Maybelle, early 1950s. Courtesy of Country Music Hall of Fame and Museum.

Tennessee parlayed their clout with jukebox operators and their small-company flexibility into good sales with their strategy of muscling in on hits. For instance, Jim Wilson and the Music City Sextet recorded a successful, pop-slanted version of Stuart Hamblen's hit song "Remember Me (I'm the One Who Loves You)." As Bill Beasley explained:

> Although the majors had distribution sewn up, they were not always too fast, and we could still sell against them on a song. Up to the first fifty to one hundred thousand, the sale to jukes was a big percentage of the whole, and we could get a good sale going. Beyond one hundred thousand, it became difficult to compete, and the majors would take over with their version.

With the philosophy that the song as much as the singer mattered, the Tennessee partners could afford to be laid back about talent searching and artist development, Alan Bubis said.

> Back then, the record business was small here, so if word got round that you were in the record business, people would start to beat a path to your door. There were so many singers and players that you had the choice, and you listened and you picked them out. Bill Beasley mainly was the one who did that.

For the most part Beasley picked successfully, but inevitably he let some good deals go by; he had the first chance to record singer Marty Robbins, who was brought to him by Ricky Riddle early in 1951. Robbins had written some songs, one of which, "Heartsick," Riddle recorded for Tennessee. The hope was that Beasley would record Robbins singing his other songs. "I passed on Robbins," Beasley remembered, "because he sang in a western kind of style, and I wasn't up on that music." Within a few years, Robbins would be one of the hottest acts in town, scoring a string of country and pop hits on Columbia, "Singing The Blues," "A White Sport Coat," and "El Paso" among them.

Billy Wallace, 1950s singer-songwriter. Courtesy of Showtime Archives [Toronto] and Colin Escott.

Perhaps Tennessee's best chance of real success came with Billy Wallace, one of the great, neglected characters of the early Nashville music scene. Born in Oklahoma in 1917, Wallace lived in Athens, Alabama, in his youth and apparently learned to play guitar from the Delmore Brothers. He moved to Nashville in 1950, pitched his songs, and landed a deal with Tennessee Records while, according to Bill Beasley, he was working as a carpenter. "Dog Hauled Around" introduced the self-pitying humor for which Wallace became known. It was an excellent record, combining Harold Bradley's uptown backing musicians with Wallace's determinedly rural vocal. Wallace made only two other records for Tennessee—the gospel offering "Reservation for Your Soul" in 1951 and "Southwind," about a train on the Louisville & Nashville Railroad—before he was signed by Paul Cohen at Decca Records and then joined Mercury.

Wallace wrote Bob Williams's classic honky-tonk recording "We're Steppin Out Tonite," which shared common ground with Hank Williams's hit "Settin' the Woods on Fire" in its depiction of country folk out for a hot time on the weekend. Hank Williams's biographer, Colin Escott, judged Billy Wallace to be "a master of using little flashes of detail to good effect. Lines like 'With the fender smashed in and one light out' marvelously evoke the image of a beaten-up jalopy just barely making it to the city limits." Wallace's big breakthrough came in July 1952 when Webb Pierce, also on Decca, covered his recording of "Back Street Affair" and took the song onto the country sales charts, which apparently annoyed Wallace until the end of his life.

A more prolific artist for Tennessee than Wallace, Bob Williams made eight discs for the label that regularly turned in sales of twenty-five thousand or so in the honky-tonk jukebox market. Born in Scottsville, Kentucky, in 1927, Williams in 1942 played on radio at WLBJ in Bowling Green, Kentucky, and organized a band that in March 1947 landed a gig at Nashville's WKDA, switching to WLAC in September. As Alan Bubis remembers: "Our records with Bob Williams were quite successful. The bestseller was 'Hot Rod Race.' Bob was working as a part-time musician and doubling as a car salesman in Nashville. He was crazy for automobiles." Williams's two "Hot Rod Race" sequels and a Jimmy Work song, "Pick Up Truck," testify to his obsession. He covered Arkie Shibley's "Hot Rod Race #2" but wrote his own "Hot Rod Race #3," suggesting how successful the original was for Tennessee. Also a hit for its writer, Arkie Shibley, "Hot Rod Race" had the boogie-woogie beat that made it cousin to the R&B smash "Rocket 88"—both fed the melting pot that Chuck Berry would soon dip into for "Maybellene."

One of Tennessee's more interesting artists was Mississippi Slim, whose "Beer Drinkin' Blues" on Tennessee was his first record. Bill Beasley had heard Slim on WSIX and invited him to record, impressed by his well-rounded tones and unruffled smoothness. Born Carvel Lee Ausborn in Smithville, Mississippi, around 1923, Slim was a Jimmie Rodgers disciple and a cousin to Opry comedian Rod Brasfield and *Ozark Jubilee* comedian Uncle Cyp Brasfield. From 1944 to 1948, he hosted *Pickin' and Singin' Hillbilly* on Radio WELO, Tupelo, Mississippi. His show preceded WELO's Saturday-afternoon *Jamboree*, and one of the local kids who listened to Slim and then got up to sing on the *Jamboree*'s amateur spot was a preteenage Elvis Presley, for whom Slim epitomized all the glamour of the music business.

To its heavily weighted list of contemporary performers, Tennessee Records added a few old-time-radio artists. Country and gospel singer Carl Tipton starred on WLAC with Big Jeff Bess and remained a staple of local radio and TV until the 1980s. He recorded both his styles for Tennessee, coupling "Going Home" with the gospel "Better Kneel and Pray." Then there was Kirk McGee of the celebrated McGee Brothers, one of the earliest acts on Nashville radio. As "Sam and Kirk McGee from Sunny Tennessee," the duo was one of the last links to the Opry's origins as a mid-Tennessee radio barn dance. Kirk McGee's "Rambler's Blues" on Tennessee headed in two directions at once, with a steel guitar and drums that point toward the future and a song that recalls Jimmie Rodgers's blues from the 1920s.

Randy Hughes, Tennessee's main man, mid-1950s. Courtesy of Bear Family Records.

But the artist Tennessee Records nurtured most in the country jukebox market was Randy Hughes, who became better known as the pilot on the flight that crashed between Kansas City and Nashville, killing himself along with the singing star he then managed, Patsy Cline; his father-in-law, singer Cowboy Copas; and another star vocalist, Hawkshaw Hawkins.

"Randy was very young when he started working for us," said Alan Bubis. "He handled stock in the warehouse and we put him on record." Harold Bradley was the session leader on Randy's first session and remembers Beasley saying that there was a young man out back who wanted to record. As Bradley recalls the meeting, Hughes was dripping with sweat, carrying boxes of records. The young man from Gum, Tennessee, was born Ramsey Dorris Hughes in September 1928, began his career at eighteen on WTOD, Toledo, Ohio, and worked as rhythm guitarist and front man with the Carter Family, Butterball Paige, Martha

Carson, Moon Mullican, and George Morgan throughout his twenties.

Signing with Tennessee Records when he was twenty-two, Hughes made nine discs in three years, displaying a voice that connected with listeners, a songwriting style that held their attention, and a fine band. With a penchant for humorous, up-tempo songs, he made "When Elephants Start to Roost in Trees" and "If I Loved a Liar I'd Hug Your Neck" before striking a chord with the jukebox audience with "Easy Monthly Payment Blues," which satirized the mushrooming instant-credit business. His fast-paced lyrics were often matched by a dazzlingly fleet electric guitar solo from Harold Bradley.

Hughes also established something of a reputation for cutting salty records. He recorded "Birthday Cake," originally written and recorded as "Take Your Hands off of It" by Billy Hughes (no relation) for Fargo Records. With its gynecological detail and the warning to "get your finger out of it, it don't belong to you," "Birthday Cake" was clearly a record aimed at jukeboxes rather than radio, and Skeets McDonald recorded a good-selling version for Fortune in Detroit. In 1955, the song would become an R&B hit for Priscilla Bowman as "Hands Off." The song's origins lie in a number of early hillbilly and blues recordings from the 1930s. Tennessee also had Hughes's version of "Tattooed Lady," which Reynold Bubis called "the first of the risqué hits in hillbilly music," even though hillbilly and blues bands had sung double-entendre songs since records were invented. With the advent of radio promotion, lyrics were becoming more circumspect, but "Tattooed Lady," the tale of a woman with an image of each state somewhere on her anatomy, found its way onto almost every jukebox and hillbilly bar in the country. In the enjoyable Autry Inman composition "Talkin' in Your Sleep," Randy Hughes again showed his predilection for suggestive songs. Like the last of Hughes's Tennessee singles, "Tapping That Thing," and "Not Big Enough," it was just innocent enough to get played.

Hughes married Kathaloma "Kathy" Copas, daughter of Opry star Cowboy Copas, in February 1952. He made his last record for Tennessee that year and started widening his interests within and beyond music. He represented Imperial Records' Travis Music publishing company in Nashville, worked for a brokerage house, and sold insurance, as well as leading touring bands on the road. He worked for promoter Hubert Long before he went out on his own, brought the emerging country and popular singer Patsy Cline to Nashville, and in 1959 took over her management. She not only saw him as the architect of her success but also brought him onto her sessions to play rhythm guitar. Hughes bought a Cadillac, some oil properties, and a Piper Comanche. When the plane went down near Camden, Tennessee, on March 5, 1963, on the way home from a benefit in Kansas City, killing everyone on board, some who had known Hughes were not entirely surprised. "I warned him against flying," said Alan Bubis. "I'd been a pilot during the war, and I knew that you had to keep your hand in it or you weren't sharp enough." Hughes's bass player, Buddy Killen, who traveled a lot with Randy, offered what could have been his epitaph: "He was a very impatient kind of person—that's what got him killed."

The Jamboree Label

Bill Beasley had set up Tennessee Records on a professional footing: It would be a union label, filing session details with the AFM for approval and paying union scale to the musicians Harold Bradley would bring in. Within a few months Beasley realized that he could cut expenses for country and blues sessions by hiring nonunion musicians, and in May 1950, the partners formed another label that would focus on local country music talent and widen their sales base on a shoestring budget.

Another motive for the new subsidiary, Jamboree—although some labels said "Dixie Jamboree"—was to test the waters in the "racking" market, selling cover versions of best-selling songs through grocery stores and other nonstandard outlets that would accommodate a rack of records, Beasley explained.

> We tried anything we could to sell a disc. Really, the main point behind Jamboree was to get a separate set of distributors and sell twice as much product. Jamboree was a nonunion label, and we sold it to distributors in any town where we already had a deal for Tennessee but where maybe there was this second outlet in town.

A third factor in setting up Jamboree was studio time, as Alan Bubis told me:

> We used the Castle studio at first, but that was not always available to us. Lack of studio time was limiting our business, so we needed to make our own studio. For a few months while we were setting ours up, we recorded up at Bowling Green, Kentucky, at a radio station, and we paid Jim McKinney to engineer those sessions for us.

Jamboree issued several discs by performers on the minor-league radio barn dance *Hayloft Jamboree,* broadcast over WKDA Saturday afternoons from Nashville's War Memorial Auditorium. Jim McKinney, the program director, worked closely with Beasley, finding artists and helping to set up recording sessions. Although Beasley said the label wasn't named for the show, the two were so closely connected that when McKinney decided to pull out, the Tennessee partners had to stop using the name. Beasley conceded that "Jim McKinney was involved at the start for a while, but he had different interests from the rest of us so we gradually dropped the label." According to Hugh Cherry, an influential disc jockey who emceed the *Hayloft Jamboree:*

> The show was the idea of the program director, Jim McKinney, who also produced some records for the Jamboree label. Some of the *Hayloft* performers were on Jamboree Records, but there was no real connection other than Jim. One time, they persuaded me to make a record for them, but I couldn't sing, and it was the second-worst record out of Nashville. The worst was a record by Audrey Williams, Hank's wife, who really couldn't sing, but somehow she persuaded me to do a narration part to it, so I was involved in the worst record, too.

According to Bill Beasley, he looked on Hugh Cherry as the barometer of success for Jamboree and Tennessee in the country music market:

> Hugh helped us a lot. I'd take a new disc over to him in the morning, and he'd play it a few times and, within a few days we'd know if we had a hit developing. We'd also do the same with other key DJs, like Dewey Phillips in Memphis, but Hugh was our barometer locally.

Alan Bubis has similar memories: "We would go sit with Hugh or Joe Allison, Noel Ball or Bob Jennings, the country deejays, and listen to what they were playing and what was selling, and encouraging them to play our discs."

The first Jamboree artist, the prolific Dick Stratton, produced a classic product firmly in line with the Beasley/Bubis philosophy, the jukebox disc "Slipping around with Jole Blon," which referenced a number of popular records by stringing their titles together. A vocalist, bass-fiddle player, and acoustic guitarist, Stratton led the house band on the live *Hayloft Jamboree* stage show and, through an arrangement with Beasley, soon led the studio band on Tennessee/Jamboree's country records. Stratton's band was tight, swinging, and accomplished, with an ensemble sound, especially in the guitar parts, that reflects players who really knew their way around their instruments—Harold "Howdy" Forrester or Boudleaux Bryant on fiddle, Allen Flatt and Bob Williams on guitar, Billy Byrd on steel or electric guitar, and Roy Hall or Del Wood on piano. Beasley remembered that the two unsung stars of the band were the Neely brothers, Mitch on fiddle and Paul on guitar.

Because Stratton and the other musicians usually had day jobs, they normally held recording sessions in the evening or later. On the Tennessee and Jamboree record labels, Beasley took delight in crediting them as the "Nite Owls." Before he moved to the main Tennessee label at the end of 1951, Stratton had four discs on Jamboree, a mix of original novelty tunes and covers of hits, notably the big-selling "Poison Love," recorded by Johnny & Jack, and Bob Wills, among others. Stratton was an engagingly rough-hewn, if limited, vocalist, and the backings were generic honky-tonk, driven by the tic-toc rhythm of the electric guitar's deadened bass strings—the sort of fare that would have gone down well in the joints around Nashville.

Bill Beasley signed another of the Nite Owls, Allen Flatt from Atlanta, for his startlingly realistic impersonation of

Ernest Tubb. By 1950, when Flatt made his first discs for Jamboree Records, Tubb was well established in Nashville and, said Alan Bubis, "would get such a kick out of the fact that this guy sounded exactly like him. Ernest had this show that went out from his record shop after the Opry, and he'd invite Allen down and get him up to sing." But Flatt, with a regular show on WKDA, had his own Nashville following. For Jamboree, he recorded "I'll Have the Last Laugh Yet," a Billy Wallace song that would have enhanced Tubb's repertoire, and "Steppin Out," which Tubb did later record, a rare example of the prophet following the disciple.

But Jamboree's biggest hit came from another *Hayloft Jamboree* artist, Johnny Talley. Born in Nashville in 1924, Talley played steel guitar in high school with a band called the Oklahoma Playboys, delivered newspapers to publisher Fred Rose's home, and made his radio debut on WSIX. A bit player in the Nashville music scene for two decades, Talley made his debut on Jamboree with "Hillbilly Sweetheart" and went on to make the first released version of Lefty Frizzell's signature tune, "If You've Got the Money I've Got the Time," Jamboree Records' biggest seller.

That Talley's record was issued in August 1950, a month before Lefty's own, was the happy result of the friendship Beasley and Alan Bubis had cultivated with a disc jockey in Chattanooga named Lloyd, who got prerelease records from the major labels. Every so often, he would slip one to Beasley, telling him it was going to be a smash. Beasley would dash out a cover version that would hit the market at the same time as the original, or, in this case, ahead of it. Although the Jamboree release caused Lefty bitter disappointment, Columbia used its clout to push his original to the top spot. Talley made one more record for Beasley, and the fact that both sides were Lefty songs suggests how well his first Jamboree disc had sold. Certainly it had caused London Records to once again exploit their connection with Beasley, with their own early version of "If You've Got the Money" by Hank Dalton.

With low overhead and good distribution, Tennessee/Jamboree looked like a winner. "Most of our early recordings were successful, and we did rather well," said Alan Bubis.

> We had national distribution and we developed a pretty heavy release schedule. Ten or twelve records a month. We were recording a lot of our own copyrighted songs and building up a big-sized publishing catalog. There was no trouble for Bill in finding country or blues artists to record in Nashville at that time. You could shake a tree and they'd fall out.

Then two unforeseen circumstances ended Jamboree's run: trouble with the musicians' union and a falling out with *Hayloft Jamboree* program director Jim McKinney. AFM leaders thought that a nonunion operation like Jamboree, and another like Tennessee that drifted in and out of compliance with the union when it felt like it, were inconsistent with Nashville's emerging status as a professional recording center in which top-flight musicians could command union scale. According to Alan Bubis:

> We did some union sessions and some nonunion. We used the Dick Stratton band for a lot of sessions, and we got into some squabbles with George Cooper at the union about that. It was touch and go there for a while, but we all survived. George wanted us to use union musicians exclusively, but some musicians didn't want to be in the union, and we didn't see why we shouldn't use them. Anyway, we couldn't wait around for George's musicians to fit us in. Bill Beasley used to get into it pretty good with George all the time. I guess they were friends really though, otherwise they would have killed each other.

When the relationship with McKinney turned sour, Beasley dropped the Jamboree name and discontinued the label in 1951, after about a year's run and some eighteen releases.

Beasley then cultivated a relationship with a second radio jamboree, the *Midway Jamboree* on WGWD in Gadsden, Alabama, organized by Chester Studdard. Tennessee recorded Lee Bonds, Sonny Sims, and other Studdard artists, and Beasley was particularly taken with Rebe and Rabe and the Sunny Valley Boys, releasing five discs by them. Revin "Rebe"

Gosdin and J. C. "Rabe" Perkins came from adjacent counties in east Alabama, were influenced by brother harmony acts, and made something of a specialty of replicating Louvin Brothers songs so precisely that many listeners couldn't tell the difference. Their cover of the Louvins' "Weapon of Prayer" proved particularly successfully for Tennessee, and their various country and gospel recordings sold well. However, according to Sonny Sims, although Rebe and Rabe assured Bill Beasley they were union musicians, they were not. This violation was discovered in April 1952 and would eventually lead to difficulties for Beasley and for Tennessee.

Tennessee's Black Pop and Gospel Series

Although issued in the largely country-oriented "lucky 711" series, Tennessee Records' first black music recordings, by Jimmy Sweeney, were in a category all their own. The first paid tribute to a popular Nashville disc jockey, Gene Nobles, perhaps an acknowledgment of the growing popularity of Nobles and other WLAC disc jockeys with white audiences throughout the South. Certainly Nobles and others were vitally important in selling R&B and gospel records over the airwaves and tapping markets that a Nashville label would not otherwise reach easily.

Jimmy Sweeney, a singer with pop leanings, recorded both "Boogie Woogie Jockey" and "Tobacco Road" for Tennessee Records early in 1950. That "Boogie Woogie Jockey" appeared on Tennessee Records at all is curious, for deejay Gene Nobles was associated with Randy Wood, who ran Randy's Record Shop and later Dot Records. The Tennessee disc certainly had Nobles's backing, for it is he who contributes the spoken interjection "boogie woogie on a Saturday night" on the recording; Sweeney sang in a sweet high tenor, and behind him Harold Bradley fronted a white country swing band.

Of Sweeney's next Tennessee disc, which Bill Beasley recorded at Ryman Auditorium, Alan Bubis recalled:

> Jimmy Sweeney was a beautiful singer and a great guy. He had a song called "Tobacco Road" that we thought was just a wonderful record. Bill [Beasley] recorded it on the stage because he wanted to try to get the big sound that the acoustics in that place could give us. It had symphonic strings and everything on it. We thought it was a hit. But we couldn't sell it.

It was a problem that would follow Sweeney for years. He moved between pop, blues, and country styles on a number of Nashville labels, using seven or eight different names: The Rhythm Rockers on Delta, Jimmy and Bob Sweeney on Tennessee, and later Jimmy Destry and Jimmy Bell and various variations, including The Varieteers.

In December 1950, Tennessee Records started a black music 100 series of gospel discs along with some country blues and R&B, recorded mostly in nonunion sessions as the Jamboree series had been. Tennessee was not the first label to record local black gospel and blues talent, but it was the first to have an affinity with the local scene. Neither Jim Bulleit nor C. V. Hitchcock understood the black music Bullet Records issued in the 1940s, and World Records had not survived long enough to make best use of the developing relationship of their session engineer, WLAC disc jockey John Richbourg, with black performers and those who distributed their music.

Bill Beasley, on the other hand, tried to understand and work creatively with all his artists of whatever style: pop, country, gospel, or blues. His partner, Howard Allison, who had developed an encyclopedic knowledge of independent label musical styles, could advise on what was selling on other labels. And in the case of the 100 series, the Bubis cousins could draw on the many connections they had established within the black community in their quest to place their jukeboxes in cafes, bars, and clubs.

One such connection was Alice Mason, the first black record distributor and sales point for black music in Nashville. Mason ran a record dealership and phonograph-machine store before the war, was at 1124 Jefferson Street by 1945, and operated for several years from various locations in north Nashville. Ernie Young's Record Mart on Third Avenue North also specialized in black music, as did Eugene Cashion's Ace

Music. WLAC disc jockey Gene Nobles himself ran a record dealership at 409 Deaderick Street in the late 1940s. Beyond Nashville, Tennessee Records had good distribution in the South through their own wholesale operation that linked into the Music Sales chain out of Memphis and other national distributors of independent label discs.

The first seven discs on Tennessee's 100 series were gospel recordings that Beasley had acquired through contacts in Kentucky while he was working on the Jamboree country recordings with Jim McKinney. His Hopkinsville, Kentucky, connections included Morgan Babb, a disc jockey and gospel singer at WHOP, and Edward Babbage, who ran the Skylark Club, part of the black club circuit. Through Babb and Babbage, Beasley was introduced to Wings over Dixie, a female gospel quartet, and the Reverend Cleavant Derrick from Knoxville, who organized the Derrick Singers. Derrick wrote "When God Dips His Love in My Heart," which became a country gospel standard.

Beasley recorded Morgan Babb's own group, the Radio Four, in April 1951 at WBDL studio in Bowling Green, Kentucky, a high-spirited "On My Journey Now" assisted by bass player Ernie Newton. This song and the mournful

Bill Beasley recording the Radio Four in his studio on Fourth Avenue South, 1952. Courtesy of Showtime Archives [Toronto] and Colin Escott.

"Sending Up This Prayer" featured Babb as a clear yet expressive lead tenor and announced him as a major talent. As Howard Allison later reported:

> That record started selling for us, far more than we expected, and then everything we could put out by Morgan Babb and his group took off and did very nicely for us. They were one of the acts we could rely on to deliver solid sales and keep the company in the forefront.

Morgan, the youngest of the seven Babb brothers, was born in 1929 in Russellville, Kentucky; five of the seven would eventually comprise the Radio Four. Their father, Giles, had a jug band that played for dances around Logan County in the 1930s, and their mother was a gospel singer in church. The brothers Cephus, Ray, Paul, and George, who sang at the Mount Zion Baptist Church in Ashburn, reportedly called themselves the Radio Four because they aspired to be good enough to appear over the airwaves. Morgan Babb started working as a disc jockey around 1948 on WHOP, a white-owned station that allowed him to play fifteen-minute slots of "race" music—blues, rhythm, gospel, and jazz—where Babb joined the genre of radio men who cultivated a jive-talking approach. He produced the *Happy Jack Show* and later described how people drove up and down the streets of town, imitating his line of jive, with "Happy Jack" painted on the sides of their cars. When he joined his brothers in the Radio Four in 1950 as arranger and guitarist as much as featured singer, his abilities galvanized the quartet, which developed a soulful style with jumping rhythms that owed something to the jug-band days.

The Four's later Tennessee discs were recorded in Nashville, where Babb thought "Tennesssee had a top-notch studio for that time. Bill Beasley had a Magnecord machine installed into the third floor of a building at Fourth Avenue South." On the strength of the Radio Four's first disc, Beasley and Alan Bubis arranged for the quartet to go out on tour and hired the aspiring local musician and composer Ted Jarrett as front man. "Ted went out ahead of us on the road," Morgan Babb said. "His job was to make bookings and to set up concerts and find hotels, that sort of thing."

Tennessee R&B: Ted Jarrett and Louis Brooks

The deal Bill Beasley made with Ted Jarrett to scout for him led Tennessee to increase its focus on R&B over gospel as 1951 unfolded. While Beasley ran the recording sessions, he said, he relied on Jarrett to bring the artists in to audition.

> With the country singers, they would just come in and find us. With spiritual and gospel music, I used Wally Fowler or Morgan Babb to suggest people I could record, and with blues it was Ted, apart from one or two like Bernard Hardison who I discovered for myself, playing piano in Nashville.

Ted Jarrett's fascination with music sprouted early. Born in Nashville in 1925 and raised by his grandparents twenty-five miles outside town, he told me:

> I had been writing lyrics and poetry, but my grandfather thought that wouldn't do me any good. I used to read magazine stories about "Make money writing lyrics," and I thought that was a means of escaping the ordinary life.

At about fifteen, he went to Nashville, took piano lessons funded by his boss at a local bowling alley where he was employed to reset pins, and attended Pearl High School. "That was when I came really to be involved in music, in school bands. After a while, playing piano in school bands and writing lyrics, that was when I got the idea to get into the music business." Jarrett used his G.I. Bill benefits to study music composition at Fisk University in 1948, while in his spare time he hung around with the Louis Brooks band, Chick Chavis, and Don Q. Pullen, immersing himself in the traditions of Nashville's black music and getting to know the principal players on the scene.

In the early 1950s, Jarrett persuaded the Bijou Theater to let him emcee some of their shows and to play piano with the bands there. Meanwhile, he said:

> I'd go along to Tennessee Records and hang around, just to be there, and I'd keep asking for a job. Eventually Bill

Ted Jarrett, Nashville's first black record producer, 1950s. Courtesy of Ted Jarrett.

Beasley gave me one. Bill was the one that helped me the most, but I did do some work for Jim Bulleit also. Jim got me a job working for Beulah Bryant. I wrote "Hold Me Tight" that sold well, and he also introduced me to Herman Lubinsky at Savoy Records who came down to my house to see me, and that was really impressive to me back then.

As road manager for the Radio Four, Jarrett did their advance work and sold their Tennessee recordings from the back of their cars as they toured from town to town.

Then, Jarrett told me:

> I started to get involved with the R&B things Tennessee was doing. I was lucky, I guess, because it was all new to me. I had some gigs early on playing piano with Louis Brooks, on the road. I had just come from high school bands, and it was a new world. The first job, Louis would say to play a shuffle. Hell, I didn't know how to shuffle. I had to learn real quick.

Between them, these two men—bandleader and saxophonist Louis Brooks and Ted Jarrett—would frame Tennessee Records' blues style.

For a time around 1952, Jarrett was a leading light in the first all-black-staffed radio station in town, WSOK, where he assimilated all kinds of musical influences that helped him develop as a session arranger and producer. Little Richard would later describe Jarrett as "*the* producer in Nashville, even though he was real young." The two men had met at the New Era Club, which, according to Jarrett,

> was where all the out-of-town singers and musicians came in: Wynonie Harris, B.B. King, Fats Domino. It was a meeting place for talent and ideas. That was where I discovered Christine Kittrell, Earl Gaines, and others that I produced for Tennessee and Republic Records.
>
> The first production job I remember was a song called 'Amen' with Edna Gallmon Cooke. Then we did "Walk Thru the Valley." Then I met a girl singer called Helen Foster. Christine Kittrell was my first real production success. I took Christine from the New Era Club onto Tennessee, then Republic, and then Vee-Jay. Tennessee did have their own studios, but right at the start we'd record anywhere, a hole in the wall or maybe a club or radio station somewhere. I didn't have a method or a style as such. I just wrote what I felt and recorded it the best way I could. I mean, I started out liking Nat "King" Cole and suchlike, but I didn't set out to work to that pattern. Our music just developed.

Ted Jarrett's fellow designer of the music that "just developed"—Tennessee's blues sound—was saxophonist Louis Brooks, who recorded the first disc in the label's R&B series. According to Brooks:

> When Bill Beasley opened his Tennessee Records, I just went by there one day. They were running through some songs, and I got involved in a jam session and wound up playing some sessions. Ted Jarrett wrote and produced some songs for us, like "Wine Hangover" and "Almost Boogie." Of course, I had known Ted for a while, as he would sit in with my band on piano sometimes. Normally, at the time of Tennessee Records, my band was Ollie Brown on bass or guitar, Lovell "Knott" Phillips on piano, Billy Sherrill on drums, who was originally the leader of the group before me. Billy was a barber who moved to Wisconsin. Sometimes Tiny Davis would be the drummer and on occasion it was Earl Gaines. Tommy McGee [credited on record labels as "McGhee"] would play saxophone with us, or Ted Jarrett would play piano when we wanted something smoother than Knott could do. We recorded with a number of vocalists over the years: Earl Gaines, Tommy Brooks, Tommy McGee, Helen Hebb, Helen Foster, Christine Kittrell, Bernard Hardison, Larry Birdsong.
>
> The music scene in Nashville before the record companies came along was just some local bands playing what they knew. Hillbilly bands, some jazz, and a small blues scene. My band played rhythm & blues, but really

Louis Brooks's band: *from left*, Lovell Phillips, Ollie Brown, Brooks, and Tiny Davis. Courtesy of Eula Brooks.

it was just the blues, the old tunes, with a little new trimming on it. It was a small group of people that had bands, and just occasionally someone would break out, like the Jimmie Lunceford band. There was a little blues, and I was also aware of people like DeFord Bailey blowing harp on the Opry along with Humphrey Bate and the jug bands and all. But it was Francis Craig and "Near You" that put Nashville on the map.

Brooks knew what he was talking about. Born Louie O'Neal Brooks in March 1911, one of thirteen children, he had watched the Nashville scene develop, learning his trade from his father, whose group, the Syncopated Five, played a style that Brooks characterized as "honky-tonk jazz, Dixieland style." Before long, Brooks was playing saxophone in local clubs and taking his talents on the road as part of a traveling circus.

When "Near You" broke in 1947, Brooks was just out of the air force, where he had the memorable experience of playing as a stand-in with Duke Ellington's band. Fellow Nashville musician Don Q. Pullen left the service at around the same time as Brooks, and they formed a band that Pullen fronted for two years until Brooks quit to form a combo that went under various names, including the Pinetoppers, the Downbeats, and the Hi-Toppers. Brooks also took a day job at the First National Bank, which he would keep for many years.

Brooks's recordings belie his assertion that his band was

basically playing "old" blues with window dressing. There was a big-city, postwar sensibility to the recordings that emerged from Nashville in the years after the Second World War. Nashville-born bluesmen like Leroy Carr or St. Louis Jimmy might have recognized some of the prewar rawness and sparseness, but Louis Brooks and his contemporaries were competing in the pre–rock & roll cauldron of small-combo jump music and sophisticated city blues.

For his first recording under his own name, Brooks chose "Almost Boogie," his intro song on the bandstand and his fallback tune in case of emergencies. "All the bands have some old tune that they kinda kick around and call their own, you know," Brooks volunteered in the enthusiastic manner that characterized his fifty-year career in Nashville music. "Mine was a boogie, almost. If you listen, the old tunes had three changes, but this song didn't quite do that." The disc had a strong piano lead by Phillips, but the drummer was busy accenting, and in comparison Brooks's sax solo was rather restrained—not almost but rather more than a boogie. "Wine Hangover" was an evocatively named moody blues instrumental whose uncomplicated piano contrasts with a rather mellow, jazzy tenor solo from Brooks. "My style just kinda came out of me," Brooks asserted, "but I always liked Coleman Hawkins as a saxophonist and Ben Webster, who had that deep tone."

By the time his first record came out, around March 1951, Brooks had a residency Thursday and Saturday nights at the Sugar Hill Club on Kellogg Street, almost as far as you could go into north Nashville before an ox-bow bend of the Cumberland River brought a natural halt to urban development. The Brooks band normally peddled a subtle blues sound based on sax and piano leads. They often had no guitarist and certainly did not employ the barnstorming, bar-walking techniques of some bands.

Louis Brooks made only one more disc in his own name for Tennessee, but he led the band for numerous other recordings, and his sound was integral to Nashville R&B for many years.

> My band played at the Sugar Hill club, and the New Era sometimes. Then we'd play hotels and the army bases, and then again we'd travel. For ten or twelve years there we were the busiest band this side of the Ohio River.

One of Tennessee producer Ted Jarrett's protégés was Helen Foster, a gospel singer for whom Jarrett eventually wrote and arranged songs, including "Blues after Sunset" and "Big Fat Daddy." Foster was from Nashville and, in Jarrett's opinion, "a real good singer. She could have become a star if circumstances had been different, you know, the right song, some publicity." Foster's vocal control was shaky on her first disc, but Jarrett proved right when Foster was moved to the associated label, Republic. In September 1952, sixteen months after her debut, Foster recorded the successful "Oop-De-Doo" with a male vocal group, the Rovers, who carried this up-tempo tune to a loping drum-and-piano beat with a driving yet mellow feel.

If "Oop-De-Doo" was a step toward Foster's moment in the sun, the flipside, "You Belong to Me," nearly put her there. "That was one that I really thought was going to go over in a big way," Jarrett recalled. "It should have been a smash." The song was a cover for the R&B market of Jo Stafford's major 1952 pop hit on Columbia, first recorded by Sue Thompson and also covered by Eddy Arnold, Bing Crosby, and Patti Page. Foster's vocal alternated from thin and uncertain to full and assured, with a male choral part midway that was effective behind her vulnerable lead voice. The lyric was adapted by western swing bandleader Pee Wee King and his vocalist Redd Stewart from an original outline by Chilton Price, a lady librarian in Louisville who started the song off as a wartime message, "Hurry Home to Me."

Despite expectations, Foster all but disappeared from the scene after her Tennessee recordings. According to Johnnie Douglas, a schoolmate then married to Shy Guy Douglas:

> Helen could have gone far. She was very smart. But she liked to party. She started hanging around shows with the Jerrie Jackson Revue. She and Jackson's daughter had a vocal group, singing gospel. She was a pretty girl, with a beautiful face, but she grew up too quick for her own good.

Christine Kittrell and Bernard Hardison

The same might be said of Christine Kittrell, a marvelous singer with all the qualities of tone and expressiveness that could elevate an independent label R&B recording from the mundane to the exceptional. Another Jarrett find, she became Tennessee's star R&B act.

Born in Nashville on August 11, 1929, Christine Porter was raised by relatives Fred and Roberta Pennington on Underwood Street. Musically, she was a product of the choir at the Progressive Baptist Church on Jefferson Street where her cousin C. J. Barner was the minister. At age fourteen, she briefly married gospel bass singer Rufus Carrethers of the Fairfield Four. At sixteen, she won a talent contest singing in the style of Ella Fitzgerald, but, she said:

Christine Kittrell, with Louis Brooks, Ollie Brown, and Lovell Phillips, and, *right,* singer Larry Birdsong. Courtesy of Bear Family Records.

> The Jefferson Street Baptist Band. That was how it all started for me, singing with the church. Then later I started singing professionally with Louis Brooks's band. That's if you can call it professionally when you were singing for all the fried fish you could eat and all the white corn liquor you could drink, and about five dollars apiece. I was all of sixteen then. We would play anywhere they would let us work. They would charge fifty cents or a dollar and give the band 40 percent of the door, and sometimes we'd have five, six, maybe ten dollars. That was the beginning of it for me, playing in places like Lawton Britten's place in Franklin, Tennessee. That was like the jumpingest place there was around then. Boy, we made big money there, because we could make all of twelve dollars each.

In the late 1940s, when the Louis Brooks band had regular gigs at the Sugar Hill, New Era, and Elks Clubs, Christine would sit in with them occasionally. By then she was married to Henry Kittrell from Columbia, Tennessee. One day, she recalled:

> Ted Jarrett had invited me for a drink at the New Era Club. Jimmy Lewis was playing there that night. He was a wonderful guitarist, and he also played bass and later worked with Count Basie. That day he was playing guitar. Someone asked me to sing "Danny Boy," and eventually I was persuaded to do it while Jimmy played guitar for me. And it was so well received that the man who owned the club offered me a job. Word got around—"There's a new singer in town"—but there wasn't a new singer. I'd been at home all my life!

Jarrett, who was playing in the club with the Brooks band, gave her a call. "Ted said, would I get together with Louis and come down the next day to audition for Reynold Bubis and Bill Beasley? And that was the start of my recording career."

"Don't Do It," recorded in the summer of 1951 and issued that fall, was the first of three Kittrell discs on Tennessee. Kittrell remembered that first session clearly.

> We recorded it at Tennessee's studio on Fourth Avenue South. It was after the club had closed, as the soundproofing in the studio had not yet been properly completed, and we had to avoid the traffic noise from outside. It was Louis Brooks and his band. Louis did all the recording with any artist they brought in at that time. There was no other band with a sound like Louis, believe me.

"Don't Do It" was a cover of a song by Nino Tempo and his sister April Stevens, who recorded it on the Society label at the end of 1950. Kittrell gave it a breathy, torchy nightclub blues vocal that was echoed by Brooks's mellow, Ben Webster–like tenor-sax solo. Kittrell was a fan of Ella Fitzgerald's ballads, Dinah Washington's blues, and singers at the pop end of the spectrum, and this was the real Kittrell. (She rated Frank Sinatra as her favorite male singer and counted the highlight of her career as singing with the Count Basie Band at the Tenth Annual Cavalcade of Jazz in Los Angeles.)

Kittrell's second disc, "Sittin' Here Drinking" released around July 1952, became something of a classic and enduring minor hit. She described writing the song with Bill Beasley in the third-floor studio Tennessee used on Fourth Avenue South.

> I was singing about my life at the time. I had found that Ted Jarrett liked to have a song recorded just as he wanted it, and I was trying to cut something in a way he did not like. I got mad and went off with a bottle. After a while, Bill Beasley came in and said, "What are you doing?" I said, "I'm just sitting here drinking," and as soon as I said it we both knew that was a line for a song. Bill and I sat there and wrote the song there and then.

On the recording, Kittrell sets up a melancholy feeling with her spoken intro, echoed in the outro. With impeccable phrasing and intonation, this was torchy, after-hours blues at its best, sophisticated late-night music for an uptown black audience. You can almost smell the smoke-filled room and the cheap mixed drinks. Louis Brooks's band is the perfect foil for Kittrell, and the spare twelve-bar sax breaks by Brooks are among the most thoughtful and melodic statements of 1950s Nashville music.

"Sittin' Here Drinking'" sold around 150,000 copies in its first year, with a success curve Alan Bubis remembered.

> That song did real, real well. It never was a national hit, but it sold more than enough records to be a national hit. It sold in one city at a time. It started in New Orleans. The distributor called us and we couldn't believe how many records he was selling on that thing down there. Then it went city to city, and over a two-year period we sold a lot of records.

On the strength of her recording success, Kittrell got bookings beyond the Nashville area. As she explained:

> Joe Turner took me on the road with him. He had a good band with him, and they were looking for a girl singer. The first show was in Little Rock, Arkansas. That paid really big. That was a seventy-five-dollar-a-week job. We went to Memphis with Joe, and then we went into New Orleans and did some shows with Big Maybelle also. Behind "Sittin' Here Drinking" I was able to stay in New Orleans and book into the Pelican Club. I worked there with Dave Bartholomew's band. That was a schooled band, a very impressive group to me at that time.
>
> Then Ben Waller out of L.A. started booking me, and I began working the California circuit. I worked there with Earl Bostic's band doing one nighters, and then I worked some with Paul Williams's band. I went back several times to the Coast, and they were some of the best times then, because the Bostic band and Williams band, they would play a little of anything. That was nice. I was able to do some of the standards and old ballads. We played all over, and I got to know some other singers real well. One was Ruth Brown; we would often run into each other. She would come to where I was playing, and she would sing, and I would do the same in reverse, that kind of thing.

Sharing venues with one of the stars of R&B at the time, Ruth Brown, hit-maker of a string of Atlantic Records classics that included "So Long" and "Teardrops from My Eyes," Christine Kittrell had come a long way from the Progressive Baptist Church.

The Nashville clubs continued to provide grist for Tennessee Records' mill, including pianist Bernard Hardison, who was playing with his band at a club when he impressed Bill Beasley. Ted Jarrett agreed, describing Hardison as "a flashy character who was one of the finest players in town. He played naturally, not in a schooled way at all, and of course that sometimes led to problems in a band context."

Singer Bobby Hebb remembers the pianist as

> a dynamic stage performer. He always got over very well, and he knew when it was time to stay and when it was time to quit. He worked the audience well. He loved Lloyd Price and Fats Domino, and he would play their songs at the Elks club on a weekend. He would open shows for people like Nappy Brown and others who came through town. He played with Big Mac on bass and Rockin' Beasley on drums. His sax man was little Tommy McGee.

Hardison's first Tennessee recording, issued around April 1951, was "Hey Little Girl." A flamboyant and temperamental character, openly gay, Hardison took a less conservative style to bandleading than did Louis Brooks, even though their bands shared and swapped players depending on who had a gig and where. Brooks said that "Bernie was a piano player who would work with his band or with anybody else he could. He worked the clubs and was a wonderful entertainer."

Bill Beasley recalled once introducing a blues singer with Hardison's band, Billie McAllister, as "Bill," only to have McAllister bristle and say: "'That's *Miss* Billie McAllister, if you don't mind.' Bernard Hardison and Billie were some of the first transsexual or homosexual people that I ever knew of in Nashville." From Hopkinsville, Kentucky, McAllister had come to town with the band of sax-player Freddy Young; both McAllister and Young had soon joined the Hardison band. Many contemporaries remember McAllister, a male cross-dresser who sometimes performed as a male vocalist but more often appeared as a woman. As early as December 1937, he was pictured in the *Chicago Defender* dressed as a woman, and described as "the boy with the feminine charm"; he had been featured at some of the best nightspots in the East and was headlining at the Cabin Inn.

McAllister's voice had a husky timbre as he sang "Walking in a Daze," issued by Tennessee around April 1951, a mellow blues with jazz-voiced stylings reminiscent of after-hours, supper-club, quasi-jazz material. The song was written by Hot Lips Page and first recorded for Columbia in October 1947. The other side of the record, "I Go for That," was a classic blues shuffle to end all shuffles. The band was tight and Freddy Young's alto-sax solo alone was worth the price. Young managed to get some Charlie Parker into the proceedings, quoting Parker's "Let's Fall in Love" at the start of his solo. McAllister's next disc appeared in 1952, combining the reflective "31 E Blues," where McAllister sang from a woman's point of view about her trip down Highway 31 to search Nashville's Fourth Avenue and Charlotte for her lover man, with the storming, excitable "Well, Alright Baby," where McAllister sang lustily, in a full-bodied way that would have done justice to Big Joe Turner or Wynonie Harris. Very possibly he learned this style watching or listening to them or Roy Brown in New Orleans. Bluesman Earl King told researcher Tad Jones about seeing the Billie McAllister Revue at New Orleans venues like the Dew Drop Café in the early 1950s: "They were all gays, and it was hard to discern whether they were female or not. That's how close they were. Wardrobe was fantastic."

As we've seen, Tennessee was recording uptown blues for the most part, often with artists who were products of the local Nashville scene, although they made a fascinating and mysterious exception for Julius King—mysterious because very few people have any recollection of him at all, and fascinating because he sang and played in a prewar style rooted in the East Coast blues. King played a ringing metal-bodied guitar, and "I Want a Slice of Your Puddin'" is close to the hokum blues and jug-band sounds of the 1930s. He delivered his lines in a voice that sounds old enough to have been around before Blind Boy Fuller made a successful recording of "I Want Some of Your Pie" in 1939 on Vocalion. The recording is all the more fascinating because someone at Tennessee in June 1952 thought this music would sell.

Piano Power: Tennessee's Popular Hits

Blues, hillbilly, and gospel were local-roots styles that seemed a natural focus for Tennessee's day-to-day record sales, and although Bill Beasley had adapted well to producing ethnic music, his expertise lay in popular dance-band music. From the outset he had intended to make Tennessee a name in the pop field and to this end recorded a number of pop-styled artists: "Bob" Sweeney with "Tennessee Waltz"; the Dinning Brothers' 1951 and 1952 recordings of "Winter Wonderland" and "The Senator from Tennessee," the latter a campaign song for U.S. Senator Estes Kefauver that was covered by Dinah Shore; and Snooky Lanson's curious mid-1952 message, "Stay away from Dixieland."

What Beasley probably hadn't foreseen was that Tennessee Records' two main successes outside of country and R&B music would come from pianists: a white sexagenarian who played honky-tonk blues, and a young woman who worked in a department store.

Alan Bubis remembered Harry Meade's "Yellow Dog Blues"—Tennessee's first big seller—because he had to rush around setting up a new record-pressing plant.

> Our second-ever record became very successful. That was "Yellow Dog Blues" by Harry Meade, who seemed to me like an elderly gentleman at that time, around sixty years old, when Bill found him. He came from Murfreesboro, and he recorded in a honky-tonk piano style. It was the second-best seller on the label, and in some areas it was almost a standard. Harry played piano with three fingers together and two apart, which was very unusual. Every jukebox in the South had a copy of "Yellow Dog Blues" on it. We sold zillions of records over several years on that item, and for as long as we were selling records we sold that one well.
>
> We had started off pressing our records at Bullet Plastics, but then our success with Harry led us to start our own pressing plant, a little-bitty plant where we could make enough records to keep us going without having to pay anyone. . . . Of course, whenever we wanted a lot of records in a hurry we had to go elsewhere, and we would then use RCA to press for us. We had a deal with RCA for a two-day turnaround. We had an office in Indianapolis with a man who worked exclusively shipping our records.

The Dixie Streamliners, February 1944, with Harold Bash, conducting; Jimmy Gossett, *center*; and Del Wood on piano. Courtesy of American Federation of Musicians and Harold Bradley.

Harry Meade made two more solid-selling juke box discs, "Harry's Blues" and "Frankie and Johnny," both cut at the Castle studio as was his first, but he never made it in the big city markets.

Tennessee had only one major pop hit, a version of the oldie "Down Yonder" recorded by a then-unknown pianist, Del Wood, who unaccountably became the label's biggest star with her upbeat instrumentals. Harry Meade's "Yellow Dog Blues" had proved that there was a market for old-timey piano solos, and Dot Records' success with pianist Johnny Maddox might also have encouraged Beasley to issue honky-tonk piano instrumentals.

Del Wood was still Adelaide Hazelwood when, as she later told the *Tennessean*, she was invited by Tennessee Records to fill in for their country session pianist Roy Hall, who had gone on the road. "I played happy," she said, identifying the hallmark of her style. Beasley put her behind Billy Wallace, Johnny Talley, and a number of other Tennessee and Jamboree recording artists. On a day when a session finished early, Beasley said, "Look, Adelaide, why don't you cut a couple of solo sides, but you'll have to change your name because it is too long. We'll call you Del Wood." The result was "Down Yonder," a million seller.

Adelaide Polly Hendricks of Clarksville, Tennessee, first sat down at a piano in 1925 at age five; her English grandmother encouraged her musical interest—she made her practice. The family moved to Nashville, where Adelaide continued her music study at East Nashville High School, then worked at the Kress Department Store's music department "until it closed out" and spent the next ten years at McClellan's Store selling sheet music and records and giving piano demonstrations to would-be music buyers. Meanwhile, she sat in with a number of dance bands, working with drummer Paul Broome in 1944 in the Dixie Steamliners and with Red Wortham's Orchestra and Wally Hopper's band in the later 1940s. She moved with her new husband, Carson Hazelwood, into a home on McGavock Pike in 1951, the same year she made "Down Yonder."

Wood later always gave the impression that this was her first record. It was in fact her fourth.

Tennessee released the first, "Nagasagi Boogie," in the spring of 1951. It had a vocal flipside, "Dreamy Eyes" by Jack Irwin. In March, Wood appeared as featured artist along with three other members of the Nite Owls on "What Am I Doing down Here." Within two months, her third disc appeared—"Wabash Blues."

In May 1951 came the famous session that produced "Down Yonder," the honky-tonk piano instrumental that launched a thousand cover versions. Alan Bubis recalled that "the disc was backed by Dick Stratton's band. They recorded in the evening. I can remember the drummer beating on the strings of Dick's guitar, and he got a sound that evidently helped sell the record." The intention had been to record "Liza Jane" and "Mine All Mine," thought to be in the public domain. "When I started 'Liza Jane' I ran into some trouble," Wood told the *Tennessean*. "The first eight bars of 'Liza Jane' are the same as 'Down Yonder,' which I had played a million times. I kept mixing them up."

Wood's record started breaking in late July 1951 and charted nationally in October. As Alan Bubis described the sales arc:

> It kicked around a few months, then it broke out of Indianapolis. There was a deejay up there that put it on the air, and it became a tremendous hit, then spread to Chicago, and then all over the country.

"Down Yonder" racked up excellent pop sales, reaching #4 on the pop charts, and went to #5 on the country charts, where it might have gone higher if Lefty Frizzell had not put four records in the Top Ten that winter.

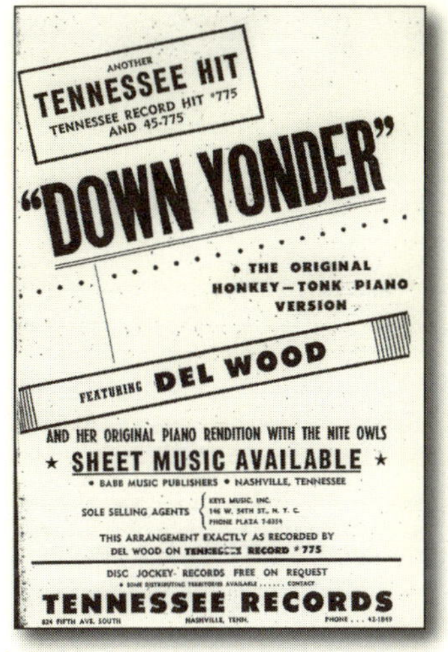

Courtesy of Showtime Archives [Toronto] and Colin Escott.

Lawsuits, Copyrights, and Union Blues

Then came the lawsuits. Just as "Down Yonder" was beginning to break, Southern Music, the song's owner, sued Tennessee Records' publishing affiliate, BABB Music, claiming that the song had been written in 1921 by L. Wolfe Gilbert, who also wrote "Waiting for the Robert E. Lee." Beasley and the Bubises held that it was based on an old fiddle tune, but in mid-August they capitulated. With seventy thousand copies sold, Tennessee needed to settle quickly because both BMI and ASCAP had refused to license Wood's version for airplay. Just about every label was in the process of rushing out a cover version, and the concern was that another company would take advantage of the situation and scoop Tennessee.

Perhaps as a necessary step in regularizing the status of the company when it started to receive unwanted attention from the IRS and others on the back of the success of "Down Yonder," Tennessee Records now formally incorporated, its charter sworn out and registered by Beasley, Allison, and the Bubis cousins on December 20, 1951.

But if the partners thought they had resolved their legal and administrative problems, they were wrong. A month later, Fred Stryker of Fairway Music slapped BABB Music with another lawsuit, reminding Tennessee that the flip side of "Down Yonder," "Mine All Mine," was not a public domain song either, having been written and recorded in 1948 by Jimmy Wakely. Stryker claimed a two-cent royalty on sales, which he insisted had passed the six hundred thousand mark. Later pressings of the record appeared with a different B side, "Dreamy Eyes" from Del Wood's first disc.

Del Wood, 1954. Courtesy of Country Music Hall of Fame and Museum.

While all the legal shenanigans took place, Del Wood made seven more singles on Tennessee. They ranged from "Ragtime Melody"—a song Bill Beasley wrote himself to be sure it would not produce another suit—and an instrumental cover of the Johnnie Lee Wills hit on Bullet, "Peter Cottontail," to "Beer Barrel Polka," and "Here Comes Santa Claus." One of Del Wood's last discs came at the end of 1952 after many months of wrangling between Tennessee/BABB and their various antagonists—"Waiting for the Robert E. Lee," perhaps a payoff to composer L Wolfe Gilbert. Among the legal players was Wood herself, who in March 1953 would be awarded five thousand dollars in back royalties from Tennessee.

At first, the legal suits surrounding "Down Yonder" were little more than an irritation to the Tennessee label partners. They took in stride paying Southern Music and Fairway Music and settling royalties with Del Wood. They brushed aside their almost daily wrangles with George Cooper at the union. The profits from a steady stream of product that had not cost too much to produce made the hassles worthwhile. Despite the flurry of major-scale record sales and the national attention that accompanied "Down Yonder" throughout the second half of 1951, Tennessee Records continued to cater to the jukebox trade, and to feed country, blues, and gospel records to southern record distributors—in particular, several country records each week right through 1952—all the time feeding copyrights to their own BABB Music Company.

But the publishing wrangles related to Del Wood's discs proved only the prelude to greater problems. In June 1950, Tennessee Music Company, the initial publishing subsidiary of Tennessee Records, had signed a contract with BMI that guaranteed Tennessee an advance per recorded song on all original songs the label issued, and BMI an assurance that the record company would place all such songs through them. To the Bubises, this seemed like a license to make money. They had no problem finding budding singers with original songs they could publish, and when they recorded an old tune, they would say they had just rearranged a public domain song. Tennessee often released songs they didn't own, claiming ownership or leaving the writer/publisher information suspiciously blank.

The cumulative effect of their neglectful or dismissive attitude to paperwork started to catch up with them. Tennessee was attracting sales on the major-label scale and with them, interest of the major-label style from music publishers, the musicians union, competitors, and the government. The American Federation of Musicians revoked Tennessee's recording license in the spring of 1952 because, according to a *Billboard* report datelined New York, March 29, 1952: "The diskery is said by AFM to have reneged on salary payments to musicians and to be long delinquent on royalty fees owed the Music Performance Trust Fund." Still, the AFM's move did not affect the nonunion sessions that were by then the label's mainstay.

Unable to follow up the massive sales of "Down Yonder" and figuring that Tennessee Records might be too localized a name for wide appeal , the partners decided to continue with Tennessee strictly as a nonunion label and to get a new label up and running—Republic. Tennessee in all but name, the label would operate on a four-square basis with proper licenses obtained from music publishers. Republic Records took its opening bow in August 1952, and the last releases on Tennessee came in November.

Tennessee Records closed at the end of 1952, and the label's charter was revoked in February 1953. Each of the principals in the company told a slightly different variant of the finale, which involved incomplete attention to contracts, copyrights, and musicians' rights, and culminated in payments of about forty thousand dollars that bounced around between Tennessee, Decca, and the courts.

Bill Beasley offered me what amounts to a conspiracy theory on the closure of Tennessee.

> It was Decca Records that was partly responsible for putting Tennessee Records out of business. The reason was that Paul Cohen [Decca's head of country recording] wanted our artists. Most of all he wanted Del Wood. What happened was that Decca went about it by getting the AFM to black-list the Tennessee label. They had a legal suit against us in connection with union legalities. See, the musicians' union was real tight, and if they wanted it that way it seemed like only eight or ten musicians were able to work at all in this town.
>
> The major labels like Decca and RCA, and sometimes Columbia, were suited by this. They were guaranteed good music and just enough of it to fit them and no one else. Decca, in particular, saw Nashville as their sole territory. They had committed a lot here, more than the other majors, and we were their main competition in town for a while there. Paul and I were pretty good friends really, but in terms of business, it was one against one.
>
> You could say that we came out of the situation well, because the laughable thing was that we bought the Del Wood items for Republic, and Del Wood eventually signed with RCA anyway, so Decca only got the rough part of the deal in the end.

Alan Bubis's take on it was this: "After we had big success with Del Wood, Decca's Paul Cohen started talking to her about a major label. We took a legal suit against him for tampering with her, for him disregarding her contract with us, and we had a judgment made in our favor." In February 1954, Republic was awarded $46,455 in damages because Del Wood had agreed to sign with Decca. Decca appealed the decision and insisted that it had been free to attempt to sign Wood because of union violations by Republic and Tennessee. "There was bad blood there for a while," Alan Bubis admitted philosophically, "but in the record business in those days you got over those things. They were everyday occurrences."

Reynold Bubis's version was the most succinct: "Eventually, over the issue of nonpayment of the 10 percent excise tax, the government closed Tennessee down. All the masters went to the government on a lien. . . . That was how it worked."

10

Republic: The Eagle Flies

In a moment of candor, Dad told me they were making a lot of money with Tennessee and Republic—a lot. But they were spending it even faster.

—Kirk Beasley

Bill Beasley founded Republic Records formally on November 12, 1952, with one hundred shares and an opening capital value of one thousand dollars—ignoring the existence of a four-year-old New York label by the same name. The charter application had been made in Franklin, Tennessee, on October 30 by Beasley and his attorneys, Dave and T. H. Alexander. The Alexanders supervised the registration by Beasley of a new office linked to the former Tennessee Records studio at 901 Fourth Avenue South, above Kraft's dry goods store, next to Morris's five-and-dime emporium. The warehouse and pressing plant were moved from Tennessee's Fifth Avenue South premises to 535 Fourth Avenue South, at the junction with Lea Avenue. Although Howard Allison and Alan and Reynold Bubis were not formal partners in Republic, the four principals from Tennessee Records ran the company at first, and in the same roles. Soon, brand-new Republic sales catalogs sported an Eagle logo and an exhortation to dealers: "Look for the Eagle—your assurance of quality in recordings—quantity in sales."

The first Republic catalog contained many reissues of discs from Tennessee, using the same songs and catalog number—only the label itself was different—but when Republic started to make new recordings, Beasley transferred just a few of his best artists to the new label. These included Christine Kittrell and Helen Foster in R&B; the Radio Four, Edna Gallmon Cooke, and Lucile Barbee in gospel; one white gospel group, J. T. Adams and the Men of Texas; and three country artists—Lee Bonds, Sonny Sims, and Allen Flatt. Beyond these, Beasley resolved to look for new talent, and the idea was that Republic would feature well-recorded, classy music across the whole range of Nashville sounds, from pop to country, gospel, and blues. The artists and records would stand up well in their own right, but wherever possible they would appeal to a wider audience.

Republic's Launch: Classy Pop and Boone's Flops

In keeping with its goals to appeal to a wider listenership with a broader range of music, the new company was launched in August 1952 not with a hillbilly act but with a pop singer, Snooky Lanson.

Snooky Lanson was a national name, a star on NBC-TV's *Your Hit Parade,* sponsored by Lucky Strike cigarettes, from 1950 to 1957, where every week he sang the top chart hits. Lanson figured that he earned around $200,000 a year and drank a good deal of it. "We spent as much as we earned—it was easy to do in New York," he later admitted. Thanks to his national reputation, the first Republic record was a minor hit. "Roll On Mississippi" was a hurrying riverboat shuffle complete with a mock Dixieland sound and a smooth yet just interested enough vocal from Lanson. The song had originally been a hit as far back as 1931, for the Boswell Sisters.

Harold Bradley was brought in to lead the session and to bring the best pop musicians in town with him, just as he had done two and a half years before on the first Tennessee label sessions. Bradley told me: "I remember cutting 'Roll On Mississippi, Roll On' in an old warehouse-type building, a temporary kind of deal. Bill was always looking to save some money. He always had an idea going of some kind or another."

In fact, Beasley was in this case investing, by upgrading the former Tennessee studio on Fourth Avenue South:

> I was always interested in getting the best quality sound I could. I had ideas on that, but I wasn't a technician. Ed Bowen had been a jukebox engineer and a radio man. He and I used to mix our brains—I'd tell him what I wanted to happen, and he'd build something that would do it, whatever it was. We had the first tape machine in Nashville. We also were the first to run the guitars straight into the mixing board without going through amplifiers in the studio. We made the first overdubs in town. We'd do anything that was different.

Alan Bubis remembered the development of the Tennessee/Republic studio:

> We put in our own studio on Fourth and Lafayette over the Kraft store. Ed Bowen was the lead engineer at WLAC, and he put it in for us. We started off with some old Magnecord machines, and that made us the first studio in Nashville to use tape because Castle still recorded direct to disc. We were able to do some overdubbing with those recorders. We heard that Les Paul had done that, and Ed called him and asked him just how he did it. It was complicated in those days, but it worked. Then we obtained a real nice Ampex two-track tape recorder around 1952. We had excellent equipment. Bill Beasley did the production and engineering, but Ed Bowen was very creative and made a lot of customized equipment for us.

Republic followed up Lanson's "Roll on Mississippi" with more releases by popular music artists: Gwen Dalton and the Ragtime Five; Joyce Paul with the Hal Bradley Orchestra (covering two crossover hit tunes, "Caribbean" and "I Forgot More Than You'll Ever Know"); and Danny Cassella, Beasley's only decent-selling act on Collegiate, who now looked for a belated follow-up hit with "The Gang That Sang Heart of My Heart." Bob Hayes recorded "Lonesome Call," Ruby Lee sang "The Mambo Reminds Me of You," Red Kirk made "Davy Crockett Blues," and the Clips and the Four Bars produced some smooth group sounds. Kentuckian Bob Harmon's boogie piano instrumentals were country-based but some, like "Shake Rag Shuffle," had a sax and clarinet behind them and probably fit all categories of jukebox.

Snooky Lanson. Courtesy of Country Music Hall of Fame and Museum.

An artist who would become a million seller in the pop field couldn't get a hit on Republic, his first record label—Pat Boone. The *Tennessean* described Boone in November 1953 as "the popular singer, college student, and recent bridegroom" whom WSIX radio owner, Louis Draughon, and his program manager, Jack Simpson, were welcoming to the staff. "He will act as part-time announcer, play records and have his own song show accompanied by Frank Bobo, staff pianist. He said this side employment will not have any bearing on his intention to follow the Ministry later." Boone described himself as "the night man"—a disc jockey, newsreader and more—and doing his homework for his classes at David Lipscomb College in between songs. He had a gospel music show and a pop show, *Youth on Parade*.

Charles Eugene Patrick Boone had arrived with his family in Nashville from Jacksonville, Florida, in 1947 when he was thirteen and was married by nineteen to Shirley Foley, a live-in med student at Mid-State Baptist Hospital and daughter of singing star Red Foley. It was Shirley who arranged for Boone to talk to Eddy Arnold about a singing career, and Arnold in turn introduced him to Harold Bradley, who remembered connecting Boone to Bill Beasley.

Pat Boone onstage, early 1950s. Courtesy of the Country Music Hall of Fame and Museum.

> Bill called me wanting to extend the pop roster on his label and asked if I knew anyone. He said, "Hey I need a pop singer." I said, "Well, Bob Johnstone." Bob was the singer with our dance band. Bill said, "No I need a young guy." So I said," Well I heard a young guy on the radio yesterday sounds like a young Bing Crosby, and his name is Pat Boone." So Bill signed him to a contract.

Boone had a promising track record. Radio and TV talent shows were much in vogue in the early 1950s, and the leaders in this market were Arthur Godfrey and Ted Mack, who both ran nationwide searches through local contests, leading to national radio and TV exposure. Boone had just won two of these national contests. As the *Tennessean* reported in April 1951, the heats of the *Ted Mack Amateur Hour* at the War Memorial Auditorium, broadcast by WSIX, listed the Modern Tones Quintet along with thirty-two other acts. The Tones were Lipscomb students and included Shirley Foley and Pat Boone. They went on to the national finals that May.

Republic released the first of four Boone singles, "Until You Tell Me So," around July 1953. Harold Bradley remembered, "Bill and I recorded Pat out at our [Owen and Harold Bradley's] studio in Hillsboro Village, him playing the ukulele and singing." Sales of the record did not live up to expectations, and for Boone's second Republic disc, "Halfway Chance with You," released around December that year, Beasley went all out to record Boone with a bigger sound. The singer was backed by a full orchestra led by James Hall, a trombonist with Owen Bradley's band. (Hall had formerly been an arranger with the Francis Craig Orchestra and went on to arrange many hit songs, including Roy Orbison's "Crying.") The results were disappointing: "Halfway Chance" was not a hit either. According to Harold Bradley:

> We had already used the Ryman Auditorium before for recordings with Jimmy Sweeney, and Bill decided to put Pat Boone together with a big band, including strings, which was unheard of. When the time came, we were all there and rehearsing and ready, and no Pat.
>
> After an hour and a half he showed up, but he really didn't know the songs. Bill had an expensive orchestra lined up and Bill was mad about it, but he recorded the band anyway. So we made tracks, which was another unheard of thing back then. Later Bill had Pat Boone sing his part over the top. It was the first overdub session I can ever remember. Bill brought Pat into our studio to sing using headphones and to try to put the voice onto the tracks. But they didn't come out very good. That session cost Bill Beasley a lot of money. That set Bill back a lot.

Beasley too remembered the session. "We wired the sound from the auditorium down the WSM link into the Castle studios at the Tulane, where they were put onto acetate discs. We recorded six songs at a time, designed for a 78 album set that was never issued. On that occasion, Pat had not rehearsed the songs properly, which was what made me mad." Beasley may not have issued his album set, but he did use two more tracks from the Ryman session. Unfortunately for Republic, the May 1954 issue of Boone's third Republic disc, "Loving You

Madly," again brought no fanfare. Beasley, who had at first been so impressed he signed Boone to a seven-year personal contract, eventually blamed the failures on an outdated style: "I got him onto the Arthur Godfrey shows in New York, and we all thought he would be big. But I cut him singing Perry Como style, and that style was just going out then."

The Departure of the Bubis Cousins and Howard Allison

Within six months of the launch of Republic, Bill Beasley found himself running the label alone. In March 1953 the original Republic Records Inc. charter was amended and the name changed to the Republic Recording Company, Incorporated. Howard Allison had been drafted, and the Bubis cousins had seen the writing on the wall. They retained their publishing interests but increasingly left Beasley to run the recording business on his own. Alan Bubis later told me that he and his cousin Reynold

> decided to concentrate on developing a chain of liquor stores and on the coin-machine business—we had a company called Reynold Amusements—because the coin-machine business was real good, and we wanted to give it more time. It was far more predictable than the record business. . . . We kept the music publishing arm of the business, BABB Music, because we knew that there was a lot of money in publishing. . . . We had a monthly advance from BMI, going back to a deal in 1950, of about $600 a month as long as we put all our songs with them. That was an income worth keeping going even after we were no longer manufacturing records. Bill Beasley kept the recording end of the label. But the problem was that Reynold and I were running other businesses, and we didn't keep up with the publishing—we didn't keep right on it day by day. We hired a girl, Lee Rosenberg, who worked for us in an office above Al's Liquor store from about 1953 to 1957, but it just went down the tubes gradually, and in the end we let the whole thing go around 1958 or so.

Howard Allison was called up for military service at about the time Tennessee became Republic, and he was out of the music scene from 1953 to 1955. He told me that "things were not going well when I left. There were several lawsuits outstanding, so I gave Bill power of attorney to do whatever he wanted with the company." Allison had been the company's anchorman, the detail person in the Tennessee Records operation, and those familiar with the demise of Beasley's labels agreed that distribution problems dealt the death blow. As Bill Beasley's son Kirk said years later:

> Dad always told me that when Howard was called up for military service in the Korean War, that was what killed Tennessee Records. Howard was the distribution guru, without a doubt. Without him, cash flow [now for Republic] was seriously diminished, according to Dad. He always said that Howard knew more about distributing R&B records and black gospel music than anyone at that time in the U.S. For years, I don't think a single week went by that Howard wasn't in our home, playing bridge or attending some party. It really hurt Dad when he had to leave.

As the hits dried up, so did the payments from distributors, Reynold Bubis explained.

> We had national distribution through independent wholesalers in each town. Our problem was that if you couldn't follow a hit record [with another hit], they didn't pay you. It was as simple as that. That's the record business. If you don't have a lever to get the money, you don't get it. Part of the reason why Tennessee failed was that the independent distributors were more geared up to R&B than country.
>
> We also tried to go into the pop music business through Snooky Lanson. Then we recorded Pat Boone, but we weren't able to do anything with him. Pat was a good singer but not great. It was a combination of the songs and circumstances that made him successful for Dot later on. We recorded good songs with him but had no luck.

Alan Bubis too blamed the hardships of distribution:

> Record distribution was a difficult business back then. When we first went into Coastline, I got quite involved in it as we started doing enough business to get by on. We were selling all the independent labels that were out there. But it was a small-scale business in those days. To do a relatively small amount of business—say ten thousand dollars' worth—you had to pack up just tons and tons of records and ship them by parcel post to get them into the stores. It was quite an operation. That was why we sold our part in Coastline in 1953. We virtually gave it to Hutch Carlock and Jimmy Green, who were the salesmen for the company.

Republic's Blues and Gospel

In December 1952, shortly after Bill Beasley formally became the sole proprietor of Republic, *Billboard* reported: "Republic Records has signed Christine Kittrell, now appearing with Paul Williams." Of Tennessee's blues artists, Beasley brought only Kittrell and Helen Foster to Republic. Kittrell's last record for Tennessee, "You Ain't Nothing but Trouble," a rumba blues with an interesting alto-sax part, had come out in September 1952. *Billboard,* which called Kittrell "the five-foot-six chirp" and "the blues find of the decade," noted that "the thrush will cut 'Gotta Stop Lovin' You' shortly with the Gay Crosse Band."

"Slave to Love" and "Gotta Stop Loving You," the thrush's promised duet with Gay Crosse in February 1953, marked Kittrell's first appearance on Republic. In "Gotta Stop," an attempt to make a pop record with an R&B band, the simple left-hand piano figure behind the vocals and the harmony between Crosse's deep, mannered vocal and Kittrell's own voice could have been made for prime time. Ultimately the song remained R&B because Crosse's Good Humor Six set up a riff from which base John Coltrane takes a considerable bluesy, screaming alto-sax solo. Certainly not pop fare.

Coltrane's contribution on "No Better for You," saxophonist Gay Crosse's first record for Republic, in September 1952, was a great solo amidst a tune kicked forward by the drums and carried along as a Louis Jordanesque shuffle. The lyric is light-hearted Jordan, too, full of advice to people who deserve no better if they can't clearly see all that is happening around them. Crosse's manager, Berle Adams, was also the longtime manager of Louis Jordan and the Tympany Five and named Crosse's band the Good Humor Six.

Born in 1916, Crosse had spent time in Ohio and New Orleans before launching a recording career on a number of West Coast and Chicago labels. When he hit Tennessee, Crosse's Six comprised himself on sax and vocals, a rhythm section of Stash O'Laughlin on piano, Alvin Jackson on bass, Oliver Jackson on drums, and an impressive improv-and-riff section of Tommy Turrentine on trumpet and John Coltrane on tenor and alto sax. Coltrane had recently become unreliable and had just left the Earl Bostic band.

"Easy Rockin'," one of two stand-out instrumentals Crosse recorded for Republic in March 1953, had nothing to do with rock & roll; it was jazz-based mood dance music designed to lead to something physical. The flipside was "G C Rock," a simply wonderful record. The piano work on the first verse, eye-opening enough, gives way to the whole band playing be-bop riffs in harmony. John Coltrane would have been no stranger to Charlie Parker's "Yardbird Suite," on which this recording is strongly based, or to "Ornithology," elements of which are also mixed in here.

Bill Beasley took out a trade advertisement touting Christine Kittrell's second Republic disc, "I'll Help You Baby" and "L&N Special": "Rush your order—20,000 sold first 7 days." On August 8, 1953, the papers listed the disc under "Coming Up Fast." On "L&N Special," Kittrell and Ted Jarrett move into the territory more often occupied by country bluesmen or hillbilly singers, lending their city-blues songwriting talents to a story about leaving on the Louisville and Nashville Railroad.

On "Every Night of the Week," Kittrell employed a band of New Orleans musicians working under the name Guitar Red and the Hot Potatoes. Red was Paul Johnson, and drummer Charles Connor has recalled that, on tour with Shirley and Lee and Smiley Lewis, the band played the New Era in Nashville for a few weeks in the fall of 1953. Ted Jarrett approached Red, who brought trumpeter Milton Battiste into the studio along with Nat Perrilliat on tenor sax. A bass player was drafted from Fisk University, as Connor recalled, and Jarrett played piano. *Billboard* reviewers in October 1953 were right in calling this "smart material and equally impressive chanting, making for a good hunk of wax." On Kittrell's "The Price You Pay for Love," Guitar Red's band appears again, and trade papers listed the disc as a "Best Bet." It was reviewed in March 1954, and the following month Kittrell was listed as one of the female vocalists "who are hitting steadily or rising in recent months."

Kittrell was hot in 1954, and she went on the road as headliner with a touring band led by Bernard Hardison. Issued around October 1954, "Lord Have Mercy" found Kittrell backed by another New Orleans aggregation, augmented by Little Richard and with Charles Connor on drums, Wilbert Smith (working as Lee Diamond) on tenor sax, and Thomas Hartwell on guitar. As Kittrell told me: "Little Richard was on my record of 'Mercy.' You can recognize it immediately because of that piano. We recorded it after hours at the New Era Club." Indeed, "Lord Have Mercy" had the same loose, swinging drive as some of Richard's earlier recordings for Don Robey's Peacock Records, and some of the good-natured, energetic, churchiness too. It opened with some tough, bluesy chords and a storming scattergun piano, leading into a New Orleans-style guitar solo.

"Call His Name," made at the same session, contains thrashing piano from Little Richard, a blasting tenor and a guitar opening straight from the Elmore James songbook. The name Kittrell called was Bobby, her boyfriend, whose other claim to fame was being "the only black policeman in town." He was there at the session, and Christine spoke of the good-natured banter between Bobby and Richard throughout—Richard joked with her about Bobby's appealing ways and joined in on the vocal refrain.

Little Richard Penniman had first worked in Nashville at the New Era and Revillot clubs for spells in 1952 and 1953 without, apparently, making any recordings. He did organize a group while in Nashville and then took the group to record for Peacock Records. He told me about those years:

Gay Crosse and two of the Good Humor Six. Courtesy of Bruce Bastin.

> It was the New Era in Nashville where I met Raymond and Mildred Taylor. They saw me singing there, fooling around on stage, and asked me to join their two-piece group. We formed the Tempo Toppers there. We played all over Nashville and then went to New Orleans and out to Texas. When I left Texas, it was on my own. I joined up with Chuck Connors and Lee Diamond who were working back in Nashville at the Club Revillot. We made about twenty dollars a night, but I remember Nashville because we could make more there. It was a hot scene then.

Richard expanded upon his Nashville days in conversation with Michael Gray:

That's where I really made my one hundred dollars a week at. I didn't make one hundred dollars a week nowhere but there, really. I stayed at the YMCA right across the corner from the Baptist publishing house. Back then the YMCA was like a hotel. It was cheap rent. Me and B. B. King both stayed there. I used to go to a R&B theater called the Bijou a lot. And Grady's blues house I used to go to. Billy Wright would come in from Atlanta. Big Maybelle would be there. Guitar Slim would come in. Big Mama Thornton—Nashville had every blues singer. The Club Revillot would have them one week, and the New Era the next. The local singers were Christine Kittrell and Larry Birdsong, who were personal friends of mine. Ted Jarrett was there.

Before 1954 ended, Kittrell was on the West Coast playing package shows, nightclubs, and ballrooms with the Johnny Otis band. Moving on to Chicago, she still went home to Nashville periodically, recording in both cities and moving from Republic to Chess, Champion, and Vee Jay before joining Federal in Cincinnati. While she was with Vee Jay, in 1962, songwriters Jerry Leiber and Mike Stoller developed a song called "I'm a Woman." Kittrell recorded it before it became a big hit for Peggy Lee and was adamant the song was intended for her.

I weighed around three hundred pounds at that time, and they had seen me perform in California and then in Chicago, and they knew my style. They wanted a big strong woman to fit the song. They wrote that song for me and were going to do a major promotion on it, but it was covered by Peggy Lee and went pop, and that wiped out mine.

In 1968, while entertaining troops in Vietnam, Kittrell was wounded with shrapnel; she never really regained her health, she told me.

When they evacuated me from Vietnam, I had my left leg in a cast, and they sent me to a military hospital near Columbus. I just stopped singing then. I just decided I was tired and I wanted a rest. I intended to take a year off, but I just didn't ever get back to it.

By the 1970s she was working outside the music business in a program for delinquent girls run by the State of Ohio. The last song she recorded was an isolated 1998 recording, "True Love Untold," on Main Street Records in Columbus.

Christine Kittrell's wonderful voice was underrecorded down through the years, and she knew it. She was perhaps Nashville's best and most successful female jazz/blues singer of the 1950s and the most talented of several Nashville-label R&B artists who never achieved what they might have. When she died in Columbus in December 2001, she left a splendid body of recordings in her considerable wake.

Although Kittrell dominated the blues releases on Tennessee and Republic, the labels recorded a number of other artists across quite a wide stylistic range. Local disc jockey George White, who had been on records with Don Q. Pullen, appeared on an R&B item, "My Gal's Got Gold," and Robert Tucker recorded a New Orleans-styled "Changeable Woman." Robert Gill's 1954 recording of "I Gave It All I Had" pointed the way to rock & roll, while Sandra Meade's "Take a Look at Me" had a swampy, Louisiana sound that pre-dated the style Excello Records would perfect in Nashville.

Republic limited its gospel releases to a few main artists, primarily Edna Gallmon Cooke, who made six singles, mainly backed by the Radio Four, and Lucile Barbee. The Smith and Gaston Singers, a female group, made one record for Republic in 1953, and the Trenton Singers, a male vocal group, made two.

Edna Gallmon Cooke, Bill Beasley told me, "was a great seller for us, an exceptional seller for a gospel artist." Her first two singles, "Walk through the Valley" and "Amen," were hits, and Beasley signed her to a personal solo contract in December 1952. Cooke was born in Columbia, South Carolina, in 1918. The daughter of a Baptist teacher, she studied in Washington and Philadelphia while developing a highly personal, sermonizing style, toured the Southeast in the 1940s, and recorded for the DeLuxe, Gospel, and Essex labels, including discs with the Dixie Hummingbirds and the Angelic Gospel Singers. Cooke was an established name when, in Baltimore in 1952, she met Morgan Babb, who persuaded her to record for Beasley.

Babb had brought another gospel singer to Beasley, Lucile (sometimes spelled Lucille) Barbee, who made "Rock Me in His Bosom" as a solo singer with piano accompaniment for Tennessee in 1952. Through 1953 and 1954, Sister Barbee recorded for Republic backed by the Radio Four, a combination Beasley persuaded Babb would achieve better sales than Barbee on her own. "Beautiful Tomorrow" and "A Little More Faith and Grace" sold well locally, and the Radio Four themselves saw four discs released on Republic through 1953 on top of their four on Tennessee.

Lucile Barbee's family moved to Nashville from Alabama when she was a child, and she grew up singing in the choir at the Twelfth Street Tabernacle Baptist Church. She worked in a dress shop in Nashville and also ran a hairdressing business, where she tended to the coiffures of touring black musicians and gospel groups. She herself occasionally toured with an all-female a cappella group, the Golden Echoes, based in Evansville, Indiana. One Sunday in early 1953, she started a radio show on WSOK, *Gospel Train*, which would have a long run—Sister Barbee remained on the show for more than fifty years, mostly on WSOK successor WVOL.

The Israelite Travelers backed up Lucile Barbee on several Republic discs and recorded "It's Alright" in their own name in 1954. A Nashville group since the early 1940s, by 1954 the Travelers included Saunders Cooper, John Phillips, Ben Vaughan, Clarence Mills, and Gene Allison. (Allison would go on to make R&B and soul records for other labels, includ-

Republic envelope, 1954, reflects Nashville's diverse music with two gospel singers, two country singers, two big-band singers, a blues diva, and a honky-tonk pianist. Courtesy of Colin Escott.

Jimmy Simpson. Courtesy of Country Music Hall of Fame and Museum.

ing the late-1957 Top Forty hit "You Can Make It If You Try," written and produced by Ted Jarrett and licensed to Chicago's Vee-Jay Records.)

Republic's only white gospel artist, J. T. Adams, was a minister and choir director based in Sulphur Springs, Texas. Atypically for Beasley, who normally recorded everything himself, he leased Adams's Texas-made recordings; he liked Adams's country gospel styling, he said, which he proved by issuing eleven Adams singles and an album.

Republic's Country Catalog

Another of Beasley's favorites was Allen Flatt, the Ernest Tubb imitator, who recorded a number of aching tales of domestic discord, among them "Get in or Get out of My Life" and "That's What She Wrote," sounding a little less like Tubb each time. If people wondered about his real voice, they found out when he switched to Mercury that it was in fact better, but it didn't sell any records.

For its country catalog, Republic also nurtured Tennessee Records' relationship with Chester Studdard, one-time Ernest Tubb sideman and promoter from Alabama. Among the performers whom Studdard connected with the label, the most likely to succeed was Lee Bonds, from Gadsden, Alabama, who had a regular spot on *Midway Jamboree,* which Studdard organized for WGWD. At the end of 1951, Bonds's first session with Tennessee Records yielded "Uh Huh Honey," a minor hit, and for Republic he made "Wild Cattin' Woman" in 1952 and "Give My Broken Heart a Break " in 1953. Another of Studdard's Gadsden-area acts, Sonny Sims, recorded "Walk Off and Leave It" and "Two Kinds of Women" for Republic; Sims also sang in a gospel quartet and as a duet with Lee Bonds on Republic.

The Gadsden connection also supplied Republic with the Smiley Wilson and Kitty Carson duo, who were playing in western bands in Alabama when they married in 1942. They joined the *Louisiana Hayride* in 1949, appeared in the movie *Square Dance Jubilee* with a who's who of West Coast country stars, and played at the WSM Grand Ole Opry in 1950 and then the *Midway Jamboree* in Gadsden. After making some discs for Apollo Records, Smiley and Kitty moved to Republic, recording "I've Found My Own" in October 1953 in Nashville with Beasley's session crew.

Apart from the Gadsden connection, Beasley found plenty of country talent to keep his label ticking, but no one to break out beyond average sales. Jimmy D. Simpson, who made some memorable country records, was an intriguing character whose songs are full of roughnecks, riggers, pipeliners, and sourdoughs, and tell the story of his long, eventful life. He was born in 1928, in Sullivan Hollow, near Ashland City, Tennessee, and, as he told Colin Escott:

> We lived back in the country quite a ways. We had an old battery-powered radio, and you had to get it to town to get it charged up. Nashville was only forty miles away, but I remember my cousin coming by the

house saying, "I'm gonna leave Tennessee. I'm going to Nashville."

Simpson quit school at fourteen, then hitchhiked and hopped trains as far as Lafayette, Louisiana, and Houston. He joined the army, then the navy, and was discharged in 1950 to his wife Marcene's hometown, near San Angelo, Texas, where his performing career began there: He appeared on the *Big D Jamboree* in Dallas and the *West Texas Roundup* in San Angelo. By 1953, Simpson was in Nashville, where he

> asked people where the recording companies were. I talked to someone at the Castle studio, and he said I should go see Bill Beasley. Beasley was in the shipping department. I brought my guitar in, sang for him, and he said, "When can you record?" Two days later I recorded. Cedric Rainwater was on the bass and Mitch Neely was on the fiddle.

Simpson cataloged some of his travels in his compelling number "Ramblin' Blues" and also wrought from personal experience "Oilfield Blues," a wonderfully detailed piece. He returned to Nashville in February 1954 to record his third and last Republic single, "Did We Overlook Each Other." In 1957, unable and unwilling to make the switch to rock & roll, he went to Alaska as a contractor, construction worker, and disc jockey. A trip to California in 1959 resulted in a brief appearance in the 1960 film *The Alamo*. In 1960, he recorded for Starday Records. Then it was back north, where Simpson worked in construction, prospected for gold, disc-jockeyed, and found time to make records on his own labels and write his autobiography, *A Vanishing Breed: The Gold Miner.*

In February 1954, *Pickin' and Singin' News* carried a story about a Republic recording session featuring Larry Dexter that described the role of Bill Beasley as label owner and record producer, or "operator" as he was termed, and the role of the session musicians: Dick Stratton on bass, Mitch Neely and Paul Neely on fiddle and guitar, Bob Foster on steel, and Papa John Gordy on piano. Interestingly, in view of the label's history, the story made much of the paperwork involved in filing the session with the union. The writer described Republic's control room as "a baffling collection of amplifiers, knobs, handles, buttons and wires, reminiscent of both a broadcasting booth and the cockpit of a B-29 bomber." *Pickin' and Singin's* interest in Dexter wasn't entirely altruistic; its proprietor managed him.

Larry Dexter came and went in a brief blaze of publicity to coincide with Republic's release of his first record, "Throwing Kisses." A twenty-six-year-old salesman from Salisbury, Missouri, he came to Nashville to seek his musical fortune and was snapped up by Bill Beasley after a fifteen-minute audition. The result is a bright outing that fit right in with the styles of a younger wave of country singers who were starting to sell in 1954—Marty Robbins, Carl Smith, Ray Price and others. Dexter's singing career was short-lived, but he remained with Beasley as a salesman into the 1960s.

Around this time, Republic also dabbled in a little political comment via the Kavaliers, whoever they were, who told U.S. Senator Joseph McCarthy to "Get That Communist, Joe." Then bass player Buddy Killen recorded a disc about the exploits of a politician, "Big Jim," possibly a reference to two-term Alabama governor Big Jim Folsom, but Killen never knew:

> The first session I made was with Jim Eanes on Decca. Then Bill Beasley asked me to play sessions at a funky little studio he had down off of Eighth on Allison. One time, he had a song and needed a singer so he asked me to sing on "Big Jim." I never even knew who Jim was. I sang the song and got in the car to go out on the road playing with George Morgan. The guys in the band were jealous and I promised to include them next time.

Killen would become a major player in Nashville with Tree music publishing and the 1960s Dial record label, which specialized in R&B and soul music.

The man who should have been the real contender on Republic toward the end was the wonderful country singer Tommy Smith, Nashville's singing barber (although Red Wortham recalls that he came from Atlanta); many country stars of the day had their hair cut at his barbershop on Seventh Avenue near Broad. Smith had first appeared on a

Front cover from the Republic sales catalog. Courtesy of the author.

short-lived label Beasley started in 1954, Tennessee Jamboree, covering the popular Mitchell Torok hit "Mexico." Beasley apparently thought better of reviving the Tennessee and Jamboree names, and switched Smith to Republic later that year.

Smith recorded the classy "Magic Girl" on Republic in December 1954 in the style that Marty Robbins would perfect, and he had much of Robbins's breezy self-assurance. Smith went on to write several songs recorded by other artists, and in 1956 he picked up a Memphis band that included Ray and Damon Saxton, who had offered Elvis Presley his first paying job, along with Reggie Young, who would become one of the best session guitarists of any generation or any style of music.

Bill Beasley's Solo Year

In January and February 1954, attorney Jordan Stokes factored the sale of the Bubises' now dormant interest in Republic to Bill Beasley, revoking the company charter and reinstating it. Beasley moved Republic Records and its American Distributing Company subsidiary across to 714 Allison Place on the corner of Eighth Avenue South. There he rented a building from the Teamsters, Chauffeurs, and Taxi Drivers Union; the deal was brokered by Louis Primm, Beasley's stepfather, known to everyone as "Buck," who was a captain in the Nashville Fire Department and occasional investor in Beasley's various enterprises. Beasley's son and Primm's grandson Kirk Beasley remembered: "Louis was a fair carpenter, and he built the baffles and so on for a number of studios Dad owned."

At this time, Beasley also started to diversify his business interests. He established Oakwood Music and other new song-publishing businesses; he briefly went into artist promotion and management with W. J. Neese, promoting Larry Dexter and Tommy Smith and yet another piano stylist, Bob Harmon; and he opened a record shop, Central Records, at 517 Union Avenue. In the Arcade, a covered pedestrian mall between Third and Fourth Avenues North, the shop was owned in part by Louis Primm. "I think my grandparents worked there and ran it for Dad with some help from Howard Allison and Ted Jarrett," said Kirk. "Dad always liked to have his hand in a number of things at one time—perhaps from necessity." It is not clear for how long Beasley controlled Central Records, but Howard Allison listed it as his place of business in 1955 after he returned from military service. Beasley also had a part with Red Wortham and disc jockey Noel Ball in a new Eagle Recording Studio (perhaps named for the Republic logo) at 232 Fourth Avenue North downtown.

Beasley was a busy man in 1954, trying to juggle his various recording, publishing, and record-distribution roles. He recorded some of his best music that year, and through artists like Christine Kittrell, Pat Boone, Edna Gallmon Cooke, Lee Bonds, and Tommy Smith he had the potential to develop a highly successful label. But the hits wouldn't come, and the next year Jordan Stokes was drawing up another set of legal papers, selling the controlling interest in Republic to Murray Nash, formerly a recording and publishing executive with Mercury Records and Acuff-Rose.

When Beasley finally had to give up on Republic, sometime in the summer of 1955, singer Jimmy Simpson later told Colin Escott:

> Bill Beasley's secretary was good friends of ours, and she called my wife to say there was some money owing, something like eighteen hundred dollars, but she said to be quick, 'cause he was fixing to go broke. I went down to see Beasley, busted into his office. I said, "Bill, I understand you're fixing to file for bankruptcy, and I understand I've got some money coming. I sure would like to get it." He laughed and said, "Jim, you're just a little late. I filed for bankruptcy this morning." I picked him up by the collar and shook him a little bit, said something to him. He said, "Nobody talks to me like that." I said, "Well, I just did."
>
> I had a '52 Cadillac, and I went and backed it into the shipping department, and there was a colored guy standing around there. I said, "You're gonna help me load my car up with my 45s." I sold those records over the years and got some of what was owed to me.

Murray Nash Associates

When Republic Records became the property of Murray Nash Associates (MNA), it was housed in the Cumberland Masonic Lodge Building next to the Clarkston Hotel on Seventh Avenue North. Although Nash took some recordings from the Eagle studio—now in the hands of Red Wortham—he soon developed his own recording studio in the basement of the Cumberland building. He had made a deal that kept Bill Beasley around, but not for long, because, Nash said:

> Bill Beasley was terrific on sessions, but you just couldn't get along with him. He was quite respected as a producer; his personal life was a little different matter. When we took over Republic, Murray Nash Associates hired Bill, until we had to fire him. Bill went on the road promoting discs towards the end, and we started getting a string of calls where he had been handing out fifteen hundred dollars' worth of hot checks. That was when MNA bought the Republic label, lock, stock, and barrel.

Robert Murray Nash's Australian father attended Bible college in Chicago and moved around as a minister; Nash was born in Campbell, Nebraska, and the family eventually settled in Gallatin, Tennessee, in the 1930s, where Nash learned to play bass and trumpet at school. He went to Knoxville in 1936 to study mechanical engineering but gave up his studies and talked his way into an odd-jobs role at C. M. McClung's, a major Knoxville department store and wholesale operation.

> I started out running the elevator, then helped with filling orders. The company was building up its wholesale business, and in 1939 they wanted me to set up a record department to help fulfill their deal with RCA. There was a big push by RCA to sell record-playing equipment for home use again. In the Depression, it had gone out. The record business had been forgotten for a number of years. McClung's went into records because RCA wouldn't give them the line of musical players without it. We would build up the number of retail outlets right across Tennessee and parts of Kentucky and Virginia. I saw it as part of the job to help the retailers set up. For example, Harvey's department store was starting in Nashville, and I sold Fred Harvey the idea of incorporating a record department.
>
> The people at RCA were impressed with our start-up packs. I had five handmade books we gave our salesmen and showed the retailers: One said how to build the physical space, another showed how to order stock, another covered inventory, and so on. In 1941 or thereabouts RCA told us we were the number-one distributor, with an unheard of number of sales for our area.

Murray Nash, *left*, and Fred Rose at work, 1954, magazine clipping. Courtesy of Colin Escott.

After a stint in the air force between 1942 and 1945, Nash went back to the record wholesale business in Knoxville, working for RCA as well as McClung's. "Later on, I started being involved in helping make acetates to send to Steve Sholes at RCA for their approval. Steve would tell us what he liked and we would then go to Chicago to record."

In 1948, Nash joined the Mercury label, where he got interested in producing records and was responsible for developing the careers of Flatt and Scruggs and other traditional hillbilly and folk artists—almost as many passed through Knoxville as Nashville. "I was my own boss at Mercury as far as what was recorded. But then Irv Green wanted me to move to New Orleans. They thought New Orleans was going to be the center of recording in the South." Nash and his family

Republic logo, 78 rpm version, in late 1955. Courtesy of Bear Family Records.

didn't want to go, and he instead joined Acuff-Rose to work in publishing in Nashville, where he appointed himself an ideas man; he said he helped set up the first disc-jockey conventions in Nashville in the early 1950s.

Another of Nash's ideas was Murray Nash Associates, a promotion, advertising, and publishing firm that also cut records. They recorded as independent producers for London, Atlantic, and Mercury Records and had plans to expand the Republic label, as Nash explained:

> When I parted from Acuff-Rose, [there was] this writer that I had been working with quite a bit, Ray Scrivener. . . . He was not the usual country writer, in that he had been more or less a pop musician years before. Well, Ray came to Nashville and wanted to back me going into the record business. He had a friend in Kentucky, Charles Bingham, that would put the money up, so I was led to believe. We split the stock in the company between the three of us, and my stock was to be the services that I performed as manager of the operation.

Scrivener was from Berea, Kentucky, where he had played in the high school band with singer Red Foley, one of several contacts in Nashville who enabled him to dabble in songwriting. He met Nash at Acuff-Rose when Fred Rose took some of his songs to be recorded, but his main business was in garage and service-station equipment. Bingham knew nothing at all about the music business. As it would turn out, Nash had not made the best of business decisions.

Murray Nash put the Eagle logo up front on the label design of his Republic discs, and for a while the post-Beasley Republic label appeared to work well. The first thing Nash did in the fall of 1955 was to re-release two of Pat Boone's Republic flipsides, "My Heart Belongs to You" and "I Need Someone," to cash in on Boone's sudden success with Dot Records. Nash next embraced the folksier end of country music with Red Kirk and the Kelleys. He also issued at least thirteen extended play discs and five LPs, mostly reissues of Del Wood material, but also EPs by Edna Gallmon Cooke and J. T. Adams, as well as "Martin and Brown, Harmonica."

For a moment, Nash and Republic seemed about to plunge headlong into the new rockabilly end of the market. In December 1955, Glenn Reeves recorded "That'll Be Love," with its distinct rock & roll feel. He also made the original demo of "Heartbreak Hotel," which was cowritten by his steel-guitar player, Tommy Durden, and songwriter Mae Axton, who had brought Reeves to Republic. Reeves was born in 1932 in Shamrock, Texas, and made his first records there for the TNT label. After Republic, he recorded for Atlantic and Decca but, as he later told Colin Escott, after several years in Nashville, "I realized I could make more money selling pencils on the street corner in Florida than I could singing in Nashville." He went to Florida and started a country music TV show that was networked in the Southeast.

Republic issued the last offerings by country stalwart Billy Wallace as well as by Christine Kittrell. Released at the end of 1955, Kittrell's "If You Ain't Sure" has a more prominent guitar and a much more professional, less funky sound than her earlier sessions. Kittrell had gone north to work with Memphis Slim in Chicago, and her flipside, "Black Cat Crossed My Trail" is a song associated with Slim; the disc was made either in Chicago or in Nash's Cumberland studio.

In January 1956, picking up the rock & roll theme, Jim Lucas cut a cover of "Tutti Frutti" on Republic, aiming to take a few sales away from Little Richard and Pat Boone. Shortly after, taking on the new rockabilly style out of Memphis, Lloyd McCullough recorded "Cause I Love You," and Lou Millet covered Eddie Bond's Decca recording of "Slip Slip Slippin' In."

Before it was possible to tell whether rock & roll could come to the fore on a Nashville indie label, the roof fell in on Republic's finances. As Nash said later:

> My partners didn't come up with the payments, and during the third year I even mortgaged my home. At MNA, we had three contracts: with London Records for thirty discs a year for their Felsted label; thirty for Atlantic; and a number for Mercury. But we needed the funds. The other two felt they could go on with it without me. Scrivener thought that he had learned enough to run it.

But all three contracts were cancelled because I wasn't there, and I was the one who knew about recording.

Without either Bill Beasley or Murray Nash, the label folded; its charter was revoked on May 25, 1956. Vee-Jay Records bought the contracts of some Republic blues artists, Nash himself bought some country masters, and others were simply never claimed. The presses were sold to Chess.

Ray Scrivener eventually sold the Republic name, but not the stock, to actor and singer Gene Autry and helped to launch Autry's new Republic label from Hollywood. Autry cut some good West Coast country artists, including Johnny Bond and Joe Maphis, and the Scrivener connection produced a few Tennessee recordings. One of these was by disc jockey Bob Jennings, singing "That's What Children Are For," an early Willie Nelson song produced by Red Wortham. In its new guise, Republic had some fifty releases in the early 1960s.

After MNA, Murray Nash formed Recording of Nashville and By Nash of Nashville, and developed an interest in all kinds of promotional and music publishing activities.

I had a studio on Third Avenue, and I did promotional work for WSM and articles for trade papers and so on. Then I moved to 1717 Division Street, the first publisher to move to the Music Row area—we did our recording at Bradley's studio then.

Nash recorded a number of artists, including Jean Chapel, a songwriter he had known at Acuff-Rose, whose "Welcome to the Club" was leased to Sun Records in Memphis as part of a recording deal that never quite took off.

Nash recognized that he was good at coming up with ideas and setting up things for other people to take forward without him. Brad McCuen, who worked with Nash at RCA, described him as "unlucky beyond words. He was a tremendous record man because he knew a good record. But Murray was also very opinionated." Eventually, Nash gave up music altogether and worked for many years at the U.S. Post Office in Nashville.

"Too Much"

In 1957 Bill Beasley and the Bubis cousins became embroiled in one of the more confusing of the many legal wrangles over hit songs out of Nashville. Early in 1955, Beasley had recorded Bernard Hardison for Republic, backed by Louis Brooks's R&B band, singing one of Beasley's own songs, "Too Much." Issued in April 1955, "Too Much" had a catchy choral refrain as well as Hardison's lead vocal, an unusual stop-time arrangement, and a wailing tenor-sax solo by Brooks. It is a genuine, solid-gold collector's item, the original version of the song Elvis Presley took to #1 in 1957.

Republic 7111, a record that triggered lawsuits. Courtesy of John Broven.

Presley came by the song via a complicated route, and when he recorded it the songwriters credited were Lee Rosenberg and Bernie Weinman. But Bill Beasley knew different.

I wrote that song with my wife. We cut it on Allison Street in my studio off Eighth Avenue South where we had an office, a little studio and a warehouse. . . . I put the session together directly with Bernard Hardison, because Ted Jarrett had moved on to work with other labels by then. Bernard played piano and sang and Louis Brooks organized the band. I had written the melody and Jean [Norris] wrote the lyrics.

Beasley published the song through Oakwood Music, the Nashville company he formed with Bernard Weinman, a part-time writer and publisher whose day job with May Hosiery had brought him into contact with Jean Beasley when she was working at Goldring's and Burke's Clothing downtown. Together, the three friends figured out how Beasley could get his money from songs he had written without this income coming to the attention of major labels like Decca with whom he was in dispute. (They even placed some of his songs with Decca, including "If I'm Called To Testify" and "Confessing My Heart" recorded by popular local singer Joan Hager.) The deal was that the Beasleys would write songs under the names of Norris and Richards—Jean's maiden name and that of her best friend, Katy Richards. Sometimes the half belonging to Norris or Richards would be published in the name of either

Bernie Weinman or Lee Rosenberg, BABB Music's and Bill Beasley's secretary, a ploy that obscured the Beasley connection completely; the Beasleys would nevertheless receive the songwriter's fee through Oakwood. Weinman would get half the publishing income, with Bill Beasley receiving the other half.

This strategy worked until the day in 1956 when Weinman pitched "Too Much" to Elvis Presley Music and supplied the writers' names as Weinman and Rosenberg. Although the original Republic recording of "Too Much" was credited on the disc to writers Weinman and Norris, Bernie Weinman and Lee Rosenberg had subsequently cut Beasley (as Norris) out of the deal. When Presley's disc hit the market, Beasley was in Texas; he immediately took legal action against Weinman but failed to prove his case because, he told me, his lawyers were outgunned.

> Bernie was laying on the couch in our house when Jean and I wrote the song. He had some kind of sickness and was resting up. He saw us write it. Later on he said he wrote it, but he didn't write any of it. Then he said we sold it to him, but we didn't. We had big attorneys on that one, but theirs were bigger still. Bernie and I were real good friends, but someone who's your friend for a thousand dollars isn't always your friend for ten thousand.

Beasley was not the only litigant in the case, which becomes more complicated with Alan Bubis's telling:

> Part of the deal when Reynold and I left Republic was that we kept BABB Music and also that Bill was to give us publishing on any song he wrote himself. Well, somehow Lee Rosenberg and Bernie Weinman ended up with publishing "Too Much," and Bill sued them to get it back. But of course we were supposed to have had the publishing from Bill anyway, so we sued too. There was a three-way legal suit on that.

Neither Beasley nor the Bubises succeeded with their cases, being unable to unravel clearly enough for the court their tangled web of publishing agreements. Weinman argued that Beasley had sold him the song. It was a reverse that irked Beasley all his life.

The Beasley and Bubis Racking Business

When Republic folded in 1956, Bill Beasley was working in Memphis with Buster Williams's Music Sales company and Lester Bihari's Meteor Records. By 1957, he had moved on to Texas, but he returned to Nashville in 1959, and he and Alan Bubis continued to feature on the Nashville recording scene well into the 1970s with the same independent spirit they brought to Tennessee and Republic. Beasley arrived back in Nashville with an idea that had been perking since Republic folded:

> I could see it coming, the racking business. I wanted to move out of recordings and into rack sales. Murray Nash had wanted the Republic label and had plans to finance it in a big way, but he was never able to do anything, and I could see this whole new business out there.

As Alan Bubis remembered, Beasley

> had the idea to buy up unsold records for two or three cents apiece from distributors—or to pick them out and pay ten cents for really good ones that had been hits or by known names. He would sell them in racks in stores for twenty-two cents, a big reduction from the normal price. We had over ten thousand racks out there at one time, and we couldn't buy enough discs. We bought millions of records from RCA, Columbia, Sun, Imperial. We would just clear their warehouses out. We could turn a huge profit just overnight. That was one of the best businesses we have ever been in.

The enterprise led them to found Record Services Inc. and the 1960s label Hit Records, an operation the *Tennessean* likened to a mockingbird:

Singing like the stars used to be good for laughs at a party—now it's the essence of a big record business that has Music City worried. The Hit label is cleaning up by kidnapping entire tunes and selling them supermarket style at one-third of the going price.

The *Tennessean* reflected the worries of some among Nashville's emerging music establishment, describing Beasley as "less a cool music cat than a copycat" and, somewhat gratuitously, as "a bland looking man with a high forehead and a fast mind."

For Hit, Beasley built a studio in the basement of his house at 3622 West End Avenue and produced union sessions with Harold Bradley and other musicians; Bobby Russell, Buzz Cason, and Connie Landers cultivated their vocal imitations while waiting for their own big break to come. (Russell later wrote several hit songs, including "Honey" and "Little Green Apples.") The Hit operation was not just a success, but fun. Landers remembered the trouble she had being Brenda Lee or Skeeter Davis until she learned to hold her nose while singing. Russell recalled practicing Robert Goulet all night, only to have Beasley require him the next day to be Elvis Presley instead. The Jordanaires were brought in to add authenticity to the session and kept telling Russell that Elvis hadn't had the same trouble with the song they were copying. Russell replied: "Elvis had more than fifteen minutes to learn to be Elvis."

Beasley and Bubis had just as much fun on another label they had formed in the wake of Hit Records—Spar, for which Beasley recorded himself as "the Tiger," who narrates a comedy record called "I Play Guitar, Too." Spoofing the payola scandals, the Tiger makes an acceptance speech for an award, relating his rise to the top and listing all the people his managers had paid off along the way. Beasley formed several cut-price album labels, too, and Jean Norris was the featured artist "Katy Richards" on a number of albums. Jean had quit singing when her two sons were born, but she was soon spending time working up demo versions of songs for Hit and Spar. Growing up in a house always full of singers and writers, their son Kirk admitted to me once that he "was in grade school before I realized that not everyone was in the music business." Kirk remembered a surf LP with an evocative Californian cover shot that Bill Beasley took with his own camera at Nashville's Centennial Park, and Beasley recalled a hardware dealer in Texas who sold so many records that Beasley put his name down as the artist on a disc: "The guy was mobbed by fans."

Hit Records was a profitable scam for many years, and the sound-alike idea expanded not only with Spar, but also with the Modern Sounds and Songs of Faith labels. However, a move into eight-track tapes proved less successful. In a repeat of the Tennessee Records pattern, the Beasley-Bubis partnership sailed into uncharted waters, and when they persuaded Howard Allison to join them in a new distribution company, National Music Sales, they overstretched. The distribution company failed, and Beasley and Allison fell out over it. Beasley and Bubis struggled on until 1973, though as late as 1976 the Small Business Administration filed suit in district court to recover a quarter of a million dollars due them from William and Dorothy Beasley and Alan and Harriett Bubis.

Around 1974, Beasley gave up on the music business in Nashville and went to run a restaurant in Gatlinburg. Alan Bubis went back to his liquor and real estate businesses along with his cousin Reynold. On and off through the fifties and into the sixties, Alan Bubis had continued to run other record labels, such as Calvert and Champion, working mainly in R&B and the emerging soul field, and often with the day-to-day direction of Ted Jarrett. These labels continued to give an outlet to the best of the local black groups, singers, and bands. Jarrett then formed several labels of his own. At this writing he was still at his office producing records and making deals, well past retirement age.

A suave Alan Bubis, about 1959. Courtesy of Nashville Public Library, the Nashville Room.

Pioneer Bill Beasley's Legacy: Tennessee/Jamboree and Republic

Bill Beasley was rather a persona non grata in his later years, and his pioneering role in the Nashville record business remains very much underacknowledged, his vision in recording an outstanding roster of hillbilly, blues, and even pop talent largely forgotten. But Sam Phillips, a competitor from

Memphis, recalled Beasley's contribution with enthusiasm. "Now, Bill was a really good record man. He had a real fine ear for music. Tennessee was a good label artistically, but their main problem was not what they recorded but money management, which is important when you are an independent outfit." According to Kirk Beasley, his father "liked to characterize Reynold and Alan as 'the money guys' while he was the 'creative force.'"

Beasley's brother-in-law, Bill Norris, confirmed Beasley's approach to life.

> He was an easy-going type of personality, always very optimistic. He always had the idea that he could hang the moon. When he went into something, he always thought he would make a million. If he didn't, he just said, "OK, that didn't work, we'll try something else." He always had his finger in something, and when he was up there he lived high on the hog, big cabin cruiser on the lake, Switzerland for Christmas, that sort of thing.

Others who knew Beasley agreed. Sometime partner Howard Allison: "Bill was creative and had many good ideas when we ran our labels, but the ideas were maybe too large for our company to handle. He was a most likeable person to work with, and we were good friends. Whatever he had, you had. But as a solid businessman, he was not." Musician Buddy Killen: "Bill was always a little bit on the flaky side, the dark side. There was no malice—people just wanted to get paid, that's all." Bandleader Harold Bradley: "Bill was very good to get on with, but the problem is that he was always behind with paying people. He didn't mean to, though, it's just the way he was."

Howard Allison died in Nashville in 1991. Reynold Bubis and Murray Nash both moved to Florida; Reynold died in 1996 and Nash in 2000. Alan Bubis stayed in Nashville and for many years continued to fund occasional recording projects with Ted Jarrett. Bill Beasley died in Arlington, Texas, in 2001.

The Tennessee and Republic enterprises remain overlooked chapters in Nashville's music history. They represent the first sustained attempts to build a large, Nashville-based independent that made Nashville-sounding music in Nashville by performers drawn from the local area. Their story is clouded to some extent by problems with practices designed to minimize tax, copyright, and royalty payments, though this was not uncommon in the independent record business at that time. Bill Beasley's musical acumen can't be denied, though, and the labels appeared in the right place at the right time. And while little made its way outside the South, there was plenty of good music to be heard on Tennessee, Jamboree, and Republic Records, including some recordings of genuine originality and brilliance.

11

Boogie-Woogie Jockeys

If you're ever down in Nashville on a Saturday night
Love to hear the boogie woogie played just right
Why don't you set your dial on your radio
And you'll hear a little jockey getting set to go
He's a real gone guy, he's on the beam
He's a boogie woogie jockey, and they call him Gene.

—"Boogie Woogie Jockey" by Jimmy Sweeney

When radio stations hit the airwaves in the 1920s, their programs cut into the mainstream popular and classical record markets, sending recording companies on scouting expeditions for ethnic music, hillbilly, and blues that would appeal to rural audiences, who often had no electricity, and thus no radios.

No wonder the early record companies and their star performers often supported the view of ASCAP and the AFM that prerecorded music on radio sounded the death-knell for musicians, and record labels frequently bore the legend "Not Licensed for Radio Broadcast"; the companies intended listeners to pay for the music they heard at home or on a jukebox, not to enjoy it free over the airwaves. Most of the Bullet discs up to 1949 carried this antibroadcast caveat, although the courts had ruled in a 1940 test case that such warnings had no standing in law.

This antiradio stance was gradually turned on its head. Capitol Records was the first to establish a radio-promotion team, handing out free records to influential stations, and by the late 1940s all the major labels had leaped on the bandwagon. Even Decca president Jack Kapp, the last holdout, warmed to the notion before his death in 1949.

As Nashville's independent recording business boomed, then, radio and radio disc jockeys boosted its success, not only popularizing new records but eventually selling them on the air via commercials for mail-order establishments like Randy's Record Shop, Ernie's Record Mart, and Louis Buckley's.

Nashville on the Air

In postwar Nashville, as elsewhere, new radio stations went on the air, eager to challenge the three established stations. These were WSM on Seventh Avenue North, founded in 1925 and now the NBC affiliate that aired the Grand Ole Opry; WLAC on Third Avenue, now affiliated with CBS; and WSIX, founded by Louis and Jack Draughon in Springfield, Tennessee, above their 638 Tire Company premises but now located on the fourteenth floor of the Nashville Bank and Trust building in downtown Nashville. The new arrivals included WMAK, on Church and Fourth in the Maxwell House Hotel; WSOK, first on Fourth Avenue North and after 1955 on Davidson in East Nashville; and WKDA, on Union Street.

WMAK's first program director, H. Calvin "Cal" Young, former Georgia disc jockey, explained that the station, which went on the air in July 1948,

> was conceived in a bomb shelter in London. Ed Kirby from Nashville and Frank Mayborn from Temple, Texas,

Ted Jarrett, musician and song writer, was formerly with the King Perry and Roy Hawkins band. Besides his talent show he doubles as "Uncle Ted" of "Teenie Weenie Time," WSOK's children's show.

Larry Dean Faulkner, program director, was formerly with WERD. Every day at 12:05 "Larry Leaps In" with rhythm and blues records.

Bill Powell is known in many top night spots as emcee and spins the discs daily on the "Bouncing with Billy" show.

George White is a musician, writer, vocalist and a member of leading Nashville orchestras. He is a staff announcer and continuity writer.

Lee (Blabber Mouth) Dorris, night club comedian and emcee is popular for his performances on WSOK's "A Train" and "Red, Hot and Blues."

Spencer Davis, WSOK's "Early Train" conductor, is a local boy who serves as an instructor in agriculture at Tennessee A & I State University.

Charles (Bugs) Scruggs was formerly with WMFS in Chattanooga. He is staff announcer of WSOK and emcees the "Club 1470," the popular show for high school and college students.

Robert Hudson, Jr. is the top newscaster that helps make WSOK a fine station reaching the vast middle Tennessee Negro market.

Charles (Chuck) Gordon hails from Charlotte, N. C. and is quite popular on his religious programs.

WSOK disc jockeys, an impressive lineup of radio talent, c. 1953. Courtesy of Country Music Hall of Fame and Museum.

were there in the services during the war, and they got to talking about their ambitions in radio. When they got back home, they eventually talked me into leaving Griffin, Georgia, to work with them on a new station, WMAK. Then, in 1951, I opened my own first radio station as owner. That was WSOK, which was largely geared to black audiences, because I had seen the success of WLAC in that area.

WSOK was indeed the first station in town to have an all-black format, and in this it followed the model set by WDIA in Memphis. Young's partners in the station were the program director, Larry Dean Faulkner—the disc jockey "long, tall, lean Larry Dean"—and Charles Webster of the National Baptist Sunday School. The December 1950 announcement of the station's premier expressed the hope that its educational and social value to the local black population would equal its commercial possibilities. It operated from studios in the basement of the Negro Masonic building downtown.

WKDA started as a 250-watt independent station in January 1947 under A. G. Beaman and T. B. Baker, former advertising manager of WLAC. WKDA's news editor, Jim McKinney from Virginia, had come to Nashville in 1944 to join WSM. McKinney later got involved in Jamboree Records and managed WMAK's *Hayloft Jamboree*, whose nonunion country artists had been a bone of contention between the AFM and Tennessee Records. (As late as 1956, the argument was still raging, when the AFM blackballed the live *Hayloft Jamboree* show at the War Memorial Auditorium for employing nonunion musicians.)

Of all the stations in town, only WLAC had a 50,000-watt signal that enabled it to match the power and influence of WSM. By 1927, Life & Casualty Insurance Company had bought into an early Nashville radio station, WDAD, and changed the call letters to WLAC; in 1935, Life & Casualty executive J. T. Ward bought the station and left the company to operate it as a stand-alone venture. WLAC, which began small, had moved by the 1940s to the Third National Bank building on Church Street, and with a full orchestra and a bevy of pop singers offered serious competition to WSM. In programming folk and western music by Charlie and Red (Charlie Head and Red Wortham), the Arizona Ranch Riders, and the Rhythm Boys, a vocal trio featuring announcer Paul Oliphant, it also carried as much rural music as WSM, though with a lower national profile.

In 1941, when there was a general frequency shift among radio stations to try to minimize airwave interference, WLAC moved to its famous 1510 slot on the dial. Sam Phillips, who served a radio apprenticeship there in 1945 and 1946, credited WLAC engineer Dave Binns with being at the forefront of radio technology—"a wonderful man, who taught me an awful lot about electronics"—and cited the part played by Charlie Dorris, another respected engineer who spent time as a consultant advising other stations. In 1942, Binns completed WLAC's move to a 50,000-watt transmitter, and for the celebratory broadcast, J. Truman Ward and manager F. C. Sowell lined up Cecil B. DeMille, Glenn Miller, Gene Autry, and the station's Charles Nagy Orchestra.

The Bijou Theater and its neighbor, the black Mason's building that housed Radio WSOK, early 1950s. Courtesy of Country Music Hall of Fame and Museum.

The station blanketed much of the United States at night. Walter D. "D" Kilpatrick, who later opened Capitol Records' first office in Nashville, remembers that while he was in the Pacific during the war, he picked up WLAC "as clear as if it was just down the street." After the war, while WSM still relied heavily on live music—mostly pop and country—WLAC headed off in a new direction: block programming record shows with disc jockeys.

"Most Popular DJ": Gene Nobles

In the 1930s men like Martin Block in New York, who joined WNEW in 1934, challenged the role of the traditional radio announcer, taking an approach radically different from the link-man concept. When Block started the *Make Believe*

Gene Nobles, the nighttime voice of Nashville's music scene. Courtesy of Country Music Hall of Fame and Museum.

Ballroom record show and became a star, others rapidly adopted his cult-of-personality approach—radio's first disc jockeys.

WLAC largely introduced disc jockeys to Nashville. To target both black and white audiences, the station cultivated country singers like Bob Jennings and Jeff Bess as disc jockeys and front men. Beyond the local area, though, WLAC eventually became known principally as a black music station because of its success programming late-night R&B and gospel music sponsored by record distributors. One of the first deejays on the late-night and early morning record shows, covering R&B, gospel, and country, was Herman Grizzard, who had started at WLAC in 1926 as a singer and made his name in sports and particularly baseball commentary.

WLAC's main men behind the microphone were white, but they often talked black, taking their lead from the man whose name became synonymous with selling black music over the radio. As *Variety* magazine commented in a report on R&B programming across the country: "Paradoxically, one of the most potent of the R&B deejays is Gene Nobles, a white jock who operates out of Tennessee. Nobles has developed a nationwide following via his WLAC stanzas."

Nobles, who moved to Nashville in 1944, gave me a rundown of his early radio career:

> I was born in Hot Springs, Arkansas, in 1913 and studied at the University of Arkansas. I worked a little with carnivals and tent shows as a huckster in the summers, and I started to learn how to communicate with people well. So I started in radio in 1935 over KTHS in Hot Springs. The pay there was practically nil, so the next year I moved over to WAPO in Chattanooga, as a junior announcer on a new station just starting out, like me. My very first disc-jockey show was on WAPO. I had an early-morning hillbilly slot, a midday Bing Crosby show, and an afternoon classics program. I also worked at night and just played whatever discs I came across. All this was for $17.50 a week.
>
> WLAC was the first station in Nashville to take up the idea of night-time deejay shows. I started my first show right after the end of the war, in 1945. The other local stations stayed with the national networks at night for some years after I started. My first program on WLAC ran from eleven to midnight but slowly was increased until, in the midfifties, I was spinning hits from ten fifteen until four.

Nobles kicked off the heyday for WLAC's black-music programming one day in 1946, when, as disc jockey Bill "Hoss" Allen told John Landes,

> some students from Fisk or Tennessee State brought some black records up and asked deejay Gene Nobles if he'd play some of their music. He was happy to do it. So he put on some boogie-woogie records, and he got so much mail he continued. And the more he played, the more mail came in from all over the Southeast, Southwest, Deep South—places where we had no idea the station reached.

Not only, as station owner J. T. Ward said, "was no other station covering the South playing R&B late at night like that," but also, influenced by segregation laws, many southern record shops carried no black music. Disc jockey John Richbourg said: "It was the thing to do for any black listener to turn to 1510. We were the only 'power' station playing black music across twenty-eight states on a block basis."

Nobles's play leaned heavily toward boogie and blues. He was regularly voted most popular disc jockey by students at campuses throughout the South, and in the process he managed to sell 1.25 million baby chicks in twenty-two weeks for one sponsor and twelve thousand pairs of bop glasses in one year for another, and to help a local distributor show the nation's biggest percentage increase in beer distribution. Keen on jokes, Nobles liked to employ double entendres; his colleague Hoss Allen recalled Nobles's pitch for the Gruen watches sold by Friedman's Pawn Shop: "Give your wife a good Gruen for Christmas."

Jockeys on WMAK and WKDA

If prerecorded music had almost won the battle over live music on radio by the mid-1940s, you wouldn't know it from spinning the dial in Nashville. WSM programmed live music almost exclusively, and a 1946 *Billboard* survey tabulated just nine disc jockeys in town playing records, most of them on WLAC and WSIX. But the tide was turning.

By August 1949, the *Banner* reported that popular singer "Snooky Lanson—labeled 'King of the Disc Jockeys' by the *Saturday Evening Post*—has his own show on station WSM every morning." Even then, Lanson sang live between records, and it would be some years before Joe Allison and Eddie Hill were running real disc-jockey shows over WSM. Even WSIX, which programmed a wide range of music and entertainment from its base at 315 Union Street, relied more on live gospel and hillbilly music shows than on disc jockeys until Ralph Emery and Noel Ball created names for themselves in the 1950s.

Noel Ball joined WMAK in 1949, often fronting the *Hayloft Jamboree*. Born in Eglin, Nebraska, in 1926, he was an established radio professional by the time he hit Nashville. In the view of music publisher Buddy Killen:

> Noel was always the number-one country deejay in town. He would engineer recording sessions at the radio studios, and he brokered record deals. He was the one who would break a song for you. He was quite a mover and shaker around town.

Ball's powerful, deep radio voice and innovative approach would take him onto WSIX-TV in the mid-1950s and into a number of recording and publishing ventures. He set up record labels of his own and helped other labels channel hit songs from the studio to the charts, including the 1958 pop hit "Oh Julie" by the Crescendos and the 1962 original of the R&B standard "You Better Move On" by Arthur Alexander.

Along with Noel Ball, the star country disc jockeys in town in the 1950s were Hugh Cherry and Joe Allison. Cherry's take on the local radio scene was this:

> Nashville was a highly competitive radio town. It was a good radio town. You had good people here. WSM had an incredibly talented staff. This was a small community—we worked and lived within two blocks of each other; we ate at the same places. There was a camaraderie among the radio people. Then, too, a lot of us drank. I was a boozer; so was Hoss Allen [of WLAC]; so was Joe Allison. I had to smuggle him out of the Maxwell House Hotel in a linen basket one day when I found him passed out.

Hugh Cherry at the WMAK mike. Courtesy of Country Music Hall of Fame and Museum.

Cherry, born in 1922 in Louisville, Kentucky, started in radio at Louisville's WKLO, because, he said, although

> there was no musicianship in my family, . . . I was always interested in music. Back in those days, we were radio buffs. We listened to big bands and all the hillbilly stuff too. In those days you had networks—Mutual, ABC, NBC, and CBS—and so in most cities you had all four stations. WKLO was independent, though. A new independent could end up with a pretty good rating if it was well planned.

He palled up with Pee Wee King and learned about hillbilly music before the war, then joined WKDA in 1948 at King's suggestion, and claims to have hosted "the first hillbilly deejay show on WKDA late in 1948, coming on right after the baseball"—his country shows included *Country Junction* and the *Hayloft Jamboree*.

> Back then, there were no stations based on one music. All the stations played everything, jazz, pop, classical, some country, and gospel, and blues. It was block programming, so long in one style and then the next block in another. They hired me because I had grown up with hillbilly music, but I liked big-band music and small-group jazz the best, and I knew a little about it all.

Cherry's fondness for jazz led to his hosting a jazz program along with his country shows, and he recalled the fun the pop

Joe Allison. Courtesy of Country Music Hall of Fame and Museum.

and country musicians had playing after-hours jazz sessions at the radio station in the late 1940s.

> At WKDA, we signed off the air at one in the morning. Then there would be a jam session. Anita Kerr would play jazz piano—this was before she cornered the market in vocal group back-up on recording sessions—and people like Owen and Harold Bradley, Jack Shook, and Tommy Jackson would join in. They all played popular music by day, backed country singers on the Opry on Saturdays, and played jazz for fun.

In 1952, Cherry joined WMAK in Nashville as program director and in the same year became involved in running the campaign of Oscar Capps to become sheriff: "The *Banner* asked me to do it," he said. "I was a member of the Colemore Club, a political club out on Murfreesboro Road, hanging out with [Mayor] Ben West and Beverley Briley and that crowd. I had a double life, really." Cherry later went on to WLW in Cincinnati, and then spent thirty years in California, mainly on KFOX in Long Beach, supplemented by extensive work in television and journalism.

Hot on Cherry's heels in the Nashville deejay sweepstakes was Joe Allison, born in McKinney, Texas, in 1924 and formerly a disc jockey in San Antonio and Paris, Texas. His recollection is that he was the first jockey brought into Nashville to play country music.

> I came to Nashville in 1949, when Eddy Arnold and Colonel Tom Parker brought me up here to work at WMAK promoting country music. I believe I was one of the first country deejays in town. Hugh Cherry was mainly playing jazz [but also some country] when I arrived, and WSM was largely a big-band pop station with some classical music, apart from the Opry on Saturdays. I had the hottest country music show in town. We started at six in the morning with the real down-home stuff, then we went to mainstream hillbilly songs of the day, then to a final late-morning block that was more urban, more pop, with Red Foley and the like.

Allison was involved in establishing the first disc-jockey convention in Nashville, in 1952, and WSM hired him in 1954 to run *Noontime Neighbors*. At one point in 1955 Allison worked at WLAC-TV, where he hosted the *Mr. Music* and *Uncle Joe* shows. He later became a network television producer, moved to Capitol in California, and then started up Liberty Records' country division there. Allison dabbled in songwriting for a time, and very successfully. In 1955 he wrote Faron Young's #1 country hit "Live Fast, Love Hard, Die Young," and he surpassed this a few years later with "He'll Have to Go," an international hit for Jim Reeves.

On-Air Record Marketing

When deejay Hugh Cherry left Nashville in 1954, he viewed WLAC as the hands-down leader of on-air music sales.

> Radio was dominated by the big commercial concerns, and WSM was mainly a general station, with little country music and not very full of new ideas. Smaller stations like WMAK and WSOK would try to innovate and, like the small record labels, they would serve the country [rural] audiences, black and white. But the real mark in musical terms was made by WLAC with their extensive air-time selling of black music.

WLAC owed this success to deejay Gene Nobles, who had introduced an innovative concept to Nashville radio: selling records by mail order over the air. Louis Buckley of Buckley's Record Shop recalled the moment he got wind of this new marketing device:

> I was listening to WLAC one night when Gene Nobles said if he could get sponsors he would stay on the air midnight to 1 A.M., and I called F. C. Sowell, the station manager, and told him I would be interested in that spot. It didn't cost much then. At first I didn't know what to do with the time because here was a powerful radio station, but I was just geared to selling records here in town. Then one day Gene Nobles said, "Why don't you tell them you'll send them C.O.D.?"

As Buckley recalled for *Billboard*:

> Those were the wheeling-dealing days. I had the 1 A.M. show on WLAC, offering packages of eight discs for $3.74. Well, we weren't prepared for the response. Gene's wife needed a job, so we put her to work filling orders. Then we got some other help. Give Gene Nobles credit for being the brains behind the mail-order record business in Nashville.

Whether or not Nobles owed his success to his use of what Bullet Record's 1947 *Bullet-In* called "slanguage" to spin platters on shows like the *Sterling Dance Hour*, the *Midnight Special*, and *Record Highlights*, something worked. Reporting on the deejay's exploits in 1954 under the headline "Pint-size Nobles Does Job of a Giant," *Billboard* reported in 1954:

> If you're the type to disbelieve the story of the mouse and the lion, you'd hesitate to accept the legends about Gene Nobles. That is, until the night you became part of a vast radio audience having its ear tweaked by this pint-sized WLAC announcer. Then you'd find yourself succumbing like everyone else; you'd be ordering phonograph records, helping make Randy's Record Shop the largest mail-order record house in the world. Little though he is, he packs a wallop.

One of the first to appreciate Nobles's talents was record-dealer Randy Wood from McMinnville, Tennessee. Wood told me in 1974, via his longtime secretary, Polly Mitchener, how he got into the record-selling business:

> I was twenty-six years old and just out of the Air Corps in 1944, and I had a pal who came from Gallatin. We decided to set up a business there with an electrical appliance store. I put up my savings, about $1,700. At the end of 1945, sometime along there, Jim Bulleit and C. V. Hitchcock started a record company in Nashville and contacted all the local traders to see who would buy some records. I decided to take seventy-five discs, just to see how they would go. Well, they went pretty good, mostly on a Saturday when people would come into town and buy extra goods on top of their basic shopping needs. We soon got to know what would sell best of all, and started to carry more and more hillbilly, gospel, and R&B discs, particularly the latter.
>
> The next year, someone suggested to me that I go by the WLAC radio studios to take a look at the way Gene Nobles operated his record show because I might be able to use him to expand my business. As a result, I took a one-minute spot advertisement in February 1947 that cost me thirty dollars a week. I said I couldn't afford the cost, and the station agreed I could pay after I made some sales. Luckily, the promotion worked so well that before long, during 1947, we remodeled the shop and turned it into Randy's Record Shop, which was geared primarily to selling records by mail through airtime advertising.

Randy's not only advertised deals over the airwaves and took orders for discs or combinations of discs—Randy's Specials—but also peddled their entire catalog, which they mailed out with an order form. As the catalog became a well-known household fixture, Randy Wood developed a national and then an international clientele.

From Randy's Record Catalog for mid-1950, for seventy-nine cents you could order just about any independent label disc or any of the major artists and labels. Through more than a dozen Randy Specials, you could buy five discs for prices ranging from $2.98 to $3.98 and get an Aeropoint needle thrown in free. You could get a pop special called "All Time Favorites" and five "Gospel Specials," including five discs by the Golden Gate Quartet, five by Sister Rosetta Tharpe, five by Mahalia Jackson, and so on. Or you could get seven special deals on boogie and blues; Special #4 included Bullet discs by Cecil Gant, Sherman Williams, Red Miller, and the Big Three Trio, and one disc on Wood's own Randy's label by Richard Armstrong.

Wood soon extended his radio advertising with additional radio slots on WLAC and ads on stations in Gallatin, Memphis, and Chattanooga in Tennessee; Cincinnati, Ohio; Atlanta and Decatur in Georgia; and Tupelo and Jackson in Mississippi. The result, Wood said, was that

Randy's Records warehouse, Christmas Eve, 1948: *rear, center,* Randy Wood; *third from left,* Johnny Maddox; *front, left,* Lois Wood; secretary Polly Mitchener with Santa, aka Stanford Brooks. Courtesy of Johnny Maddox.

Randy's Record Shop's second location, Gallatin, Tennessee, 1952. Courtesy of Sumner County Museum/Allen Haynes Collection.

> we sold records to over half the states in the U.S. By the end of a year of advertising, our record sales had gone up from two hundred a week to about four thousand. Before long, I bought into my own radio station in Gallatin, WHIN.

Billboard reported how Wood's operation and marketing philosophy differed from those of other dealers trying to sell records over the radio:

> Randy thinks that many other record dealers have made mistakes by taking time on a radio station and then not following through with the programming end. Randy makes sure to confer constantly with Gene Nobles, and they both say that lining up a list of platters with sales potential for each show is harder work than the broadcast itself. Shrewd sales packaging has enabled Wood to move a lot of his dead stock, too. For instance, he has set up a special offer of five discs for $2.98 (and two of them dogs).

Billboard also reported that Wood tried out his discs on WHIN in Gallatin, the radio station he partly owned, and that, when he had a new record due out, he usually called several youngsters into his private office to hear the record and comment on it.

One of Randy's employees at the record store, Johnny Maddox, offered some insight into what made Wood tick and what accounted for his success:

> Randy was just a go-getter, a real hard worker. When I worked in the store in the late forties, he would still be personally involved, filling orders himself, packing up discs, and the like. Randy started to get stacks of money through the mail-order business. I remember when he first started it—he would go down to the bank, and because there were so many money orders and it was so bitty, the bank wouldn't take them, refused to tally them up. Well, Randy went right over to another bank, and they were delighted to have his business, and the money just rolled in. That first bank regretted that to the tune of thousands. I mean, he had a tremendous mail-order business going. Soon, he had four or five people just filling those orders. And when his whole business had taken off, he still had a guy back there repairing radios just like at the start.
>
> At first, people in Gallatin didn't take kindly to Randy. There were a few families that had been running business and social matters here for years. They looked down their nose at him. The post office didn't like it because they had to pay for broken records. Randy had a round with them about that. Told them they were insured and they had to pay. But Randy was so very personable that soon he persuaded everyone of what he was doing, and most people then thought he was the most wonderful thing in the world. I later met people from all over the U.S. who only associated Gallatin with Randy's Records.

John Richbourg at the microphone with an influential group of early Nashville country players: *from left*, Marshall Barnes, Zeb Turner, Jabbo Arrington, and Bob Foster. Courtesy of Country Music Hall of Fame and Museum.

Nashville DJs and Payola

Two well-known Nashville deejays, John Richbourg and Bill "Hoss" Allen, got caught up in the payola scandal that swept the nation in the late 1950s, although both felt that the charges against them in fact defined accepted practice among deejays.

From Charleston, South Carolina, John Richbourg had studied theater before moving to New York to appear in stage shows and play character parts in radio soap operas in the 1930s. Back in the South, he joined WTMA in Charleston and then Nashville's WLAC, where he worked as a general announcer rather than a music man. When he left for a three-year stint in the navy, Jim Bulleit and Sam Phillips took over his role. Returning to WLAC in 1947, Richbourg worked both with hillbilly and black music programs and was particularly associated with the *Ernie's Record Parade* show. His heyday as radio personality "John R" came in the 1950s and 1960s, and he threw himself energetically into radio selling, advertising an idiosyncratic line of products from gutted car mufflers that roared to weight-control tablets; he touted the tablets for six months as "Weight-On" and for the next six months as "Weight-Off." He meanwhile moved in and out of the recording business, supervising some sessions for the Cheker and World labels at WLAC studios, and, much later, taking a leading role in his own R&B and soul label Seventy-7 Records.

In 1960, Richbourg was charged with taking money from Nashville's Southern Record Distributors, located at 147 Lafayette. The Federal Trade Commission said he had "misled purchasers into buying the exposed records by advancing their popularity." John R. said at the time: "This doesn't amount to anything. What they refer to was accepted trade practice."

Bill "Hoss" Allen agreed that taking money from record labels to give their discs greater exposure was a common perk of the deejay business, at least until the IRS changed the applicable law in 1958:

> Many record companies would send discs that had not yet been issued, to test them. They'd say, "I'm sending you a dub by somebody new—listen to it or play it on the air and see what happens." Now that was a money challenge. If they said "play it on the air," you didn't have to ask how much he was sending. There was an understanding. It was the customary way of doing things. The stations were not paying much, and if you could make it on the side, it suited them. Up to 1958, when the IRS made it illegal, we would declare it on the IRS forms, and they would accept it.

Allen was from Gallatin, where as a child he had learned to like gospel songs from a black housekeeper; he remembered going to the local black church with her. He started in Gallatin radio on WHIN, before Randy Wood bought in, with a black music program called the *Harlem Hop*, playing Count Basie, along with some blues and gospel music. In the late 1930s, he got his first taste of jazz at Buckley's jukebox warehouse, listening to Andy Kirk, Chick Webb, Jimmie Lunceford, and other big bands. "I wanted to be a big-band drummer," he once said.

Instead, he went into the army and played drums in Special Services during the war, and then to Vanderbilt and into theater work. He started at WHIN as a sideline and arrived at WLAC in 1949. By the time Allen joined the on-air staff, black music dominated WLAC's evening hours. Allen took to selling over the radio as well as he did to black music. Along with other WLAC jocks, he advertised baby chicks every November; he sold Bibles, and he promoted Royal Crown hairdressing and the Silky Straight hair treatment.

As for the payola scandal, deejay Hugh Cherry shared Richbourg's and Allen's opinion regarding the relationship between deejays and record labels; he said he too took gifts—but not money—from record companies.

> I benefited from payola, but I never charged anybody to play records. They gave me things. The first TV set I had was payola. I would play the Perry Como golf tournament every year and Randy Wood would buy the airline ticket. Jimmie Davis would come to meet me and shake hands and in his hand would be money to play his records. What am I going to do? Turn down the governor of Louisiana? That's the way it was in those days.

Randy's Records

Randy Wood's entry into the independent recording field was gradual and inauspicious, considering where that road would finally take him. He remembered that around 1949,

> one time when I was visiting Gene Nobles at his studio, he said that I should go with him to see one of the other WLAC employees, a black fellow named Richard Armstrong who had composed two tunes for Gene. It was put to me by Gene that we should record those songs, "Gene Nobles Boogie" and "Gene Nobles Blues," and put them out on disc as Gene's theme tunes. So we put the songs out on a label that we called Randy's Records. That was the start of my involvement in the record business.

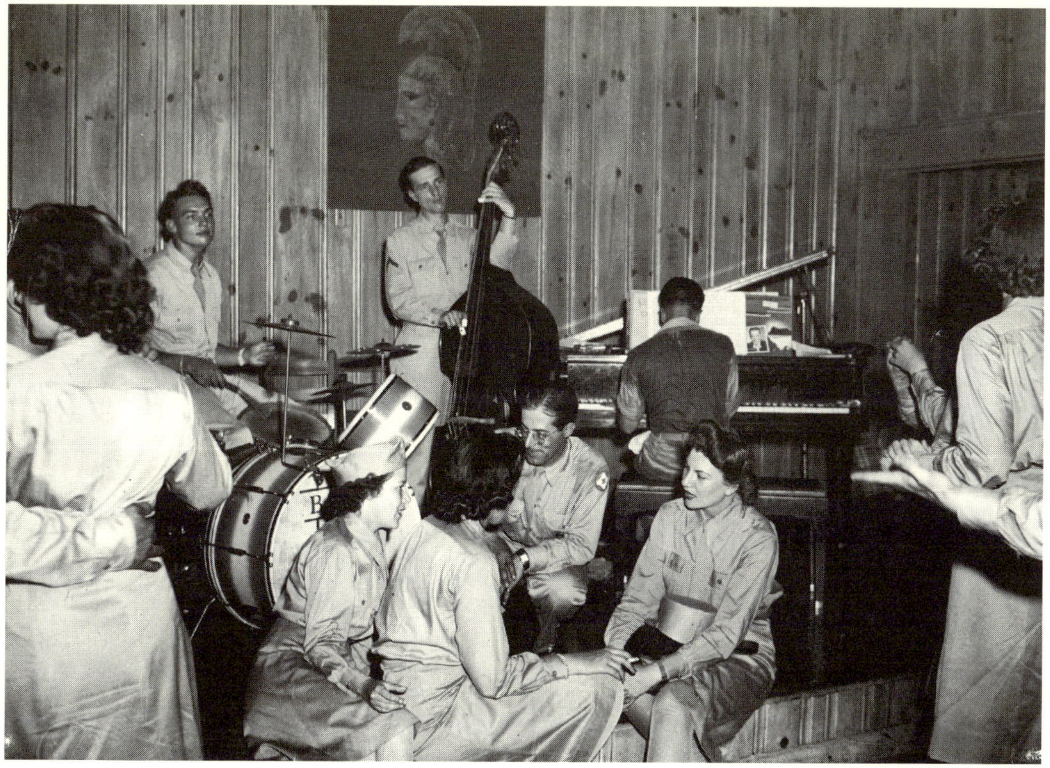

A young William "Hoss" Allen as a jazz drummer, early 1940s. Courtesy of family of Hoss Allen and the Country Music Hall of Fame and Museum.

The tunes' composer, Richard Armstrong, was a friend of Tom "Shy Guy" Douglas and in the band that recorded with Douglas on Delta/MGM in 1949; a pianist, he also went with Douglas to Memphis to record for Sun in 1953 (unissued at the time).

The Armstrong tunes about Nobles were not in fact newly recorded for the Randy's Records label, and what Nobles actually pitched to Wood was the idea to reissue the cuts already made for Cheker by Maurice Likens. Interestingly, the issue number, 104, was the same on both labels, even though Randy's 104 appears to have been the first disc on the label. Apart from that disc, Randy's issued two brief series of gospel recordings. One featured singer and guitarist

Sister Alexie Barney, following the style of the popular Sister Rosetta Tharpe, and the other series contained recordings by the United Spiritual Singers, the Sincere Singers, and the Five Blind Boys. This series was manufactured for Randy Wood's mail order catalog by agreement with Palda Records of Philadelphia, owned by Dave Miller, who would soon discover and record Bill Haley. Randy Wood had seen enough of the record-manufacturing side of things to realize in the fall of 1949 that his future might lie in the record business. He may have bought out the Cheker and World labels' stock at this time, and he definitely had a part in a label called Raba, according to Hoss Allen who told researcher John Broven:

> Randy and I, in Gallatin, started a little label, R. A. for Randy and B. A. for Bill Allen, Raba. I cut some [records] out at Tennessee State University where they had the Tennessee State Collegians, this great dance band. It was a big seventeen-, eighteen-piece band that was a cross between Count Basie and Jimmie Lunceford, who had started his band at Fisk, and it had a lot of individual good jazz players—and so this is what I wanted to record. I mean, I was bugging [Randy] all the time after I met him. We cut a couple of sessions; nothing really happened.

These were mere diversions, though, and in October 1949 Wood launched a new label, Dot Records, based in Gallatin alongside his mail-order operation. Soon, Nashville's radio stations and disc jockeys would be able to take some credit for creating the climate that enabled Dot and several new Nashville labels, including Nashboro and Excello, to develop as offshoots of companies that marketed records via the airwaves into highly successful independent record companies.

12

Dot Records: Raising the Standard

I know what I like. It's the sound I'm interested in. I like nothing better than to go into a studio and come out three hours later with a song a million people will pay a dollar for.

—Randy Wood

Dot Records and Tennessee Records, under way within weeks of each other in the early 1950s, took entirely different trajectories: Ten years later, nearly every record buyer in the United States owned a Dot record, and Tennessee and its successor, Republic, were all but forgotten. Ironically, Pat Boone, an artist who struggled and failed on Republic, made Dot Records into a major name.

Jim Bulleit, in at Dot's beginnings, recalled a meeting at his Ash Street offices in 1949:

> Randy Wood came to see me, together with some people from WLAC, and they asked me what was involved in setting up a record label. We sat around for a while and dreamed up this scheme for the business that eventually became Dot, though at the time Randy used other names like "Randy's." I told him that he had to have a name that was short and simple in order to stick in the minds of the distributors and deejays.
>
> I set up Randy's initial distribution system for him, working with Howard Allison. When Randy got going a little, he wanted to be less reliant on WLAC for recording, and to be able to test out performers for himself. So I put him in touch with Ivin Ballen of Gotham Records, who had a Magnecord tape machine for sale, and Dot Records was off and running on its own.

When he settled on the Dot name, Randy Wood probably didn't know that there had been other Dot labels. Two were listed in *Billboard* as late as 1948 and 1949, one in Federalsburg, Maryland, and another in Shaker Heights, Ohio.

Early Days at Dot

Wood's Dot Records was formally incorporated on April 12, 1950, with $10,000 capital stock in the names of Randolph Wood, Lois Wood, and Willis Lowery Jr. (a trumpet player with a local Gallatin dance band, the Rhythm Masters). Nashville lawyer Jordan Stokes handled the incorporation papers, and Bullet Plastics made the first Dot pressings. At the same time, Wood formed the Dot Publishing Company, although it was not chartered formally until October 1951, when it was registered in the names of Randolph Wood, Gilbert Brown, and Jordan Stokes.

Dot was not a Nashville label, despite Wood's ties to WLAC, Nashville publishers, and Nashville musicians and songwriters. Gallatin is thirty miles northeast of Nashville, and its identity was more distinct in the early 1950s, before the Nashville metropolitan area expanded to embrace much of middle Tennessee. Pianist Johnny Maddox said that

> Randy never saw himself as part of the Nashville scene, even though Nashville people come from here [Gallatin]. Bill "Hoss" Allen was from here, and Murray Nash, and Beasley Smith's family. And Francis Craig lived here as a teenager. But Nashville was the big city compared to here.

Nevertheless, Dot drew initially on the same talent pool the Nashville labels dipped into, although Wood would set a new standard in how to operate an independent record business—in a sense, Dot became everything Bullet and Republic had wanted to be.

Dot's First Discs

That Randy Wood formed Dot mainly so he could produce records to fill Randy's Record Shop's mail-order packs is clear from the sixty discs issued before mid-1951: a few local country artists and a lot of blues and gospel by artists such as the Fairfield Four and Cecil Gant, reissued from other labels.

The very first record, Dot 1000, was "Bluejack Boogie" and "Late Hour Blues" by the Blue Jacks. It hit the stores, or at least Randy's Record Store, at the tail end of 1949. Jim Bulleit said he acquired the recordings and sold them to Wood as a package.

> Randy wanted to get into the record business, but he had no real knowledge of the recording aspect of it. So I set up some deals for him as far as getting records pressed and distributed. I also let him have the recordings for his very first records. But then he soon found his way.

Musically, the first Dot record was odd rather than impressive. It had something of the easy feel of the jug-band era of Southern street blues; however, the piano is to the fore, with churchy undertones, and the vocalist sounds like a gospel singer persuaded to sing some prewar blues.

The second Dot, "Boogie Beat Rag" and "Honest Heart" by George Toon and the Tennessee Drifters, appeared after Christmas and was reviewed in the trade papers in January 1950. It became something of a minor jukebox hit, and its relaxed mix of popular and hillbilly influences set the initial direction for Dot toward the pop market. But it was a local Gallatin boy, Johnny Maddox, who got the Dot label noticed.

Ragtime Pianist Johnny Maddox

Johnny Maddox's discovery is a variation on the classic movie script about the kid down the block who was in the right place at the right time and became a star. Wood didn't even have to look down the street for his star; Maddox worked right there at his record store.

A member of the sixth generation of Maddoxes in the area, Johnny was born in August 1927. As he told me:

> My family had lived on the same street, Winchester Street, here in Gallatin since 1867, when my great-grandfather came here after the Civil War. My great-aunt played piano, and she had performed ragtime at the St. Louis World's Fair in 1904. When I was about three years old, she would put me at the piano stool and tell me to play. I learned violin, trombone, and organ as well, but it was my great-aunt who taught me all the instrumental rags. Later, I studied with a teacher here in Gallatin, Lela Donohue, and picked up her style of playing somewhat.
>
> I started taking music [lessons] in 1932, but I never dreamed of making a living at it, and then Randy Wood gave me a chance. I was working at the J. C. Penney store across the road from Randy's shop, and he offered me a job at his record store because he knew I was interested in music.

Wood hired the twenty-year-old in 1947 because he knew classical music—Wood had to take the classics along with all the other genres from the record companies who supplied him—although Maddox sometimes joined the team of people filling mail orders.

> Randy had people filling orders as fast as they could, and I would do some of that work to help them. But often you couldn't read the writing to save your life, so I would

just put them back in the pile and let someone else get them. Sister Rosetta Tharpe, I remember, was a big seller, "Didn't It Rain" and "Strange Things Happening Every Day." And Dinah Washington's records sold a lot. People would write in and call her Diana, and Rosetta they called Rosella, I remember all those type of letters. They would write things like, "My records was broke"—mostly from people from the lower South.

Wood had a wire recorder in his electronics shop "for fun," Maddox recalled, "but I took it home and fooled with it and tested some things I was playing. The wire was always breaking, but the sound was fine." Wood certainly thought so when he heard Maddox's home recordings. He already knew that his employee played with a band on evenings and weekends. Maddox had joined the Rhythm Masters dance orchestra in Gallatin in 1939 at the age of thirteen and worked with them on and off through the 1940s, and it was their leader, drummer O'Donnell Templeton, who suggested to Wood that Maddox should be on records.

It was May 19 of 1950," Maddox recalled precisely, "when we went up to the WHIN radio studio here in Gallatin and recorded "Crazy Bone Rag." I had O'Donnell Templeton and Bobby Charles Baker from the Rhythm Masters with me, and I used an Aquasonic studio piano. I remember that Randy stopped me from putting my foot on the pedal. He said it gave a "wow" sound, and he didn't want that.

Wood later told researcher John Michlig about the session and its results.

> Johnny had made a study of ragtime piano, and he was good. I noticed at the civic clubs and evening meetings Johnny was always very popular. We decided we'd make a record with him. We had a local radio station that was off the air during the night hours, and we went out there with a little microphone and a tape recorder and we made something called "Crazy Bone Rag." I put it on the radio, and before long we had many, many mail orders from across the country.

The Rhythm Masters, late 1940s: Betty Alderson; Johnny Maddox, piano; Bob Wynn; Jewell Templeton; Marvin Baker; J. O. Templeton, drums; and partner in Dot Records, Willis "Sonny" Lowery, trumpet. Courtesy of Johnny Maddox

Maddox's first disc was a hit on jukeboxes as well, and Maddox told me he was

> known primarily then as a jukebox artist. Randy sold many of my records that way. He would really work those records with his distributors. That's how he was; he would take something and really push it. "I'm hot one minute and cold the next," he would say. And that's how he really was with things.

Maddox continued to record hits, both at WHIN and in the Castle Studio in Nashville, mainly old songs in a ragtime style. "I Get the Blues When It Rains," "Alabama Jubilee," "Stardust," and "Johnny Maddox Boogie" were all steady sellers. In September 1951, Wood moved Maddox to Dot's new 15000 series of popular music, where his very first record, "San Antonio Rose," became his biggest hit so far. An even bigger sale came in 1955, as Maddox recalled:

> It was a cover record, really. Decca had some German recordings by "Der Shrager Otto," which strangely caught on. Bill Randle, the Cleveland disc jockey, heard one of the tunes and got me to copy it. Bill named it the "Crazy Otto Medley," and Randy issued it. The thing sold over two million copies.

Randolph C. Wood. Courtesy of Country Music Hall of Fame and Museum.

For a time, Maddox stayed around the mid-South, performing and developing an act. He cultivated an old-time riverboat look with a candy-striped shirt and armbands, and flew the flag for ragtime music wherever he went.

> When I started to become popular, they didn't know what to do with me, so often they would put me on country music shows, which is what the local bookers knew. I worked a lot with Eddy Arnold, and later on with Ray Price and Andy Griffith. I played with Jamup and Honey, who had an old-time, black-face, tent-show kind of deal. Their theme song was "The Nashville Blues." We played up in east Tennessee and Virginia and the Carolinas. I worked all over with Lonzo and Oscar, Pee Wee King, Lew Childre, the Duke of Paducah, Minnie Pearl, Kitty Wells, all of those artists. I didn't know anything about country music, but I could play "Beer Barrel Polka" or "Ragtime Cowboy Joe" and so on, and it sort of fitted in; people knew those songs.

Maddox signed with MCA to book him beyond the country circuit in 1952 and played all but two states of the Union, with high-profile engagements in New York, Los Angeles, and Las Vegas. Before this, Maddox had worked briefly as a session pianist for Dot recordings, as he told me in his matter-of-fact way:

> There wasn't anyone in Nashville who played like I did at that time. Randy liked my sound and wanted to use it. This was before Del Wood came out with her piano solos, of course. I backed up Big Jeff Bess on "Juke Box Boogie," also Mac Wiseman, and Jane Grant, who recorded "Goody Goody." I played behind Bob Lamm on "Waiting for the Robert E. Lee," which did well for us. Randy recorded him out here at the radio station in Gallatin—clarinetist Marvin Baker from the Rhythm Masters recorded with him. Later on I recorded "Sweet Georgia Brown" with a local Gallatin girl who sang on Dot, Carol Woodward.
>
> We'd go out to a radio station and record in the evening when they were off the air. Didn't take me long to record because I always had an idea of what I was going to do and how. But the piano is a difficult instrument to get a true recorded sound with, and they spent a long time on putting the mikes around correctly even though the whole thing was rather primitive in those days. Randy would put everything onto big old tapes. He always used tape right from the start, didn't fool with acetates like the Castle studio did.

Once Maddox had a few hits, other musicians wanted to work with him. Francis Craig wrote "Learning" for Maddox and suggested to Randy Wood that he might want to issue a record by the two pianists, Francis Craig with Johnny Maddox. "Randy thought for a minute," laughed Maddox, "and then cleared his throat and said, 'Yeah, well, Johnny Maddox and Francis Craig would be on one side and Francis Craig and Johnny Maddox on the other.' " Beasley Smith arranged several of Maddox's songs, including "Beg Your Pardon" and the "Whistling Piano Man." Later, Smith and Matty Matlock arranged a jazz album on Dot, *Dixieland Blues*, of which Maddox is uncharacteristically proud, calling it "one of the best I ever made."

Nowadays, Maddox rather dismisses his own records: "They didn't mean anything to me then and they don't mean anything now, most of them. Because I just don't think about it. When I am working, I play piano; when I'm not, I don't. That's all there is to it." Nevertheless, Maddox is a considerable student of ragtime, and he takes care to explain the origin of the style and of his pieces, right back to Charles L. Johnson's "Crazy Bone Rag," and to explain that "Yellow Dog Blues" was really "Pattona Rag."

Dot's R&B and Gospel Rosters

While Dot was developing Maddox as a major recording artist, the label relied on the steady sales of country, R&B, and gospel music, the same strategy Bullet and Tennessee used when they started. Dot issued more than a hundred R&B and black gospel records in the 1000 series between 1950 and 1957. The Cap-Tans were the first to hit, with "I'm So Crazy for Love," in September 1950.

The Griffin Brothers, from Norfolk, Virginia, and based in Washington, D.C., were the main black-music act on early Dot releases and scored several big R&B hits with a tight, small-band style light-years away from the Blue Jacks. Their Top Ten R&B hits on Dot included "Street Walkin' Daddy" (featuring vocalist Margie Day), "Little Red Rooster," "Tra La La"/"Hoppin," "Pretty Baby" (by Tommy Brown with the Griffins), and "Weepin' and Cryin'," which hit #1 in December 1951. Margie Day continued with Dot for some years, recording interesting songs like the blues standard "Ace in the Hole" and the risqué "The Clock (Let Your Pendulum Swing)."

Day, the Griffin Brothers, and other R&B artists gave a strong black profile to the first year or two of Dot's operation. Despite this, Randy Wood himself recorded little black music, buying or leasing most of Dot's gospel and R&B catalog from other labels.

Wood had bought Delta masters of the Fairfield Four from Jim Bulleit in May 1950; bought the titles by the Cap-Tans from Lillian Claiborne's D.C. label the same year, along with Cecil Gant recordings made for Bullet; and in 1951 obtained a block of three- to five-year-old former top-selling songs from Leon Rene's Exclusive label on the West Coast. He purchased blues from Gold Star Records in Houston, and another block of Bullet masters when that label closed down in 1952.

All these deals gave Wood low-cost filling for his Randy's Record Shop prepacks. Through the 1950s and beyond, he developed his leasing strategy, extending it to cultivate an impressive array of contacts among disc jockeys and publishers who would alert him to potential hits on minor labels. As Johnny Maddox observed: "Randy knew the record business by the time he got into it himself, because he had been in distribution first, and he knew what would sell."

Dot reissued big-name records like "The Honeydripper" by Joe Liggins and established a solid back catalog of items by the Big Three Trio, Gant, and the Fairfield Four. Gant's last hit, "Waitin' for a Train," hit the jukebox sales charts in 1951, but the R&B roster didn't score heavily again until 1954, when the Counts' "Darling Dear" and "Hot Tamales" saw some chart action. Bobby Marchan recorded "You Made a Fool of Me" early in that year, a regular visitor to Nashville before he gained some fame out of New Orleans as vocalist with Huey Smith and the Clowns. Saxophonist Rusty Bryant recorded some tough instrumental discs, including "All Night Long," an R&B hit in 1953 that Wood had recorded with a one-microphone portable recorder in a night club in Columbus, Ohio. Then Wally Mercer, formerly on Mertone in Florida, weighed in with "Rock around the Clock" (not the hit song recorded by Bill Haley).

Randy Wood and his growing daily mailbag for Dot Records, captured in an early 1950s *Gallatin Examiner* press call. Courtesy of the author.

Dot's original 1000 series also featured many gospel reissues from Bullet and other labels. The Fairfield Four and Sam McCrary, the Gateway Quartet, and Joe Warren all stayed in the catalog as strong sellers for many years. Otherwise, Dot issued the influential but underrecorded Brewsteraires, with

"That's Enough" and "More of Jesus and Less of Me," and vocalist and guitarist Sister Rosa Shaw made four records for Dot in early 1952, including one whose title offered secular advice: "Stop Playing the Numbers." The Golden Voice Trio recorded for Dot in 1953, as did the Singing Stars, a male vocal group led by Tommy Ellison.

Hillbilly on Dot

As with its gospel and R&B lines, Dot's hillbilly roster relied on mainstays of the Nashville scene like Big Jeff Bess to rack up mail-order and jukebox sales—Big Jeff recorded "Juke Box Boogie" as one of his first Dot outings. Bess always kept a tight, tough band that played on the raw edge of the hillbilly sound. "Fast Women, Slow Horses and Wine" followed, along with a reprise of "After We Are Through," which first appeared on World Records. In June 1951, Big Jeff recorded the old blues refrain "Step It Up and Go," one of the best expressions of honky-tonk hillbilly music.

Dot was the closest Big Jeff ever came to a major label, but he was a big star in Nashville, where he and his wife, Hattie Louise (known as Tootsie), ran a succession of joints. In 1961, shortly before their divorce, the couple opened the bar that became Tootsie's Orchid Lounge on Nashville's Lower Broadway. Tootsie got it in the divorce settlement and made it into a Nashville landmark; she died in 1978. Jeff suffered a stroke around 1980 and also battled diabetes and Parkinson's disease. Once a Nashville institution, he lived alone and virtually ignored in a trailer north of the city in Goodlettsville until his death in 1998.

Lonzo & Oscar, and Jamup & Honey were among the other Nashville radio personalities to record for Dot, along with disc jockey Andy Wilson, who recorded good-selling cover versions of "Faded Love" and "Hillbilly Boogie." Promoter and recordman Gabe Tucker, who had a hand in a number of recording and publishing deals in town, found time to record a couple of novelty country discs himself, "Cracker Barrel Farmer" and "Streamline Country Girl"; he also appeared on a short-lived Dot 200 series of country recordings. Tommy Jackson, originally from Birmingham, Alabama, but for years the fiddle player of choice on Nashville recording sessions, made a number of instrumental discs, including some 78-rpm albums that sold well during a square-dance revival in the 1950s.

Once Randy Wood had exhausted his own local contacts in country music, he signed up Mac Wiseman both as contracted artist and A&R man. A bluegrass pioneer from Crimora, Virginia, Wiseman was playing bass with country singer Molly O'Day when Jim Bulleit referred him to the new Dot label. "I didn't know who was doing who a favor," said Wiseman. "The biggest Dot distributor at that time was the back seat of Randy Wood's car."

Nevertheless, Wiseman started with a small hit, "'Tis Sweet to Be Remembered," in June 1950. A number of homely country-folk titles followed, including "Little White Church" and "I Wonder How the Old Folks Are at Home." In 1954, Wiseman recorded "Goin' Like Wildfire" and then had a big hit with "Love Letters in the Sand."

Joe Allison, then a disc jockey and Capitol representative, recalled a minor turning point in Dot's early history:

> It was in 1952, wintertime, and Randy Wood and I were on the road somewhere and we got snowed into a hotel room. Bill Beasley and Al Bubis from Tennessee Records were there, too, and Randy was talking about making his label more uptown. I mean not only the label as a business but also the actual record-label design. Well, I used to be a commercial artist, so I sat down and designed him a new label. We took all those funky little dots off it and made it look professional.

By 1954, sales of pop music had raised Dot's profile significantly, and Wood wanted to score as well in the country field, rather than relying on successful spin-offs from mail orders. In April 1954, Jimmy Newman from Louisiana recorded "Cry Cry Darlin'," which became a significant seller, followed by "Daydreamin'" in 1955; Newman's mastery of plaintive hillbilly ballads with a Cajun inflection continued through "Blue Darlin'," "Honky Tonk Tears," and "Fallen Star." Just as successful was Jimmy Work, who had been on Bullet and a number of labels before landing on Dot in September 1954 and hitting the charts with "Making Believe," which Kitty

(Opposite): Early Dot catalog—the slogan wasn't far wrong. Courtesy of Country Music Hall of Fame and Museum.

Wells and several others covered. Work followed up with a number of other classic honky-tonk hillbilly numbers, among them "That's What Makes the Jukebox Play" and "Let 'Em Talk."

The initial Dot 1000 series lasted until 1957, largely as a country label. Although little of this hard-core hillbilly music made the transition to Dot's pop series, Nashville session players, including guitar virtuoso Hank Garland and pianist Marvin Hughes, recorded standards that did.

Dot's Pop Boom

By September 1951, Johnny Maddox had been so successful that Wood started a new series, Dot 15000, which embraced pop and country-turned-pop. Dot's early releases had included little popular music, apart from Johnny Maddox. In the first year or so, only Jane Grant, Bob Lamm, and Wes Britt and the Rhythm Masters were recorded in that style, along with George Toon and the Tennessee Drifters. But once Wood decided to get into the more lucrative pop market, he issued more than four hundred pop discs between 1951 and 1955. Dozens of these were by Johnny Maddox, who carried the label for the first couple of years. Soon though, Maddox moved over to make room for Beasley Smith, Billy Vaughn, and Dot's most successful early act, the Hilltoppers.

A smooth-singing group from Western Kentucky State University in Bowling Green, the Hilltoppers saw their first disc, "Trying," become a Top Ten pop hit in August 1952. The Hilltoppers were the brainchild of Billy Vaughn, born in Glasgow, Kentucky in 1919, a mature student who was playing piano in a band in Bowling Green when he met lead singer Jimmy Sacca and his friends Don McGuire and Seymour Spiegelman. The four took their name from the University's basketball team. Vaughn had written "Trying" some years earlier and after several years of effort found in Randy Wood a man who was prepared to take a chance on it. Wood told researcher Rob Finnis that he recorded the group in the college auditorium, "on a very small portable machine that ran at the wrong speed. We had one microphone and no band, just a piano. We allowed the acoustics of the auditorium to influence the sound and it came out so well one dee-

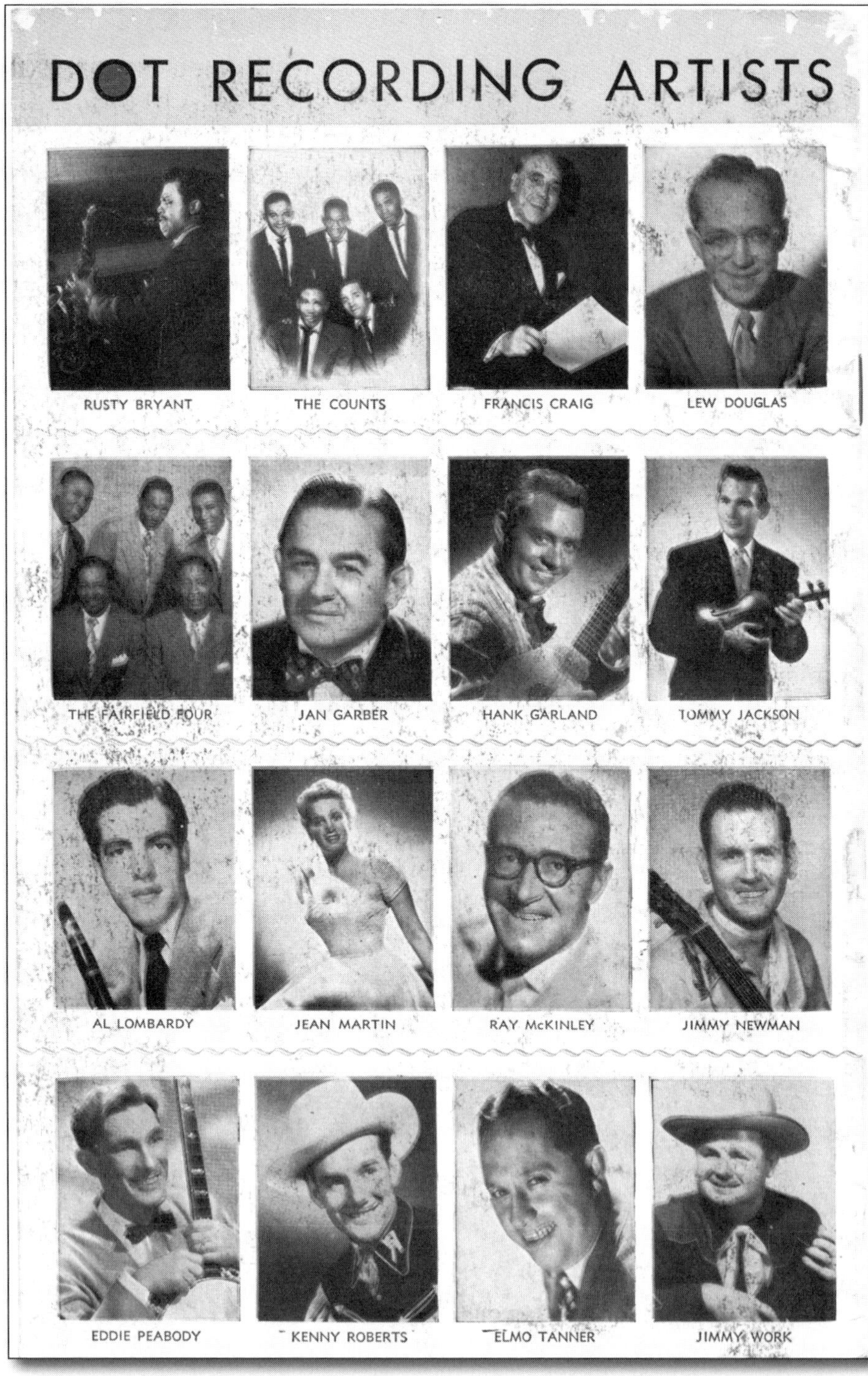

jay thought it was a twenty piece orchestra. It was one giant rumbling sound."

The Hilltoppers were promoted in university sweaters and caps as wholesome boys with a clean-cut style and clear diction, their voices very much to the fore. This would set the trend for Randy Wood's production style for many years. The Hilltoppers followed "Trying" with two other million-sellers: "P.S. I Love You" and "I'd Rather Die Young." On the popularity of these hits, the group toured Europe in 1955 with a band from Nashville led by jazz musician, Karl Garvin. Billy Vaughn did not tour with the group and instead became the musical director at Dot and recorded with his own orchestra. He hit with "Melody of Love" in 1953 and later had a big hit with "Shifting, Whispering Sands." His trademark sound included two saxophones playing lead in unison.

Alongside Vaughn, Randy Wood signed up Al Bennett as his head of promotion. Bennett was renowned for a blisteringly intense and irresistible sales approach, and together the top team at Dot became one of the most successful outfits in the record business.

Popular bands and singers who didn't break any sales records but who kept the label in the limelight included Tony Almerico and the All Star Dixieland Band; Don Estes and Dottie Dillard, both regulars on WSM; Eddie Peabody; Al Lombardy; and the Ray McKinley Orchestra. McKinley was a Texan who had been the drummer in Beasley Smith's band before working with Benny Goodman and the Dorsey brothers and then forming his own orchestra in New York in 1942.

In October 1954, *Billboard* dedicated a six-page feature to Dot's fifth anniversary, visiting with enthusiasm bordering on awe the main stations on the label's journey to success:

> Much has been written in various ways about many examples of the American system of free enterprise in action. Examples can be gleaned from many eras and many industries. Few, though, will be as striking as the example of Randy Wood and Dot Records.

The extended feature pointed out that Wood started in 1946 with a stock of 75 records and no thought of running a record label himself. Now, five years later, he had 30,000 records in stock on 125 different labels, was selling 60,000 records a month across thirty-five states, and owned a record label worth over a million dollars. *Billboard* reported that R&B represented 60 percent of Randy's Records mail-order sales, with Dot Records geared to pop music and hillbilly; that Wood had given over the day-to-day running of Randy's Records to Gilbert Brown, his store manager; and that the staff filled orders continuously from eight to five, with Randy in his private office talking on the phone to some distant city while Billy Vaughn checked new songs or arranged for a new release. According to *Billboard*, an unidentified New Yorker who had recently visited the operation concluded: "This place is all business."

And all this before Randy Wood signed Pat Boone.

In 1952, Johnny Maddox remembered, he visited West End High School in Nashville and played for an assembly program.

> While I was there I also played accompaniment to some students. One was Pat Boone, who sang some popular songs. The first thing I did was to tell Randy what a great voice he had. Randy wanted to record Pat, but he was under contract. Later on, Randy was able to audition Pat, and that was the start of his success.

Meanwhile, discouraged by the recording business, failed Republic artist Pat Boone had relocated with his family to Denton, Texas, where Pat planned to attend North Texas State to study English and music, and to get a singing job on the side. A three-time winner of *Ted Mack Amateur Hour* shows, Boone was living in Dallas when he was invited to New York for the national finals. While there he auditioned for, and won, another contest, the *Arthur Godfrey's Talent Scouts* show.

Boone was stopping over in Nashville to visit his folks when, on the recommendation of disc jockey Hugh Cherry, he met Randy Wood and made an oral agreement to record for Dot Records, even though he was technically under contract to Bill Beasley. Beasley was unable to enforce his contract and decided instead to sell some master recordings of Boone to Dot. Jim Hall, who led Boone's backing orchestra on Republic, also joined Dot as an artist at this point.

Pat Boone opened his Dot account with "Two Hearts" and "Tra La La" in January 1955. Wood had signed Boone in May 1954 but waited a while for the legalities to be settled with Bill Beasley and for the right song to come along. Wood felt that "Two Hearts" was the one, and arranged for Boone to fly to Chicago to record the song at the Universal Studio. "We cut all of Pat's early sides in Chicago," he told Rob Finnis, "which used to surprise people, but it worked very well with an engineer called Bill Putnam, who used to do a lot of R&B sessions." "Tra La La" was a cover of the Griffins' R&B hit on Dot, setting a precedent; in June, Dot issued Boone's covers of the R&B and country classics "Ain't That a Shame" and "Tennessee Saturday Night." Two more discs in 1955 kept his name out front, and then in January 1956 Boone hit the big time with a million-selling cover of Little Richard's major hit "Tutti Frutti." It is unlikely that Boone ever caught Richard's original lyrics at the New Era—"Tutti Frutti, good booty"—and in fact he sanitized Richard's hit Specialty-label version. Adding insult to injury, Boone covered Richard's "Long Tall Sally" in April 1956.

Deejay Hugh Cherry recalled telling Randy Wood he should record Boone back when he was on Republic, and when Wood called Cherry to tell him what they had recorded, Cherry told me: "I said, 'Randy, Pat is a balladeer, not a rock & roll singer,' and he said, 'Well, I think you're right, but I want to break him with a youthful audience, and I think this will do it.' " It did.

Between 1955 and 1959 Boone was on the charts continuously with hits such as "At My Front Door," "I Almost Lost My Mind," and "Love Letters in the Sand." For his part, Boone was always unstinting in his praise of Wood. "Randy was the most energetic guy, indefatigable guy, a dynamo," Boone said. "He picked the songs, he recorded them, he promoted them. I'd probably be winding up a schoolteaching career right now, preaching on Sundays, if it hadn't been for Randy Wood." Instead, after a successful recording and movie career, Boone turned to gospel music and remains active in that arena today.

Dot Records continued to rack up huge pop hits throughout the mid-1950s. In January 1955, the Fontane Sisters were #1 on the pop charts with another R&B cover,

Courtesy of Country Music Hall of Fame and Museum.

(Opposite): Back page of Dot's catalog, with Dot's second string, a fairly proportional reflection of Nashville's music scene: three country singers, five jazz bands, three popular singers, one gospel group and one R&B artist, and two country-pop instrumentalists. Courtesy of Country Music Hall of Fame and Museum.

"Hearts of Stone." In December, they were back with "Daddy-O" at #11. The sisters from New Jersey, Bea, Margie, and Geri, were billed as a blonde, a redhead, and a brunette when they went on the Perry Como radio show in New York in 1945 and took the town by storm. By 1948, they had their own show in Chicago.

Snooky Lanson had joined Dot by the midfifties, but it was another radio star, Gale Storm, who became a Dot headliner when her cover of Smiley Lewis's R&B hit "I Hear You Knocking" weighed in at #2 on the pop charts late in 1955. She scored eleven pop hits between 1955 and 1957. Born Josephine Cottle in Bloomington, Texas, Storm moved to California and appeared in various movies before she went on to a big TV career.

By 1955, Wood had hired veteran bandleader Beasley Smith to help with A&R, and together they formed the joint publishing venture Randy Smith Music. Dot, meanwhile, was shipping 750,000 singles a month, peaking at 1.1 million singles that November.

What people were queuing up to pay for was not groundbreaking stuff. Like all the other independent labels, Wood issued country and gospel and R&B music, but he specialized in what he called

> middle-of-the-road music. Songs that I knew a whole range of people would like. Most record buyers are teenagers, but not all of them want the louder rock & roll music or the older styles of country or black music. I took artists I liked and I tried to mold their style to what I knew would sell. Pat Boone had done some pop records for a country and western label, Republic, but they hadn't sold well, and he was discouraged. He quit show business and went off to school in Texas. When I met him he wanted to record again so I decided I would see if I could get him released from Republic. Then I heard Gale Storm, who [later] starred on TV in *My Little Margie*, and called her for months and months trying to get her to record for me. Eventually she signed, and we are having great success. It's not the money that's important to me, it's creating something that will be heard and enjoyed.

Dot's success with Boone, the Hilltoppers, the Fontane Sisters, and Gale Storm convinced Wood that he needed to get out of Gallatin.

From Gallatin to Hollywood

On July 6, 1956, Wood hosted a buffet at the Hermitage Hotel in Nashville to celebrate Pat Boone's success and to mark the move of Dot Records to the West Coast. "Don't think it's easy for us to leave," Wood told the entertainers, reviewers, and TV and radio personalities present, "but we've got to get closer to the hub of the industry to do the job better." Having achieved twenty-five top-selling discs over five years, Wood was now set on tapping into the movie connections that Nashville could not offer. For their part, many of the movie studios wanted to add a recording arm.

Dot's move to Hollywood had been in the making for a while. Wood had been on the road all through 1952 and 1953 tying up recording and publishing deals in New York, Chicago, and Los Angeles. In 1954, he realized that although Nashville was developing as a recording center, his music was more suited to the big-city markets; he started cultivating contacts on both coasts, and in 1955 opened offices in New York and Hollywood. In May 1956, the *Nashville Banner* reported that Dot Records, "the youngest of the major record labels," had signed a long-term lease on the former Capitol Records home on the corner of Sunset Boulevard and Vine Street in Hollywood.

When Frank Clement, then governor of Tennessee, visited Wood in Hollywood, he said: "I am sorry to see Randy leave Tennessee, but I'm proud to see him succeed. He is a warm and good friend, and one of the great success stories that makes this country what it is."

Wood wrapped up the move to California by July, and later in the year, the *Banner* visited his new offices to tell "the success story of 1956 or any other year." Describing Wood as a "quiet, good looking man speaking with a soft Tennessee accent," the newspaper reported that you'd never suspect that he was the driving force behind the company that outsold all the veteran major record labels that year. "He's a calm fellow who can't play an instrument, can't sing worth a hang, and never was in show business," yet he had made stars of Pat Boone, Gale Storm, the Fontane Sisters, the Hilltoppers, and Johnny Maddox. Wood told the *Banner* by way of explanation: "I know what I like. It's the sound I'm interested in. I like nothing better than to go into a studio and come out three hours later with a song a million people will pay a dollar for."

Mac Wiseman told music researcher Colin Escott that Wood moved to California with the express intention of selling the label to a movie company:

> He had the label for sale, and label chiefs would come to Gallatin from New York or Los Angeles and couldn't believe a shoestring operation from a podunk town could be worth the asking price. So Randy moved to California, tacked another million dollars onto the asking price, and got it. He told me he got the best night's sleep he'd ever had after he sold it.
>
> Wood sold Dot to Paramount Pictures in 1957 for around $3 million and was hired back as president of Dot Records. By the time he renewed the deal in 1962, Wood had widened his distribution to seventeen factory-owned branches, grossing more than $5 million a year.

Life was not all smooth sailing, though, and Dot had its share of writs. One, from Patsy D'Aughbeny, claimed she had written a song country singer Ernie Ashworth had cut for Dot called "Boogie Woogie Baby from Nashville, Tennessee." Dot's attorneys denied all such claims. Often, as in this case, they added insult to injury by submitting to the court that "most of the copies sold were returned."

McNeill Stokes remembers that "Randy Wood kept Dad [Jordan Stokes] on retainer for years after he sold Dot to Paramount, even after he was not legally needed, because Randy did not want to forget someone who had been an inspirational adviser to him in the early days." Wood looked after his other colleagues too: Gene Nobles retired from WLAC on the money he made from the sale of his 10 percent of Dot stock, and Hoss Allen took over his spots; Al Bennett used his share of the Dot money to buy into Liberty Records and eventually assumed ownership.

Plaque at the site of the second Randy's Record Shop; in the center of the row of stores opposite, Wood's original electric shop and store. Courtesy of the author.

Wood stayed on as president of Dot for two five-year terms. When the label was revamped as ABC-Dot after Paramount's takeover by Gulf+Western in 1967, he left and started Ranwood Records, which he subsequently sold to Lawrence Welk. In retirement, Wood was in a bad auto wreck and afterward became a recluse, but Randy's Record Shop did business at the last of its three Gallatin locations until August 15, 1991. The building is still there, now housing a flower shop, just around the corner from Wood's first electrical repair shop. The building from which Dot Records really took off is now a parking lot, with only a roadside plaque to mark Wood's achievements.

13

The Record Center of the South: Nashboro and Excello

Ernie was a good businessman. He had the foresight to see the market for black music in Nashville. But he also liked that music and wanted to do something with it.

—Cal Young

Ernie Young, proprietor of Ernie's Record Mart, had been around a lot longer than Randy Wood and had started in the record-sales business earlier. Although Young started Nashboro and Excello Records a year and a half behind Wood's entry into the recording arena, the suggestion that he was in any way secondary to the founder of Dot Records rankled him.

Ernie Young and the Record Mart

Ernest Lafayette Young, born in Giles County, Tennessee, on December 2, 1892, worked around Nashville for more than twenty years before he founded the Record Mart, as Alan Bubis recalled: "Ernie Young was someone I knew from way back, before either of us was in the record business. Ernie was in the grocery business originally, and my father used to deal with him selling coffee." Young set up a jukebox operation to avoid having to pay someone else to supply music to the restaurants he then owned, and he started his record stores partly to sell off the records he removed from the jukeboxes. By 1944, he was advertising his first store in the Nashville city directory:

"Ernest L Young, 191 Second Avenue North, Automatic Phonographs—All the latest hit tunes are placed weekly on our automatic phonographs."

The next year, Young was advertising the Record Shop at 8 West Hillsboro Road, and by 1946 he had moved all his business into the Record Mart, established at 177–179 Third Avenue North. At an age when someone else might be contemplating retirement, Ernie Young found new purpose in the record business, as Cal Young observed:

> Ernie was in his fifties when he founded the Record Mart. He was a guy who never clicked with anything very much until he found the record business. That was his forte, his niche if you like. Ernie was a good businessman. He had the foresight to see the market for black music in Nashville. But he also liked that music and wanted to do something with it.

Ernie's Record Mart soon doubled as an independent one-stop distributor with a strong reputation for blues and gospel music. As Young later reminisced to Howard Allison:

> I started out the Record Mart with a small stock of Bullet records. Then I had some blues and gospel things from

independent distributors in other cities. Back then it was not as easy to buy a record as it is now. It was only after the war that a few people started putting in specialized record stores. Before then it was mostly an aside to the furniture or electrical business, certainly in the South.

Nashville Globe **advertisement, January 25, 1946. Courtesy of National Baptist Publishing Board.**

Within two years, Young was doing more business selling records than he was selling phonographs. In January 1946, he touted his wares in the *Globe,* reminding customers that his Record Mart was open until nine on Saturday.

In May that year, Young apparently thought buyers still needed directions to his store and advertised in the *Globe*: "The Record Mart—just a few steps off Church Street." He had competition, after all, not only from the Cashions and Hitchcocks of the town, but right next door, at 169 Third Avenue North, where Capitol Vending Machine Company was selling "Latest Hits—New and used Records—Cecil Gant, Lionel Hampton, Johnny Moore." Within a few years, no one needed directions; everyone knew where to find the store that had been renamed Ernie's Record Mart—in "the Record Center of the South," as he often advertised.

By 1953, Ernie was also regularly advertising his sponsored radio shows:

> You'll find your favorite records at Ernie's Record Mart—Listen to Ernie's Record Parade on WLAC and on WSOK each afternoon at 3 p.m.

His main pitchman, WLAC disc jockey John "John R" Richbourg, took over as host of *Ernie's Record Parade* after initially substituting for Gene Nobles. Record producer D Kilpatrick remembered Young's start with Nobles as his promoter:

> Ernie was an honest and a fair man. He treated you right. That was why he was able to build up his shop and the reputation of his mail-order business. And he was interested in what he sold. He was a real student of gospel and R&B music, and he monitored carefully what WLAC was playing.
>
> When Randy Wood started to use Gene Nobles to promote his store, Ernie straightaway got himself a radio slot with Nobles. And he was smart, very astute. When I was at Mercury in the middle 1950s, I had a dub of a new recording by Dinah Washington that Ernie had wanted to hear. Well, I gave him the dub to listen to for his own pleasure. That same night I tuned into WLAC and there it was being played over and over with a plug to order it from Ernie's—and it hadn't been released yet.

Young's savvy paid off. As Richbourg told Dave Booth: "Ernie's averaged, for years, better than three or four hundred orders per day, of anywhere from one record to twenty-five. That's a lot of records." Ernie's nephew Cal Young confirmed the scale of the business:

> Back in those days of radio selling, the first thing Ernie Young would do was to weigh the morning mail, not open it. He wanted to get an estimate of what the daily take was going to be and he had a formula down to an art.

RCA Victor field manager Brad McCuen described the balance he tried to maintain among Nashville's record sellers: "Victor had a very precarious relationship with Ernie Young, Randy Wood, Louis Buckley. We couldn't play favorites.

Ernie Young, *left,* and Ted Adams, Ernie's Record Mart manager, 1961. Courtesy of Country Music Hall of Fame and Museum.

These fellows were so competitive, trying to find out what the others were doing."

Murray Nash, who during his days heading Mercury's country division knew Young well, told much the same tale:

> Ernie was a very religious and humble man, a behind-the-scenes kinda guy. He didn't put his name up front on all the record production he did, like maybe an Owen Bradley. He let others take the credit. But you had to treat him right, too.
>
> When I was heading distribution for RCA out of Knoxville in the later forties, I would let the main dealers have advance copies of our releases. And I always had to bear in mind the intense rivalry between Ernie Young and Randy Wood. If I let Randy have the new Eddy Arnold record before Ernie, then, hell, Ernie sure let me know about it.

Bill Beasley spoke of a marked difference between Young and Wood: "I'm proud to say that I knew Ernie way back in the beginning of my involvement in records. Coastline sold a lot of our records through Ernie, who was a nice guy, down to earth. He wasn't at all flashy like, say, Randy Wood." Lawyer Jordan Stokes, who was caught up in several squabbles between Young and Wood, recalled one case in particular that put him squarely in the middle of the record dealers' wrangling.

> I always had a philosophy that you have to act fair and do the right thing, and over the years I got several clients from both sides of an argument because of that. I represented Randy's Record Shop, which was programming record shows for black people on WLAC. They were quite successful, but one day Randy Wood called me and said: "Mr. Young at Ernie's Record Mart, his announcer John Richbourg is talking jive talk and copying the style of Gene Nobles on my shows."
>
> So I went down there and I said to John R, "Why'd you do that?" He said, "Well, Mr. Young told me to do it." Then there was a legal hearing set by Randy, and that was when I got a call from Ernie Young, asking "Would you represent me?"

Nashboro Records: Focus on Gospel

In June 1951, Ernie Young and his wife, Roberta, consulted Jordan Stokes about launching Nashboro Records, and Young set about turning seven years' experience with Ernie's Record Mart into a successful recording business. He had been around long enough to know that there was a large market for gospel music and, like Randy Wood, he saw the advantages of being able to fill out prepacks of records with his own product. Young's Nashboro label, the first founded in Nashville with a primary focus on black music, would issue some ninety discs between 1951 and 1955, mostly gospel music. According to Murray Nash, in the early years Roberta Young "was the bookkeeper, office manager, and so forth and had a lot to do with the running of the Nashboro company, because it was her money that started it."

The Nashboro 500 gospel series opened in June 1951

with a slew of quartets, known and unknown. Young sometimes found the groups himself, but more often Morgan Babb acted as talent scout and contact man, a role he had performed for Bill Beasley at Tennessee for some months. With the Record Mart just a block from WLAC, Young first hired the radio studio to make recordings but soon switched to a cheaper makeshift studio in the front of his Third Avenue store after it closed for the day. Later he built a better studio upstairs.

Out-of-town artists made all of Nashboro's earliest discs: the first, "I'm Looking for My Jesus" by the Silvertone Jubilee Singers from Cincinnati, the second, "Blessed Saviour" by Tasso Zachary's Heavenly Gospel-Aires, a female group from Kentucky; and then discs by the Chosen Gospel Singers from Los Angeles, who had recorded on Specialty in 1952. The Singers' first Nashboro release, "It's Alright," featured singer Lou Rawls, who would go on to a successful secular career. The group, minus Rawls, would continue with Nashboro for many years, later as the Gospel Keynotes.

The lead tenor of the Chosen Gospel Singers, James Brumfield, joined the Radio Four in 1954 or 1955; the Four had left Republic, and their first session for Young's Nashboro label, in November 1955, featured Ernie Newton on bass, moonlighting from his usual jobs with country sessions and jazz bands. The mainstay of the group on Republic, Morgan Babb, sang at that session, which produced the classic "An Earnest Prayer," but then Babb left the group. The Radio Four, who for years remained one of Nashville's best gospel quartets, went on to record a number of Nashboro discs without Babb.

Morgan Babb's fame as "Happy Jack" on WHOP in Hopkinsville, Kentucky, won him a job with Nashville station WSOK (later, WVOL), where he became chief announcer. Babb sang and played guitar as a hot gospel singer and ran talent contests for others; formed the Philco Singers and Voices of Nashville; and also wrote pop and country songs, including the #8 R&B hit "I Miss You So," recorded on Excello by Lillian Offit in 1957. Babb would stay at WVOL for over thirty years until 1983, when he formed his own small Nashville radio station, WMDB, dedicated to black music and community relations. By then he was a minister, having founded the King Solomon Baptist Church on Tenth Avenue North in 1965.

Nashboro's 500 series boasted an embarrassment of fine gospel groups, some of whom stayed with the label for decades. All prolific recorders, they included (but were by no means limited to) the Skylarks, the Flying Clouds, the Fireside Gospel Singers, the Blair Gospel Singers, and the Spiritual Five.

The most productive of these, the Skylarks, started as an offshoot of the Fairfield Four in 1950 and first appeared on Nashboro in 1951; the success of early records like "The Rock" and "Life's Burdens" led to another two dozen discs on the label over the next twenty years. For the most part, the group on Nashboro comprised Willie Jefferson and Wilson

Morgan Babb of the Radio Four, broadcasting from Ernie's Record Mart on Third Avenue North. Courtesy of Dr. Morgan Babb.

(Left): Trade-paper advertisement, early 1953, with the Skylarks: *from left,* Robert Crenshaw, James Hill, Lindsay Starks, and Isaac Freeman. Courtesy of Jerry Zolten.

(Right): The Jewel Gospel-Aires: *from left,* Canzetta Staton, Maggie Staton-Peebles, and Naomi Harrison-Manning. Courtesy of Naomi Manning.

Paige, based in Greenville, Alabama, along with Fairfield Four members Edward Thomas, James Hill, and Isaac Freeman. As the 1950s progressed, Ernie Young tried to get the group to record secular material as well, similar to the gospel-to-pop metamorphosis of Sam Cooke and Clyde McPhatter, who were then enjoying big careers in rock & roll. "I just couldn't do it," said James Hill, "I wasn't brought up that way. Some of [those artists] would change and wouldn't last long, wouldn't live long."

Another group long faithful to the Nashboro label, the Flying Clouds of Detroit led by Elmer Stallworth, first joined Nashboro in 1953. The Flying Clouds normally comprised Ruben Willingham, Charles Bramwell, William Crawford, Rufus Washington, and James Anderson. Their "Sit Down Servant" and "On My Knees" were particularly good sellers for the label, and the group remained with Ernie Young right through the 1960s.

A longtime group formed as early as 1943 as the Fairfield Four Juniors became the Fireside Gospel Singers, renamed by Ernie Young when they joined Nashboro; "Gabriel Sound Your Trumpet" was the first of their five discs on the label between 1951 and 1953. Ben Vaughan and Willie Lewis both performed in the Fairfield Four and the Firesides over the years, but the group that recorded for Nashboro comprised Forrest Wiggins, Edward Hall, Irvin Tucker, Albert Phillips, and Thomas Gilbert.

The Swanee Quartet also made the first of their long string of recordings for Nashboro, "Walk in the Light," in 1951, and the Blair Gospel Singers made five discs for the label between 1952 and 1955. Their "Forgive Me Lord" was a good seller, according to Howard Allison, who remembered orders for the disc coming in over many years. J. B. Blair led the group, which featured the three Pullom brothers. Finally, the Spiritual Five, who had recorded for other labels, did their best work for Nashboro with recordings that featured bass singer Jimmy Jones. (Jones also appeared in the Sons of the South, who made five records for Young in 1954 and 1955.)

Around 1955, Ernie Young acquired a number of new artists, many of whom had recorded for other labels and some of whom would become Nashboro staples into the 1960s and 1970s. These included the Angelic Gospel Singers, led by Margaret Allison, Josephine McDonnell, and Thomas Mobley; Professor Harold Boggs; and the Consolers, who were Sullivan and Iola Pugh from Florida, sharing vocals and guitar.

Young picked up Lucile Barbee's contract when Republic

folded, and in 1956 she recorded for Nashboro backed by two local groups, Clarence Mills's Israelite Travelers and Bobby Jones's Royal Gospel Singers; she continued recording for Nashboro into the 1970s. In 1955, Edna Gallmon Cooke also left Republic to join Nashboro, for whom she recorded dozens of influential discs over several decades.

A female quartet, the Jewell Gospel Singers, recorded for Aladdin Records on the West Coast in 1953, but by the time the Singers—Bishop Jewell and Maggie and Canzetta Staton—got to Nashville, they were billed as a trio and renamed the Jewel Gospel-aires. They made five records for Nashboro with quite a large musical backing group, which gave discs like "Take My Hand, Precious Lord" and "The Gospel Ship" a full sound; they sold well down through the years, although Canzetta had a bigger career in popular music as Candi Staton.

A Touch of Blues and Hillbilly

Nashboro released the occasional blues disc in the 500 series, most notably "You've Gotta Stop That Mess," credited to the Fat Man with the Sunnyland Slim Trio. Recorded in 1951 for release on JOB Records in Chicago, the disc appeared on Nashboro that December. The Fat Man was Alfred Wallace, a well-known session drummer around Chicago from the early 1940s. Curiously, Nashboro also issued discs by another Chicago-based drummer, Jack Cooley, but these may not have been Chicago recordings. Cooley worked often with pianist Albert Ammons, who frequently played the New Era Club in Nashville, and it is possible that "It's So Fine" and "Tom Tom Boogie" were made in Tennessee.

Local musicians recall husky-voiced blues singer Sherman Johnson performing around town at the start of the 1950s, when he recorded "Back Alley Boogie" and "Nashville after Midnight," issued on Nashboro in September 1951. The next year, Johnson had a regular radio show on WTOK in Meridian, his hometown, and two discs on Jackson, Mississippi's Trumpet Records. Label boss Lillian McMurry remembered one particular session: "We could have strangled him, as he insisted on imitating Cecil Gant, but badly."

One of the rare discs from Nashboro's forgotten hillbilly series.

A short-lived 1000 series designed for hillbilly music joined Nashboro's original 500 series within a few weeks of its beginnings. As Ernie Young recalled in conversation with Howard Allison: "I did record some hillbilly things, but I found that Tennessee Records, Bullet, and the majors had a secure foothold in that market. For me, black music was more successful."

Vance Morris and the Alabama Play Boys monopolized Nashboro's early hillbilly releases with accomplished, zestful tunes like "Crazy 'bout the Boogie" and "Slap Happy Pappy." That Morris, born in 1919, grew up near Oklahoma City probably accounts for the heavy western swing influence in the band's repertoire. He went to Mississippi in 1934, then on to Huntsville, Alabama. A local promoter, Robert "Big Deal" Vann, got him on Nashboro. There were two sessions, no royalties, and only a little airplay.

One of the few Nashville independents to take a stab at bluegrass recordings, Nashboro stumbled on the Dixie Ramblers, a fine band with a curious style. Their "Lonely for You" was a routine bluegrass record until a trumpet appeared with a couple of fills on the bridge before taking a solo. On the West Coast, western bands had added brass instruments to their sound throughout the previous decade, and Al Dexter's million-selling popular hits such as "Pistol Packin' Mama" were well-known; the eastern variant works well here. Led by Woody and Lena Hix, the Ramblers had several more discs on Nashboro, suggesting that they must have sold well.

Excello Records

In August 1952, Ernie Young phased out his hillbilly series and started Excello Records, which, he explained, developed for pragmatic reasons into a mostly blues label:

> The reasoning there was originally to issue secular music of all kinds, keeping Nashboro purely as a gospel label so as not to confuse people. We did start with blues and hillbilly on Excello, but the blues was what we were best set up to sell, so once again the country element gradually dried up.

Courtesy of Bear Family Records.

Young had cultivated his affinity with black music during his years of selling appliances to black customers, some of whom not only patronized his record store but supplied him with performers for his records. "When I started Ernie's," he said later, "it seemed like everyone was a singer or musician or knew someone else who was. People came along to the store and would ask to record." Young soon found that recording songs in his record store after hours was limiting, and so converted his third floor into a studio. "It was easier to audition performers that way. People like Louis Brooks, Arthur Gunter, Kid King, they just were around. All I had to do was to try to pick who was going to do some good in sales."

Issued in January 1953, the first R&B disc on Excello was "Allotment Blues (Dear John)" by the Charlie Dowell Orchestra, with vocals by Willie Lee Patton. While not typical of what was to follow on Excello, it was highly typical of the contemporary music scene in Nashville's black clubs and theaters. Dowell likely used the Jerrie Jackson Revue band as his "orchestra"—he managed the revue, which appeared regularly at the Bijou Theater, and was an occasional vocalist, a more regular tap dancer in the revue, and the organizer of a meeting place for black musicians at his mother's house in north Nashville. Jackson Revue blues singer Willie Lee Patton sang her vivid "Dear John" message to her absent man, a familiar theme in light of the strain on relationships during the Korean War. (In the country field, Jean Shepard and Ferlin Husky scored a major hit on Capitol with the similarly themed "A Dear John Letter" just six months later, in July 1953.)

Next up on Excello was Del Thorne, a competent jazz-based singer and pianist/organist, no stranger to the hipper cabaret-club scene. "I Let Him Move Me" followed the West Coast genre of slick female bluesicians like Nellie Lutcher, Camille Howard, and Hadda Brooks. From San Antonio, Thorne had first played in Nashville in 1946 with Wynonie Harris on a package show at the Ryman Auditorium, when the *Globe* called her "a double threat bombshell whose skill as a vocalist and pianist is hard to separate—she is outstanding in both departments."

Another artist with an off-on connection with Nashville was Max "Blues" Bailey, whose "Delinquency Blues" had appeared on Bullet. From Huntington, West Virginia, and also known as "Little Maxie" or "Scat Man," Bailey had sung with the Buddy Tate Band during the time he was on Bullet in 1949 and showed up on Excello with "Brown Skin Woman Blues," an interesting recitation on the blues and the sociology of skin color. It followed a tradition of blues songwriting far more acceptable and meaningful in black society in the 1930s, 1940s, and even when it was released in March 1953 than today.

Although Ernie Young said he designed Excello as a secular label, early on it issued not only R&B but also gospel discs—four by the Boyer Brothers vocal duet and several by the Hendrix Singers, Brother Henry Edwards, and the Young Gospel Singers. The Boyer brothers, born in Winter Park Florida—James in 1934 and Horace in 1935—went to high school in Nashville, where Horace helped direct the Faith Holy Temple Choir. The brothers had worked out a close vocal harmony style, and both were pianists—still in school in 1952 when they cut eight sides for Ernie Young in the back of the Record Mart.

The Hendrix Singers were organized by James Hendrix of Nashville, their pianist, singer, and manager. Brother Henry Edwards was a cook at the Andrew Jackson Hotel who promoted his gospel shows on his WSOK radio show. Finally, Leroy Waldo organized the Young Gospel Singers (not named for Ernie Young), who shared some personnel with the Waldo Singers on Nashboro and also with the Sermonaires, a mixed vocal group who recorded for Excello in 1953.

Many of Excello's blues sessions were arranged by pianist Skippy Brooks (no relation to Louis), who had been a leading player in Sherman Williams's band on Bullet and toured with Williams and then with Texas-based R&B guitarist Gatemouth Brown. Back in Nashville in 1949, as the *Commentator* crowed, Brooks formed a band at the New Era Club:

> It's the inimitable Skippy Brooks, the Boogie Woogie man, running up and down the keys like electricity. And he's playing to a happy, happy house. The Combo has taken a rejuvenation since playing with Skippy Brooks. . . . Yes, you'll get a kick with your chick, if you bring her to hear Skippy Brooks.

By the early 1950s Brooks had joined drummer Kid King, saxophonist Freddy Young, and bass player Clifford "Big Mac" McCray in what was effectively the Excello house band, a gathering of experienced musicians who could play jazz,

Willie Lee Patton, singer with the Charlie Dowell Orchestra and the Jerrie Jackson Revue. Courtesy of Irene (Jackson) Irvin.

blues, or R&B. Brooks himself was the leading player, with his distinctive, high-register piano voicings, followed closely by alto-sax player Freddy Young. Bass player McCray recalled that he was to the fore in working out the band's arrangements, but he was not the leader because Ernie Young liked the sound of drummer Lee Arthur King's working name, Kid King, and named the band the Kid King Combo.

"Skip's Boogie" / "Banana Split" was the first of nine Kid King Combo discs on Excello, along with one credited to Skippy Brooks, and gave the label its first hit when "Banana Split" in November 1953 made #6 on the national R&B juke box chart. The record had been released around May, and in August Excello took out a trade ad: "It's a hit—Banana

THE NASHVILLE COMMENTATOR

WELCOME

AT THE NEW ERA

"Hello! Everybody hello!
Watcha know everybody hello!"
"Every time I hear the train
It makes me think of you
It's been a long time baby
Since I heard your name."
*"I get a kick from my chick
Alcohol doesn't feel at all
Being with my baby that's all
I get a kick from my chick."*

Yes! you have it. It's the inimitable Skippy Brooks, the Boogie Woogie man, running up and down the keys like electricity. And he's playing to a Happy, Happy house. The Combo has taken a rejuvenation since playing with Skippy Brooks. You wouldn't know them at all now. Not at all. Yes you'll get a kick with your chick, if you bring her to hear Skippy Brooks.

WHAT THE FAT MAN SAYS

AT THE RITZ

"RED RIVER"

with

JOHN WAYNE

WAIKIKI DINNER CLUB

—Now Open—
AMERICAN LEGION CLUB
37 Factory St.
Ben Taylor, Mgr.

RECORDS
Spirituals—Boogies—Blues
Listen To "Record Parade"
WLAC 4 times weekly
THE RECORD MART
179 3rd Ave., No.
(Between Church & Commerce)

Shop Phone, 6-3808
Home Phone, 6-7791

YOUTHFUL BEAUTY

Recommendation for the New Era Club, *Nashville Commentator*, 1949. Courtesy of the Nashville Public Library, the Nashville Room.

Split—order from Monarch, Los Angeles," a location that gave weight to the press's assertion about the disc that "the West Coast is eating it up."

Flushed with success, Excello and the Combo had a difficult call in deciding on a follow-up for their hit. A bluesy instrumental was the order of the day—one side slower, one side faster—but they also needed a gimmick. The unsubtle solution they came up with was to name the moody, bluesy piece "Brass Rail" after the nightclub the combo often played, and to title the tune on the faster side "Gimmick." Ernie Young was a lover of smooth jazz, and this is about as close as he came on Excello. *Billboard's* reviewer heard "very competent soloists doing excellent riffs in a frankly modern jazz vein. Exciting music." The disc was closer to the day-to-day sound of the combo than to the music they made as house band for a blues label.

Roscoe Shelton, who worked with the band on and off in those days, said that Skippy Brooks "was probably the best—well, there's no probably about it—he was *the* blues pianist in Nashville back then." As versatile as Brooks, who could play R&B, blues, jazz, or society cocktail music, bassist McCray had developed a leaning toward jazz during his music studies at Tennessee State, where he played with the Collegians band under Chick Chavis. McCray, who named as his idols Oscar Pettiford and Ray Brown, talked about the combo's relationship with Ernie Young in the Excello studio:

> He'd make us a little mad sometimes because he wouldn't balance everything just right. But we'd tell him, "You need to raise things up," and he was the kind of man, when he saw certain records were good sellers, he'd say, "I'm sure glad you all told me that."

Later discs by the Kid King Combo were made without King himself, who when he left sold the name of his combo for a nominal sum to Ernie Young. Sam Beasley took over the drums in the Excello house band; Tommy McGee, who had been playing with Louis Brooks, replaced alto player Freddy Young; and young guitarist Bobby Hebb also joined the combo. McGee, less experienced than Freddy Young, in time became an exciting player, more attuned to the meaty sound of R&B and later soul stylings.

By the time he came to record, Sam Beasley was working as vocalist with Skippy Brooks and, billed as "Good Rocking Beasley," made "Happy Go Lucky," a song by Ted Jarrett about playing the numbers—a cultural period piece of the Leiber and Stoller type. On "Now Listen Baby," credited to the Kid King Combo, Beasley presides over the melodic twelve-bar blues that work the "Baby, don't you want a man like me?" theme. (Little Richard recorded the song as "Baby" at his first session for Specialty Records.) Beasley had been a song-and-dance man at the Bijou Theater on Sunday nights since the early forties and was fond of the big-band singers of the blues, people like Jimmy Rushing, Joe Turner, and the other shouters.

Part of a package with the Kid King Combo, Bijou veteran Tom "Shy Guy" Douglas came into the studio in the spring of 1953. The first in a series of fine blues recordings he made for local labels paired "Detroit Arrow" and "New Memphis Blues," which followed "Raid on Cedar Street," his initial outing for Delta and MGM. Douglas had previously recorded "New Memphis Blues," written and engineered by Red Wortham, for a release on Sun that never happened.

The Blue Flamers, who recorded the powerful "Driving down the Highway" for Excello, were a Clarksville, Tennessee, band that featured vocalist Bob Elliot and three brothers named Suggs. Charles Suggs later told Michael Gray that their band was named for the Blue Flame nightclub in Guthrie, Kentucky, and that John Richbourg produced their disc for Ernie Young at the WLAC radio studio.

Blues Hits after Hours

An acknowledged blues classic, Arthur Gunter's 1954 Excello disc "Blues after Hours" was recorded with Skippy Brooks on piano and Kid King on drums. The record introduced Gunter's pleasing, dry voice and his overall back-porch style, often compared to the sound prevalent in the Carolinas or to artists like Blind Boy Fuller or Big Bill Broonzy.

Gunter had recorded as part of the Leap Frogs and on guitar had occasionally backed other Excello artists, made records in Georgia as part of the Gunter Brothers gospel group, and written "I'm Down Here Lord Prayin' in Your Name," recorded by Sister Rosetta Tharpe. His father, William, was a preacher; Arthur, born in Nashville in May 1926, took to gospel singing and tried out different instruments along with his elder brothers, Larry and Jimmy, and his younger brother, known as Little Al. As a gospel group they performed with cousin Junior in the Nashville area and in Georgia. Gunter later told blues researcher Jim O'Neal:

> All of my family was connected with music. My daddy would write music, print 'em, and put them in the store to be selled. My grandfather, he used to print music. My aunt, my niece, cousins, and brothers, all of them.

The Kid King Combo, with King on drums and Edward "Skippy" Brooks at the piano. Courtesy of Bear Family Records.

Arthur Gunter, briefly a star, 1955. Courtesy of Bear Family Records.

Once his brother Larry had taught him the rudiments of the guitar, Arthur took a liking to the blues. "When I first bought a guitar, I listened to different people—Blind Lemon, Tampa Red, Sonny Boy Williamson. I don't read music, but anything that I ever heard that I want to play, I just play it."

In the early 1950s, Gunter and his younger brother, Al, started to hang out around Ernie's Record Mart, meeting Skippy Brooks and other musicians and briefly forming the Leap Frogs. Gunter also played gigs with the Kid King Combo on small local tours.

"Baby Let's Play House," initially the flipside of Gunter's debut, was a romping mix of country and blues shuffles that reworked the old blues lyric about finding the right girl—"I'd rather see you dead little girl, than to be with another man." Released right at the end of 1954, "Baby Let's Play House" was a simple, primitive, even sloppy, recording but a classic nonetheless. Arthur Gunter was a marvelously laconic vocalist. The song was #12 on the R&B charts by January 1955.

On the strength of his hit, Gunter went out touring around Georgia, Alabama, Mississippi, and North Carolina, as well as the Nashville area. His record came to the attention of Sam Phillips at Sun Records in Memphis and to Phillips's main country artist, Elvis Presley. Although Presley's Sun recording, issued in April 1955, was essentially a copy of Gunter's beat and mood, a telling lyric change altered getting religion to getting a pink Cadillac, and Presley added the mumbling rockabilly intro, "Baby, baby, baby . . . come back, baby." Gunter later recalled that he never met Presley but added: "My first royalty check off Presley's record was six and a half thousand dollars. I was satisfied with that." Arthur bought a new station wagon to get him to the full-house shows that he thought would continue. They didn't, and Gunter eventually moved to Michigan. His luck remained variable; he won the state lottery, but he died relatively young, in 1976.

Ted Jarrett, who produced some of Excello's local R&B artists from the spring of 1953 onward, worked as an independent producer with Ernie Young.

> Gradually, things began to happen for me in terms of making a name at record production. After I had had my first big artist, Christine Kittrell, then I went over to see Ernie Young at Excello. He liked what I had done with Bill Beasley and asked me to see if I could do the same for him. I worked there in his studio at Third Avenue.

Jarrett did some producing for Young while he was still working for Republic Records. He was never a staff producer at Excello—or at Tennessee/Republic, for that matter—as he explained to me.

> I always did my own thing, and worked on my own music and productions, and didn't pay too much attention to the others. How it worked with Tennessee was that Bill Beasley would run the sessions, and I would just work with my own artists. He did the rest. Same thing with Excello. Ernie Young was a very fair man, but he was tough. He kept his word on whatever he had told you he would do for you, but he never would promise much in the way of money or guarantees, so I had to find other ways to go with my career.

Although the work of Ted Jarrett as writer, producer, and sometime pianist is all over Nashville recordings of the 1950s, his Excello recording of his own song "Love Love Love" was a relatively isolated instance of his coming up front as featured artist. Jarrett was a fine arranger, and on this classy example of the pop end of R&B his tenor vocal was backed by a vocal group and brassy, baritone-led sax riffs.

The disc sold only about five thousand copies, according to Jarrett, but country singer Chuck Reed recorded it on Mercury in March 1955, Johnnie Ray covered it on Columbia for the pop market, and country star Webb Pierce recorded it in July 1955 and made it a #1 country hit by the time Jarrett's own version was released. Jarrett picked up a songwriting award for "Love, Love, Love," but only just—when he turned up on presentation night among the other Nashville record people, all of whom were white, the doorman wouldn't let him in until he called someone from the record company to go in with him.

Apart from Ted Jarrett, a number of other artists who had worked with Bill Beasley on Tennessee/Republic eventually recorded for Excello, including, by the early spring of 1954, bandleader Louis Brooks.

> The way it came about, was that Ernie Young wanted me to work for him, but he also wanted something different. Tommy McGee had been playing with me at the New Era Club as alto-sax man and vocalist, so we decided to issue discs with Tommy up front. The problem was, he would often sit in with us, and for a while we tried to make him a regular, but he never was very reliable. We never could depend on him.

Tommy McGee's recording of "Late Every Evening" featured Louis Brooks's band augmented by Skippy Brooks. The other side was "Poppin'," written by ex-con Robert Riley, who had penned several songs for the Prisonaires and other Nashville acts. Written and copyrighted as "Poppin' at the Era" in honor of the New Era Club, the song may owe a debt to the Griffin Brothers' "Hoppin'," a big hit on Dot in 1951.

The first disc on Excello under Louis Brooks's name, "Bus Station Blues," came in April 1954 with his band the Pinetoppers, a name Brooks would soon change. "There was a group in New Hampshire somewhere with the same name, and they soon let us know about it, so we stopped causing confusion with it," he told me. Drummer Tiny Davis talked in the mellow, driving blues instrumental penned by bass player Ollie Brown; and Louis Brooks drew a plummy vibrato from his tenor sax, not unlike that of J. T. Brown in Chicago. The bus-station theme, not a new one, evoked a venue poignant in the minds of the many black people who traveled often between the South and northern and western cities.

Louis Brooks and his band, now the Hi-Toppers, were the complete package; they could play not only the R&B of the moment but any kind of blues or rhythm music. On their ever-changing roster of vocalists, Larry Birdsong piloted "Pleadin' for Love," cut at the end of 1955 and released in February 1956, to #11 best jukebox seller. He was one of Jarrett's main protégés after Christine Kittrell and Gene Allison, and Jarrett, who produced him, remembered cutting a deal with another label for the singer.

Ted Jarrett, *center,* holds copies of recordings of his hit song, "Love, Love, Love." He is congratulated by Ernie Young, *right,* and Ernie's store manager, Ted Adams, *left.* Courtesy of Ted Jarrett.

> We had a hit with Larry Birdsong, "It Won't Be This Way Always" and "Pleadin' for Love," and then Vee-Jay Records came in and wanted him real bad. So I said, "Well, you gotta take Gene Allison and some other artists I was working with as well." They didn't want Gene Allison at all, but as it turned out we sold a lot of records for them with Allison, and Larry never did sell.

On "Pleadin' for Love," Birdsong's soulful vocals, at their churchy, melodic best, combine with a fine deep sax solo by Louis Brooks and the trademark tinkling Excello piano of Skippy Brooks. As Hank Davis suggested to me upon listening to a number of Excello blues discs, Brooks's piano was almost like director Alfred Hitchcock's walk-on part in each of his movies—even when his piano didn't add much to the plot, you just expected it to be there.

Earl Gaines. Courtesy of Earl Gaines and Fred James.

Earl Gaines was about the first and most successful of the vocalists who worked with Louis Brooks and the Hi-Toppers, although Brooks recalled him as highly independent.

> Earl worked with me and with Ted Jarrett from around the time we started making records. Sometimes he would sing and sometimes he would play drums, and Earl was in and out of our band. One day we were at Bill Thomas's club in Dyersburg. Ted Jarrett had written this song "It's Love Baby (24 Hours a Day)," and Earl was singing that night. I said, "Let's try that song out tonight." Well, the people began to get very interested in it. So we recorded it, and the thing broke loose. They bought that number left and right. But Earl was the kind of feller to be around one minute and not the next. He never did sign any contracts, so Ernie Young put the record in my name.

Gaines offered a different take on this story. The Brooks band, he said, had recorded the song once in the early spring of 1955 at a fast tempo. In Dyersburg, they took it at a slower tempo to suit Gaines, and when that went over well with the crowd, Brooks went back to Ernie Young, pleading to record the song again in the slower version. By July that version made the R&B best-seller and jukebox listings and spent fifteen weeks on the charts, eventually reaching #3 among best-sellers and #2 among juke hits. A cover on Federal in August by Hank Ballard and the Midnighters scored a #10 hit, and Ruth Brown's cover on Atlantic made #4 in September. On the strength of his hit Gaines won places on package tours with Big Joe Turner and Bo Diddley that year—heady stuff for a twenty-year-old.

Born in Decatur, Alabama, in August 1935, Gaines had lived in Nashville in his teens. "It's Love Baby" was the first of four mid-1950s discs he made on Excello. He went on to record frequently for Nashville labels, had one more Excello disc in 1962, and made an album of soulful material on Hanna Barbera in 1966. In 1973 his "Hymn Number 5" was a minor hit on Seventy-7 Records, but none of his later recordings approached the success of his first Excello disc.

Vocal Groups, Rock & Roll, and Swamp Blues

In the spring of 1955, Red Wortham took Ernie Young into the Tennessee State Penitentiary in the hope of repeating the Prisonaires' success story with Sun Records. Although the Prisonaires had broken up, leader Johnny Bragg had lost no time in forming another prison-based group, the Sunbeams, which then became the Marigolds. When Young recorded them, the group comprised Bragg, Harold Hebb, Willie (Billy) Wilson, Henry Jones, and Al Brooks; "Rollin' Stone," another song from ex-con Robert Riley, had an endearing, friendly, homemade feel to it. The tenor lead by Bragg is wonderful, and the piano and maracas backing, which sounds latinesque at moments, is calypso based.

Issued around March 1955, "Rollin' Stone" by the Marigolds was a hit; it entered the R&B best-seller lists in June and made #8 on the jukebox-seller list. The Cadets covered it on Modern for the black West Coast market, as did the Fontane Sisters on Dot for the white pop market. The disc also marked the start of a push into the secular vocal-group market for Excello, which hitherto had concentrated on solo singers and instrumentals. Ernie Young, of course, was a fan of gospel quartets, and he would have had little difficulty relating to the music of the Marigolds, and particularly to their lead tenor, Johnny Bragg.

Another of the leading Marigolds was Harold Hebb, who belonged to a large and well-known Nashville family of musicians and who in the early 1950s had gotten into a little trouble that sent him to the pen. His parents, William and Ovalla, both blind, had met at the Tennessee School for the Blind; they had four sons and four daughters. Harold performed as a child song-and-dance entertainer with Jerrie Jackson's Hepcats at the Bijou Theater, aided by his younger brother, Bobby, who debuted on the Bijou stage on his third birthday in 1941. "We never had much money and we had a very hard childhood," Bobby Hebb recalled, also explaining that Jerrie Jackson was something of a father figure to the two Hebb brothers and to dancer Henry Allen, with whom they worked in a tap routine as the Typewriter Brothers.

When the Prisonaires split up, it was Harold Hebb who persuaded Bragg to start over with the new group that became the Marigolds. Upon his release from the penitentiary, Harold became floor manager at the Club Baron on Jefferson Street and was killed in 1963 in a knifing incident outside the club, the day after the JFK assassination. These two incidents sparked his brother Bobby's thoughts, from which sprang the lyrics for the pop, soul, and jazz standard "Sunny."

The Marigolds made five more discs for Excello over the next year or so, one as the Solotones; their last, "Jukebox Rock 'n' Roll," represented an unsuccessful attempt at reaching a wider audience. Johnny Bragg was released from prison and recorded for Decca in 1959, but he was back behind bars for robbery and attempted murder between 1960 and 1967. He then recorded for his own Elbejay Records but with little success. Bragg was again briefly imprisoned in 1970 and 1977. When he died in September 2004, Nashville lost one of the truly great voices in black music.

Although few of the Prisonaires or Marigolds had much luck in life, Robert Riley carved out a career as a songwriter and came along with both groups as part of the package. He worked informally with Ernie Young's groups on the production side of things and was at one point almost a fixture at Ernie's, tidying up songs and making suggestions. But Riley's hustling know-how equaled his songwriting skills. As one contemporary summed him up:

> He was a writer, a promoter, a crook. He was one of the smartest recordmen in town, but always a step ahead of you. You never knew what was the truth. He would pretend to promote things and take the money. But he could do it if he wanted to. He was good.

Riley brought soul hit maker Joe Tex to Buddy Killen's Dial label and was on the payroll at Tree Music until Killen discovered some checks missing.

A name familiar from Bullet Records, Rudy Green, weighed in on the Excello roster almost ten years later, in December 1955. The new drive he displayed is partly attributable to the influence of Little Richard. When asked about Green, singer Bobby Hebb replied immediately: "Well, that was Little Richard's friend. That's the man— 'Tutti Frutti, Oh Rudy.' "

Green's "My Mumblin' Baby" was a mighty-sounding rocker complete with heavy backbeat and wailing sax that owed a debt to the emerging sound of New Orleans (and to a now politically incorrect 1950s vogue for songs about vocal impediments); Green, something of a chameleon stylistically, had spent time with the New Orleans musicians who frequently played in Nashville. The song was actually the "Mumbles Blues" recorded on Chess in 1952 by Bobby Lewis. Rudy Green recorded again in Nashville a few years later, but his time had largely passed, and he never found the fame his abilities warranted in any of his many styles.

Ernie Young put no sustained effort toward the country or pop markets, although, as he had initially intended, Excello put out an occasional country record by a local writer or singer who caught his fancy. Don Haggard sang with Judy Bess—Big Jeff's daughter—on a couple of songs, and the Rainbow Valley Boys weighed in with a bluegrass-tinged item. Songwriter Jackson Toombs was on the label, as was Ray Batts, who recorded "Maybe It's You, Maybe It's Me" in 1954. Both Toombs and Batts had recorded their songs for other labels—Ernie Young merely bought up the masters.

After 1955, Excello went on to have significant national chart action with the Gladiolas' "Little Darlin'," Lillian Offit's "Miss You So," and the Crescendos, whose "Oh Julie" came out on Nasco, the teen-oriented label Young launched in 1957.

By 1956, Excello Records was ready to branch out. Starting to hit with Nashville R&B, the label at the same time started to embrace the swampy beat of Louisiana through a critical affiliation with producer, promoter, writer and Louisianan J. D. Miller from Crowley, who wrote Kitty Wells's signature hit "It Wasn't God Who Made Honky Tonk Angels." Murray Nash introduced Ernie Young and Miller in 1955, and Miller provided Excello with an ongoing supply of Louisiana blues. He told researcher John Broven that "Ernie was a very fair man, but tight with his money, always finding a good reason for not increasing my royalty rate. He was a very, very ultraconservative businessman." Miller's first royalties came from the sales of "Lightnin' Blues" by Lightnin'

Slim, issued in October 1955, a raw blues, starkly recorded, that sold well over the Nashville airwaves via WLAC.

A second Lightnin' Slim disc at the start of 1956, "Sugar Plum," opened the floodgates for a wave of "swamp" blues artists who would help carry Excello into a new era. Lonesome Sundown, Lazy Lester, and others with equally evocative names reigned alongside Excello's later R&B artists. The most successful was Slim Harpo, whose "Rainin' in My Heart" was an R&B and popular hit in 1961.

Ernie's Record Mart: "A Good Place to Visit"

Ernie Young ran most of the Nashboro and Excello sessions himself; he used arrangers and producers like Ted Jarrett far less often than was once thought. But the secret of Young's success was not cutting-edge record production (his labels, Excello particularly, display a variety of styles and varying quality in their arrangements) but marketing—specifically the marketing of his six-pack specials by mail order through John R's WLAC radio show.

The packs always included the R&B hits of the day with at least one Excello-group record. It's telling that many Excello recordings, particularly those by one-shot artists, had loose arrangements at best and slightly chaotic openings and endings, as if Young wanted to give the artist a chance but at the same time knew that well over half the resulting discs would be giveaways with radio packages.

John Richbourg's *Midnight Special* show and *Ernie's Record Parade* generated a large percentage of Excello's sales. Ernie had the WLAC spot down to an art, continually putting together new specials with catchy names; listeners would be seduced by, for example, "Ernie's Whiz-Bang Blues Special" or "Ernie's White Cross Spiritual Special."

When Shannon Williams took over as manager of Ernie's store and promoter of much of Ernie's product in 1962—Young had suspected his former manager, Ted Adams, of favoring discs on Chess and Atlantic for the radio shows and taking payola in the form of a Pontiac and house furnishings—Williams found that he was responsible for programming John R's entire show every day. As Young himself and then Adams had done before him, each day Shannon scheduled recordings, put together the special mail-order offers, and by 5:30 got the running order and discs over to WLAC for the late-evening show, *Ernie's Record Parade*. Every two weeks, WLAC returned a batch of these discs, and Ernie Young placed them in his store racks ready for sale.

Shannon Williams recalled the family atmosphere he found at Ernie's when he started working there:

> Ernie's secretary, Dorothy, had placed an ad for help in the store. She and Ernie Young were the only ones at Nashboro/Excello up to then apart from Ted Adams, who ran the store, and the stockroom staff. I worked there filling mail orders from thirty-six states, often just letters saying, "Send me that new record by such and such." It was fun. I was on the first floor of 177 Third Avenue with the stock. The store was at ground level. The second floor had the packing room and one girl who took care of exchanges and returns. The third floor had the studio and the offices of Ernie Young and his secretary, Dorothy Keaton [formerly Duncan].
>
> The back door at third-floor level opened out onto Printers Alley, full of strip joints and beer taverns. Ernie Young always entered and left through that entrance. Sometimes we would not see him in the store. He would spend his time mostly upstairs, but we always knew he was in the building, as he smoked cigars and the distinctive smell would filter around the place.

Memphis recordman Sam Phillips, who had regular occasion to visit Ernie's in the mid-1950s, saw the Record Mart as

> a good place to visit. You had the right feeling as soon as you entered the building. It was businesslike but friendly. You felt you were going to be treated right. Ernie himself was a fine old gentleman, very honest. I truly liked him, though he could be a little aloof until you knew him. And then his wife became an invalid in the midfifties and he devoted a lot of time to her, too. Fortunately, his staff was devoted to him in return—people like Dorothy, his secre-

tary; Willie Hendrix, the sound man; and Jimmy Clifton, who could tell you every record number ever made.

Almost uniquely for a local independent record producer, Young is recalled equally well by the musicians who came and went through his studio. Al Garner called him "my man. Anything I asked for, he would let me have—a little money, an advance for car repairs, whatever. And not just me. He was giving dudes breaks who couldn't get a break in a china shop." One man who got a break from Young was singer Earl Gaines, who was adamant in his praise.

> I never did hear anyone who ever had a bad word to say about Ernie Young. He was a Christian man; he didn't believe in taking advantage of people. He was a sharp businessman, but he always paid you your three cents a disc. And he would help people. Many musicians would sell songs to him for cash, but often he would sell them back if the song got to be a hit. He'd say: "You have it, it's your song!" And he didn't have to do that.

In 1967, Young announced he would sell Excello/Nashboro to the first buyer who could meet his price. When John Richbourg and Ted Adams failed to get a solid offer together in time, Young sold the labels to the Crescent Amusement Company, with Bud Howell and Shannon Williams at the helm. In 1967, Nashboro moved to an old theater building on Woodland Street, where they had built the Woodland Sound studio. The label continued issuing records until 1974, when an investment group, AVI, bought its catalog, which eventually ended up at MCA/Universal.

After his gradual retirement in the late 1960s, Young stayed at 1031 Overton Lea Drive in the Nashville suburb of Oak Hill, where he had lived since the 1950s, an address celebrated in an Excello instrumental title. He still played an extensive collection of easy-listening music that he had built up at home while he was recording Nashville's finest roots sounds at work. Shannon Williams recalled the contrast.

> His personal taste was far different from the music he recorded. He did like church music and jazz, but mainly the shop would order special things for him—Mantovani, Al Martino, Sinatra. Ernie's taste was elevator music, really.

This revelation should perhaps be unsurprising: Young was a businessman years before he was a recordman, and unlike the Atlantic Records partners or Sam Phillips, he had no artistic vision that he wanted to realize. That he recorded his elevator music on reel-to-reel Excello session tapes that he took home was also of a piece with his much-described parsimony, but as a result, many of the original masters were irretrievably lost.

14

Broke Waiting for a Break: The Small Labels

All that effort, to make about one thousand records and then not sell them was a real disappointment.

—Frank Innocenti

Several small record labels started up in Nashville in the early 1950s, most now forgotten and some barely heard from at the time; they remain significant because their existence contributed to the development of the music-business substructure and the growth of Nashville as a recording town. The best of the rest was Speed Records, which operated between about 1951 and 1955; its founders, John Dunn, Frank Innocenti, and James Gann, were all already involved in the music business.

Mecca and Speed Records

In 1951, Frank Innocenti and Fred Shoemake both worked at the Mecca Club at 870 Murfreesboro Road, and Shoemake also played Dixieland jazz piano at the Hermitage Dinner Club. Their discouraging first foray into recording was with 4-Star Records, based on the West Coast; Innocenti recalls cutting the instrumentals "Redwing" and "Keyboard Rag" at Red Wortham's studio on Fourth and Union Street.

> We worked a little bit as a country music duo. We recorded for 4-Star Records, which had a base here in Nashville in those days run by Bob Jennings. We made those things here in Nashville, but they didn't sell anything. So then Fred and I had the idea to set up a label of our own. This was Mecca Records, which started in 1951 and had just a few releases.

The first two discs on Mecca were by Buddy Estes, who is sure they were made a couple of years earlier than Innocenti described, and his story perfectly illustrates the fluid environment in which many independent labels worked. Earl "Buddy" Estes was originally from West Palm Beach, Florida, moved to Harrisburg, Illinois, and started singing popular and country tunes over WEBQ having been influenced, in turn, by Bing Crosby, Gene Autry, and Eddy Arnold. His radio show was heard in 1949, when he was twenty-four, by Fred Shoemake's wife, and Buddy recalled his resultant visit to Nashville:

> I met Fred Shoemake at his house and he played me several songs on the piano that they owned, and he asked me to select the four I liked best to record. Then we made the recordings—two versions of each song—at the studio in the Tulane Hotel. I played rhythm guitar and was accompanied by Fred's son, Del, on mandolin and violin; the steel guitarist from my own band, Bob Murphy; and a studio musician on the bass. Then I sang one of the four songs on the Ernest Tubb Record Shop radio program,

backed by Del Shoemake and the Sundowners. I never saw any of them again after that; I went to California, and then in 1950 I was drafted into the army and spent two years in England. I never heard from Mecca Records, and never received any royalties from them.

Estes's records were aimed at the market for smooth, pop-flavored country music. "With All Your Heart," the best of his four sides on Mecca, is representative of his soothing vocal style and the influence of Eddy Arnold. In striking musical contrast, the only other known record on Mecca was by Tommy Brooks's tough R&B band. A powerful record with a solid stomp rhythm, Brooks's "Steam Pressing Woman" forged something of a link between big-band swing and hard-edged R&B; its unusual lyric uses a steam press as a metaphor for a sexually demanding woman. Innocenti and Shoemake had already written the songs Brooks made for Bullet, "Drying My Blues" and "Where Did You Go," issued early in 1951, and Innocenti recalled meeting Brooks at Ernie's Record Mart and arranging to put out a second, unissued, session that Brooks had already recorded for Bullet.

Both the Brooks discs are important in the context of Nashville music, for Innocenti recalled that the band on the recordings was a combo derived from the jazz dance band of trumpeter Chick Chavis—he was possibly referring to the Tennessee State Collegians, with whom Brooks had been trombonist and sometime singer when Chavis was leader. Chavis worked with this small combo all over Nashville between 1951 and about 1955, but no other recordings have turned up.

With little capital for promotion, the Mecca discs did not sell, and in 1952 Frank Innocenti decided to go in with John Dunn and James Gann on a new project.

I got the idea for the new name when the change came in the industry from 78- to 45-rpm [singles], and to 33-rpm albums. The question of what speed was going to prevail in the business was on everyone's lips and in the record buyers' minds. "Speed" proved to be a good name. Most all the Speed records were issued on 78s, but we did issue some 45s also.

Buddy Estes in 1950, just after he recorded for Mecca Records. The sound was Eddy Arnold, though the image was more Woody Guthrie.

Innocenti was a musician and sales rep, while Dunn and Gann were in the record-pressing business. They all saw Speed as a sideline, something to work on in the evenings and on weekends. Innocenti would do most of the recording, while Dunn and Gann would take care of manufacturing and publishing. Innocenti gave me some background:

I came to Nashville in 1942 as an air force sergeant. I was leading the 353rd Show and Dance Orchestra in the Special Services. I was born in a small coalmining town, Snowden, Pennsylvania, in 1916, just five years after my parents had come there from Italy. They passed through Ellis Island as millions did, with only the clothes on their backs. I have two brothers and two sisters, and we all had to start from scratch.

The tall, black-haired Innocenti and his wife, Lucy, moved into a home on Riverside Drive in east Nashville, and Frank kept the books at Capitol City Glass Company until

John Dunn, preparing a drink at the Gerst Haus in the days before he became a record-pressing mogul and owner of small record labels. Courtesy of John Dunn Jr.

1949. He became a semiprofessional dance-band saxophonist and featured player in the Bob Young band at the Legion Club on Ninth Avenue. He was well known around town and had even made records, which gave him a degree of experience his Speed partners needed. In 1949, he had written songs for Ernestine Woodard and backed her as Frank and the 4 Beats on Jim Bulleit's Delta label. He was working as a salesman of hillbilly and blues music when he met Dunn and Gann at Hermitage Music.

> I worked for Buster Williams's Music Sales distributorship from Memphis. I stayed in Nashville, but I was on the road from 1951 to 1954. I called on jukebox operators and record shops, selling. I was very busy, and it seemed we carried all the independent lines going—Chess, Peacock, Apollo, Sun. We had all the screamin' labels in those days. I would travel Tennessee and all down into Mississippi and Arkansas. I knew everyone in those days. I knew Sam Phillips real well. I knew Hank Williams. We were friends and did a lot of fishing in this area. Hank was helpful to me in suggesting artists to record.

Speed partner John Dunn had been involved in music since 1946, when he joined C. V. Hitchcock's Hermitage Music Company. Born in McEwen, in Humphreys County, Tennessee, in June 1920, he had dropped out of high school at age thirteen when his mother died, and he helped his father run a grocery store. He married in the late 1930s and briefly moved to east Tennessee to run a restaurant, then settled in Nashville in 1940 to work at the Vultee Aircraft Company. After a stint in the air force he set up the Magnolia Café, where he first met C. V. Hitchcock and took the job at Hermitage.

In 1947, Dunn took charge of the Bullet Plastics record plant. When Bullet started pressing discs in the old army barracks at Berry Field, Dunn had been among the first people involved, and in 1949 he became vice president. When Bullet Records folded, he changed the plant's name to Southern Plastics and moved the operation to 512 Franklin, between Fifth and Sixth Avenues South. The Franklin premises were next to Hamilton Machine Company and Weisman's restaurant, where Hitchcock and Dunn ate every day.

Dunn's son, also named John, remembered his father as

> one of those guys who came up the hard way. He was born in a little-old one-stoplight town, and he had to make his own way. He wasn't able to go to college, but he had a good business head on him. He made some good money in the record business, and he had some interesting times. I remember him having various run-ins with people, and not always about business. One time in the 1940s he was stabbed in the neck, but that was for dancing with the wrong woman.

John Dunn's role at Speed was largely organizing record manufacture and production, he said, and he was persuaded to go into the business mainly for financial reasons.

> I could see that Bullet and Tennessee Records and so on were making a little money, and so I decided to have a try at that business along with James Gann, who worked with me. We needed someone to organize the recording side of it, and so we had a musician friend in Frank Innocenti, who took that on and produced the sessions. We used a band run by Chuck Gregory on most occasions. We recorded wherever we could, mainly at the former Brown Brothers' studio and at WMAK Radio.

Hillbillies on Speed

The Speed label kicked off with "Flyin' Saucer Baby" and "Jig Saw Puzzle Heart" by Georgia Jim Odom, who arrived in Nashville from Cedartown, Georgia, in 1951. "I stayed three or four days up there," he told Colin Escott. "I just walked up and down and I saw this sign that said Speed Records. A guy listened to the songs and signed me." Disc jockey Noel Ball produced the session, and Odom found the experience disappointing. "Noel Ball signed me to a publishing contract. They sent me some records, and then Noel

Ball and Red Wortham said they would send me publishing royalties, but they never did."

Frank Innocenti explained how Speed Records came by its first real contender:

> In the summer of 1952, I met Lattie Moore as I came out of the Ernest Tubb Record Shop on lower Broadway. Lattie was a writer and guitarist who wanted to make a record, and he sung right there in the busy sidewalk for me to listen. The song was called "Juke Joint Johnny." I thought it was so good, I gave him a song contract and recording contract and cut it that very afternoon. In a hurried moment, I quickly found Noel Ball, a deejay who did some engineering for records, and three musicians: piano, bass, and drums. Lattie played guitar and had [a steel] guitarist with him.
>
> We went to a makeshift studio above the Buckley Record Shop that Noel Ball sometimes used for WMAK. No one in the band knew the song except Lattie and his [steel] player, so to fill out the sound I told the engineer to bring the drums in as loud as possible to fill out the sound of the piano. The song hit the jukeboxes fast and good. I think this was about the first rock & roll record out of Nashville, and in those early days we didn't know it.

John Dunn at Bullet Plastics had pointed Lattie and his steel-player friend Bobby Phillips toward Frank Innocenti. Moore's "Juke Joint Johnny," Speed's first classic, was the quintessential honky-tonk song delivered with vigor, although slightly suspect musicality. The disc wasn't a charted hit, but artists on major labels covered it, and forty years later it got an unexpected second lease on life when it showed up in the Matt Dillon movie *Big Town*.

Lattie Moore, born in 1924 in Allen County, Kentucky, played guitar, bass, and mandolin and first performed on WLBJ, Bowling Green, Kentucky, in 1949. He made his first record for Arrow Records in Indianapolis, then took a trip to Nashville to try out for Bullet Records. He moved on to King Records and recorded a string of drinking songs that come no finer than his "Here I Am Drunk Again" or "Out of Control."

Another singer who worked in the honky-tonk hillbilly style was Roe Hollingsworth, "Tennessee Slim," who was playing in Paris, Tennessee, when Frank Innocenti arrived there scouting for talent. Innocenti scooped up both Slim and Billy Bun Wilson, who shared a band for a while. Speed recorded Slim's "Dog House Blues" and "One Sided Love Affair" and Wilson's "Confess That You're Mine" (as Little Bun Wilson).

Tennessee Slim, born in Benton County, Tennessee, in 1918, moved with his family to Cleveland, Ohio in 1927, where he got his first guitar and formed his first band, then headed back to his home state. Wilson was a familiar face on Nashville's music scene; he had worked with everybody around for the best part of thirty years.

Guitarist Chuck Gregory hung around Speed Records and worked on Ernest Tubb's *Midnite Jamboree* in addition to his day job as a painter. He directed many Speed sessions, in addition to writing some of the songs, and produced his wife, Mary "Chickie" King. For someone with little professional experience, she sounds confident and assured on "Lov-ie Lov-ie," a rollicking boogie number on Speed. Singing was never more than a hobby for her, though, and her only public appearances were on Tubb's *Midnite Jamboree*. Raised in Santa Cruz, California, Chickie had met Gregory when he was working there and returned with him to Tennessee in 1941.

In Betty Jo, Speed recorded a very different singer; her pop-flavored vocal led a spirited pianist and drummer through "You'll Need My Help," an answer to the Carlisles' smash "No Help Wanted." Mary Catlett, Betty Jo's actual name, was a Texas singer who had begun her career in San Antonio. Openly lesbian, she performed in androgynous trouser suits years before they were common. By 1951 she was working in Houston with the cream of western swing musicians; her group the Saddle Chaps included both the influential fiddler Leon Selph and pioneering steel-guitarist Bob Dunn. But Betty Jo's move to Nashville was not successful, and she drifted out of music after recording for Speed.

Innocenti was the first producer to record writer and singer Jackson "Jack" Cleveland Toombs, a fixture of both the Nashville music industry and the town's taxi business for

Lattie Moore. Courtesy of Bear Family Records.

Jack Toombs. Courtesy of Showtime Archives [Toronto] and Colin Escott.

more than forty years. Jack recorded only one single on Speed, "Pinball Fever," and he couldn't quite remember how that came about, as he told Colin Escott.

> Jim Bulleit had wanted me to record when I was with Morris Furniture. I can't remember how I got hooked with Speed, but Frank Innocenti came into it somehow. I had lunch with Gann and Dunn. Met them at Linebaugh's, and we got to be pretty good friends. I don't remember who worked the session. It was a black bass player and a black piano player, and it was recorded at a studio right next to Speed's pressing plant.

The studio was in fact Bullet Records', as was the pressing plant, and the piano player was Shy Guy Douglas, according to session engineer Red Wortham.

Born in Murfreesboro, Tennessee, in 1925, Jack Toombs came to Nashville with his family in 1937; he started driving a cab in 1950, after his stint with Morris Furniture. His first music job was on WHOP in Hopkinsville, Kentucky, in the mid-1940s, and he started writing with Vic McAlpin around 1950. Their first song, "I've Got Other Fish to Fry," was recorded by Ricky Riddle on Tennessee; their first hit was George Morgan's "Almost."

Jack went on recording and appeared on other labels, cutting a spirited cover version of Big Mama Thornton's R&B hit "Hound Dog" under the name Cleve Jackson on Herald Records in 1953, three years before Elvis Presley's version. Then Frank Innocenti acquired the publishing rights on Toombs's greatest hit, "You're the Only Good Thing That Happened to Me":

> I quickly signed that song, and hurried a copyright because Jack had the habit of selling songs, and I didn't want it to get away. I arranged a recording session for the song on a cold, wintry Sunday night at the WLAC radio station. Jack said he had the musicians all lined up, but they proved too weak and we called it off. We cut it the following Sunday. The song hit so well it now is a standard country classic.

But not on the Speed label. Innocenti sold his share of Speed just after the Toombs session and sold those tapes to Ernie Young. "You're the Only Good Thing" eventually emerged on Excello in May 1954, one of the great country love ballads, touching in its simplicity and in its understated pledge of fidelity. Gene Autry, Billy Walker, and Ernest Tubb also recorded it, and George Morgan recorded both a hillbilly and a pop version in March and December 1959; it finally became a charted hit.

Toombs wrote for Sure-Fire Music and Cedarwood and began using a pseudonym, Jacky Trent, to cut rock & roll. His "Little Andie," on the Excello subsidiary Nasco, sold well, but Toombs never gave up his day job with the cab company.

Speed's main claim to fame was not scoring a hit record but giving Bobby Helms his start before he moved on to record "Fraulein" and other major hits for Decca. Helms was working on WWTV in Bloomington, Indiana, when he recorded "Yesterday's Lovin'" and "Hangin' Around" for Speed at the WFIU studio there. "It was no big thing," he told journalist Jimmy Guterman. "Just cut 'em, and they didn't go anywhere. We just cut 'em to sell 'em on the show."

Robert Lee Helms was born in Bloomington in 1933. His father, Fred, hosted a local country music show, and Bobby and his brother, Freddie, were already a fairly big noise in Bloomington when Bobby made his debut on Speed. When Ernest Tubb got a tape of him to Paul Cohen at Decca, Cohen signed Helms despite his similarity to Webb Pierce; at the second Decca session he recorded "Fraulein," which spent an incredible fifty-two weeks in the pop charts—eleven of them at #1. Helms also hit with "My Special Angel" and his 1957 Christmas record "Jingle Bell Rock."

Although Speed was geared to country music, in 1952 the label issued one R&B record: "Pitch a Boogie Woogie" by Charles Ruckles, a somewhat out-of-control, call-and-response item that Frank Innocenti said

> was a give-away kind of deal, a split-second decision on a guy who approached me with a song one day on Broad

Street and performed a quick audition there and then. I decided to see if there was any mileage in starting an R&B label.

Innocenti whisked the artist into either WMAK's or WLAC's studio in the fall of 1952. Charles Ruckles's music is long forgotten, but the tenor saxophonist for this one-off recording for Speed was John Coltrane, then playing in Nashville with the Gay Crosse Band.

People around Nashville remember Ruckles, a singer and pianist who worked with Louis Brooks's band on and off, as a local man, well-mannered, with a nice attitude, who played pretty good blues piano. His song's title, "Pitch a Boogie Woogie," was an in-vogue slang phrase among the black community in the 1940s. Quite how Ruckles came to the song is unknown; he probably saw it as a variation on the theme of a tune Nat Cole wrote with Cab Calloway and recorded, "Pitchin' Up a Boogie." But just maybe Ruckles had seen or been in the 1947 all-black, twenty-five-minute movie short made in Greenville, North Carolina, called *Pitch a Boogie Woogie*, a showcase for local musicians that Lord-Warner Pictures promoted as an "all-colored cast musical comedy featurette."

Frank Innocenti, John Dunn, and James Gann ran Speed for about two years. Dunn recalled the label with some pleasure but had no regret in selling it: "This was purely a part-time activity and did not do any good, so after a few years we ceased operation." Although Frank Innocenti too saw they needed to sell the label, he was less sanguine about the results of the work the partners had put in:

> I had married my wife here in Nashville. We had a daughter and twin boys, and with my duties on the road I found producing sessions and signing songs a hard job. The work of writing lead sheets, filing copyright forms, studying what to record was all too much. We all tried but we came to a point where we couldn't go on. All that effort, to make about one thousand records and then not sell them was a real disappointment.
>
> We sold the label to a man named A. C. Reed who wanted a label to promote a child star he had going. Not being a recordman, he had no pedigree in the business and the label died in 1955 sometime.

Real estate salesman A. C. Reed had decided on a whim to go into the record business. He filed incorporation papers for the new version of Speed Recording and Publishing Company in October 1953, retaining Frank Innocenti, who would soon start a new career as a mailman, as a partner, along with Reed's attorney, Walker Casey. Reed and Casey were both based in the same office building on Fourth and Union downtown.

Bobby Helms. Courtesy of Bear Family Records.

Reed's "child star," sixteen-year-old Bob Rogers, based in Kentucky, had been singing since the age of five. Speed released his "A Little Bit Late for Lovin'," a teenage date song written by Jack Toombs, in November 1953. Reed managed to keep Speed going for only two more releases, one by Little Bun Wilson and the other by Bobby Helms, both discs culled from session tapes Reed inherited from Innocenti and Dunn.

By now, John Dunn had moved on to focus with C. V. Hitchcock on their rapidly-developing record-pressing business; Southern Plastics was soon pressing for eighty labels. In 1966, C. V. Hitchcock sold his part in the company for $1.5 million to former session steel-guitarist Joe Talbot and his partners George Mecyssne and Ozell Simpkins who, with Dunn, formed United Record Pressing.

In the later 1950s, John Dunn and James Gann went into partnership with Leonard Chess to set up Dunn Record Pressing in Chicago, which Gann ran. John Dunn Jr. recalls his father's involvement with Chess and particularly with Motown Records: "He would talk to Berry Gordy of Motown at least twice a week even after he retired, and Gordy visited us frequently. He came to mother's funeral. Motown set [Dad] up with a retirement policy too."

Another World: Getting Up to Speed

While Speed Records was the biggest of the small local labels that set up in the early 1950s, the existence of several others helped boost Nashville's reputation as a recording town. The singers and songwriters that Alan Bubis felt fell out of trees couldn't all end up on Tennessee or Republic, let alone on a major recording label, and there were plenty of other people willing to start a label and try to offer an alternative recording option. New labels to appear at this time included Gold, Belmont, Hillbilly All Star, and second incarnations for World and Delta, as well as a number of vanity and promotional labels.

Just as the original owners of Speed were making plans to exit the record business, their house bandleader, Chuck Gregory, decided that he could use the same studios and pressing contacts to start his own label. Motivated by the belief that he had brought artists to Speed with little reward, Gregory formed Gold Records with his brother-in-law, Peter Petrarca, around 1953. Among the artists he had steered to Speed was his wife, Mary—"Chickie" King—whose "I Need Your Lovin'" was Gold's first release. Gregory claimed that Chickie's second record for Gold, "Just Walkin' in the Rain," was the original version, insisting that he acquired the song through Red Wortham, who for his part insisted that the Prisonaires' version came first. That version became a hit on Sun, as did Johnnie Ray's on Columbia.

Gold also issued a disc by Billy Wilson, and Gregory said that he recorded Jack Toombs and others on a number of small labels in later years; these would essentially mark the end of his many years on the Nashville music scene. A Kentuckian, Gregory had come to town as a child in the early 1930s and was singing and playing in clubs with Al Hicks and his Hickory Sticks by the time he was drafted ten years later. A good guitarist, he was spotted by Bill Monroe and worked show dates with him, met Ernest Tubb at the Opry, joined Tubb's traveling show, and then took on the management of Tubb's *Midnite Jamboree* and simultaneously formed his own band.

> I had a good band at that time, and we worked shows with many of the top artists. We worked mainly in the local area. We did go on some longer tours, but we certainly didn't travel full-time. I had a job as a painter that I kept up most of the while. I fooled around with all parts of the music business for years and years, but never could quite make a good solid living at it. I retired in 1956 from playing and painting after an accident, and I took on the role of business manager of the painters' union.

In June 1953, four months before A. C. Reed bought into Speed Records, Michael Thrower, a real estate agent who worked with Reed in the Commerce Union Bank building on Union Street, established World Records Inc. with partners G. C. White Sr. and G. C. White Jr. One of the Whites worked in the record-pressing business with John Dunn, and the Bob White who performed on half the four known World discs was probably a relative. Whether or not World Records Inc. made some arrangement with Jordan Stokes over the use of the World name, the new labels bore a completely different design from the former World logo. And although World registered all its songs with Dot Music as publishers, the company had no obvious relationship with Randy Wood.

One of World's two numerical series comprised just one record, World 1651 by the Burt Henry Septet, "Blues Impromptu," apparently aimed at the jazz market. The other, a 1400 series, comprised two discs by Bob White and the Folklanders, "String Band Boogie" and "My Heart Depends on You," subdued, folksy items and not the strongest recordings in the marketplace.

The only other disc in this series marked the first recordings by R&B musician Ted Jarrett—his "Love Me a Long Long Time" and "The Road." Jarrett told me that WLAC announcer John Richbourg engineered the session at the radio station; he mainly recalled his euphoria at making a record at all.

> That was my first involvement with recording. It was set up through John Richbourg, the deejay, who acted as the in-between man. I never knew who the label was, I just cut the session. We were just high on having a good time and on getting recorded and being on records. I was just so proud to have a record out that I never did take too much notice of the business side of the deal. It was just a thrill to be on record at that time. We wanted to make things happen.

In fact, Jarrett thought, wrongly, that World Records was an out-of-town label. It is also possible that the recordings were made a little earlier than the World label's incorporation in 1953, because Fats Domino recorded "The Road" under the title "Long Lonesome Journey" in April 1952. Jarrett could have made his own version as a demonstration disc or to cash in on the release of Domino's version. On his recording, Jarrett moans a downcast story about traveling a dark route, an interesting disc that combined all kinds of old and new elements, original and unoriginal ideas from the budding producer. He is revealed as an adequate vocalist on the midpaced "Love Me," although the arrangement contains a little of everything, including a mambo kick in parts presaged by a bongo effect in the intro. Saxophonist Louis Brooks remembered being on the session, and indeed the tone and style of his playing come through clearly. The songs were credited to "Daddy Dean," for no reason that Jarrett could recall—"It was just a name that appealed to me"—although he might have wanted to avoid upsetting his emerging production roles with Republic and Excello.

The 1953 version of World Records was not the only short-lived recording business that year. Mrs. A. Lettie Sweeney operated Belmont Records as an experiment from her house at 1110 Sixteenth Avenue South near Belmont College, in an area that is now part of Music Row. Sweeney was yet another person who moved into records from the restaurant business; in 1940 she had been a cook at a restaurant at 211 Woodland in Nashville.

Belmont Records issued only three discs, all rather curious. One pairs the white gospel Victory Quartet with Lonnie Hooberry narrating "The Christ Child's Story." (Hooberry may have been connected with Hooberry's Bookstore at Commerce and Fifth Avenue.) The other two records both feature Jesse Harrison's forgettable pop-country recording of "Someone New," backed on one disc by Bill Cooper, and on the other disc by "The Smoke House," recorded by Liza Lee, who sometimes billed herself as "Nashville's only woman undertaker."

Joe Reavis "was a screwy little guy who ran a cheap and fast studio," recalled Joe Allison, who used the Reavis operation for Capitol. "It was a demo studio really—everyone used him to cut demos—but he always wanted to be in the record business himself." Reavis briefly achieved that objective with a vanity label, Reavis Records, which custom-pressed records for clients. Some of these seem to have been issued at least semi-seriously as commercial discs; the Becker Sisters' "Campfire Capers" was one, with a piano backing reminiscent of Del Wood.

Reavis operated variously from locations on Beech Avenue, Church Street, and Fourth Avenue North before moving to 420a Broadway, next door and upstairs from Mom's Restaurant, now Tootsie's Orchid Lounge. He had sold the studio by 1957 to the partnership of local attorney Kenny

Marlow and songwriter Gary Walker. Marlow went on to run several small labels in the late 1950s, including Deb, Mark, and Image. Walker was active in music publishing for many years before he launched a Nashville-based chain of used record stores, the Great Escape.

Although promotional discs were rarely pressed up as commercial ventures, one that turned up in flea markets around Nashville was Big Jeff Bess's record for a label called, improbably, Ma An' Pa Say, on which he extols the virtues of Hom-Bru Beer. Bess recalled that Hom-Bru was brewed locally by a German family that owned Nashville's only German eatery, the Gerst Haus, but he couldn't say with certainty when the disc was recorded. Both songs give a good sense of what Jeff's early-morning listeners heard on WLAC. His band is as tight and sharp as legend has always insisted.

A different kind of promotional effort was the label named Wally Fowler, which the gospel singer started around 1951 and promoted over WSM as a "Record of the Month Club." Releases by the Goodman Family and the Oak Ridge Quartet dominated, largely recycled from Bullet sessions.

Different again was the Artist label, formed early in 1955 by two men who spent most of their careers in Alabama radio; disc jockey, singer, and promoter Happy Wilson, and guitarist and bandleader Slim Lay. Wilson moved to Nashville at this time to work for Capitol Records and to promote his wife, singer Marion Worth, while Lay remained in Huntsville, Alabama, but brought talent to Nashville to record. Artist Records were made mainly for the artists to sell at live performances, though Wilson hoped to feed songs and performers to Capitol. Slim Lay had earlier recorded a song about "Susie" for Jim Bulleit's Delta label, and on Artist he developed the obscure theme with "Susie's Poodle Dog." The label folded within a couple of years, but not before it had released a song by two gospel singers, Ollen and Dennis, about a fatal collision between a train and a busload of children, the "Tragedy of Spring City."

The Red Wortham Orchestra at the Andrew Jackson Hotel, early 1940s. Red on guitar. Courtesy of the author.

Red Wortham: Wheeling and Dealing

Finally among the smaller record labels were Hillbilly All Star and Delta, both run by Red Wortham, who was part of the cement that kept the local record business together. Like Murray Nash, he turned his hand to a range of promotional, publishing, and recording activities. Like Nash, he played a major role in the scene but exaggerated it so much that people disregarded his real achievements as a musician, studio owner, songwriter, publisher, and promoter.

Wilburn Clyde "Red" Wortham came to Nashville from Stewart County, Tennessee, in 1929, aged nine, and developed into a fine dance-band guitarist. At age fifteen he was playing over WLAC when the station manager F. C. Sowell put him together with mandolin player Charlie Head on the "Charlie and Red" show, playing folk and hillbilly tunes as well as jazzier, popular songs; the show lasted well into the 1940s. Guitarist Billy Byrd also worked with the duo, and as "Bill and Red—Guitar Twins," Red and Billy appeared in theaters and traveling package shows—"Stars from the Grand Ole Opry"—typically headlined by DeFord Bailey and with WLAC musicians actually dominating the bill.

Around the age of twenty, in 1940, Wortham contracted tuberculosis and was hospitalized for a year or so. There was no question of his being drafted, and he spent the next few years as a musician, having formed a dance band that toured the country, playing on the coattails of Francis Craig, Beasley Smith, and Owen Bradley.

He got to know Owen and Harold Bradley through a fellow musician, he told me.

> Charlie [Head] and I also used to work with a bass player called Golden Stewart who lived on Lucille Street, near to Owen and Harold Bradley. I became acquainted with them at that time. Harold was trying to learn guitar, and I used to help show him chords and strokes. He was a real nice guy.

Harold Bradley has noted that Wortham had one of the first electric guitars in town, a Gibson ES 250; which Wortham remembers buying on the spot:

> I went with my friend Billy Byrd to a demonstration by a man from the Gibson company at a store on Eighth Avenue. The man had three different guitars and was taking orders. I said I liked the one he was playing and wanted that actual one. After some argument, I was able to walk out of the store with it that day. It caused a real stir around town. One of my regrets is that neither my orchestra or the WLAC duo ever made any recordings at that time, so the sound of that guitar is now lost.

Not surprisingly, Wortham met his wife-to-be, singer Phyllis Spain, from Kingston Springs, Tennessee, through a musical connection,

> the tenor-sax man in my orchestra, who was Jack Gregory. She was at WSM radio applying for the job as a singer with the staff orchestra on networked shows. Jack and I were having lunch at the Hermitage Hotel, and he asked if he could bring her so that she could talk about singing with my band. She was a very attractive young lady, and I called an audition with my band, and she passed with flying colors. I worked cocktail hours in the evenings with a small unit, and dances at night with my full band. She sang and traveled with me on all engagements. We worked hotels and clubs all over the country in the late 1940s. Being together so much I became very attached to her and proposed.

Billy Byrd, playing Red Wortham's Gibson, early 1940s. Courtesy of the author.

When Wortham developed muscular dystrophy, he gradually gave up playing in favor of songwriting and wrote "Imagination" (not the popular Van Heusen-Burke tune) in 1947 for his wife. He also recorded Phyllis under a new name for Bullet.

> She was a pop singer, but when I started writing country songs I raised her key range a tone and a half so she would sound like a hillbilly singer. I changed her name to Tabby West for this purpose. I didn't want a hillbilly singer with a pop orchestra. The first time we presented

her as a country singer was at Fort Campbell military base when we did a show for the 101st Airborne. They liked her, so I kept her as Phyllis Spain with the orchestra and Tabby West with the little country band, which included Grady Martin on guitar and Del Wood on piano.

Her first efforts at recording were "Tennessee Hayride" and "Last Night I Heard Somebody Cry." I wrote both sides, and they were covered by Sue Thompson and some other people. It was a successful record, by no means a hit, but it got a lot of airplay and made money. There was also "Invading My Dreams." Bullet records had a very small studio upstairs over the pressing plant. This is where we recorded Tabby. I was the engineer on those sessions. Red [Hitchcock] originally had another man to produce sessions but he got drunk and passed out on the floor one day, so Red Hitchcock asked me to do the production more and more. I was presenting songs to all record labels and I had to make demos for artists, so I used to ask Tabby to sing on them. This is how Decca got to hear of her.

Owen Bradley called and asked if the singer on the demos would record a session for their subsidiary label, Coral. He said could I have her ready that night. You should have seen the look on his face when I walked in with Phyllis. He knew her well and knew she was a pop singer and just couldn't believe she was the person demoing the country songs. She recorded on Coral for a while and then moved to Decca. Tabby got a real break when she landed a spot on the *Ozark Jubilee* show with Red Foley. But that meant her going in one direction and me another, and we grew apart and got divorced.

Tabby West relocated to Springfield, Missouri, took part in successful television and touring shows with Red Foley, and had some minor recording successes with Decca and Capitol, but Wortham stayed to became one of the first wheeler-dealers in Nashville. He pitched songs or master recordings to Decca, Mercury, or whoever would listen; he arranged and engineered sessions, soon forsaking pop music for country and blues; and he wrote songs. One lucrative songwriting deal he remembers began

at Owen Bradley's first studio, at Second Street [Second Avenue South] in Nashville, where Paul Cohen was trying to record Billy Wallace on "Back Street Affair." The session was going nowhere and Paul was starting to get comfortable in the control room, with his girlfriend massaging his neck. Paul decided he was hungry and asked her to go out and get some food, and he pulled out a wad of money. She said, "I don't want your money, I want your time." This played on my mind and I woke up that night at three and wrote a song with that title. It was the B side of Kitty Wells's first big hit.

The record was made in May 1952 at the Castle studio along with the top side, "It Wasn't God Who Made Honky Tonk Angels," a major hit for Decca.

But Wortham's publishing experiences were mixed, he said, and he held strong views on that side of the music business.

"I Don't Want Your Money" was put on the publishing company Paul Cohen controlled. But I didn't get paid and I had to sue for it. He asked me why I was suing, and I explained. He called his bookkeeper Joe Diamond, who was supposed to have paid me. He had used the money himself. Paul got me my money. Not all writers are as lucky. There was a lot of Joe Diamonds around. . . .

Hits like "Near You" started to attract a lot of out-of-town publishers. They started moving in, trying to sign writers and singers. That would have been good, but at the same time along came the hip-pocket publishers. They thought of us as dumb hillbillies. Their contracts were so one-sided you couldn't get anything. Syd Nathan of King Records was laughing at the deejay convention one year about his policy of withholding publishing royalties below five hundred dollars. If people sued, he would settle. Otherwise he would keep the money. He said: "Five hundred dollars is not much unless you have hundreds of songs. Then that becomes a nice sum."

Owen Bradley signs singer Tommy Smith. Courtesy of the author.

Still, Wortham may have been quick to learn some of these practices; other writers and singers have told a number of Wortham-didn't-pay stories.

In the later part of 1952 Wortham spent some time in Florida managing the Rebels Quartet gospel group for Jim Bulleit, but early in 1953 he was back in town to set up a publishing and recording business at 232½ Fourth Avenue North behind a cigar store, next to Krystal's hamburgers.

> I recorded anything, including Eddy Arnold transcriptions for radio, but mainly I recorded black musicians. No one would touch black music except Ernie Young, so I decided to do that. I leased recordings to Decca, King,

> Chess—those labels. I made some of Jim Bulleit's J-B recordings there, too. Paul Cohen at Decca used a lot of my R&B cuts. One time he took a group to New York, but they couldn't record anything there. They had to have someone who knew about improvised instruments and sounds. We used tubs and string as a bass fiddle, and bouzoukis and saws on early R&B cuts. They would never play the same song twice and you only had single-track tape, so you had to keep on your toes. I often made demos for people. Joe Reavis had a demo studio, but he didn't often record blues. I did, and if it was any good, then I'd see what I could do with it. Because promotion was my main business. I had other people to help in the studio, Noel Ball and engineers from WLAC, mainly.

Wortham's most spectacular promotional activity was with the Prisonaires, of course, but they were not the only group at the Tennessee State Penitentiary he recorded that year. He told me:

> I had a black gospel group, the Canaan Jubilee Singers. I set up the deal in November 1953 with D Kilpatrick at Mercury, and the warden at the prison let me go down to the Bradley studio at Twenty-First Avenue South in Hillsboro Village. That was a good studio. We recorded "I Bowed Down and Cried Holy."

Wortham and Phyllis lived at 1315 Riverside Drive in east Nashville in 1951, three blocks from Frank Innocenti of Speed Records. By 1953, they had moved to nearby Ordway Place, where Wortham established the short-lived label Hillbilly All Star.

The two known discs on Hillbilly All Star were both idiosyncratic. The first, Rod Taylor and his Blue Valley Boys performing "Too Wet to Plow," was an out-of-the-ordinary song complete with falsetto calls as the singer laments his bad fortune. The second disc was "Chili Dippin' Mama" by Vernon Way and his Carolina String Band. It has an engagingly coy feel—a smutty song delivered with suspect intonation and timing—and is a wonderfully compelling record. Vernon Way had been the manager of the Two Legs clothing store in the building opposite Wortham's Fourth Avenue Studio since the mid-1940s.

In 1955, Wortham reactivated Delta Records, having acquired the name from Jim Bulleit. Some of his 1500 series of releases promised much, but Whitey Pullen's "Broke Waiting for a Break" turned out to be the label's most apposite title. Delta's best hope was Tommy Smith, the polished country singer who had recorded for Tennessee/Republic. Wortham discovered Smith, the "hillbilly hairstylist," back cutting hair at Harvey's Department Store. Smith's riveting version of "I'm a Fool" was covered by Slim Whitman in February 1956, though Whitman's record credits Bob Nolan as composer rather than Smith.

Smith, a major-league vocalist, eventually recorded briefly for Decca in 1956. By then, though, his haunting, beautifully poised hillbilly music was slipping from favor. He wrote several songs for Ernest Tubb's music-publishing company, but Wortham regretted that Smith never reached his potential. "Tommy was basically a nice guy," he said. "We got along together, but other people couldn't get along with him. He wasn't always very cooperative."

Overall, Red Wortham succeeded in his music-business wheeling and dealing, and like Murray Nash and disc jockey Noel Ball, he ran an operation that enabled the recording of many more discs in Nashville than the few main studios could cope with.

Record Distribution: Faith and Hard Work

The one area that Wortham did not get into was record distribution, a vital part of Nashville's postwar music activity. The sharp rise in the number of independent record labels after the war led to an increase in independent distributors. The largest in the area, and one of the earliest, was Music Sales in Memphis, which handled around twenty lines as early as 1946. That year, apart from the Bullet/Hermitage/Volunteer outfit, Nashville had only a handful of smaller distributors, most handling one or two labels. The biggest of these was Tennessee Music Sales, which handled Mercury and three others, until it was joined by Coastline.

The first serious local challenge to Music Sales came

in 1953 when Hutch Carlock started Music City Record Distributors. Carlock, who was from Gallatin, started out with Bullet Records, probably the first salaried salesman working out of Nashville for a Nashville-based record company. His story covers a lot of postwar Nashville music ground, ten years of personalities, recordings, and distribution.

> I joined the old Bullet company as an on-the-road salesman early in 1947. Bullet was expanding at that time and Jim Bulleit advertised for two employees. Jimmy Green and myself were taken on and we set about the task of selling country records to local stores all through Tennessee and to the wholesale distributors wherever we could. We started out with records by artists like the York Brothers, who were a big act with "Hamtramck Mama" and other tunes, and Minnie Pearl and the other Opry regulars. This was before the company had its really big hits.
>
> I think I got the job because of my experience in selling and in traveling. I first came to Nashville just after the war, in 1945. I was born in 1923 and I came to the big city looking for work. I had several jobs. My first big job was selling insurance, and then I became a surveyor for the Rural Electrification Program. That entailed me traveling all through west Tennessee and gave me useful local knowledge. Through 1947 we were involved primarily in selling copies of "Near You." We moved about three million of that title real fast during the year. I left Bullet in 1948 when they hit distribution problems and did away with their sales department. I went into record distribution again, working with Bill Beasley in a company called Coastline. Then, just before Christmas 1952, Jimmy Green and I formed our own operation, Music City Record Distributors, which commenced trading in January 1953. We would take turns at running the shipping and receiving department and traveling on the road. We started with a capital of five hundred dollars and ended our first year with one employee and a net profit of eighteen thousand dollars.
>
> The early days in Nashville were hard. At first our suppliers offered quite lenient credit terms and were protective to us, giving us a chance, but our limited capital meant we never could keep up, and it was many years before we were established. The first year we had a turnover of stock valued at a million dollars was 1958, but as late as 1955 we turned over only $345,000 and made just $40,000 net. The music business in Nashville was expanding all the time, but it took a lot of faith and hard work to make it all happen.

15

Publishing Folk Tunes: Fred Rose and Hickory Records

Fred Rose took hillbilly music over the mountain. He took it to people who had never heard of it.

—Hugh Cherry

If the development of local recording companies in Nashville began with the work of Jim Bulleit, music publishing in the city was even more closely identified with the efforts of Fred Rose. From a pop music background, Rose was a singer, songwriter, radio performer, pianist, recording artist, and record producer. He became the driving force behind the internationally renowned Acuff-Rose Publications and helped lay the foundation for today's Nashville music scene, as longtime music-industry personages Hugh Cherry and Alan Bubis attest.

"The most important man the industry in this town had was Fred Rose," Hugh Cherry claimed. "He wrote hits, and he stole nothing. He's all but forgotten and that angers me. Fred Rose took hillbilly music over the mountain. He took it to people who had never heard of it." Bubis said that Rose

> really got things going around here. He was very well liked and he gave the songwriters a shot at making some regular money, where before most of the publishers from up north would come down and take the songs and hardly pay anybody. Acuff-Rose really helped start the music business in Nashville—or at least gave it a kick up the road, put it that way.

Fred Rose and Music Publishing

When Indiana-born songwriter Fred Rose and east Tennessean singing star Roy Acuff had joined forces in 1942 to set up Acuff-Rose Publications, their publicity warned the world to look out for folk tunes and popular hits from Nashville; the company delivered spectacularly on both in the succeeding years.

In 1946, Rose began a professional relationship with a songwriter from Alabama with a reputation for being unreliable, Hank Williams. He went on to produce Hank's recordings for Sterling and MGM Records, helping the singer achieve just the right balance between the raw, almost outdated folksiness he started out with and a more crafted popular music. By the time of Williams's early but almost inevitable death just seven years later, major pop acts were covering many of his hits like "Hey, Good Lookin'," "Cold Cold Heart," and "Jambalaya"—and Hank Williams was the greatest star in country music.

The relationship with Williams sometimes obscures Rose's achievement in publishing other hits in the ten years after the war, of which two of the biggest—"Jealous Heart" and "Tennessee Waltz"— were not Hank Williams tunes. Rose himself wrote seventeen top-selling songs during this time, including "Take These Chains from My Heart," "Roly Poly," and "Blue Eyes Crying in the Rain." Originally an ASCAP writer, he placed his new songs with Acuff-Rose's ASCAP affiliate, Milene Music—a name derived from the names of the partners' wives, Mildred Acuff and Lorene Rose. For a brief period in 1942–43, Rose also wrote under the name Floyd Jenkins for the BMI-affiliated Acuff-Rose itself, until ASCAP rules required that he publish through Milene.

At first, the local competition for Acuff-Rose was limited to self-publishers and gospel-music companies. The first serious moves came in 1946, by which time Wallace Fowler Publications was operating from a WSM-owned office on Seventh Avenue North. That April, the ASCAP giant Leeds Music opened a Nashville office under the direction of singer Riley Shepard. Until 1949, Bullet Music was the only publisher associated with a local recording company; Jim Bulleit acquired Wallace Fowler Publications that year, and the West Coast publisher Fred Stryker's Fairway Music opened an office at 311 Church Street. In 1950, Tennessee Records started Tennessee Music in conjunction with veteran New York publisher Dave Dreyer, then launched BABB Music.

More publishing companies specifically associated with independent record labels sprang up, following Bullet's and Tennessee's lead, less to acquire and promote copyrights as Acuff-Rose did than to avoid paying an outside company to publish their discs. The independent labels usually tried to own at least one song per disc; then, if a singer on a larger label or a pop orchestra cut one of their songs, the windfall would be substantial. Randy Wood formed Dot Music in 1950, and the pace quickened in 1951: Ernie Young opened Excellorec Music, while Randy Wood and Beasley Smith formed Randy Smith Music, joining Milene as an ASCAP island in a sea of BMI affiliates. In 1952, Vic McAlpin opened an office for Melody Trails, and Gallatin Music followed in 1953. Red Foley formed a short-lived company, Old Hickory Music, and attorney Kenny Marlow organized Kenny Music at 535 Church Street. In 1954, musicians Hank Garland and Roy Wiggins formed Harpeth Hills Music in Brentwood.

Acuff-Rose and publishing, recording, and political heavyweights: *at rear, from left:* Bert Hutchison, Frank Kelton, Wesley Rose, Tennessee governor Gordon Browning, Murray Nash, D Kilpatrick, Fred Rose, Randy Wood; *front row, from left*: Pee Wee King, Audrey Williams, George Morgan, Hank Williams, and Tex Williams. Courtesy of the author.

Tree Music: Jack Stapp and Buddy Killen

WSM program manager Jack Stapp, in partnership with Louis Cowan, a New York–based broadcasting production executive, formed Tree Music, the first in Nashville to follow Acuff-Rose as an unaffiliated local publisher.

A 1951 meeting in the Drum Room at the Andrew Jackson Hotel between longtime radio man Stapp and Cowan, his boss during the war, changed the direction of Stapp's life and significantly extended the publishing arm of Nashville's music business. As Stapp later recalled:

Buddy Killen. Courtesy of Country Music Hall of Fame and Museum.

> Lou Cowan said to me, "Jack, why don't you go into some form of record or music business? This town is popping wide open and you're working yourself to death. Try to build something for yourself." So I said to him that I didn't have the time or the money, but he said that he would run the office end of it from New York. He said, "You just get the songs recorded and get you some writers." His wife, Polly, thought it was a good idea and drew a tree on the back of a menu right there in the Drum Room. She said, "You can talk about the branches growing and the company taking on roots and being alive."

Polly Cowan, heiress to the Speigel catalog business, in fact bankrolled Tree Music. Louis Cowan owned a radio production agency and was later involved in pioneering TV game shows like the *$64,000 Question*. Nashville native Jack Stapp, born in 1912, grew up in Atlanta and began his career programming the music piped into rooms at the Winecoff Hotel, then joined the Georgia State Tech station, WGST, in 1929. He went on to become evening network manager for CBS in New York and returned to Nashville in 1938 as program manager at WSM, where he intended to create programs that could be networked, such as *Sunday Down South*. Soon afterward, he was instrumental in getting the Prince Albert Tobacco–sponsored portion of the Opry onto NBC.

After a stint in London working on psychological radio warfare in the early 1940s, feeding information programs out to European countries, Stapp continued to work mainly in radio and got his first taste of the music-publishing business when he was credited as cowriter of the 1950 smash "Chattanoogie Shoe Shine Boy." "It was about a black guy called Clifford, a porter at WSM who used to pop a shoeshine rag to make extra money," said Stapp's later partner, Buddy Killen. Stapp's claim that he and WSM manager Harry Stone wrote the song was the subject of a major legal action by the wife of the late David "Bunny" Biggs that year. The suit claimed that Biggs wrote a similar song and before he died showed it to Stone. The reality is that Fred Rose wrote the song and gave it to Stapp and Stone in return for their having used Acuff-Rose songs on WSM.

Tree got going in 1951 but existed on advance royalties from BMI until late 1953, when Stapp hired bass player Buddy Killen for thirty-five dollars a week to work with writers, artists, and record producers. The company took off under the energetic and enthusiastic Killen, who at first did not even have an office; he brokered deals in the studios or corridors of WSM or at Mom's Restaurant. As Killen told me:

> Jack didn't run Tree at all. He had [steel guitarist] Jerry Byrd working it for him but nothing happened. I had done some demo work he liked and he employed me instead. I shared an office with [music journalist] Charlie Lamb until 1956, when we moved to the Cumberland Lodge Building.

Killen was instrumental in running the company from 1954 right through to 1991.

As one of eight children, Buddy Killen, born William Doyce Killen in 1933, had as a child worked in the fields near Florence, Alabama: "Back then, if you could walk you could work, at something," he wrote in his autobiography. Killen and his Florence neighbor Autry Inman learned to play guitar together, and by 1951, Inman was writing songs and recording with Bill Beasley and, for a time, with Decca. That September he got Killen a job playing bass with Jamup and Honey and then with George Morgan on Opry road shows. Killen found Nashville inhospitable at first: "In 1951, the country music community was not accepted in Nashville. There seemed to be a feeling about the music business that said, 'If you don't feed it then it will go away.'" Unperturbed, he wrote songs for George Morgan and Ray Price and recorded for Bill Beasley as a featured artist, but by then he was demoing songs for friends who wanted to get published, and Jack Stapp had already talked him into trying that line of business.

One of Killen's early successes was his business relationship with songwriter Mae Axton, from whom Killen and Stapp were able to acquire "Heartbreak Hotel" at the November 1955 Disc Jockey Convention. When Elvis Presley joined RCA and recorded that song in Nashville, Tree secured its place in the wider world of popular music.

Cedarwood Music: Jim Denny

Jim Denny, with backing from Webb Pierce, formed Acuff-Rose's next major competitor, Cedarwood Music, in January 1953, along with a parallel company with Carl Smith, Driftwood Music, that was eventually assimilated into Cedarwood. When he organized the company, Denny was the Opry House manager and ran WSM's booking department; like Stapp, he at first ran his new business from the WSM offices. He moved to his own office on Seventh Avenue North in 1954, still working at it part-time until 1956, when he left WSM to concentrate on Cedarwood and launch his booking agency. He later moved to offices on Sixteenth Avenue South, across from the Bradley studios in an area that became known as Music Row—one of the first music executives to relocate to what was then a residential area.

Jim Denny at his Cedarwood desk. Courtesy of Country Music Hall of Fame and Museum.

Born near Difficult, Tennessee, in 1911, Jim Denny arrived in Nashville in 1922 with forty cents and instructions to go live with an aunt. On leaving school, he worked for the National Life and Accident Insurance Company as a mail delivery boy. He was fascinated by WSM and the Opry, and became an usher and bouncer before taking over the Opry concessions; by late 1947, the self-made Denny was managing WSM's talent agency. For the next ten years, promoters who wanted to hire WSM or Opry talent had to work through him. As a result, he became influential, if not always well liked.

At the end of Denny's ten years in charge of the agency, *Billboard* named him Country Music Man of the Year, which the *Music Reporter* expanded upon by calling Denny a colossus looming over the field of country music: "Besides his personal contacts, his name carries weight so that his judgment is constantly sought and freely given. As Music City developed, he early recognized what was happening and threw himself into the expansion." Denny died of cancer in 1963, leaving his wife, former dancer Dollie Dearman, to run the business with his son, Bill Denny, another successful figure in the Nashville music business.

Fred Rose's Hickory Records: Stone Country

In December 1945, Acuff-Rose had brought in Fred Rose's son, Wesley, an accountant and auditor, as general manager, freeing the elder Rose to develop new writers and artists, most notably Hank Williams. Hired the following March, songwriter Mel Foree became the first music-publishing promotion man in Nashville. When the company moved to new offices on Franklin Road in 1949, accountant Bud Brown joined the staff, followed in 1951 by former Mercury producer Murray Nash, who helped recruit and pitch songs, promote records, and work with artists.

Fred Rose was first and foremost a writer and publisher, but the deal he had with Hank Williams and MGM Records drew him more and more into the recording end of the business. He recorded many other artists for MGM, including himself, none of whom were remotely successful. Either Rose's disillusionment with MGM or MGM's disillusionment with Rose after Williams's death may have set him on the road toward forming his own label.

Murray Nash thought there was another factor—exclusive recording-company arrangements that favored one publisher over another. Acuff-Rose had a special arrangement with MGM because of Hank Williams, and both Mercury Records and Ken Nelson at Capitol were open to recording Acuff-Rose songs. However, RCA, Decca, and Columbia each had their own publishing tie-ins and favored contacts. According to Nash:

> The biggest conflict in the publishing business was the advantage that Jim Denny and Jack Stapp had in country music, with their WSM connection. Fred was quite bitter about it and didn't know how to handle it or to better it.

Whatever the motivating force, Fred Rose was formulating plans for a record label by September 1953, some nine months after Hank Williams died. Bud Brown, the new label's manager during the 1960s, explained how Rose named his company: "Fred wanted to have a regional identity, something with dignity yet also a country flavor. Hickory was the name given to President Andrew Jackson and reflected his Hermitage home nearby Nashville with its hickory trees."

When Rose launched Hickory Records in January 1954, he told the music press that "Nashville was selected as our base since very few record manufacturers actually operate their country music activities from the area where country music is actually made. Nashville is the natural center."

Hickory's early years were its most vibrant, if not its most successful. Fred Rose supervised most of the releases and cultivated a string of locally based songwriters and performers, including Tommy Hill, Danny Davis, Boudleaux Bryant, Howard White, and Opal Jean. He also recorded Jimmy Sweeney, formerly with Tennessee Records and one of the first black singers to work in the Nashville country music industry, and the more traditional McCormick Brothers and Wilma Lee & Stoney Cooper.

Although the label's inauspicious first release was a song by Bobby Dick, "The Lord's Last Supper," Tommy Hill was the first musician to record a Hickory session. He had been recording for Decca, he said, when Fred Rose approached him at the 1953 Disc Jockey Convention in Nashville.

> Fred said that he had heard me on Decca and seen me play and that he heard something in me that he thought was commercial. He took me and Paul Cohen from Decca to one side and he said to Paul: "I'm starting a new label and I've got plans for this boy and I would like you to release him from Decca." He told me he thought he could do something special with me and he took me and some others under his wing both as artists and writers.
>
> At that time, Fred saw Hickory as a project that could turn into a major label. Fred wanted nothing but the best. He had a fine studio on Franklin Road and he employed the best musicians. My sessions were not made

with my road band. We had Chet Atkins, Floyd Cramer, Jimmy Day, and Jerry Byrd—men of that quality. And Murray Nash was a good session engineer. It was a real quality set-up.

Tommy Hill's first Hickory record, "The Life That I'm Living," struck the high moral tone that Fred Rose liked as a recovered alcoholic and Christian Scientist; it was a small hit for the new label. (Rose didn't like drinking songs unless drinking was framed negatively, as in this piece.) The Hickory session logs note that it was recorded in December 1953 at Rose's home studio. Hill had several small hits on Hickory, the best being a catchy honky-tonk number from 1955, "Mr. Jukebox."

Born in 1929 on a farm near San Antonio, Hill had grown up listening to country music on the powerful Mexican border radio stations and worked as a musician with Big Bill Lister and Smiley Burnette. He joined Webb Pierce as hired fiddle player in February 1952, moved to Shreveport, where Pierce was a star on KWKH's *Louisiana Hayride*, and gave Pierce half-interest in a song Hill had recorded for Imperial, "Slowly," which Pierce took to #1 for seventeen weeks. Hill subsequently launched his own band in Shreveport, featuring his sister Goldie, who soon became a Decca star in her own right. In 1954, he moved to Nashville.

After his discs for Hickory, Hill continued performing, sometimes as opening act for Lefty Frizzell or Jim Reeves, until 1959, when he launched a career as a producer and engineer with Starday until that label was sold in 1968. Later, he organized Stop Records with Pete Drake, and then worked for Gusto Records.

The first female singer on Hickory was Opal Jean Amburgey, born in Neon, Kentucky, in March 1925. She broke into the entertainment business with her sisters, Irene (later known professionally as Martha Carson) and Bertha, working as a hillbilly band called the Sunshine Sisters on WLAP in Lexington, Kentucky. Their other aliases included the Coon Creek Girls, the Hoot Owl Holler Girls, and the Amber Sisters. Opal's second husband, Salty Holmes, brought her into his act, and they became Salty and Mattie O'Neill.

Fred Rose had lined up Martha Carson's deal with Capitol that resulted in a major gospel hit, "Satisfied," on which Opal Jean sang backup, and Rose clearly kept her in mind for Hickory. Her "Tennessee Courtin' Time" was a Fred Rose–Hy Heath song very much in the style of a song Rose cowrote for Hank Williams, "Settin' the Woods on Fire."

Ernie Chaffin's two Hickory records came from a single session in May 1954, and "I'm Gonna Salt My Sugar Away," particularly, underlined the excellence of his voice. Born in Water Valley, Mississippi, in 1928, Chaffin grew up listening to the Opry. He met Murphy "Pee Wee" Maddux playing at a club, and Maddux brought Ernie to Nashville in 1954. They met Jim Denny, who introduced them to Paul Cohen, saying, "I got a boy here sounds a little like Eddy Arnold, a little like Red Foley, a little like Marty Robbins, but not a lot like anyone." Cohen offered a four-year deal, but Chaffin didn't like his attitude.

"Then we went to see Fred Rose and he was a different kind of person altogether," recalled Ernie. "He was a fine person. Made me feel relaxed." "Get Me on Your Mind" was the best of the four cuts, but Rose was disappointed with the sales of Chaffin's Hickory singles. Chaffin and Pee Wee Maddux subsequently started Fine Records and then went to Sun in Memphis, where Chaffin made "Feelin' Low," quite simply one of the best country records of the 1950s.

With the release of the McCormick Brothers' "Red Hen Boogie," Fred Rose dipped his toe into string-band music—what would soon come to be known as bluegrass. A class act, Lloyd, Kelly, and Haskel McCormick arrived on records at just the wrong time for their style.

Wilma Lee and Stoney Cooper played West Virginia mountain music without many concessions to the changing times. On their Hickory debut, "Just for a While," Wilma Lee sang in the passionate, slightly off-key style of Molly O'Day, and on "Row Number Two, Seat Number Three" in her full-throated mountain style, backed by a weeping steel guitar. Without the electric instruments, this disc could have been made in 1935 as easily as 1955. In 1956, the Coopers scored a hit with "Each Season Changes You," and they stayed with Hickory until 1965.

(Above): Rusty and Doug Kershaw, just up from Louisiana. Courtesy of Bear Family Records.

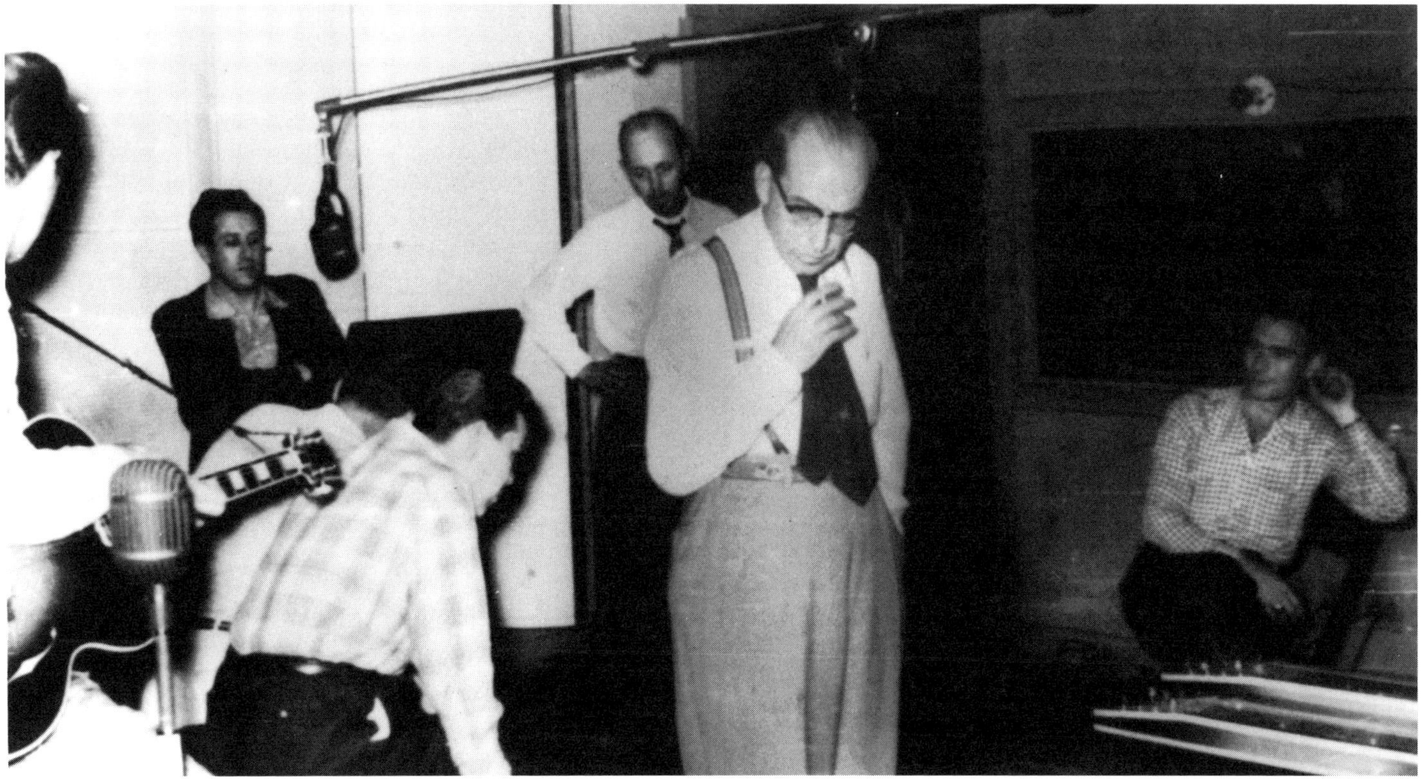

(Right): Fred Rose at a Hickory recording session, with singer Al Terry at the microphone, November 1954. Courtesy of Country Music Hall of Fame and Museum.

Hickory's Louisiana/Cajun Sounds

Besides recording budding Nashville songwriters and artists at the folk end of the music spectrum, Hickory Records issued a strain of recordings with a Louisiana–East Texas feel. The catalyst for this development was J. D. Miller, the songwriter, record producer, and promoter from Crowley, Louisiana, who brought Lightnin' Slim and other acts to Excello.

Miller came by the Acuff-Rose offices one day in late 1953 during the Disc Jockey Convention, pitching songs by Al Terry and others. Fred Rose already knew him as the writer of Kitty Wells's "It Wasn't God Who Made Honky Tonk Angels," which Acuff-Rose published. Rose and Miller entered into an arrangement whereby Miller sent his artists to Nashville to be recorded for Hickory, and Rose helped Miller work recordings of copyrights the producer owned.

Miller's star act was Al Terry—Allison Theriot, born in Kaplan, Louisiana, in 1922. Hickory struck gold early with the release of Terry's "Good Deal Lucille," which he had recorded as a demo for Miller. "Jambalaya" had shown Rose just how successful a simple faux-Cajun tune could be, so he had no hesitation in issuing "Good Deal Lucille," with its engaging mix of French and English phrases. Recorded in Nashville in December 1953 with Tommy Jackson on fiddle, Chet Atkins and Velma Williams on guitars, Kenny Hill on bass, Al's brother Bob on steel guitar, and Floyd Cramer on piano, the Hickory disc beat out every cover version and rose to #8 on the country charts.

Al Terry stayed on Hickory for several years but never repeated his success. Rusty and Doug Kershaw and Wiley Barkdull followed his trail from Louisiana to Hickory, and Louisianan Jimmie Collie weighed in with a novelty approach on "Cajun Lingo."

Rusty and Doug Kershaw's "So Lovely Baby," recorded in

May 1955, was the first of a rich vein of the Cajun-inflected variety of the brother duets that for years provided saleable items in country music. The Kershaws did much to popularize Cajun music, and Doug will be remembered for penning "Louisiana Man," a song recorded more than 850 times. He was born on a houseboat near Tiel Ridge, Louisiana, in 1936; his brother Rusty was born in 1938. The two began working with their older brother in Pee Wee Kershaw's Continental Playboys and by 1953 were on KPLC-TV, Lake Charles. They moved to the *Louisana Hayride* and in May 1956, joined the *WWVA Jamboree* for a year, and, as Rusty and Doug, stayed with Hickory until 1963. They split up the following year; while Rusty continued to play the joints in Louisiana, Doug become a media celebrity in the 1970s and ended up on a ranch in Colorado.

The spirited and appealing nature of the Kershaws' "So Lovely Baby" owed something to Wiley Barkdull's bass vocal, which wove in and out of the song. On his own Hickory recordings, like "I'll Give My Heart to You," Barkdull's delightfully laconic bass vocal is one of the unsung treats in country music. He first recorded for J. D. Miller's own Feature Records, came to Nashville with the Kershaws in May 1955, and continued to record through the 1960s, but never again quite captured the quality of his Hickory records.

Pop on Hickory: Jimmy Sweeney

"Deep Blues" by Jimmy Sweeney was a real departure for Hickory, in content and concept as stone country a label as you can imagine. But Fred Rose had been a pop tunesmith, and he recognized talent when he saw it. Jimmy Sweeney had it. He wrote well and he sang well. When his Tennessee recordings didn't sell, he joined MGM and then Acuff-Rose, an atypical black songwriter and singer who worked across all styles of music.

With the release of Sweeney's recording of "Deep Blues," Hickory took a big advert in *Billboard* in March 1954 proclaiming: "A New Song Stylist . . . A Voice to Thrill You"—the label could almost have been talking about Ray Charles. The song, written by Rose, was in the tradition of vintage West Coast trio music with shades of Nat Cole or Charles Brown. A good solid disc, which Red Foley covered on Decca, it featured Sweeney's soaring pop-blues vocal and a chanting black vocal group, the Varieteers, all counterbalanced by Chet Atkins on guitar and a country rhythm section.

Sweeney made two other Hickory discs, issued under the Varieteers' name. They took a smooth, pop-flavored approach to "Call My Gal, Miss Jones" and "I Pay with Every Breath," but Sweeney's talent did not translate into hits. He returned to the ranks of Nashville songwriters, making occasional discs for small labels before he attracted the attention of Columbia in 1958. The label issued three singles by him and then transferred him back to Hickory for another five releases between 1960 and 1962. Sweeney also recorded the first release on Louis Buckley's Buckley label in 1962, scoring his only hit record, under the name Jimmy Bell, with "She Wears My Ring," a rerelease from Hickory. Written by Boudleaux Bryant, who worked closely with Sweeney, the song entered the R&B chart in July and made #24 later that summer.

Over a long career, Sweeney wrote a batch of songs for country singers, smooth bluesmen, and pop singers alike. He wrote and performed both country music and supper-club blues in the days when such crossover was unusual for a black artist. Before Sweeney, aside from the Fisk Jubilee Singers, perhaps the first crossover performer in Nashville was harmonica player DeFord Bailey, who played, recorded, and operated in the country music world rather than that of the blues and was always seen to some degree as a novelty act. Another black man, Pee Wee Marquette, worked with the Francis Craig Orchestra in the 1930s and 1940s, but he undertook mascot duties and provided comical interludes, a long way removed from making one's way on equal terms across all fields of music. Young Bobby Hebb was a member of Roy Acuff's Smoky Mountain Boys, dancing on the Opry shows and later playing sessions and writing songs for country, pop, and R&B artists in Nashville, but in the early 1950s he was also viewed as a novelty act. Jimmy Sweeney alone was plowing an independent but equal furrow in the local industry.

He spent four years with each of the big Nashville stations from 1950 to 1958 and was equally at home on WLAC blues programs and on WSM's *Sunday Down South* with pop singer Snooky Lanson. Hickory's Buddy Killen spoke of

Jimmy Sweeney at a recording session with, *from left,* musicians Hank Garland, Floyd Chance, Boudleaux Bryant, and Floyd Cramer. Courtesy of Elmer Williams.

Sweeney as "a nice guy who hung around my office all the time. But he had a little slicker sound than he needed to if he was going to happen. He was neither fish nor fowl in his style."

Disaster for the Hickory Label

By December 1954, things looked promising for Fred Rose and Hickory. They had scored a charted country hit with Al Terry's "Good Deal Lucille" and signed several good artists to their roster. Then Fred Rose had a heart attack in the Castle Studio and died soon afterward, on December 1, 1954. His death spelled disaster for, among others, Murray Nash and Tommy Hill, both of whom pointed the finger at Wesley Rose for their disappointment. Murray Nash:

> When Fred Rose hired me in 1951, it was with the understanding that I would be a partner, but Acuff-Rose was set up so that no one else could buy in. I was there over two years when Fred came into my office one night and said he'd talked to Roy Acuff and he'd found a way to bring me in. He said he would organize Hickory Records, because that way we could produce things that we couldn't get recorded by other labels, and when it had gotten to its feet, it was to be handed to me.
>
> Despite Fred's promise to me, Wesley Rose decided to keep me out of Hickory. Wes Rose and I had a problem. It started when we were at a convention in Chicago and we needed three rooms at the last minute. Wes had tried the Palmer Hotel but I knew the people and walked in there and got the rooms. You can see the clash that started from this. Then I recorded some things for Hickory, but Fred and Wesley Rose went ahead on issuing other things. They were keen on Al Terry.
>
> It was mostly about Jimmy Newman—I had gotten Fred to approve recording him. We brought him to Nashville and made a session at Castle that I was on cloud nine about. "Cry Cry Darlin'"—I thought it was a hit. But Wesley was just beginning to get interested in the recording end of things and he couldn't see Jimmy Newman. Fred was on the fence. So Jimmy wanted his record out. I told him to take the four sides we had to Randy Wood, and so we sold the session to Dot. After Fred died, I wanted Acuff-Rose to stay country, but Wesley wanted to diversify.

Tommy Hill:

> Fred did not live long enough to make his plan come about, and Wesley took over. Wesley and I could not get along after a while. He had no talent like his dad did. Fred would sit me down and have me play ten songs for him, saying, "No, no, maybe, no," like that, partway through each song. He would focus you on what was good. When he came across one he really liked, he'd jump up and do a kind of Indian rain dance around the room.
>
> But Wesley had none of Fred's perception. Fred was a great writer and producer and he had the connections and the manpower to do something big. Wesley didn't know songs or music. He just wanted to be a big shot. He should've employed someone who knew what they were doing to run Hickory.

In time, the label for which Fred Rose had such hopes became little more than a vanity label for Acuff-Rose protégés. Hickory had some success in the 1960s and 1970s, but as a stand-alone commercial venture, it would not have survived as long as it did had it not been underwritten by Acuff-Rose. Still, Fred Rose deserves great credit. He helped bring Nashville to the notice of the music-publishing world and helped build a bridge between pop and country music; it is not overstatement to call him the prophet of the Nashville Sound.

Career Country Songwriters and the Pop-Market Pot of Gold

The increasing sales of country records in the early 1950s and the growth of local music publishers in the wake of Acuff-Rose had led to a slow increase in the ranks of career country songwriters. As Jim Bulleit said:

> The record business was a penny business. A company had costs that were broken down into so many pennies for this, and so many for that. Copyright payments were an important part. As Nashville got bigger in the music world, so the question of who owns the songs became important. And then it became more and more important to have good songs. If you wanted to make something of a performer it helped if they had their own songs, but to keep them on top you needed access to a continuing stream of good tunes.

Felice and Boudleaux Bryant, who numbered among the first professional writers, became early role models for those who followed. Boudleaux told their story:

> When we were just married and still living back in Moultrie, Georgia, we wrote and sang just for fun. I was a musician and Felice was an amateur singer. We never even thought of selling our songs. The country or hillbilly artists wrote their own material. It was only gradually after the war that there came a market for songs. Artists were more in demand and the distances they traveled were greater. Some used this time to write, but others didn't or couldn't, yet these people all needed to get a hit song or two to ensure they followed on well from their last hit.
>
> We came to Nashville after we had written to several publishers and after Fred Rose had accepted our first published song, "Country Boy," in 1949. I was playing in Detroit with a singer named Rome Johnson, and he told Fred Rose about "Country Boy." Eventually that song became a small hit for Jimmy Dickens, and after that we were on our way. We were then the first people in town to do nothing but write songs.

A *Tennessean* feature in 1952 titled "Everybody's Writing Songs" estimated that its hometown songwriters were generating five hundred new songs a week and further that Nashville, "the acknowledged capital of hayloft harmony, probably has more writers per capita than Philadelphia has lawyers." The subtext, though, was that no one was making a full-time living at songwriting. Although the article cited Vic McAlpin and Jack Toombs as among the more successful songwriters, Toombs hadn't given up his day job as a taxi driver, and McAlpin was the local representative for the New York publisher Melody Trails.

Boudleaux Bryant also did more than write songs. Working out of Nashville, he served as a representative for Acuff-Rose and for New York–based Tannen Music, and he recorded for MGM and Hickory as "Bood" Bryant until the mid-1950s, when he became a career songwriter.

The pot of gold for country songwriters was the pop market, as the Bryants learned in 1953 when they wrote "Hey Joe," a country #1 for Carl Smith, and then saw what a difference pop sales made to the bottom line when Frankie Laine recorded it. A hit song netted the writer around one cent per record, three cents for every copy of sheet music, and airplay royalties on top of that—in other words, one or two thousand dollars for a country hit and many times that for a pop hit.

The Bryants' strength was their adaptability. When rock & roll burst upon the scene, Felice and Boudleaux crafted a string of million-selling pop ballads and teenage playlets for the Nashville-based country duo the Everly Brothers, from "Bye Bye, Love," and "Wake Up, Little Susie" to "All I Have to Do Is Dream."

By the time of Fred Rose's death, Acuff-Rose had penetrated the country music business to an even greater extent than statistics now reveal. Those statistics are impressive: Between 1944 and 1955, Acuff-Rose had 14 percent of all the country songs that made the Top Ten, some seven hundred titles. Only New York–based Hill and Range fared better, with 26 percent.

But Jim Denny, Jack Stapp, and Wesley Rose represented a new, business-focused approach in Nashville's music industry. While there was little limelight for the music-publishing business, they recognized that copyrights last longer than most recording artists. The companies they headed retained their preeminence well beyond the mid-1950s, so that decades later they became part of the major media corporations that took the music industry into another phase. By then, the world routinely described Nashville as Music City USA.

16

Music City USA

You can hear them on your radio, wherever you are,
Everybody jumping to the solid beat, of a guitar pickin' out an eight to the bar,
If you're living in some distant town, then brother, pack your rags and come right on down,
They used to call it Nashville, but I'm here to say, that now they call it Music City USA.

—Bill Beasley, Dick Stratton, and Ray Anderson,
"Music City USA," Jamboree Records

What could have become Nashville's theme song, "Music City USA," made its low-key appearance in August 1950 on a small label, Jamboree, by a little-known artist, Dick Stratton, and it has never been revived. Barely even a local hit at the time, the song has garnered significance because it deals with Nashville's emerging status as a music town.

The Selling of the Image

Local papers referred to Nashville as Music City USA in 1950 and 1951, and the Jamboree disc was the first recording that touted the city by that name. It was written by Bill Beasley, Ray Anderson, and Stratton when the Music City part of Nashville was confined to a few small hives of activity. Some of these were despised by the city administration, which saw the hillbilly-music business as inconsistent with Nashville's reputation as the Athens of the South.

Who first coined the phrase "Music City USA" is debatable. WSM announcer David Cobb has asserted that he came up with the term serendipitously when announcing Red Foley's network radio show one day in 1950. It was a play on WSM's tradition of originating radio shows for network broadcast and recognition of Foley's status at the top of the popular music charts with "Chattanoogie Shoe Shine Boy."

Each of the many WSM and WLAC programs from that period needed its own theme. The best-known themes, of course, were those of *Sunday Down South* and the Grand Ole Opry itself. But it was the smaller-scale *Hayloft Jamboree* on WKDA that took up "Music City USA," and Stratton sang it there regularly.

As late as December 16, 1951, Cobb was selling the alternative concept "Tin Pan Valley." A script from a WSM broadcast networked over NBC that day had Cobb opening the show with

> Welcome to Tin Pan Valley. This is WSM in the music capital of the world—Tin Pan Valley. This is Nashville, Music City USA, the new mecca of singers, musicians, composers, and recording artists—the birthplace of some of today's top tunes.

Music followed by Dottie Dillard, Beasley Smith, and "Tin Pan Valley Man" Johnny Maddox, among others, before Cobb signed off with: "Come back and see us next Sunday night right here in Tin Pan Valley. Tin Pan Valley came to you from WSM in Nashville." It all added up to one reference to Music City USA, one to the new mecca, one to the music capital of the world, and fifteen "Tin Pan Valleys." Regardless

The Owen Bradley Orchestra setting up to play on *Sunday Down South*. Courtesy of American Federation of Musicians and Harold Bradley.

of which phrase has endured, all the networked programs from Nashville were selling the image of the town as a popular music center with an endearing folksy tinge.

In July 1951, the *New York Times* devoted a feature to the success of songs such as "Tennessee Waltz" and "Chattanoogie Shoe Shine Boy," and the failed attempts of New York's Brill Building songsmiths to duplicate the music "of the hitherto harmless city of Nashville, Tennessee." WSM announcer Louie Buck, quoted in *Coronet* magazine the following year, announced that

> Nashville has become the Broadway of country music because it gathered native tunes from all sections of a big country . . . it is more than hillbilly. It is valley-billy, river-billy, desert-billy and blues-billy as well. . . . Tied in with Nashville's goldmine of country talent is one of the biggest "country" music firms, Acuff-Rose; three locally owned recording firms—Tennessee, Bullet, and Dot—and a backlog of songwriters who have made Nashville their home since it became the Broadway of country music.

Not everyone perceived Nashville as the up-and-coming center of country music or of any other kind. RCA field representative Brad McCuen, who observed the Nashville scene in some depth between 1948 and 1955, didn't much like what he saw.

> There wasn't what you'd call a permanent music business fraternity here, certainly on a [major] record-company level. Most people would come into town to do business. I lived in Charlotte. If you didn't gamble, there wasn't an awful lot to do in Nashville at night. You'd go to the movies or a cafeteria, or drop into the radio stations. Music people tend to be night people. There was Nickerson's cafeteria on Sixth Avenue opposite the Hermitage Hotel; it was open twenty-four hours a day. It made sense for one area to wind up as the center in the South, but it could so easily have been Knoxville or Atlanta. Nashville has never been a good record town. The record tastes were such that you can't base any national view [on them]. What sells in Nashville won't necessarily sell anywhere else.
>
> When [Nashville] people detected I was in the record business, I quickly noticed a sort of suspicion that would come across them—my southern university frat brothers—and it was quite a joke among their set about what the Grand Ole Opry people would get up to. The Belle Meade crowd could care less about country music. If you were in the music business you couldn't join the country club.
>
> Nashville was corrupt in the late 1940s and early 1950s—to me it seemed corrupt. If money was your kick, then the publishers had ways of getting it to you. But I was doing what I loved, and I wasn't interested. It was a town where there were call girls operating openly and

freely. There were whiskey stores here, and if you wanted a bottle at two in the morning, a policeman would help tell you where to go for it. There were strip joints in Printers Alley, and there was gambling activity.

Interestingly, the country artists who lived here or came in for the Opry didn't want anything to do with country music. The jukeboxes wouldn't have a Hank Williams or Ernest Tubb record. Eddy Arnold would be the only Nashville-oriented record. The jukeboxes and little bands in the clubs would be playing easy-listening or adult pop music.

The Early Music Hubs: Downtown Seventh and South Nashville

Over the years, the international reputation of Music City USA has been associated either with the Opry or with the large number of recording studios, publishers, promoters, and especially major-label recording companies that gathered in the Music Row area between Sixteenth and Eighteenth Avenues South, just southwest of downtown. But none of this infrastructure was in place in 1950 when Beasley, Stratton, and Anderson wrote "Music City USA," nor is it certain the major labels would have solidified and expanded their Music City presence had it not been for the efforts of the local industry pioneers.

Seventh Avenue North downtown was the original hub of the music business because that's where WSM, National Life, and various hotels and theaters were. The Ryman and all the early studios were nearby, as was the musicians union, which, Harold Bradley explained, was "on Church Street back in the early days because that was where everything was at that time. We were in a place called the Bennie-Dillon building, and then we went to the Warner Building, and then we built at 1806 Division Street, and it was not until 1977 we built on Music Row."

Virtually all the premises of the Bullet, Coastline, and Tennessee companies were located south of Broadway in the lower-rent business area. In South Nashville, with its mix of residential and commercial development, the buildings were older and rent was cheap. Local resident Jim Stephens lived in the early 1950s on the block next to Tennessee Records, near the intersection of Lafayette Street and Fifth Avenue South, and he confirmed the thriving commercial nature of the area that was home to many record and jukebox dealers:

> We lived a little ways from Hermitage Music on Lafayette and marveled at the big Wurlitzer jukeboxes and pinball machines that they had in their back room—we kids snuck in when they weren't looking. Most of the elegant homes of Lindsley, Fifth, Fourth, and Ash Streets had seen their better days. Most of the businesses in the area, except Sears and a couple of big supermarkets, were small one-owners such as radio repair, motorcycle shops, taverns, and corner grocery stores. Many of the elegant homes were now rooming houses, and the older families had moved on to West End, out by Vanderbilt.
>
> It was a working-class neighborhood. There were lots of Jewish families who owned small businesses or rooming houses, and lots of us kids, too. First through Eighth Avenues south of Broad was my neighborhood. We swam in the Cumberland, played in the old trolley barns, shined shoes in the country music bars on Broad Street, and sold papers. Lafayette was Main Street to us.

When he toured Republic's Fourth Avenue recording premises with his father, Bill Beasley, Kirk Beasley remembers:

> The first floor below the studio was empty. Fourth Avenue South and Lafayette were and are commercial districts. Sears, Roebuck had moved their main store from Eighth and Commerce to Seventh and Lafayette in that era. The Tennessee studio was at Fourth and Mulberry, only a block or two from the first Krispy Kreme doughnut shop in town. A little farther out Fourth, near the feed mills, was Nashville Phono-Matrix where masters and stamping plates were made. I think they were open at all hours due to the demand to convert wax masters to metal quickly. Parts of the neighborhood were residential, very poor, and in those days almost entirely black. The image that

comes to mind is a row of tarpaper shacks on Fourth near the old City Cemetery. All this was just before the "Row" developed. South Nashville was really the industrial heart of the Nashville record business back then.

Early in 1946, when Bullet Records was starting out, even the idea of downtown Nashville, let alone South Nashville, as a "Music City" area would have made people laugh. Apart from the radio studios, there was nowhere to record music, although like most towns after the war, Nashville had plenty of entrepreneurial people willing to make the most of new technology. Around May 1945, Jim Denny and another WSM employee, Rogers Glenn, briefly opened a recording studio at Fourth Avenue North and Union, apparently set up so that service personnel could make songs and messages to send home; it reportedly closed by September.

One who joined the vogue for using war-surplus recording equipment for home recordings was Lional Henderson, who operated in the black part of town and advertised his recording service in the *Globe* in April 1946: "Keep a Record—I Will Record Anything in Your Own Home—Family, Party, Songs, Groups." Another alternative was the recording booths placed in stores, such as the Wilcox Gay Coin Recordio-gram machine, which made a cardboard-backed disc and at the same time sold a special mailing envelope for five cents. The *Commentator* still regularly carried advertisements for the machine in 1949.

Nashville Recording Studio

Between 1946 and 1949 the city directories listed the Nashville Recording Studio at 403½ Union Street—the Commerce Union Bank building, which housed a number of offices and businesses. In 1946 the listing credited the studio's ownership to two friends, James O. Michelinie and W. Harold Walker, who may have taken over from the personal recording service set up by Jim Denny. Evidence indicates that Denny had access to a studio facility downtown to record demonstration discs, air checks, and the like. Michelinie recalled that after he got out of the army, he had nothing particular to do. Harold Walker was still living in the neighborhood, and I told him I'd had the idea to go into the recording business, and he was interested. I had heard the country music on the radio and I had seen some early television shows. I knew that there were musicians and performers who wanted to know what they would sound like on a record, and I thought that a recording studio might be profitable as a business. I had heard about two rooms that were available on Union Street; it was a front office and a small studio on the second floor of a three-story building. The recording equipment was already there, to be sold with the lease. So we bought the place and started up in business around the end of 1945. We called it the Nashville Recording Studio.

James Michelinie was born in Alderson, West Virginia, in October 1913 and came to Nashville at age twenty to study data processing at Vanderbilt. He worked for the Veterans Administration, and he and his wife, Lanelle, became friendly with the Walkers, their neighbors in the Franklin area, just south of Nashville, in the late 1930s. After two years in England and France with the First U.S. Army running the Thirty-Second Mobile Records Unit, keeping track of information on servicemen and casualties, Michelinie returned to Nashville in August 1945 and started to look for work. At Nashville Recording, he and Walker

worked for anybody who came in and wanted recordings made. Sometimes we went out and recorded parties and weddings and the like. Mostly, we worked from the studio, though. I was there full time and Harold part time, as he had another job. We both took turns about, so that someone was always there. Some people came in to record speeches and talks or even just to tell jokes; they wanted them for home use. Others who came in were singers or musicians who wanted something more professionally made than they could get elsewhere . . . a few were up-and-coming performers from the Grand Ole Opry and WSM radio. They were mainly individuals or small groups. It was all kinds of music but mainly country, I would say. I can't recall any of them now by name, and I've often wondered whether any of them became stars later on. We made transcription discs in three different sizes and speeds.

We ran the studio for at least a couple of years. Ninety-nine percent of our business was by word of mouth or from local flyers we put around town. We bought a little new equipment, and at first we did well enough and had sufficient to get along, but we didn't have the funds to make the business bigger, and eventually we were not making a lot of profits and we decided to give it up.

Michelinie went back to work for the Veterans Administration and eventually moved to Louisville and St. Louis to set up IBM systems for the VA there. Walker remained in Nashville.

The extent of the Nashville Recording Studio's impact on Nashville's music business remains unclear. James Michelinie told me that "several WSM employees came down to see us when we started out, and a couple of fellows came down to make some radio jingles, too." He remembered that one of these was WSM engineer and Castle recording-studio pioneer Aaron Shelton. Jim Bulleit knew of Michelinie's studio but didn't remember ever using it for Bullet; in his opinion, "Nashville Recording Studios was pumped up, I think, in the hurry to get in on the ground floor after the Castle Studios started."

James Michelinie, before he founded the pioneering Nashville Recording Studio, 1930s. Courtesy of James Michelinie.

Castle Recording Laboratories

In terms of commercial music, it was Aaron Shelton's Castle Recording Laboratories that made the Nashville recording business possible. Shelton had joined WSM in 1928 and was a vastly experienced radio engineer by the time he, George Reynolds, and Carl Jenkins started Castle with the tacit agreement of their employers at WSM, who stood to gain in studio fees and goodwill. The recording service was conceived in 1944, triggered by RCA's need for a studio where they could record Eddy Arnold. Bullet then kept the Castle partners in work, even though the business was more virtual than real, operating after hours when WSM's radio studios were not in

(Opposite page): Fourth Avenue stretching through South Nashville, 1952, with the premises of Coastline (1), Tennessee (2), and Republic Records (3, 4) highlighted along Fourth, Fifth, and Ash and the Bullet building (5) on Broadway highlighted in the foreground, beyond the roof of the Ryman Auditorium. Courtesy of Nashville Public Library, the Nashville Room.

An early Castle studio acetate.

The Hotel Tulane at the northeast corner of Church and Eighth, which housed the Castle studio from 1947, shown here in 1951. Courtesy of Nashville Public Library, the Nashville Room.

use. The Castle partners used Studios B or C in the National Life building on Seventh and Union and piped the signal to another WSM building for cutting master discs.

Shelton, Castle's front man, was born in Erin, Tennessee, in 1910, moved to east Nashville in the 1920s, and became fascinated with sound the first time he saw a radio in a general store in 1924. He started to build his own receivers and got an amateur broadcasting license. When WBAW (named for Braid Electric Company and Waldrum's drugstore) put in a station near his home on South Twelfth and Jack DeWitt and George Reynolds built the transmitter, the young Shelton persuaded them to let him help. Shelton said later that "George Reynolds then invited me up to Sixth and Church, where they had the radio studio above the Capitol Theater, and I was helping out and playing records."

The part-time Castle facility, though soon in heavy use, still wasn't a full-time business for any of the partners. So in mid-1947 the engineers moved to a location that could be worked continually on a rotating basis, ensuring that someone was on hand practically all the time—a large, wood-paneled room on the mezzanine level of the Tulane Hotel at 206 Eighth Avenue North, formerly the home of President James Polk. As George Reynolds told *Billboard* in 1961:

> We took a Scully lathe from our previous location to cut sixteen-inch acetates, aluminum discs. This was quite presentable equipment for the time. We would cut records all day in three or four sessions, each taking a turn. We had other WSM employees working with us, men like Elmer Alley.

Castle's move to the Tulane was in part linked to a decision by Decca Records' country music A&R man, Paul Cohen, to make recordings in Nashville. Two-and-a-half years had passed since Eddy Arnold first recorded in Nashville for RCA, but Cohen had just seen a Nashville record label, Bullet, top the sales charts with a Castle recording, "Near You." According to Owen Bradley, though, it was Ernest Tubb who had the final say in Cohen's decision. "If Ernest had said no, we wouldn't have done it," he told researcher Ronnie Pugh. "He was that big."

On August 30, 1947, *Billboard* reported: "Milton Estes and Red Foley cut their first Decca platters in Nashville two weeks ago. Previously, all cutting was done in Chicago, but many waxeries are now using WSM's new studio. Majestic also cut a series of sides there." What *Billboard* called "WSM's new studio" was of course the relocated Castle Studio. Majestic recorded Jimmie Selph there, and the Decca sessions, which also featured Tubb's first Nashville recording, "That Wild and Wicked Look in Your Eye," were held on August 11 and 13, 1947. Decca's Paul Cohen soon relied heavily on Owen Bradley and Beasley Smith to line up session musicians.

Aaron Shelton kept detailed notes for the years 1952 and 1953, which reveal something of the range of Castle's clients then. Bullet was no longer using Castle in 1952, but the studio was getting regular bookings from Dot Records. The biggest out-of-town independent, King Records of Cincinnati, also made use of Castle from the fall of 1952, recording its WSM artists. And all the large record companies except RCA Victor recorded there. Decca recorded Webb Pierce, Tommy Hill, Ernest Tubb, and Red Foley, among other top-selling country acts. MGM, via Fred Rose, recorded Hank Williams, while Capitol recorded the Louvin Brothers and Faron Young. Columbia scheduled sessions with Ray Price, Carl Smith, Curley Williams, Don Gibson, and other country artists, as well as pop singers including Rosemary Clooney. Stars were thick on the ground in Nashville.

Charles Brown, *seated*, radio recording and advertising expert, discussing a show with western and country talent: *from left*, Tom Mix, Ernest Tubb, and Eddy Arnold. Courtesy of Bear Family Records.

Monogram Radio Productions: The Brown Brothers

Castle's first competitor after Nashville Recording was Monogram Radio Productions, owned by two brothers from Springfield, Missouri: Sherman William "Bill" Brown and Charles H. Brown. At Gardner Advertising Company in St. Louis, the Browns had come up with an idea for expanding sales for a client, the farm feed-products company Ralston Purina—country music. In January 1943 the first Purina advertisements appeared on WSM.

Around this time, Charles Brown saw singer Eddy Arnold working in a tent show in Arkansas with the comedy duo Jamup and Honey, and he was impressed with Arnold's voice and stage presence. The Browns were looking to set up their own advertising agency and soon they quit Gardner and moved to Nashville. They booked Eddy Arnold on a one-hour show they sponsored over the Mutual network, which broadcast from the Andrew Jackson Hotel in 1944 and 1945. Arnold was the host and singer, and Owen Bradley led the band. The Browns' production business was grounded almost entirely on producing and transcribing radio jingles and advertising.

Jim Bulleit used the Browns' studio on occasion when Castle was unable to accommodate a last-minute Bullet session, but he felt the Browns had little commitment to recording for records because they were "so deeply involved in radio

The Monogram Recording studio, also known as Brown Brothers studio, above the Royal Cigar Store at 240 Fourth Avenue North, November 1951. Courtesy of Tennessee State Library and Archives.

work for WLAC and WKDA and other stations. They also produced the Purina-sponsored show on WLAC that starred Eddy Arnold. The Browns were radio men basically, though one of them did photographic work also." In 1944, Bulleit was an announcer on the Purina show, regionally networked through NBC and sometimes known as the *Checkerboard Show*. He seemed impressed by the Browns' financial acumen.

> They were quite a substantial advertising agency here for a while. They put up a stock issue and sold stock in their company and raised an awful lot of money. They would come up to WSM and buy time, and they'd hire WSM artists to appear on the Purina show for thirty minutes at 7 PM. They would do fifteen-minute transcriptions for various and sundry shows. First they used the WSM studios for this—one of the three studios, A, B, or C, which was the larger one for the big bands. This was when the studios were not in use for their regular duty.

When the Browns needed even more studio time, they leased the second-floor premises at 240½ Fourth Avenue North, above the Royal Cigar Store, in a building where Andrew Jackson formerly practiced law. They may also have leased the office in the Commerce Union Bank building, diagonally opposite Royal Cigar at the northwest corner of Fourth and Union, once the home of the Nashville Recording Studio. James Michelinie told me that when he and Harold Walker sold Nashville Recording, "it was bought by a couple of men who had ideas to retain the business and improve it. We sold the equipment and the lease to them. I can't remember their name."

Harold Bradley made radio transcriptions at the Browns' studio for the Brown brothers with Slim Whitman singing, and

> we did Morton Salt transcriptions with Snooky Lanson. It was about three or four blocks away from WSM and the Hermitage Hotel. . . . The Browns were show producers, too. They sent Slim Whitman and me out on the road as the Light Crust Doughboys working for Burrus Mills Flour. I left college after three years because I was going to be bandleader for Slim Whitman, who was here at that time, on a show the Browns recorded. I was making $150 a week, and I was living at home and had a new car. I saw that I was not going to be a classical musician, so I got work with the Brown brothers doing transcriptions. The Willis Brothers and I were like the house band there. Cliff Thomas was the writer. Charlie Brown was more the PR guy, and his brother was more the hands-on guy. I remember cutting records in their studio, too, with Eddy Arnold and Steve Sholes.

RCA Victor in Nashville

The occasional use of the Monogram studios, also known as Brown Radio Productions, for demo recordings as well as for prerecorded radio transcriptions led to a deal between the Browns and RCA that made the studio effectively the first RCA studio in Nashville. RCA had used several southern locations, but the idea of having one base had increasingly appealed to their country music A&R director, Steve Sholes. Brad McCuen, Sholes's field representative for the South after 1948, explained that

> Sholes was making the tours of cities until about 1950, when he figured it would be better and cheaper to bring people into one central place to record, rather than keep hopscotching, as had been the tradition since Ralph Peer did it in the 1920s. Steve didn't use Castle. There was a union problem because Steve wanted to use an RCA engineer.

RCA's Eddy Arnold had used WSM engineers briefly in 1944, before those engineers started Castle, but RCA generally had a stipulation that its own engineers must be used on all sessions. This did not sit well with Castle at all, but the Browns had no objections to giving over their facility to the engineers Sholes brought with him from New York.

Born in Washington, D.C., Sholes at eighteen had joined Victor Records as a messenger in 1929, the year RCA took over the company; he would remain with RCA Victor his entire working life. In 1939, his boss, Frank Walker, asked him

Chet Atkins. Courtesy of Country Music Hall of Fame and Museum.

to coordinate some field sessions in Atlanta, and those became Sholes's introduction to country recording. McCuen, on the other hand, although a New York City native, came south as an RCA field representative based in Charlotte, North Carolina, because he had been educated in the Carolinas and knew the area a little.

> My job as a field rep was to do seventeen different things—I was the link between the factory, manufacturer, distributor, and worked with the salesmen and the DJs. I liked Duke Ellington, but I soon found that that didn't make much of a stir from the sales viewpoint. I could make my quota in the South selling just Eddy Arnold records.

In 1950, when RCA started using Nashville as a regular recording location, McCuen and Sholes came into town, got their business done, and left, going their separate ways. Tired of being accosted by musicians downtown, Sholes stayed at the Mercury Court Hotel on Murfreesboro Road. "He kept it a carefully guarded secret for many years," said McCuen.

From mid-1950 until late 1952, Steve Sholes and an engineer—Jeff Miller or Fred Lynch—came in from New York to run sessions at the Browns' studio. This suited the Browns, who wanted to get out of the transcription business; they sublet their premises to RCA and went back to Missouri. When RCA was using it, what people knew as "the Brown Brothers studio" was effectively run by the Browns' former engineer, Cliff Thomas. As McCuen described RCA's studio practice in Nashville: "There was a little, dinky control room, and Jeff Miller, Steve's recording engineer, would set up a day or so early, and Steve would come in with the artist later. The studio itself was surrounded by piles of sixteen-inch transcriptions. But the sound was great."

RCA and Cliff Thomas moved to a studio in a large metal building near Broadway at 109 Thirteenth Avenue North in 1952; what had started out as a storage location for RCA's recording equipment briefly became the label's main Nashville studio. In 1953 and 1954, Sholes was Cliff Thomas's biggest customer among the record labels, but in late 1954 RCA began renting the Methodist Television, Radio & Film Commission (TRAFCO) Building on McGavock Street, Brad McCuen recalled. "RCA used it when they [the Commission staff] weren't using it. It had a big Nipper dog and RCA insignia out front of it."

Sholes had signed Chet Atkins to RCA as a singer and guitarist in 1947. Atkins had worked with Wally Fowler and the Carter Family and spent time in Nashville off and on for some years. He recorded briefly for Bullet at Castle, but when he joined RCA his recordings were made in Chicago or Atlanta. After stints in Springfield, Missouri, and Knoxville, Atkins moved to Nashville in June 1950, drawn by Fred Rose's assurance he could find session work there—and Rose proved right. Sholes increasingly relied on Atkins to line up sessions and do spot production, as he had earlier relied on others as his eyes and ears in Nashville, principally Bob Ross beginning early in 1949; Ross was well connected, the stepson of promoter "Colonel" Tom Parker and the manager of singer George Morgan, among others. When RCA moved to the TRAFCO Building studio in late 1954, Atkins began running sessions there.

Atkins summed up the series of events that led to his taking over the studio altogether:

> During the late forties and early fifties, I was really just a musician who played sessions. I spent a good deal of time studying record producers like Fred Rose and Owen Bradley, just to see how it was done. Gradually, I became an assistant or stand-in producer, mainly for Steve Sholes whenever he was unable to meet commitments in Nashville. I spent a lot of time organizing sessions and making arrangements for musicians and studios to be available on behalf of RCA. When RCA thought of having their own studio in Nashville, Steve Sholes was to retire from the A&R business, and he came to me and asked whether I would like to take over and run the studio. I very quickly agreed.

Steve Sholes's big coup came in November 1955 when he signed Elvis Presley, who recorded "Heartbreak Hotel" at the McGavock Street studio with the front lobby as an echo chamber. Sholes's Elvis-related workload from that point ensured that routine Nashville productions increasingly fell to Chet Atkins. In 1957, when Sholes's reward for signing Elvis was a promotion to head of Pop Singles, RCA put the country division entirely in Atkins's hands.

Decca in Nashville

The role Chet Atkins played for RCA in Nashville was foreshadowed for Decca by Owen Bradley in the years after Decca's Paul Cohen decided to make maximum use of Nashville's Castle studio from 1947 on.

It's hard to overstate Owen Bradley's role in the development of Nashville's music business. A recording artist, bandleader, session pianist, and composer, he left his most telling mark on the scene as an arranger and producer.

In terms of his own recordings, Owen Bradley had followed his success on Bullet with several good-selling records for Decca, often profiting from Decca A&R man Paul Cohen's advice. "Paul Cohen told me to take the Delmore Brothers country hit 'Blues Stay away from Me' and to put an organ on it and get a couple of background singers, and I could make a hit. We did just that, and it sold half a million copies."

Bradley also arranged Red Foley's hit 1949 recording "Chattanoogie Shoe Shine Boy" for Decca, although asking drummer Farris Coursey to come up with a sound to simulate a shoeshine rag proved the simplest of production concepts. Owen's brother Harold recalled the scene:

> Owen asked Sap (that was Farris's nickname, back to the days when he was our next-door neighbor) to think about the sound, and Farris came up with the idea of slapping the palm of his hand onto his leg. He beat on it so hard that he bruised his leg and had to go onto the other one to finish up the song.

Foley's version of "Chattanoogie Shoe Shine Boy" made #1 in country for thirteen weeks and #1 pop for eight; covers appeared by Frank Sinatra, Bing Crosby, and a number of lesser names, making it a top-selling song of 1950.

Owen Bradley told John Rumble that getting to know

The major-label producers: *clockwise from rear left*: Steve Sholes of RCA, Ken Nelson of Capitol, D Kilpatrick of Mercury, and Paul Cohen of Decca. Courtesy of Bear Family Records.

Paul Cohen redirected his own ambitions. Cohen was based in New York but eager to use Nashville as an auxiliary recording base, and Bradley "tried to play the piano and make Mr. Cohen happy. I thought I was a pretty good piano player, but I didn't know anything about the recording business. I told him almost immediately that I wanted his job when he got a promotion, which I knew would happen someday."

It was as a session producer and arranger that Owen Bradley found fame. Having tasted success with Bullet records, and having flirted briefly with the Select label, he fell into a pattern at Decca. He knew enough about big bands, and he was happy to learn all he could from Cohen, a northerner who taught Bradley more about country music than he had picked up in thirty years in the South.

Native Chicagoan Paul Cohen started in the record business with Columbia in 1927 at age nineteen and joined Decca upon the formation of the English label's U.S. division in 1934. In 1944 he took control of all folk and hillbilly

Owen Bradley and Paul Cohen. Courtesy of Country Music Hall of Fame and Museum.

recordings, succeeding Dave Kapp, brother of American Decca's cofounder Jack Kapp. Cohen recorded in Chicago, Cincinnati, and in various field locations before employing Bradley and committing to Nashville in 1947, a commitment that extended to racking up substantial gambling debts at the city's Plantation and Downtown clubs.

Calling Nashville "my second home," Cohen flew in frequently from New York and, relying on Bradley to do his groundwork, signed an impressive roster of performers that included Kitty Wells, Webb Pierce, and Bobby Helms. When asked in 1964, he counted as his three favorite productions Red Foley's "Peace in the Valley," Bobby Helms's "My Special Angel," and "the song I've just recorded." The general consensus holds that Cohen had ideas and overall vision, but because he wasn't a musician, the real producer of many of his recordings was Owen Bradley, who replaced him at Decca when Cohen left to head the label's Coral imprint in 1958.

Like many record producers, Cohen also had substantial song-publishing interests, although, as Hugh Cherry observed, Cohen's abrasive nature alienated many in the music business. "Paul had the same problem with Decca that Jim Denny had with WSM. Paul got wealthy by picking up songs and publishing what he recorded. Paul had a harsh façade, and a lot of people didn't like Paul Cohen, but he did this town a lot of good."

Owen Bradley studied Cohen's methods in order to make progress as a producer, he told John Rumble:

> Paul Cohen had been a promotion man and a salesperson, and he used to snap his fingers a lot and tell everybody how great it was. He had worked out of Paducah, Kentucky, and Chicago, and he was much more informed than I was about country music. Aaron Shelton always said he enjoyed working with Paul Cohen because he was so enthusiastic. Paul would say, "It's a smash," and when it was, you remembered it and forgot about all the others.

One of Cohen's precepts, as he told the *Nashville Banner*, was to "remember that the song is the thing. If you haven't got it before the session starts, you sure as hell won't have it when the record is released." And as Bradley learned:

> We could do different versions of a hit song and sell it in different ways. I remember on "Goodnight Irene" we had a big record by the Weavers on Decca. Guy Lombardo did it. Red Foley and Ernest Tubb did it. We had a black artist named Cecil Gant. He did it. Paul was not a musician. He liked to have a beat. In fact, he used to talk about "the Decca beat" all the time. He liked to have drums.

Owen Bradley produced sessions for Bullet, Select, and Decca before taking over from Paul Cohen as Decca's head of country A&R in 1958, a job he held for nearly twenty years.

He produced Kitty Wells's monster 1952 hit, "It Wasn't God Who Made Honky Tonk Angels," a pivotal disc in female country music, and over the next decade he specialized in developing female singers, producing Goldie Hill, for instance, and framing many of Patsy Cline's best recordings, such as "Walkin' after Midnight," "I Fall to Pieces," and "Crazy." He developed young Brenda Lee into another Decca star and then signed Loretta Lynn to the label in 1961. His male stars included, among others, Webb Pierce ("Slowly"), Bobby Helms ("Fraulein"), Bill Anderson ("Still"), and the Osborne Brothers ("Rocky Top"). After retiring from Decca, he produced k.d. lang's 1988 album *Shadowland.*

As Bradley analyzed his own achievements:

> Over the years, we recorded many #1 hits, country and pop. My dual base in Nashville, being a bandleader but also working in more-or-less traditional country music with Ernest Tubb or Kitty Wells, was really what enabled me to combine the pop sound with country later on, with Brenda Lee or Patsy Cline and the other so-called crossover artists.

The Start of the Studio System

Harold Bradley, Owen's brother, who eventually became president of the Nashville chapter of the American Federation of Musicians, was in the first wave of Nashville-based session musicians who gradually became as important to the city as the producers. In 1946, when Bullet Records started recording, featured artists usually recorded with their own local band members or touring musicians. This practice persisted for some years, but as recording increased in importance and time became money, a label or producer relied on musicians more experienced in recording techniques than full-time road musicians tended to be.

Harold Bradley went on his first paid gig at age fifteen with his cousin Fred Shoemake and made his first recording session in Chicago in 1946 with

> Pee Wee King's band for RCA. Redd Stewart played electric guitar, but he was needed to play fiddle on the session so they hired me on guitar. "Tennessee Central Number 9" was a hit from that session. We rehearsed at Eighth and Church in a building used by Joe Frank's School of Music that later became Hank Snow's record shop.

Harold gradually became a regular in Owen Bradley's bands and at the Castle Recording Studio when it moved to the Tulane Hotel: "My brother Owen and I played the first-ever notes at Castle. They were for a radio jingle sung by Snooky Lanson."

Harold Bradley also worked at the Brown Brothers' studio and the Tennessee Recording Studios before setting up the various Bradley studios with Owen beginning in 1952. He played not only on a slew of top-selling country and pop records—he was featured on a famous 1952 session at the Ryman Auditorium when Capitol recorded the Ray Anthony Orchestra there—but also for the local Nashville labels, appearing on many Tennessee-label hillbilly discs and on Snooky Lanson's Republic label debut. "In those early days," he said, "the recording business was in the hands of just a few people, and they got to know who the good musicians were, so that those musicians would often play for various labels and in different styles."

In November 1947 Harold recorded his first R&B session, with Ivory Joe Hunter and horn players Sonny Turner, Sammy Ford, and Andy Goodrich of the Tennessee State Collegians, along with bassist Jimmy Lewis and drummer Johnny Jarette. "All States Boogie" was one of the Hunter sides recorded that day at Castle, Harold remembered:

> I was all over the record, playing like a fool. Somebody had called me and asked me to come and do the session. He had a black band of his own but needed a guitar. He took his shoes off and played piano. Curly Fox and Texas Ruby were at the session, and they kept coming out and wanted me to play hotter and hotter, and I'm thinking I'm playing as hot as I can, you know. But it's okay, it fits the record quite well.

Harold Bradley lists two generations of "A-team" players who forged the Nashville Sound, among them Farris Coursey,

Paul Broome at drums, with guitarist Hank Garland, 1950s. Courtesy of the American Federation of Musicians and Harold Bradley.

the Bradleys' next-door neighbor and Owen's drummer, who Harold calls "a fine big-band drummer. He was on everything until he had a back operation, and Owen started using Buddy Harman. Farris had had heart trouble for years, too, and before too long he had a heart attack and died." Harold spent years in recording studios with other former school friends and neighbors. "Bob Moore went to East High School here, and he used to lug the bass home from school when it was bigger than him. Tommy Jackson was a great fiddle player, and he was always around in Nashville."

Harold Bradley's take on the session players before, as he said, "the A-team became crystallized, along about the time we moved out to Hillsboro," included

> the pioneers who played at Castle and the downtown studios. The pioneers were Owen, Farris, Jack Shook, Don Helms, Jerry Byrd; and then Chet played some, I played some, Hank Garland, Billy Byrd, Grady Martin played some (he played the solo on "Chattanoogie Shoe Shine Boy," and I played rhythm). Right at the start you had Zeke and Zeb Turner, but nobody knows who they are now. Farris Coursey was important to Nashville's rhythm because, although his drums were often off-microphone, the rhythm guitarist sat right in front of the drums, and he would pick up the rhythm. Jack Shook was the premier rhythm player because he played left-handed, upside down, and hit the treble strings first, and it sounded like a drum. Jabbo Arrington made a few sessions but actually he died pretty early.
>
> You had Ernie Newton on bass and Walt Summers. Tommy Jackson and Tommy Vaden were on fiddles. Bob Foster played steel guitar back at the start. And Billy Robinson played steel with Red Foley's sessions. This was all before the A-team as such came into being, back in the days when people used whatever group of musicians they wanted, but they were picking from a kind of A-team pioneer list.
>
> Then came the move to Music Row. Some of us survived the transfer here, and a lot didn't. Buddy Harman replaced Farris. Jack Shook didn't make it because he played upside down and couldn't play the range of instruments necessary out here. Most of the pioneers were gone before we moved out here in '55.

In the R&B world, members of the Louis Brooks, Kid King, and Don Q. Pullen bands were the equivalent of the emergent white A-team of the country-pop world. The best all had something in common. Each could move from a late 1940s life in local pop or jazz orchestras, or in hillbilly or blues road bands—playing the occasional recording date—to a lifestyle in which sessions were far more frequent, planned, and professionally executed. With the proliferation of recording studios came the rise of the career session man.

And then there were the background singers. As much as it relied on musicians, what became known as the Nashville Sound relied on vocalists to fill out and sweeten the sound. In the wake of their work with Elvis Presley, members of the

Jordanaires gospel group, who had their origins in the John Daniel and Wally Fowler groups, became the sought-after combination.

Their main competition came from Anita Kerr, a Memphis native born to Italian immigrant parents. She sang and played on Memphis radio as Anita Grilli, then married in 1947 and moved to Nashville the next year with her radio-announcer husband. She took jobs as a radio announcer on WKDA, as staff pianist on WMAK, and as leader of a five-girl vocal group on WLAC. She was a good, jazzy piano player, well-known from working with local bands before and after Jack Stapp asked her to set up a vocal group for WSM's *Sunday Down South* in 1949. This developed into a full-time career on recording sessions when Paul Cohen heard her on the radio and asked her to work on a background vocal sound with Red Foley. One of the creators of the Nashville Sound, she formed the Anita Kerr Singers in 1956, working recording sessions in Nashville along with the *Arthur Godfrey Show* in New York.

Dottie Dillard joined the Anita Kerr Singers and sang on many hit recordings as a backing vocalist, winning all kinds of awards, including a Grammy. Dillard was also vocalist on "Forever," a Top Ten pop hit of 1960 credited to the fictitious Little Dippers.

Recording Studios: The Road to Music Row

Along with Nashville's top-drawer session musicians and background singers, the proliferation of recording studios helped cement the city's role as Music City. When RCA Victor began operating at the McGavock location in 1954, Castle was fading from the scene; at the end of 1955 the partners received notice that the old Tulane Hotel would be demolished to create a central shopping district parking lot, and at about the same time got an ultimatum from WSM president Jack DeWitt, who had decided that his employees' moonlighting took up far too much time. Shelton, Jenkins, and Reynolds decided to stay with WSM and move to the new growth industry, and new technical challenges, of WSM-TV.

Television had blown into Nashville five years earlier, in 1950, as Harold Bradley remembered: "We played the first broadcast for WSM-TV. Owen and I were on camera together with Dottie [Dillard]. It was called the *Harvey's Has It Show*, sponsored by the [Harvey's] department store." Owen became convinced that TV and film would be his destiny rather than records. In a move that was way ahead of its time, in 1952 he and Harold built a studio to make promotional films that would accompany TV or music programs—early music videos.

At the same time, other interests looked upon television differently. Certainly it was competition for the disc jockeys. The decision to establish an annual disc jockey convention in the fall of 1952—inviting the nation's influential disc jockeys to town and plying them with news, interviews, and other incentives to promote Nashville and country music—was not unrelated to warding off the influence of the new medium. The decision was linked to several key names in the town's music business. Disc jockey Joe Allison was involved at the outset. Murray Nash, who said the idea was his, often described how he persuaded people to let him set the wheels in motion. But WSM's Irving Waugh recalls that the convention—officially the Grand Ole Opry Birthday Celebration—was the idea of a secretary at WSM, Harrianne Moore (later Condra), and that Nash merely came up with the invitation list of DJs. Waugh told me:

> I started the Disc Jockey Convention as part of my sales and management role at WSM. The idea was to generate some promotion and publicity for country music. I took over from a fellow who spent a lot of time with his feet on his desk and his mind in neutral. My job was, as Edwin Craig told me "to promote the home company and to promote a service, and I'm not opposed to making a dollar along the way." The concern was the effect that television was starting to have on country radio shows. We wanted to keep up the interest in the Grand Ole Opry and Nashville's music.

The Bradleys forged ahead with their recording studios, audio and visual, with the philosophy that they were not mutually exclusive activities. Harold Bradley listed the various incarnations of the Bradleys' studios that put them out in front of the pack by 1956.

> Right after I got married, in 1952, I was only working in music with the dance band and some sessions with the Tennessee label and other local things, plus the early morning radio and TV shows. So I had some other time that I could fill. Owen said, "Well, I've been thinking about getting a recording studio." So we went to look at a building on Second [Avenue] South and Lindsley, on the third floor above the old Teamsters Union building.

He gave the details to John Rumble:

> We rented Second and Lindsley for some astounding figure, like twenty-five dollars a month or something. And we did it, myself and another guy, we physically boarded up the windows and did a lot of work on it. But we didn't do that much recording there, film or sound. We were just kinda feeling our way. At the end of the year they tripled the rent.

Searching for cheaper premises, but still geared up for film as well as sound, the Bradley brothers took a property in Hillsboro Village southwest of downtown, as Owen told me:

> Over the space of a few years, Decca became more and more successful in Nashville, but the Castle Studio got more out-of-date and less easy to use, so my brother Harold and I opened the Bradley Film and Recording Studio. In 1954 we moved out to Hillsboro on Twenty-First in an alley opposite McClure's department store.

Harold remembered both the timing of that move and the problems the new location presented.

> It was where the Acme School Supply service was located for years after us. We were there just two years, from 1953 to 1955. We made some promotional films for Genesco and for Springfield Woolen Mills and so on. But it clashed with the recording of sound sessions because we had a low ceiling and couldn't get the lights high enough, and the sound would bounce off them.

Nevertheless, the Bradleys recorded several top-selling country discs for Kitty Wells at the Hillsboro location, producer D Kilpatrick used the studio to record artists for Mercury, and Bill Beasley used it on occasion for Republic Records.

When the wrecking balls knocked down the Tulane in December 1956, the balance of recording power shifted to Music Row, where Owen and Harold Bradley's new Bradley Film and Recording Studio at 804 Sixteenth Avenue South was becoming the studio of choice for Decca, Columbia, Mercury, and out-of-town independent labels.

But an impressive number of other recording studios were in operation at the end of Castle's ten-year reign, including the RCA Studio at 1525 McGavock, the Nashboro Studio at 179 Third Avenue North, the Reavis Studio at 420a Broadway, and the Theater Recording Company at 1506 Eighth Avenue South, as well as the Wortham Studio on Fourth Avenue, the Acuff-Rose Studio, and Murray Nash Associates Studio. A number of new operations were getting started, feeding not only the home-recording market but more importantly the aspirations of the increasing numbers of songwriters and performers eager to get on in the music world—the B&L Recording Company, for instance, which advertised from 212 Fourth Avenue:

> B&L, Nashville
> Home of Grand Ole Opry
> We will record anywhere at any time
> Masters or Audition Dubs, Professional or Amateur

When the Bradleys' studio was in Hillsboro Village, Paul Cohen had talked to Owen about possibly moving with him to Dallas to set up a Decca recording headquarters there at the Jim Beck studio. Jim Beck had a better echo facility than the Castle Studio in Nashville, but Harold Bradley reported the deal that kept Cohen in town:

> We moved to Sixteenth Avenue because Paul Cohen was considering moving his base of operation to Dallas, where he felt there were better studio facilities. We didn't want to lose his business, so we said that if he guaranteed a hundred sessions a year, we would build a better studio again.
>
> Paul said, "I want echo on my records." But Owen didn't want to go to Texas because he had his dance band here, his radio work, and we had our studio and session work. So he said, "Harold and I will build you a studio, and we'll have echo," and Paul said, "Great."

The Bradleys bought a house on Sixteenth Avenue South and set about putting in the studio Decca promised would guarantee them $10,000 a year. They removed much of the first floor of the building to get the studio into the basement and give it a high ceiling, with a separate control room above. Later, they hired the Joe Crane Company to build a Quonset hut alongside the house for filmmaking. "We paid $7,500 each for the house and for the Quonset hut," Harold recalled, "and we were still paying it off when we sold the studios in the early 1960s."

The Quonset hut and a later studio, Bradley's Barn, which they opened in nearby Mt. Juliet in 1965, became famous as venues where the "Nashville Sound" was created. By then the Decca recording business had grown so huge that Owen Bradley had let the film aspect go, but as 1956 rolled around, the Bradleys were still using the house studio on Sixteenth for sound recording, Harold said.

> We made some records there before we decided to move into the Quonset hut for sound recording. Gene Vincent recorded "Be Bop a Lula" there, and Sonny James made his hit "Young Love." Marty Robbins made "Singing the Blues" there, and I played on a session with Buddy Holly there for Decca.

Major Decisions

By 1956, all the major labels had a decision to make as far as their presence in Nashville was concerned. We've seen that Steve Sholes and RCA Victor's folk and country catalog increasingly relied on Chet Atkins and the group of highly competent session musicians he was able to deliver to order in Nashville, but Decca and Mercury were the first major or quasi-major record labels to establish full-time offices in the city. Owen Bradley was Decca's local representative, and Mercury started locally with Wally Fowler, whom Irving Green replaced briefly in August 1947 with Les Hutchens, followed in turn by Murray Nash (operating out of Knoxville), former Capitol salesman D Kilpatrick, and Lloyd Cook, who took over when Kilpatrick moved to Mercury's home base in Chicago in October 1953.

MGM president Frank Walker, one of the pioneers of field recording and perhaps the only major record-company boss with firsthand knowledge of country music, spent time with Columbia and RCA Victor before he launched MGM Records in March 1947. His biggest coup was signing Hank Williams via Fred Rose, who acted on MGM's behalf in Nashville from 1947 until 1954.

Beginning in 1938, Columbia Records' country A&R was in the hands of two Englishmen, Arthur Satherley and his assistant, Don Law. Between them they signed or recorded the famous blues singer Robert Johnson along with an impressive array of country artists: Roy Acuff, Gene Autry, Johnny Bond, Al Dexter, Jimmy Dickens, Roy Rogers, the Hoosier Hotshots, the Sons of the Pioneers, George Morgan, Tex Ritter, Bill Monroe, Bob Wills, Marty Robbins, Lefty Frizzell, and Carl Smith, among others. In 1951 Columbia divided responsibility for its country division between Satherley and Law. Law headed the territory from El Paso east. Satherley, based in Los Angeles, took care of the territory west of El Paso; he retired in May 1952, and took up fishing, golfing, and working as a night watchman at a laboratory.

Satherley and Law had set up a good working arrangement with Jim Beck in Dallas, and a large number of Columbia's releases in the 1940s and early 1950s came from Beck's Texas studio rather than from Nashville. There

Don Law with a hot product. Courtesy of Country Music Hall of Fame and Museum.

was, in fact, a consensus in the industry that Beck's was better equipped than Castle. But with several artists based in Nashville, including Carl Smith and Marty Robbins, Law spent an increasing amount of time there, especially after the Bradleys opened their Sixteenth Avenue studio. Songwriter and music publisher Troy Martin, who became Law's eyes and ears in town, lined up deals that led to several of Law's signings, including Johnny Horton, Flatt and Scruggs, and the Everly Brothers.

After Beck died in May 1956, Columbia recorded all its eastern-based artists in Nashville, Law said.

> I moved my headquarters over here to Nashville. I lived at the Andrew Jackson Hotel first, then I stayed at the Hermitage Hotel for a while, and finally I took an apartment. We used the Castle Studios, but gradually the business grew and grew, and I started using Owen Bradley's studio.

In 1962, Columbia bought the Bradley Studio outright.

Of all the major labels, Los Angeles–based Capitol Records was least committed to Nashville. During his tenure with Capitol, D Kilpatrick briefly opened an office in town, but when he left the label in 1951, Capitol's head of country A&R, Ken Nelson, flew into town to record his Nashville-based artists—Faron Young, Hylo Brown, and the Louvin Brothers, among others—and then flew out again. Nelson later hired Opry pianist Marvin Hughes as a point man in Nashville, but Capitol didn't establish another office in town until the 1960s.

Alone among the majors, Capitol resisted the notion of Nashville as "Music City USA." MGM was so heavily associated with Hank Williams, and, by extension, with Nashville, that its otherwise fitful contact with the town during those years was barely noticeable. For RCA, Columbia, Decca, and Mercury, the words "Nashville" and "music"—particularly "country music"—were by 1956 already more-or-less synonymous.

17

The End of the Beginning

Nashville looked down on the record business at that time. The citizens of Nashville thought of the people as fly-by-nights. Anybody in the business was just not stable. That lasted well into the 1950s, until the money really started to roll in.

—Hutch Carlock

The first ten years of recording in Nashville left a few people rich, some fulfilled, some trained fo bigger and better things, and others bitter or confused. Inevitably, everyone involved had their own slant on what happened and why.

Giving Credit to the Independents

In the postwar years before the major labels arrived, Harold Bradley points out, making a record was a novelty for him and for his brother Owen and for nearly anyone else in Nashville. "People today come into Nashville and they can't imagine the town like it was when I grew up, that there was not a recording studio here at all. There were no records before Bullet and little else apart from Bullet for several years."

He gives a great deal of credit to the town's independent labels in the 1940s and 1950s, and in particular to Bill Beasley and Bullet:

> Bill Beasley was very good to me. Some people had trouble with him, but I never did have any trouble with him. I'm sorry he didn't have more success than he did. Because he sure tried, and he kinda kept everything going here. We had the major labels coming into town, but after Bullet there were a lot of other artists looking for a label who had no place to go. People had a place to go when Bill was here. Later on we had Hickory and Monument, and they performed the same function.
>
> You need more than the majors if the local economy is going to work properly. You need the smaller ones to keep the business going and be like a farm club where people can develop their talent. I wish we had someone like Bill Beasley in town today.

Noteworthy about Nashville's indie record business of the 1940s and early 1950s, too, is that the small labels recorded music of a technical standard comparable to the majors. In contrast, during the period that would follow, the first few years of rock & roll, a plethora of one-man labels recorded a lot of very basic music very badly; in Nashville's early years, only some of Excello's recordings approached that low standard. In the main, Bullet, Tennessee, Speed, and the rest all used good studios and good musicians, and, for the most part, decent pressings.

Chet Atkins told me he credits the musicians themselves, along with the first recording studios, with the growth of Nashville as a music mecca:

> When I was first in town, we used to go to Atlanta to make records. Other folk and country singers went to

Church Street, 1950, looking east. Courtesy of Metropolitan Nashville Government Archives.

> Chicago or Dallas. But people quickly found that there were a lot of fine musicians in Nashville—pop, country, gospel, and black. Once some studios sprung up here, this town was made.

Aaron Shelton, co-owner of Castle Studios, took a similar line, pointing to Nashville's string of top-selling records as the final link that drew musicians to town, as he told *Billboard* in 1975:

> People took time to be sold on Nashville. Artists were not sure that it was the right thing to do, to record in a hick town in Tennessee. What made people come here was hits. Castle's first big smash was "Near You," then we had Red Foley's "Peace in the Valley" and "Chattanoogie Shoe Shine Boy." When we started to produce million sellers, then the top artists in all musical fields came to town.

Longtime R&B bandleader Louis Brooks echoed Shelton's view. "It was a smaller scene in the thirties or forties. There was some jazz and blues for sure, but when Francis Craig had the big hit with 'Near You,' that was what put Nashville on the map."

But blues performer Al Garner, speaking from the point of view of local musicians; feels that Nashville was always a difficult place, that country singers had to compete with the WSM stars, and that

> Nashville has always been a hard town for blues too. Nashville is cold-blooded. You have to be like a champion before anyone will accept you. A lot of local blues players made records, but there was not the big distribution available. The Nashville scene was oriented to Tennessee, in blues. Unless you could get with the Shaw Agency or whatever and get really promoted, like Christine Kittrell did there for a while.
>
> I have lived in Nashville and in Texas, and the difference was that in Houston, Duke Records managed and promoted their acts, like Bobby Bland and Junior Parker. They kept you in work. The Nashville labels like Tennessee and Excello did not do that.

Certainly, blues singers had few big-time promotion outlets from Nashville; along with big band and popular singers they had to look to the New York and West Coast based agencies. The promotion of country artists was a developing business in Nashville, though, even if the independent record companies didn't grasp hold of it. Red Wortham and Murray Nash were among an increasing number of small publishers and promoters, but they didn't fully link up with Bullet or Republic to create concerted recording-publishing-promotional packages. This was something at which established managers like Joe Frank excelled, and increasingly Nashville felt the impact of the wheeler-dealer, Colonel Tom Parker, who set up base in Nashville and latched-on, in turn, to Jamup and Honey, Eddy Arnold, Hank Snow, and Elvis Presley.

In the 1940s and 1950s, Nashville's local record labels were trying to make a living from a slice of an industry whose size and ownership were still in question. The local dealers in jukeboxes and amusements were happy to set up a record label and see what would happen. The national record labels were happy to develop a base in Nashville and take from it what they thought could contribute to the wider balance sheet. To an extent, these interests developed in parallel. It was in the middle ground, where a local interest occasionally started to have an impact on the national picture, that conflict emerged.

As Alan Bubis of Tennessee Records reminds us:

> It's hard to realize now how small the record business was back then. Everyone knew everyone else, and the music business wasn't such a big deal in town. You could have taken the whole record industry of Nashville and put it in a good-sized room in 1950.
>
> There weren't that many large independent labels in the whole country back then. The major labels did all the business, really, on a national scale. There were just scraps laying around for the independents to pick up. We were in the jukebox business, then records. We were just looking for a way to turn a dollar.

Although Bill Beasley agreed they were all just trying to make a buck, he thought the independents missed an opportunity in the 1950s.

> We were each doing what we could, of course, but for a while there, Tennessee was the only country label in town, going head to head with Decca. We didn't become a major distributor as we should have done. Decca and RCA Victor in particular were keen to dominate Nashville. They were desperate that they might lose out to the surge in the independent sector of the music business.
>
> There was a tremendous scrap going on, and over the years the publicity machines have glossed over the old days, and success has bred more success, such that the real story has never been told. Looking back at it, in reality I think we all contributed something to it, in our different ways.

The Advent of the Major Labels

There is no doubt that the first independent recordman in town, Jim Bulleit—dubbed by Bill Beasley "the best salesman I ever saw, the Barnum & Bailey of the music business"—dreamed the big dream; but he couldn't realize it. Tennessee Records, though successful for a time, never managed to fulfill its potential or to become more than a fringe operation. Nashboro and Excello settled into comfortable niches with gospel and blues, respectively, but Excello's stab at the pop market with Nasco Records in 1957 soon died. By the dawn of 1956, Republic Records was on its last legs; Bullet, World, Speed, and other labels had come and gone; Hickory was still in business, albeit without the guidance of Fred Rose; but only Dot was flourishing, and it was on the verge of moving to the West Coast.

Jim Bulleit saw the major labels, eager to preserve their domain, piggybacking on the work done by the local independent companies.

> I believe that they never would have based their companies here had it not been for the emergence first of companies like Bullet. They had to come to Nashville, or to use Chet and Owen to represent them, so that their label was here on the spot, to stop labels like ours from picking up the best country artists from the Opry whenever they became available. Then, given that, Nashville was a convenient center to record other music, particularly blues and gospel.
>
> The first indications that people were coming into Nashville to record came through the Castle studio and later the Bradley studios. Some of the most important people to the music business development were the out-of-town record executives and producers—men like Art Satherley and Don Law, Paul Cohen, and Steve Sholes. Those men contributed a lot. Then it was Owen Bradley who began the whole Music Row scene. He was the important man.

Joe Allison developed from his role as a small-station disc jockey in Nashville into a recording executive on the

Looking north across Broad Street at Seventh Avenue, 1952. Courtesy of Metropolitan Nashville Government Archives.

West Coast, and this helped shape his forthright attitude. He agreed that the major labels carried the ball in terms of transforming Nashville into Music City USA, but for him the key men were not the out-of-town producers but the labels' local representatives.

> There were only ever the four majors that counted, and all the local labels in Nashville or anywhere else were just spinning their wheels, taking amateurish swipes at it. Their main role was in gaining an occasional hit and in maybe developing a few artists to sell on to bigger labels. Fred Rose had been very keen to develop Hickory into a substantial concern, but he died, and Wesley was no Fred Rose. Dot was only formed originally to stuff those mail order packages with ballast, and it grew by circumstance, almost by accident, though it moved to the West Coast to really become a force. Bullet was successful briefly, but most of those labels were never going to break out nationally. They didn't have the distribution. The Tennessee people were good distributors, but they had no earthly idea how to run a record label, and that was why they hit so many problems. They were on the fringe. They wouldn't have employed a union musician to save their lives.
>
> So the really vital people, I believe, were those locally based people who worked to establish the major labels here. Ultimately, you come back to Chet Atkins working with RCA, Owen Bradley working with Decca. The independent labels were never going to compete with them.

The former Hermitage Music and Bullet Records premises, 421 and 423 Broad, awaiting rediscovery. Courtesy of the author.

Evolution or Revolution

It was RCA's local representative, Chet Atkins, who in January 1956 put the band together for Elvis Presley's first Nashville recordings. The session was held at the RCA Studio, in the TRAFCO building, and apart from Presley's own rockabilly musicians—guitarist Scotty Moore, bassist Bill Black, and drummer D. J. Fontana—the cast included one of Nashville's top guitarists, Atkins; a relatively new country pianist, Floyd Cramer, who would go on to help define the Nashville Sound; and three stalwarts of Nashville's gospel quartets: Gordon Stoker from the Jordanaires, and Ben and Brock Speer from the Speer Family. Although the session produced two rockers and the uncategorizable "Heartbreak Hotel," which was published by Tree Music, it also featured two country-based ballads and set the scene for the "popularizing" of Presley's sound. Evolution was the word from the first, even if the world thought it heard revolution in this session.

The same week, *Billboard* published the list of top #1 hits of 1955. In sequence, they were: "Hearts of Stone" by the Fontane Sisters, "Sincerely" by the McGuire Sisters, "Ballad of Davy Crockett" by Bill Hayes, "Rock Around the Clock" by Bill Haley, "Sixteen Tons" by Tennessee Ernie Ford, and "Memories Are Made of This" by Dean Martin. In the year ahead, the top hits would include Presley's "Heartbreak Hotel," "The Great Pretender" by the Platters, "I Almost Lost My Mind" by Pat Boone, and "The Green Door" by Jim Lowe.

For a time in 1956, it seemed that Nashville might embrace other movers in the new music. Owen Bradley recorded three Decca sessions with Buddy Holly in the Bradley studios during 1956, including the original version of "That'll Be the Day." Bradley also recorded, for Coral, Johnny and Dorsey Burnette's Memphis-based Rock & Roll Trio in June 1956, capturing in titles like "The Train Kept A Rolling" and "Honey Hush," both R&B songs, some of the rawest rockabilly music ever made. Ken Nelson recorded Gene Vincent's hit "Be Bop a Lula" in the Bradley studio in May 1956. Columbia had already recorded Marty Robbins's rockabilly versions of "That's All Right" at Castle, and "Maybellene" and "Singing the Blues" at Bradley's. And then Roy Hall—former piano-boogie man on Bullet, session player at Tennessee, and Nashville nightclub owner—popped up as a rock & roller on Decca with a song he had cowritten called "Whole Lotta Shakin' Going On," soon to become a major hit for Jerry Lee Lewis. The same year, 1957, Cadence Records used RCA's Nashville studio to record "Bye, Bye Love," the first in a string of hits by the Everly Brothers.

Presley represented both a challenge and a triumph for Nashville. Performers and record-label executives who had built up a solid country image now faced the threat of a new, younger musical form, rock & roll. But RCA's country music division would be ever more firmly wedded to the concept of Nashville as its recording base, and Nashville's real response to rock & roll was to make country records, and R&B records for that matter, less "ethnic" and more mainstream. Pop airplay would surely result.

The piano, the electric guitar, and the vocal chorus increasingly replaced the signature instruments of postwar country music—the steel guitar and fiddle. Strident hillbilly singers became less in vogue than singers capable of bridging pop and country. Nashville has remained a recognized center for blues, soul, and gospel recording throughout, but never the major center, and the black-music dream has never been as prominently promoted in the city as the pop-country one. From his vantage point as a pioneering black R&B producer, Ted Jarrett saw the major labels occasionally bring their black stars into Nashville to record; he reflected that, "later on, you could record R&B or gospel and your market could be international. Originally, your market was national at best and almost solely black, in the days before Elvis Presley."

Briefly in the early 1960s, with Roy Orbison and others, Fred Foster's Monument label became the most successful independent Nashville-based label since the demise of Bullet. But all the major companies were represented in town by the 1960s, and the major labels increasingly dominated the headlines in the recording news that came out of Nashville.

For the Record

The how, why, where, and when of the early Nashville record labels is a story worth knowing—if only to remind us who the responsible players were, and that they were there. Most of the literature about Nashville and the music business over the years has lost sight of them, yet each played a part in the creation of a legend.

Not that Bullet Records or Tennessee Records should replace Chet Atkins or Owen Bradley in the forefront of histories of Nashville music—although maybe Jim Bulleit, along with the roller-coaster history of Tennessee and Republic Records, deserves more than a passing nod, as do the contributions of Nashboro and Excello to the story of black American music.

Of the independent music–industry locations from the 1940s and early 1950s, the old Bullet and Hermitage Music buildings at 421 and 423 Broadway remain, their history surely unknown to most passersby. Even if designer bars and restaurants have replaced the former vibrant business and commercial uses of the lower blocks of Broadway, the buildings there still retain something of the outward look they had in the 1950s.

It would be interesting to know what Jim Bulleit, Wally Fowler, and C. V. Hitchcock would make of the modern-day equivalents of Linebaugh's or, indeed, of the giant, glass-fronted Country Music Hall of Fame and Museum just behind Broad, a grand repository of Nashville's musical history—a history that now includes just a little bit more about them, their contemporaries, and the early days of the independent record business. Perhaps they would agree that Red Hitchcock was right to think, that late fall day in 1945, that it was possible to "make a go of recording" in Nashville.

(Opposite): Map of Nashville Record Company Offices and Studios, 1945–1955, adapted from a Jersey Farms milk route map, late 1940s. Courtesy of Country Music Hall of Fame and Museum.

1 Castle Studio (1)
(WSM at 301 7th Ave N)
2 Hermitage Music/Bullet (4)
Bullet Plastics (2) (421/423 Broadway)
3 Bullet (1) (119 7th Ave N)
4 Bullet (2) (2320 12th Ave S)
5 Bullet (3) (1710 Portland Street)
6 Select (Memorial Hotel
at 325 7th Ave N)
7 World (Warner Building
at 535 Church Street)
8 Castle Studio (2)
(Hotel Tulane at 206 8th Ave N)
9 Cheker Studio, (726 Benton)
10 Bulleit Enterprises (415 Ash Street)
11 Coastline/Tennessee (1)
(417 Ash Street)
12 Tennessee (2) (824 5th Ave S)
13 Republic (1) (535 4th Ave S)
(Studio at 901 4th Ave S)
14 Republic (2) (714 Allison Street)
15 Eagle Studio (232 4th Ave N)
16 Republic (3)/MNA (319 7th Ave N)
17 Nashboro/Excello (177 3rd Ave N)
18 WLAC radio studio (170 4th Ave N)
19 WSIX radio studio (315 Union)
20 WKDA radio studio (324 Union)
21 WMAK radio studio (207 4th Ave N)
22 WSOK radio studio (4th Ave N)
23 Belmont (1110 16th Ave S)
24 Speed/Gold (421 Broadway)
25 Hillbilly All Star (1724 0rdway Place)
26 Wally Fowler Records
(714 Warner Building)
27 Acuff-Rose (220 Capitol Boulevard)
28 Dot Records (in Gallatin, Tennessee)
29 Brown Brothers Studio/RCA (1)
(240 4th Ave N)
30 Thomas Recording Studio/RCA
Studio (2) (109 13th Ave N)
31 RCA Studio (3)
(1525 McGavock Street)
32 Reavis studio (2014 Beech Street)
33 Reavis studio (2) (417 Church Street)
34 Reavis studio (3) (230 4th Ave N)
35 Bradley Studio (1) (2nd/Lindsley)
36 Bradley Studio (2)
(21st Ave S/Hillsboro Rd)
37 Bradley Studio (3) (804 16th Ave S)
38 Nashville Recording Studio
(403 Union Street)
39 Ryman Auditorium (116 5th Ave N)
40 Hickory Records/Acuff-Rose (2)
(2510 Franklin Road)
Off the map, in Gallatin, TN
See detail area below
Present day Music Row
Scale: approximately 1 mile

Acknowledgments

During the thirty-year genesis of this project, I frequently remembered a cartoon where two people find themselves face-to-face at a party. One volunteers enthusiastically, "I'm writing a book." With cynical realism, the other replies, "Neither am I." And for many years, it looked like it was going to turn out that way.

That this project has now come to fruition reflects the enthusiasm and assistance of so many people who have helped over the years. I have had the benefit of several types of help: general support and advice from a few especially involved individuals; specific information from many record collectors and music writers; assistance from a number of professional researchers; and the vital input of those interviewed about their roles in this story.

I have discussed aspects of this work with Colin Escott and Hank Davis, in person and by letter, telephone, and e-mail, for the best part of thirty years. Colin has continually sent me unsolicited information over the years. He has offered important insights and encouraged me to summarize in an effort to enhance rather than diminish the story. He worked with me on two boxed sets of Nashville-based music CDs a few years ago, as did Hank Davis and Kevin Coffey, and I think they might recognize a few of their phrases within this text. Richard Weize of Bear Family Records is the only person in the world who would have dreamed of allowing me to produce two complex 8-CD boxes, and he worked personally and enthusiastically on them.

Looking back over a mountain of correspondence, I found a large pile of letters from Bill Daniels, full of information, ideas, and enthusiasm about dating of record releases. These helped set the structure of this book many years ago.

It was important at the outset to understand the scope of the record labels themselves. How many were there? When did they operate? Exactly what records were issued? At one time, I had a big stash of Nashville-label 78-rpm discs that I had collected. I also had access to some record-company catalogs and to pioneering discographical works such as the Blues Research listings by Anthony Rotante and Paul Sheatsley. But I needed the expertise of several heavyweight collectors to help fill in the label listings and point out linkages and stylistic similarities. Bill Daniels worked hard in the early days to send me a stream of helpful listings, acting above and beyond the call without ever being asked. Dave Sax played a major part in the work connected with the record label listings included here, and with the CD boxed sets, clarifying record releases, producing copies of impossibly rare discs, and being generally enthusiastic. He made the ultimate sacrifice when a pile of 78-rpm records was broken in the cause of research. I spent time trying the patience of Phil Tricker and Al Turner with interminable questions about label listings and the origins of obscure items. I am also indebted to other collectors, including the late Bob Pinson, who first gave me the run of the Country Music Foundation's 78-rpm archive (now named in his honor), Doug Seroff, Bruce Bastin, John Broven, Ray Topping, George Moonoogian, and Mitch Drumm. Lars Lundgren copied a lot of country discs for me some thirty years back. More latterly, Mike Smyth and Michael Gray have volunteered invaluable help and produced copies of very rare recordings.

The record labels on pages 87, 108, and 169 are courtesy of Bear Family Records; on page 48, courtesy of Jeff Knutson; and on page 110, courtesy of Dave Sax. The Collegiate label on pages 81 and 266 and the World Records label on page 299 are courtesy of Mike Smyth. Unless otherwise indicated, all other labels are from the archives of the Country Music Hall of Fame and Museum or from my own collection.

The detailed knowledge of other record collectors, writers, and researchers was inspirational. Over the years I have gained navigational aid and encouragement, discographical and biographical information, and general help and enthusiasm from Bill Millar, Chris Bentley, Wayne Russell, Tony Russell, Richard Peterson, Bob Laughton, Bob Fuller, Robert Loers, Jim O'Neal, Fred James, Bruce Bastin, Tony Collins, John Pearson, John Broven, Rick Coleman, Tad Jones, Les Leverett, Jim Stephens, Dave Penny, Bruce Nemerov, and some I am sure I have quite unforgivably forgotten to record.

As I was finishing this book, between 2003 and 2005, I was able to draw on professional help from a number of organizations in Nashville. At the Nashville Public Library's Nashville Room, I had the considerable benefit of the knowledge of Ronnie Pugh and the help of Beth Odle and others who pulled a phenomenal number of files and guided me through them. At the Metropolitan Government Archives of Nashville and Davidson County, I enjoyed the help of Linda Center, and I found Susan Gordon and Robert Lee similarly helpful at the Tennessee State Library and Archives in Nashville.

At the Country Music Foundation in Nashville, Bob Pinson, Robert Oermann, and Kyle Young had been involved in the beginnings of this project many years ago, and in 2003, Kira Florita, Daniel Cooper, and Jay Orr persuaded me that this book had to be placed with the CMF Press and Vanderbilt University Press. In the final stages, I was pleased to have the full weight of the experts at the Foundation behind me. Dawn Oberg, Denny Adcock, Michael Gray, Alan Stoker, and Becky Miley helped me pick my way through oral histories, information files, photographic files, and the record library. In particular, this book would not be as well sequenced or as readable without the phenomenal efforts of Daniel Cooper to help me put things in the right place and to drop information that was of marginal relevance. John Rumble provided many invaluable comments and insights, and helped me avoid some potentially embarrassing mistakes. Leia Buchanan pulled the photographic research together, provided a brilliant day-by-day link point, and occasionally told me to stop sending e-mails at midnight.

Jay Orr undertook the editing role for the Foundation, coping with my occasionally bizarre mixture of U.K. and U.S. spellings and language. Then Bobbe Needham took on the daunting task of copyediting. She has helped immeasurably by proposing sequencing and phrasing that make best sense of my sometimes bewildering array of facts. Both Jay and Bobbe made me really think about the meaning of the words I was stumbling to use, and theirs is a rare skill, if not an art.

At Vanderbilt University Press, Betsy Phillips showed considerable enthusiasm and amazing resilience as the deadlines came and went and I kept finding new reasons to revise the manuscript. Dariel Mayer worked long and hard to turn my text, photographs, and ill-expressed layout suggestions into a really outstanding design that certainly enhances the raw materials I gave her. Sue Havlish led the marketing of the work with enthusiasm and panache, and I'm sure that Betsy, Dariel, and Sue resolved all kinds of problems I didn't even know I'd caused, along with some I know I did.

Together, every one of these people has helped me turn a mere manuscript into a real book, and one of which I think we are all proud. I really hope that I have not wasted all their efforts and that I have done justice to them, and to everyone else who helped. Still, I would love to hear from people with additional information, and I hope that anyone with questions or comments will contact me through Vanderbilt University Press.

As I got further into this project, of course, many of the principal characters in the story passed away, and I found myself talking to their children, other relatives, and acquaintances. Many of these people welcomed my enquiries warmly and produced all kinds of information and photographs that I might have hoped for but not really expected. I am indebted particularly to Gayle Bulleit Moses, Kirk Beasley (my man in Hawaii), John Dunn Jr., Richard Cashion, Tony Ganong, and Ogden and McNeill Stokes. They all provided help either with family information or photographic sources, and displayed considerable enthusiasm and good humor, without ever becoming too irritated by my questioning.

Finally, none of this would have been worthwhile without the time taken by the people featured in this book, the pioneers of the independent record business in Nashville, from whose reminiscences and supply of factual data I have been able to piece together this story. Many of them made themselves available for interview, and they are listed in the References section that follows. Mostly, they fed back to me a real enthusiasm to see this book written about a world and music that were so very different from today. This really is their story, and I have deliberately told it in their own words where possible. It is a shame it took me so long, and that many of them didn't live to see it.

References

Author Interviews

The following are the principal personal interviews relied upon in this text. They were supported by a number of other supplementary telephone interviews, letters, and e-mail exchanges. N.d. indicates that the exact date of an interview has not been recorded.

Howard Allison, May 29, 1974; and April 12, 1981
Joe Allison, June 1998
Chet Atkins, April 1979
Bill Beasley, May 12, 1974; n.d. 1981; January 27, 1982; September 1998; June 24, 1999; August 19, 1999; and November 1999
Harold Bradley, June 8, 1998; March 1999; April 2003; November 2003; and February 2004
Owen Bradley, April 3, 1981
Louis Brooks, April 1985; May 1985; and n.d.
Paul Broome, n.d. 1996; January 1998
Alan Bubis, April 23, 1998; April 25, 1999; September 1, 1999; April 2003; n.d. 2003
Reynold Bubis, March 30, 1981
Louis Buckley, May 1975
Jim Bulleit, May 1973; May 11, 1974; April 16, 1975; April 1981
Hutch Carlock, May 8, 1981; December 9, 1981
Hugh Cherry, n.d. 1997
Dottie Dillard, n.d. 1998 and 1999
Johnnie Douglas, October 12, 1999
John Dunn, March 12, 1982
John Dunn Jr., n.d. 2003 and 2004
Earl "Buddy" Estes, January 7, 2006
Earl Gaines, June 1999; September 1, 1999
Al Garner, September 1999
Chuck Gregory, n.d.1997
Roy Hall, May 28, 1974
Buddy Harman, n.d. 1999
Bobby Hebb, n.d. 1998 and 1999
Helen Hebb-McCray, n.d. 1998 and 1999
Tommy Hill, June 9, 1998
Frank Innocenti, April 8, 1982; n.d. 1995, 1996, and 1998
Ted Jarrett, April 8, 1982; n.d. 1995, 1996, and 1998; April 28, 2003; October 2003
Buddy Killen, December 2003
D Kilpatrick, n.d. 1998
Christine Kittrell, May 1985; n.d. 1992, 1997, and 1998; May 6, 1999; August 11, 1999; February 13, 2000; n.d. 2000
Johnny Maddox, February 2003; April 26, 2003
Kenny Marlow, December 28, 1981
Dean May, April 3, 1981
James O. Michelinie, May 11, 2005
Bob Moore, April 2005
John Moore, 2003
Cam Mullins, 1997
Murray Nash, n.d. 1992 and 1997; September 14, 1999
Gene Nobles, November 1, 1981; December 1981
Bill Norris, March 17, 2004
Richard Penniman, November 2003
Sam Phillips, July 5, 1983; May 1999
Tommy Scott, n.d. 2003
Red Sovine, April 1974
Rufus Thomas, October 1999
Arthur Weinman, August 18, 1999
Shannon Williams, n.d. 1998 and 1999
Mac Wiseman, April 1974
Randy Wood, March 31, 1982 (via Polly Mitchener)
Red Wortham, May 1975; October 1982; n.d. 1996 and 1997; August 27, 1998; n.d. 1999 and 2000
Cal Young, n.d. 1997 and 1998
Ernie Young, June 1974 (via Howard Allison)

CMF Oral Histories

I have sometimes quoted from or cross-checked my own interviews against the following interviews conducted by Douglas B. Green, John Rumble, and others as part of the Oral History Program at the Country Music Foundation:

Harold Bradley, September 15, 1988; September 28, 1988; and January 17, 1974
Owen Bradley, n.d. 1993/1994
Jim Bulleit, February 10, 1976; May 4 and 9, 1983
Hugh Cherry, February 28 and 29, 1996
Don Law, May 14, 1975

Brad McCuen, March 11, 1974; May 8, 1974; June 19, 1974; January 27, 1975; April 23 and 29, 1975; May 8, 1975; July 22, 1975
Murray Nash, April 25, 1974; May 2 and 13, 1974; June 8, 13, 14, and 15, 1983; June 14 and 21, 1984; June 18, 1987
Jack Stapp, August 8, 1972

Interviews by Colin Escott

Information summarized from Colin Escott's contributions to the Bear Family CD boxed sets came from, among other sources, interviews with: Ray Batts, Jeff Bess, Alan Bubis, Rachel Bulleit, Chuck Gregory, James Grishaw, Ruby Hollingsworth, Wes Holly, Kathy Hughes, Frank Innocenti, Chickie King, Murray Nash, Jim Odom, Myrtie Payne, Leon Selph, Jimmy Simpson, Sonny Sims, Jack Toombs, Buck Turner, and Zeke Turner.

Library Resources

I have drawn information from the following:

Fisk University, Franklin Library, Special Collections, Nashville
Frist Library and Archive of the Country Music Hall of Fame and Museum, Nashville
Metropolitan Government Archives of Nashville and Davidson County
Nashville Room, Nashville Public Library
Tennessee State Library and Archives, Nashville
Vanderbilt University Special Collections Archive, Nashville

Publications

I have quoted from, drawn information from, or cross-checked my own information against the contents of the following books and periodicals:

Adams, G. Rollie. *Nashville: A Pictorial History*. Marceline, Mo.: Walsworth, 1982.
Allen, Duane, and Jesse Burt. *History of Gospel Music*. Nashville: Silverline Music, 1971.
Bear Family Records. CD boxed set booklets, various.
Becker, Paula. *Let the Song Go On: The Speer Family*. Nashville: Impact Books, 1971.
Billboard, 1945–1956
Billboard supplements (record labels, distributors, jukebox dealers), 1940s
Boone, Pat. *Together: Twenty-five Years with the Pat Boone Family*. Nashville: Thomas Nelson, 1979.
Broome, Paul, and Clay Tucker. *The Other Music City: The Bands and Jazz Musicians of Nashville, 1920–1970*. Nashville: American Press, 1990/2000.
Burt, Jesse. *Nashville: Its Life and Times*. Nashville: Tennessee Book Company, 1959.
Cashbox, 1945–1956.
Cooper, Daniel. *Lefty Frizzell*. New York: Little, Brown, 1995.
Crain, Charles R. *Music Performance and Pedagogy in Nashville, 1818–1900*. PhD diss., George Peabody College for Teachers, 1975.
Cusic, Don. *Eddy Arnold*. Nashville: Rutledge Hill Press, 1997.
Daniels, Bill. Disc-Dating Guides, 1940s and 1950s. Salem, N.H.: Daniels, 1981.
Delmore, Alton. *Truth Is Stranger Than Publicity*. Nashville: CMF Press, 1977.
Doyle, Don. *Nashville in the New South, 1880–1930*. Knoxville: University of Tennessee Press, 1985.
———. *Nashville since the 1920s*. Knoxville: University of Tennessee Press, 1985.
Escott, Colin, and Martin Hawkins. *Good Rockin' Tonight*. New York: St. Martin's Press, 1992.
Gart, Galen. *American Record Label Directory, 1940–1959*. Milford, N.H.: Big Nickel, 1990.
———. *First Pressings*. Milford, N.H.: Big Nickel, 1995.
Gentry, Linnell. *History and Encyclopedia of Country, Western, and Gospel Music*. Nashville: Clairmont, 1969.
Godrich, John, and Robert Dixon. *Blues and Gospel Records*. London: Storyville, 1969.
Goff, James. *Close Harmony: History of Southern Gospel*. Chapel Hill: University of North Carolina Press, 2002.
Harris, Sheldon. *Blues Who's Who*. New York: Arlington House, 1979.
Hayes, Cedric, and Robert Laughton. *Gospel Records, 1943–1969*. London: Record Information Services, 1992.
Heilbut, Tony. *The Gospel Sound*. New York: Limelight, 1985.
Ikard, Robert. *Near You*. Nashville: Hillsboro Press, 1999.
Jensen, Joli. *The Nashville Sound*. Nashville: CMF/Vanderbilt University Press, 1999.
Journal of Country Music (Country Music Foundation). Various editions, including Bullet records by Martin Hawkins, 1981; Castle Studio Logbooks by John Rumble, 1978.
Killen, Buddy. *By the Seat of My Pants*. New York: Simon and Schuster, 1993.
Kinkle, Roger. *Encyclopedia of Popular and Jazz Music*. New York: Arlington House, 1974.
Knoxville Sentinel
Leadbitter, Mike, and Neil Slaven. *Blues Records, 1943–1966*. New York: Oak, 1968.

Malone, Bill. *Country Music USA*. Austin: University of Texas Press, 1968.
Morton, David. *DeFord Bailey*. Knoxville: University of Tennessee Press, 1991.
Nashville Banner
Nashville City Directories, annual publications by Marshall-Bruce-Polk.
Nashville Chamber of Commerce. Statistical records of Nashville. Various dates.
Nashville Commentator, 1949 and 1951
Nashville *Globe & Independent*
Nashville Musician (Journal of AFM Local 257). Various dates.
Nashville Scene
Pavlow, Al. *The R&B Book*. Providence, R.I.: Music House, 1993.
Rumble, John. *Fred Rose and the Development of the Nashville Music Industry*. PhD diss., Vanderbilt University, 1980.
Rust, Brian. *The American Dance Band Discography*. New York: Arlington Press, 1975.
———. *Jazz Records*. London: Storyville, 1969.
Shaw, Arnold. *Honkers and Shouters*. New York: Collier, 1978.
Smith, Wes. *Pied Pipers of Rock and Roll*. Athens, Ga.: Longstreet Press. 1989.
Spinney, Robert. *World War II in Nashville*. Nashville: University of Tennessee Press, 1998.
Tennessean
Warner, Jay. *Just Walkin' in the Rain*. Los Angeles: Renaissance Books, 2001.
Watkins, Clifford. *Jordan "Chick" Chavis*. Nashville: Tennessee State University, 1979.
Whitburn, Joel. *Joel Whitburn's Top Country Singles, 1944–1993*. Menomonee Falls, Wis.: Record Research, 1986.
———. *Joel Whitburn's Top Pop Singles, 1945–1972*. Menomonee Falls, Wis.: Record Research, 1973.
———. *Joel Whitburn's Top R&B Singles, 1942–1988*. Menomonee Falls, Wis.: Record Research, 1988.
Wolfe, Charles. *A Good Natured Riot: The Birth of the Grand Ole Opry*. Nashville: CMF/Vanderbilt University Press, 1999.
———. *Classic Country*. New York: Routledge, 2001.

Music Sources

I listened to the music on Nashville's independent record labels from the following main sources, apart from my own collection:

Bob Pinson Recorded Sound Collection, Country Music Hall of Fame and Museum, Nashville
Disc copies from the collections of Al Turner, Phil Tricker, Dave Sax, Lars Lundgren, John Broven, Mike Smyth, and Richard Weize.

Currently Available CDs

These compact-disc reissues should still be in catalogs or obtainable from specialist and secondhand dealers.

Blues and R&B

Nashville Jumps: Blues and Rhythm on Nashville's Independent Labels, 1945–1955
Bear Family Records (Germany)
BCD 15864 HL

This is an eight-CD boxed set containing more than 210 recordings from all relevant labels (except Dot) and interviews with Jim Bulleit and Christine Kittrell. It contains a 276-page, LP-sized booklet with detailed analyses by Hank Davis and me of all the recordings.

Night Train to Nashville: Music City Rhythm & Blues, 1945–1970
CMF Records / Lost Highway
B0002100–02

A two-CD set covering the range of blues, R&B, and soul music recorded locally from the 1940s to the 1970s. Produced by Daniel Cooper and Michael Gray, it contains a thirty-two-page booklet and many rare illustrations.

Night Train to Nashville: Music City Rhythm & Blues, 1945–1970, Volume Two
CMF Records / Lost Highway
B0005228-02

Follow-up to the first volume, also produced by Cooper and Gray.

The Excello Story, Volumes 1–4, 1952–1975
Hip-O Records (Universal)
HIPD 40149/50/56/57

Four CDs containing all the hits and significant blues and R&B (mainly), rock & roll, and country recordings on the label. Gatefold sleeves and detailed notes by John Broven.

Across the Tracks: Nashville R&B and Rock & Roll
Ace Records (England)
CDCHD 493 and 672

Two CDs from the Kit, Calvert, and Champion labels operated from 1956 on by Al Bubis and Ted Jarrett.

Various Excello CDs
Ace Records (England) CDCHD 400 (Excello Hits), 604 *(Deep Harmonica Blues)*, 652 *(No Jive: Country Blues)*, 653 *(Wail Daddy: Nashville Jump Blues)*, 662 *(Southern Rhythms)*, 684 *(Ernie's Record Mart)*, and 686 *(Record Center of the South)*.

Country

Tennessee Jive: Country Music on Nashville's Independent Labels, 1945–1955
Bear Family Records (Germany)
BCD 15854 HL

This is an eight-CD boxed set containing more than 210 recordings from all relevant labels (except Dot) and interviews with Jim Bulleit and Hutch Carlock. It contains a 276-page LP-sized booklet with detailed analysis by Colin Escott, Kevin Coffey, Charles Wolfe, and me of all the recordings.

Gospel

Radio Four: 1952–1954
Heritage Records (England)
HT CD 42

Tennessee and Republic recordings, including Lucile Barbee and Edna Gallmon Cooke.

Radio Four: There's Gonna Be Joy
Ace Records (England)
CDCHD 448

Nashboro recordings made at the end, and just after the period this book covers.

Popular and Jazz

Francis Craig: Near You
Hillsboro Press (CD included in a book by Robert Ikard)
Contains early recordings, hits, radio shows.

Nashville Record-Label Listings, 1945–1955

This section attempts to list all the records issued on independent labels based in Nashville during the period 1945–1955. It also includes Dot and associated labels from nearby Gallatin.

While country, blues, and gospel music were the mainstays of these labels, there was nevertheless a significant amount of other music issued: popular tunes, dance-band jazz, or novelties of some kind. The Bullet label, for example, issued records in five different numerical series covering country, blues, gospel, pop, and Mexican music separately.

The record labels are listed alphabetically, with each separate numerical series identified, and an indication of the time-frame within which the series existed. Where a label issued records beyond the end of 1955, the listing has been terminated at an appropriate cut-off point. These are all single records, mainly issued on ten-inch discs at 78 rpm (revolutions per minute) although, from about 1950 onwards, many of them were also issued on seven-inch discs at 45 rpm. A few of the labels repackaged their music into Album sets of 78 rpm discs and, later, Extended Play 45s (with four songs per disc) and ten or twelve-inch LPs (with around twelve songs) at 33 rpm—none of which have been included here to save space.

Where possible, I have listed the performers and titles exactly as shown on the record labels, spelling mistakes included (except that articles and conjunctions have not been capitalized), but otherwise I have relied on spellings from sales catalogs that are not always totally accurate. Then again, some records were pressed at more than one place and time, resulting in spelling inconsistencies on labels of the same record. In any case, the prime purpose of these listings is to give the reader a thorough picture of what music was issued, not to produce a word-perfect discography.

It is likely that some records were issued that have not survived to be heard or listed, and I have indicated apparently-lost records as "unknown." However, the vagaries of some of the companies' release schedules mean that gaps in these listings may be just that, with no record having ever been issued.

I have based these listings on record company catalogs and sales lists from mail order companies, along with information from my own record collection and from pioneering discographies such as those in *Record Research* and *Hillbilly Researcher*. But over a thirty-year period many record collectors have readily contributed their own information. It is only through their assistance that these listings have become anywhere near complete. Those who helped include, principally, Dave Sax, Al Turner, Phil Tricker, Lars Lundgren, Bill Daniels, and the late Bob Pinson; also Ray Topping, Doug Seroff, Richard Weize, Mike Smyth, James Zurek, and Bob Laughton. My apologies to others who undoubtedly made contributions that were not recorded over the passage of time.

Artist (800 series) (Country)
First issue: circa 1955
Last known: 1955

Label	Artist	Side A	Side B
800 - 804	unknown		
805	Slim Lay and The Home Folks	Susie's Poodle Dog	I'll Never Find Another You (vocal by Carolyn Gossett)
806	unknown		
807	Ollen and Dennis–The Gospel Singers	Tragedy of Spring City, Tennessee	Mother's Dead and in Heaven

Belmont (300 series) (Popular)
First issue: October 1953
Last known: 1953

Label	Artist	Side A	Side B
300	Victory Quartet	Have Faith and Pray	
	Lonnie Hooberry		The Christ Child's Story
301	Jesse Harrison	Someone New	
	Bill Cooper		All the Time
302	Liza Lee	The Smoke House	
	Jesse Harrison		Someone New

Bullet (100 series) (Country Gospel)
First issue: April 1946
Last known: 1952

Label	Artist	Side A	Side B
100	Baxter Quartet	They Have Gone Away	Just What He Promised
101	Stamps-Baxter Mixed Quartet	Who Is That	You Better Get Down and Pray
102	John Daniel Quartet	Careless Driver	Headin' for the Pearly Gates
103	John Daniel Quartet	In the Valley of the Moon	Goin' Forth to Win
104	John Daniel Quartet	Crossing Over Jordan	No Disappointments Up There
105	John Daniel Quartet	Gonna Row My Boat	No Darkness Can Hide My Lord from Me
106	Rangers Quartet	Just a Little Talk with Jesus	Looking for a City
107	John Daniel Quartet	You've Got to Move	I Want That Kind of Blessing
108	John Daniel Quartet	On the Glory Road	I Have Everlasting Peace
109	Rangers Quartet	Down On My Knees	I Couldn't Begin to Tell You
110	John Daniel Quartet	I Love Jesus Best of All	He Is the Best Friend
111	Wally Fowler and the All Night Gospel Singers	Lead Me to That Rock	Just a Closer Walk with Thee
112	Wally Fowler and His Oak Ridge Quartet	I Got Faith	You Must Have the Pure Religion
113	John Daniel Quartet	Looking Beyond	More of Thy Grace
114	Wally Fowler and His Oak Ridge Quartet	Pray, Pray, Pray (for the U.S.A.)	Hold to God's Unchanging Hand
115	Wally Fowler and His Oak Ridge Quartet	No Pass to Heaven	Perfect Joy
116	Wally Fowler and His Oak Ridge Quartet	I'm a Bible Lovin' Man	I'm Free Again
117	Goodman Family	A Mansion Over the Hilltop	Lead Out of Bondage
118	Wally Fowler and His Oak Ridge Quartet	I Wanna Rest	Land Where Living Waters Flow

Label	Artist	Side A	Side B
119	Goodman Family	I'm Free Again	Looking for a City
120	Speer Family	Peace in the Valley	My Burdens Have Rolled Away
121	Speer Family	Won't We Be Happy	Dig a Little Deeper
122	John Daniel Quartet	Get Aboard This Train	One by One We'll All Be Gathered Home
123	Wally Fowler and His Oak Ridge Quartet	One Day	Looking for a City
124	John Daniel Quartet	Praise the Lord I'm Coming Through	I Want a Golden Mansion
125	Speer Family	It Is No Secret	The Land of Perfect Day
126	Wally Fowler and His Oak Ridge Quartet	I've Found a Hiding Place	Mother's Voice
127	Wally Fowler and His Oak Ridge Quartet	Dig a Little Deeper (In God's Love)	Lead Me Gently Home, Father
128	Wally Fowler and His Oak Ridge Quartet	Victory Through Jesus Only	He Bought My Soul at Calvary
129	Wally Fowler and His Oak Ridge Quartet	Roll On Jordan	He'll Understand and Say Well Done
130	Speer Family	O Rock of Ages, Hide Thou Me	Looking for a City
131	Wally Fowler and His Oak Ridge Quartet	Peace in the Valley	It Is No Secret
132	unknown		
133	Daniel Family Quartet	Gonna Row My Boat	'Tis the Name of Jesus
134	Wally Fowler and His Oak Ridge Quartet	My Journey to the Sky	I Dreamed of Heaven
135	Wally Fowler and His Oak Ridge Quartet	A Mansion Over the Hilltop	Do You Call That Religion?
136	Crusaders Quartet	My Journey to the Sky	Welcome to Gloryland
137	John Daniel Quartet	How Beautiful Heaven Must Be	Don´t Be Knocking
138	John Daniel Quartet	Just Wait til We Get to Heaven	I'll Leave It All Behind
139	Speer Family	Some Morning Fair	Rock-A-My Soul
140	Goodman Family	Thank God I'm in His Care	Weapon of Prayer
141	John Daniel Quartet	My People	Sing a Happy Song
142	Speer Family	You Sure Do Need Him Now	The Old Time Faith Is What We Need
143–144	unknown		
145	Wally Fowler	Bound for the Kingdom	Jesus´ Love Just Bubbles Over
146	Wally Fowler	The Love of God	Hide Me, Rock of Ages
147	Wally Fowler	Where He Leads Me	Weapon of Prayer
148	Wally Fowler	He Bought My Soul At Calvary	Victory Through Jesus Only
149	John Daniel Quartet	Singing Keeps Me Happy	Rocking on the Waves
150	Speer Family	He Bought My Soul At Calvary	unknown
151	Wally Fowler and His Oak Ridge Quartet	I Went to Heaven in a Dream	Rock-a-My Soul
152	Jack Rogers	Christ Over Korea	Have You Heard from the Man Upstairs
153–154	unknown		
155	Wally Fowler and His Oak Ridge Quartet	Revival Day	
	Joe Allred		Something Within Me
156	Speer Family	Satisfied	I've Been to Heaven in a Dream
157	unknown		
158	Speer Family	Someone to Care	Lord, I Want to Make It Up There
159–161	unknown		
162	The Speer Family	My God Is Real	Miracles Will Happen on That Day
163	Daniel Family Quartet	By and By	He's Just the Same Today

Bullet (250 series) (Blues, R&B, Gospel)
First issue: April 1946
Last known: May 1952

Label	Artist	Side A	Side B
250	Cecil Gant	Nashville Jumps	Loose as a Goose
251	Wynonie (Mr. Blues) Harris	Lightning Struck the Poor House	Dig This Boogie
252	Wynonie (Mr. Blues) Harris	My Baby's Barrel House	Drinkin' by Myself
253	Fairfield Four	Who Stole My Old Shoes	Better Leave That Liar Alone
254	Fairfield Four	Don't You Want to Join That Number	Where Shall I Go
255	Cecil Gant Trio	Train Time Blues	Sloppy Joe's
256	Cecil Gant Trio	If It's True	Boogie Woogie Baby
257	Cecil Gant Trio	I'm All Alone Now	Anna Mae
258	Cecil Gant Trio	Ninth Street Jive	It's the Girl
259	unknown		
260	Rudy Greene Trio	This Happened When I Gave You My Heart	Evil Man Blues
261	Rudy Greene Trio	No Good Woman Blues	Deep in My Heart
262	Red Calhoun and His Dallas Swingsters	Here Comes the Man with the Gin (vocal by Thomas Ross)	I Can't Make My Way
263	unknown		
264	Cecil Gant Orchestra	Every Minute of Every Hour	Boozie Boogie
265	Cecil Gant	Go to Sleep Little Baby	My My My
266	Rudy Greene and His Orchestra	Buzzard Pie	Florida Blues
267	unknown		
268	Four Clefs	Am I Still Your Baby	The First Thing in the Morning
269	unknown		
270	St. Louis Jimmy	I Ain't Done Nothing Wrong	Goin' Down Slow
271	unknown		
272	Cecil Gant Trio	I Wonder	I Believe I'll Go Back Home
273	unknown		
274	Big Three Trio	Get Up Those Stairs Madamoiselle	Lonely Roamin'
275	Big Three Trio	Signifying Monkey	You Sure Look Good to Me
276	Sherman Williams and his Orchestra	Sherman's Boogie (vocal by Skippy Brooks)	Keep Your Man at Home (vocal by Iona Wade)
277	Sherman Williams and his Orchestra	I'm Lucky with My Brown Gal	Baby, Don't You Want to Go
278	St. Louis Jimmy	My Trouble	Sittin' and Thinkin'
279	unknown		
280	Cecil Gant Trio	Another Day-Another Dollar	Three Little Girls
281	unknown		
282	Littlejohn and the Three Silhouettes	Pennies from Heaven (Vocal by Dick Morgan)	One Rose (Vocal by Ernie Chesson)
283	Sherman Williams and his Orchestra	Red Head Blues (My Flamin' Gal) (vocal by Skippy Brooks)	Skippy's Blues (Baby, Please Don't Go) (vocal by Skippy Brooks)
284	Fairfield Four	Standing in the Safety Zone	Don't Let Nobody Turn You Round

Label	Artist	Side A	Side B
285	Smokey Hogg	Hard Times	Goin' Back Home
286	Vicki Zimmer	He's a Bad Man, but He Treats Me Good	Take Another Guess
287	Buddy Moore	Big Fat Poppa	Blow Top Blues
288	Boogie Evans	Low Land Blues	Savoy Boogie
289	Cecil Gant	I'm a Good Man but a Poor Man	Cecil's Jam Session
290	Rose Oden	You Can't Love Me Baby	Call Me Every Mornin'
291	St. Louis Jimmy	Now I'm Through	Mr. Brown's Boogie
292	Fairfield Four	When I Get Up in Heaven	Amazing Grace
293	Evangelist Singers of Detroit	I'm Tired	One Day
294	Famous Jubilee Singers	Sweet Little Jesus Boy	Go Tell It on the Mounatin
295	Red Miller Trio	Bewildered	Nobility Boogie
296	unknown		
297	Pepper Neeley	Fanny Brown	Lorita
298	unknown		
299	Cecil Gant	I Ain't Gonna Cry No More	Screwy Boogie
300	Cecil Gant	I Hate to Say Goodbye	My Little Baby
301	unknown		
302	Ernie Fields	T-Town Boogie	E. F. Boogie
303	Joe Costa	Don't Wanna Letcha Go	I Couldn't Begin to Tell You
304	Sherman Williams	Oo-Wee Baby Gee	Take a Ride
305	Walter Davis	Move Back to the Woods	You've Got to Reap What You Sow
306	Max (Blues) Bailey	Delinquency Blues	Sting-a-Ree
307	Fairfield Four	Canaan	I'm Going to Live the Life That I Sing About
308	Fairfield Four	You've Got to Move	Just One More Moment in God's Kingdom
309	B. B. King	Miss Martha King	When Your Baby Packs up and Goes
310	Max (Blues) Bailey	Rockin' the Blues	Coming Home Blues
311	Walter Davis	Wonder What I'm Doing Wrong	I Would Hate to Hate You (Like I Love You)
312	Tuff Green and His Orchestra	Let's Go to the Liquor Store	I Love My Baby
313	Cecil Gant	I'm Singing the Blues Today	Rose Room
314	Margaret Barnes	Saviour Don't Pass Me By	Dig a Little Deeper
315	B. B. King	Got the Blues	Take a Swing with Me
316	Abe Baker Trio	Don't Ask Me Why	Just You and Me
317	Don Q. and his Q-Tones	Thanksgiving	Major Alteration
318	Fairfield Four	Steal Away	Noah
319	Roosevelt Sykes	Candy Man Blues	Why Should I Cry
320	Cecil Gant	What's the Matter	You Can't Do Me Right (And Do Me Wrong)
321	Walter Davis	Santa Claus Blues	Got to See Her Every Night
322	Chuck Merrill	Rag Mop	Chattanooga Shoe Shine Boy
323	Doc Wiley	Play Your Hand	The Doctor's Jump
324	Fairfield Four	John the Revelator	Elijah
325	Ebenezer a.m.E. Church Gospel Choir	He Knows My Heart	I'm So Glad

Label	Artist	Side A	Side B
326	Walter Davis	Stop That Train in Harlem	So Long Baby
327	Mr. Swing with Bobby Plater's Orchestra	Beer Bottle Boogie	Gonna Bring My Baby Back
328	Walter Davis	My Life Depends on You	Come on Baby
329	Jerome Richardson with Bobby Plater's Orchestra	She's Gone Again	Phillips Sent Me
330	Don Q. and His Q-Tones	Private Property Blues	Baby I Don't Need You Now
331	Glen Abner	Silent Night	Jingle Bells
332	Glen Abner	O Come All Ye Faithful	O Little Town of Bethlehem
333	Glen Abner	First Noel	It Came upon a Midnight Clear
334	St. Mary's Choir	Adeste Fideles	O Little Town of Bethlehem
335	St. Mary's Choir	Silent Night	First Noel
336	St. Mary's Choir	O Holy Night	Joy to the World
337	Joe Williams	Jivin' Woman	She's a Married Woman
338	Tuff Green and his Orchestra	She Ain't No Good	Bounce with Benny
339	Tommy Brooks Orchestra	Drying My Blues	Where Did You Go
340	Wee Willie Kirk	Come on Home and Quit Your Looking	Your Love Was So Nice and Warm
341	Walter Davis	I Just Can't Help It	You are the One I Love
342	Cecil Gant	So Tired	Bullet Boogie
343	Fairfield Four	Moving Up the King's Highway	The World's in Bad Condition
344	Cecil Gant	Take It and Get	Don't Worry About Me
345	Walter Davis	Lonely Nights	Good Morning Baby
346	Dusty Brooks and the Four Tones	Chilli-Dogs	Whoa Mule
347	Tucker Coles	TC Blues	Don't Get Excited
348	Little Eddie	Darling You Know I Love You	My Baby Left Me
349	Tucker Coles	That's All I Ask of You	House Rocker's Jamboree
350	J. D. Horton	Cadillac Blues	Why Don't You Let Me Be

Bullet (600 series) (Country)
First issue: January 1946
Last known: October 1952

600	Brad Brady and His Tennesseans (1st pressing)	Wave to Me, My Lady (vocal by Joe Carroll)	Zeb's Mountain Boogie
	Owen Bradley and His Tennesseans (2nd pressing)		
601	Turner Bros. (Zeb and Zeke)	Guitar Reel	No One Will Ever Know
602	Pete Pyle	Living in Sorrow	Talking the Blues
603	Sheb Wooley	Oklahoma Honky Tonk Gal	I Can't Live on Without You
604	Jimmy Selph	Dream Castles Shared with You	Times a Wastin'
605	Ford Rush (The Singin' High Sheriff)	Remember Sweetheart	Your Only Arms
606*	Owen Bradley and His Tennesseans	The Call of a Broken Heart (vocal by Zeb Turner)	Tennessee Limited
607	York Bros. (George and Leslie)	Mine in Dreams	I'm Not Fooling
608	Clyde Moody	If I Had My Life to Live Over	I Worship You
609	Texas Troubadours	That's All She Wrote (vocal by Jack Drake)	Why Should I Cry Over You (vocal by Jack Drake)
610	York Bros.	Yesterday's Love	Blues, Why Don't You Leave Me Alone

*Note: A later pressing was numbered 600/606, coupling "Zeb's Mountain Boogie" with "Tennessee Limited"

Label	Artist	Side A	Side B
611	Clyde Moody	I'm So Lonesome	You Care No More for Me
612	unknown		
613	Minnie Pearl with Pee Wee King and the Golden West Cowboys	I'm Lookin' fer a Feller	Jealous Hearted Me
614	Frankie "Pee Wee" King and the Golden West Cowboys	That Cheap Look in Your Eye (vocal by Jimmie Wilson)	You Were the Cause of It All (vocal By Jimmie Wilson)
615	Bradley Kincaid and his Kentucky Mountain Boys	Now the Table's Turned on You	Ain't We Crazy
616	unknown		
617	Chester Atkins and the All-Star Hillbillies	Guitar Blues (Pickin' the Blues)	Brown Eyes A-Cryin' in the Rain (vocal by Jack Shook)
618	York Bros.	Hamtramck Mama	My Tears Will Never Make You Change
619	York Bros.	Hop, Skip and Jump	Let's Talk It Over Please Do
620	Johnnie Barfield and Chattahoochie Valley Boys	Doin' the Boogie Woogie	I Hope I Break Your Heart
621	unknown		
622	Tommy Scott	Ain't Love Grand	Broken Heart
623	Milton Estes and the Musical Millers	That's Why I Worry (vocal by Jimmie Selph)	Say You'll Be Mine (vocal by Jimmie Selph)
624	Ramblin' Tommy Scott	Sweet Woman Blues	My Little Moonbeam
625	unknown		
626	Pete Pyle	I Know That I Have Lost Your Love	Love Turned to Hate
627	unknown		
628	Jack Gillette and the Tennessee Ramblers	Nothing to Lose (vocal by Bud and Benny Kissinger)	In the Same Old Way (vocal by Benny Kissinger)
629	Zeb Turner	Chattanooga Boogie	Ain't Had No Lovin'
630	Zeb Turner	I'll Drift Along (vocals Zeb Turner with the Dixie Dons)	When Love Is Gone (vocal by Zeb Turner)
631	Owen Perry and the Happy Hillbillies	Louisiana Stomp	Two Can Play the Game
632	unknown		
633	Pappy Howard and His Connecticut "Kernals"	Cool Water (vocal by Pappy Howard and Trio)	I Wanna Go Fishin' (vocal by Pappy Howard and Trio)
634	Blaine Smith with Pappy Howard and His Connecticut "Kernals"	I Hope I Never Wake Up	Darling, Don't You Love Me Anymore?
635	unknown		
636	Zeb Turner	Coal Miner's Blues	You Never Done Me Right
637	Bill Nettles and his Dixie Blue Boys	Too Many Blues	High Falutin' Mama
638	Bill Nettles and his Dixie Blue Boys	Hungry	You're Breaking My Broken Heart Again
639	Tex Justus and the Texas Cowboys	Y-O-U Are My Sweetheart	Lonesome for My Texas Sweetheart
640	Tex Justus and the Texas Cowboys	I'll Get by Somehow (vocal by Tex Justus)	Old Kentucky Moon (vocal by Charlie Gillan)
641	York Bros.	Mother's Not Dead, She's Only Sleeping	Got Blues on My Mind
642	York Bros.	Blue Ridge Mountain Blues	I'm a Soldier for Jesus
643	Merl Lindsay and The Oklahoma Night Riders	When You Come Home Again	It's Been Too Late Too Long
644	Merl Lindsay and The Oklahoma Night Riders	What's to Become of Me	You Laughed at My Tears
645	Jamup and Honey	Feudin' and Fightin'	Lion's Cage
646	Jamup and Honey	Used Car Blues	Little Red Wagon
647	Merl Lindsay and The Oklahoma Night Riders	Old Timey Christmas	Safety Pin Rag

Label	Artist	Side A	Side B
648	unknown		
649	Leon Payne with Jack Rhodes and His Lone Star Buddies	Don't Try It	Lifetime to Regret
650	Pappy Howard and The Connecticut "Kernals"	That Guy's Out Gunning for You	Pal o' Mine
651	Zeb Turner	Don't That Moon Look Lonesome	Guess That's Why I Love You
652	Tommy Dillbeck and His Rock Candy Mtn. Boys	Now I've Seen Everything (Mother, I've Come Home to Die)	Right Next Door to Tennessee
653	Zeke Clements and His Western Swing-Gang	Brown's Ferry Boogie	In the Valley of My Dreams
654	Smiley Burnette and His Rancheros	It's My Lazy Day	Hominy Grits
655	Smiley Burnette and His Rancheros	Swamp Woman Blues	Catfish, Take a Look at That Worm
656	Tommy Scott	Alley Cat Blues	Lovely Blue Eyes
657*	Leon Payne with Jack Rhodes and the Lone Star Buddies *(Some copies of 657 were mislabelled 647)	Empty Arms	Lipstick Trail
658	Merl Lindsay and the Oklahoma Night Riders	I'm a Plain Talkin' Man from the West (vocal by Ted Haff)	Your Troubles Are My Troubles (vocal by Ted Haff)
659	Bob Manning and His Riders of the Silver Sage	I'm a Fool to Care (vocal by Bob Manning)	Reading Your Letter with Tears in My Eyes (vocal by Billy Gray)
660	Al Clauser and his Oklahoma Night Riders	Sally Goodin'	I'm Not Lazy, I'm Just Tired
661	Zeb Turner	Things Just Happen That Way	Big Fat Papa
662	Tommy Scott	Ain't Love Grand	Broken Heart
663	"Cowboy Pal" Loyd Weaver	Kute-Te-Kue	Too Many Tears
664	Art Davis and His Rhythm Riders	T-Town Sue	Booga-Boo Baby
665	Dub Adams and His K-Bar Ranch hands	Cripple Creek (Jelly Green - fiddle)	Arkansas Traveler (Jelly Green -fiddle)
666	Ken Curtis	It's in the Cards	When the Organ Played Nearer My God to Thee
667	unknown		
668	Zeke Clements	I Won't Be There	I Dreamed I Spent Christmas in Heaven
669	Joe St. Clair - Cowboy of Air	Red Long Fingernails and a Cigarette	Tears
670	Leon Payne	Lost Highway	Baby Boy
671	Leon Payne	What's the Need	Rolling Stone
672	Leon Payne	They'll Never Take Her Love from Me	I Found Someone New
673	Dick Dyson	Time After Time	You'd Better Change
674	Paul Blunt	Sweetheart of Hawaii	You Promised Me
675	Smiling Ed Gregory and the Rocky Mountain Boys	Down at the Zoo	Black Snake Blues
676	Smiley Burnette	House Trailer Blues	I Hope You're Having Fun Hurting Me
677	Bob Manning	Time on My Hands	Yesterday's Heartaches
678	Joe St. Clair	Too Proud to Cry	Waltz of My Heart
679	Leon Payne	Cheaters Never Win	I'll Stick by You
680	Dale Belmont and Her Texas Townsmen	Gonna Go Back to Texas	Gonna Ride to the Rainbow
681	Sunny Skylar	Amigo	Be Fair with Me
682	Autry Inman	It May Be	You've Got to Leave Those Other Guys Alone
683	Bill Drake	I've Got News for You My Darling (I Won't Be Coming Home)	What Used to Be Love
684	Don Curchill and His Texas Mavericks	Texas Plains	One Year Ago Tonight
685	Butterball Paige	The Girl At the End of the Bar	Honky Tonk Pete

Label	Artist	Side A	Side B
686	Pete Pyle	Lovin' Lies	I'm Walking Right Out of Your Life
687	Autry Inman	Double Cross	In My Imagination
688	Bill Drake	When You Have No One to Love You	Let's Start All Over Again
689	Pete Pyle	Think Twice	Why Don't You Haul Off and Love Me
690	Annie Lou and Danny Dill	Dime a Dozen	My Loss Is Another Man's Gain
691	Cousin Wilbur and Blondie	Blues Stay Away from Me	Why Not Confess
692	Banjo Murphy McClees	Blues You Want to Lose	Five Foot Two Eyes of Blue
693	Charley and Bonnie Barley	That Solid Rock	John 3:16
694	Charley and Bonnie Barley	Miner's Welfare Fund	John L's Contract Tune
695	Butterball Paige	I'm Too Old to Boogie Anymore	Heart Please Be Still
696	Johnnie Lee Wills and His Boys	Near Me (vocal by Leon Huff)	Rag Mop (vocal by Johnnie Lee Wills)
697	Annie Lou and Danny Dill	I'm in Love up to My Ears	There's a Rainbow in Your Tears
698	George Lee	Goodbye and Good Luck	My Mind Won't Have a Care
699	Jimmy Work and His Tennessee Border Boys	Mr. and Mrs. Cloud	Hospitality
700	Johnnie Lee Wills and His Boys	Peter Cotton Tail	Shattered Dreams
701	Ray Price	Jealous Lies	Your Wedding Corsage
702	Tani Allen and His Tennessee Pals	Tennessee Jive (vocal by Buck Turner)	Rockin' Chair Boogie (vocal by Buck Turner)
703	Calvin Tubb	Lonely Traveler	Heart, Don't Complain
704	Roy Hall and His Cohutta Mountain Boys	Old Folks Jamboree (vocal by Frankie Brumbalough)	Mule Boogie (vocal by Frankie Brumbalough)
705	Sonny Daulong	Heartaches Too Late	Folk Dance Schottische
706	Paul Blunt and the Frontiersmen	Walking Up Stairs	Shovin' My Lovin'
707	Charlene Arthur	Is Love a Game	I've Got the Boogie Blues
708	The Frontiersmen	Guitar Shuffle	Honky Tonk Hop
709	Hamm Bros.	He Saved My Soul	When He Reached Out His Saving Hand
710	Johnnie Lee Wills and His Boys	I'm That Way About You (vocal by Curley Lewis)	Champagne Polka (vocal by Leon Huff)
711	Johnnie Lee Wills and His Boys	Coyote Blues (vocal Trio)	Boogie Woogie Highball
712	Roy Hall and His Cohutta Mountain Boys	Ain't You Afraid (vocal by Hal Clark)	Turn My Picture to the Wall (vocal by Hal Clark)
713	Tani Allen and His Tennessee Pals	I'll Still Love You (vocal by Buck Turner)	Just Checkin' On You (vocal by Buck Turner)
714	Wally Fowler	Wanted, Someone to Love Me	Linger Longer
715	Tex Milligan	Nashville Moon	Flowers on Lovers Lane
716	Jimmy Wallace	My Green Eyed Darling	You Lied Your Way into My Heart
717	Johnnie Lee Wills and His Boys	A Bad Deal All Around (vocal by Leon Huff)	Tom Cat Boogie (vocal by Leon Huff)
718	Jimmy Wallace	One Love	Don't Ever Call Me Darling Again
719	Wiley Jordan and The Sons of the South	God Bless You Darling	Feel Like the World Belongs to Me
720	Al Clauser and His Oklahomans	Move It Over Rover (Dog House Blues)	My Sweet Mama
721	Johnnie Lee Wills and His Boys	This Room Is Too Crowded	Si' Te Amo (Yes I Love You)
722	Calvin Tubb	She Slipped out on Me	I'm Trying to Read between the Lines
723	Boots Woodall and the Radio Wranglers	I Cry Each Night over You	It's No Secret
724	Johnnie Lee Wills and His Boys	I Like You Best of All (vocal by Leon Huff)	I'm Leaving (Yes Indeedy) (vocal by Leon Huff)

Label	Artist	Side A	Side B
725	Hardrock Gunter and the Pebbles	My Bucket's Been Fixed	The Little Things You Do
726	Johnnie Lee Wills and His Boys	Oklahoma That's for Me	I Needed You
727	Hardrock Gunter	Maybe Baby, You'll Be True to Me	Rifle, Belt and Bayonet
728	Hal Howard and the Pearl River Boys	Fat Gals, Skinny Gals	Don't Ever Trust Your Chicken
729	Bob Swerer	Don't Be Careless with My Heart	Your Picture in My Heart
730	Calvin Tubb	Portigue Gal	Two Shadows on a Window
731	Si Jenkins and the Ozark Rangers	Warm Beer and Cold Kisses	Secret Treasure
732	Boots Woodall and His Radio Wranglers	Two Timin' Baby	Who's That Kissin' My Honey
733	Ray Melton and His Country All Stars	She Hit the Ceilin' (When I Hit the Door)	I Love Every Little Thing You Do
734	Tani Allen and His Tennessee Pals	I'm Back in the Army (vocal by Buck Turner)	Suspicion Blues (vocal by Buck Turner)
735	The Sapphires	All You Gotta Do Is Behave	Blue Jean Rumba
736	George Lee	Station Door Blues	Memories Never Bother Me
737	Johnnie Lee Wills and His Boys	The Band's a Rockin' (vocal by J.L.Wills)	I'm Not Sorry (I Cried over You) (vocal by Leon (Huff)
738	Si Jenkins and His Ozark Ranchers	One Dollar Boogie	My Play Around Heart
739	Al Clauser and His Oklahoma Outlaws	Last Night (vocal by Al McDaniel)	Green Apples (vocal by Al McDaniel)
740	Tani Allen and His Tennessee Pals	Little Blue Eyed Blonde Goodbye (vocal by Buck Turner)	On Our Shotgun Wedding Day (vocal by Buck Turner)
741	Johnnie Lee Wills and His Boys	Careless Me (vocal by Leon Huff)	Big Chief Wamp-Pa-Setti (vocal by Leon Huff)
742	unknown		
743	Johnnie Lee Wills and His Boys	Levée Blues (vocal by Leon Huff)	I'll Make You Happy (vocal by Leon Huff)
744	Tani Allen and His Tennessee Pals	Fatty Cake (vocal by Buck Turner and E.G. Frazier)	Empty Hands, Empty Heart (Empty Pockets) (vocal by Buck Turner)
745	Tabby West	Tennessee Hayride	Last Night I Heard Somebody Cry
746	Tani Allen and His Tennessee Pals	I Don't Want You Now (vocal by Buck Turner)	When Hillbilly Willie Met Kitty from the City (vocal by Buck Turner)
747	Zeb Turner	I Lost Everything	Love That Will Never Be
748	Chuck Bridges	Black Eyed Angel	Country Love
749	Shorty Ashburn	Are You Lonely Too	Triflin' Heart
750	Buddy Beason and His Barn Dance Buddies	Bill Bailey	John Henry
751	Don Reynolds	All Alone	I Tell Myself a Lie
752	Shorty Ashburn	There Is Always a Tomorrow	More and More
753	Chuck Bridges	Lonesome Life	Heart Breakin' Darlin'
754	Ray Batts	Wild Man Boogie	Bear Cat Daddy
755	Buck Turner	I'll Put My Dreams Away	Honky Tonk Bounce

Bullet (1000 series) (Popular)
First issue: January 1947
Last known: March 1952

1000	Eddie Wiggins Sextet	The Bullet Bounce	Babe, You Know You Like It That Way
1001	Francis Craig and His Orchestra	Red Rose (vocal by Bob Lamm)	Near You (vocal by Bob Lamm)
1002	Francis Craig and His Orchestra	Sometimes I Wonder	Hot Biscuits
1003	The Wagners and Their Music	I Do, Do, Do Like You	Honey
1004	The Wagners and Their Music	Hold Me	Ja-Da

Label	Artist	Side A	Side B
1005	Russ Carlyle and his Orchestra	Why Don't You Answer the Phone	Chapel in the Moonlight
1006	Russ Carlyle and his Orchestra	It's All My Fault	Hanging on the Garden Gate
1007	Ray Pearl Orchestra	Flaming Mamie	Please Don't Tell
1008	Ray Pearl Orchestra	Pick-In-Icking (In the Park)	Please Don't Tell
1009	Five Bars	I'm All Dressed Up with a Broken Heart	To Make a Long Story Shorter
1010	Five Bars	Deep in My Heart	Bars Boogie
1011	Seger Ellis	Little Jack Frost, Get Lost	We Just Couldn't Say Goodbye
1012	Francis Craig and His Orchestra	I'm Looking for a Sweetheart (vocal By Bob Lamm and the Dixie Dons)	Beg Your Pardon (vocal by Bob Lamm and the Dixie Dons)
1013	Francis Craig and His Orchestra	Foolin' (vocal by Bob Lamm)	Do Me a Favor (Will Ya?)
1014	Seger Ellis	Let's Drive Out to Joe's Drive-In (vocal by Seger Ellis and the Dixie Dons)	Moon After Moon
1015	Ray Herbeck	Little Fellow	Nuff Said
1016	Denny Beckner and His Orchestra	Texas (vocal by Dale Belmont)	Seven Days a Week (vocal by Denny Beckner and The Harmony Hilltoppers)
1017	Murray Peterson	Honey Bear Polka	Iron Horse Boogie
1018	Owen Bradley Orchestra	I'd Love to Live in Loveland (vocal by Bob Johnstone)	Baby, Don't Be Mean, Be Mine (vocal by Dottie Dillard)
1019	Hi, Lo, Jack and the Dame	I'm A-Comin' A-Courtin' Cora Belle	Cut the Knot, Turn Me Loose
1020	Bob Crosby Orchestra	It's Got to Be	You're My Everything
1021	Patti Clayton with the Russ Carlyle Orchestra	A Man Could Be a Wonderful Thing	Nickels, Quarters and Dimes
1022	Bobby Breen	One Raindrop Doesn't Mean a Shower	The Thrill Is Gone
1023	Adrian Rollini Trio	Dardanella	
	Peggy Mann and Adrian Rollini		You're Gonna Get My Letter in the Morning
1024	Bob Chester and His Orchestra	Melancholy	Just One More Chance
1025	Les Elgart Orchestra	Doodle Doo Doo (vocal by The Uptowners)	I Lost My Heart in Hartford (vocal by The Uptowners)
1026	unknown		
1027	Jack Shook Quartet	It's the Truth	All of Heaven I Ask
1028	Les Elgart Orchestra	I Went Down to Virginia	What Do You Want to Make Those Eyes at Me For
1029	unknown		
1030	Dean Hudson and His Orchestra	Fat Mama Boogie	I'll See You in My Dreams
1031	Bob Berkley	Ain't She Sweet	She Don't Wanna
1032	Ronnie Deauville	My Happiness	You Can't Be True Dear
1033	unknown		
1034	Bob Chester and His Orchestra	I Don't Want to Meet Anymore People	Hold Me
1035	Bob Troup Trio	Bye Bye Blackbird	Heidi
1036	Bobby Breen	It's a Sin to Tell a Lie	Molly Malone
1037	Russ Carlyle Orchestra	My Favorite Friend	Whisper a Word of Love
1038	unknown		
1039	Patti Clayton with the Russ Carlyle Orchestra	It's a Lonesome Old Town	Shut the Door (They're Coming thru the Window)
1040	Francis Craig and His Orchestra	I Still Get a Thrill	Disallusioned

Label	Artist	Side A	Side B
1041	Al Trace and His Orchestra	Kickin' up Dust in the Nursery	I Can't Spell Schenectady
1042–1043	unknown		
1044	Danny Cassella and His Orchestra	Hawaiian War Chant	Cruel Love
1045	Bob Crosby Orchestra	My Donna Lee	Til We Meet Again
1046–1047	unknown		
1048	Jack Shook Quartet	My Hillside Heaven	To Make a Mistake Is Human
1049	Dean Hudson Orchestra	Moon Over Miami	What Is This Thing Called Love
1050–1051	unknown		
1052	Lesley Grey	I've Got a Right to Sing the Blues	My Ideal
1053	unknown		
1054	Jack Caldwell Trio	That's My Gal	You'll Always Be My Sweetheart
1055	Bob Troup Trio	Baby, Baby All the Time	I Found a Million Dollar Baby
1056	Pepper Neely and the Ace Trio	Rendezvous with a Rose	Everything Reminds Me of You
1057–1058	unknown		
1059	Bob Reid	Christmas Candles	Rogue River Valley
1060	Billy Bishop and His Orchestra	Don't Bring Lulu	Annabelle
1061	Adams Brothers	Our Love Will Never Die (vocal by Bob Emmett)	I'll See You in My Dreams
1062	Red McEwen Orchestra	(When I Woke up This Morning) It Was My Lucky Day	Lalito Linda
1063	Red McEwen Orchestra	I Wish Upon a Star (And Wonder Where You Are)	I've Been Hearing Rumors
1064	Patti Clayton with the Russ Carlyle Orchestra	Say It Isn't So	He Tickles My Fancy
1065	Francis Craig ad His Orchestra	It Hurts Me More Than It Does You	Hot Biscuits
1066	Bob Crosby Orchestra	Saturday Night Mood	Gone Home
1067	unknown		
1068	Adams Brothers	Indian Love Call	Dark Eyes
1069	unknown		
1070	Smoothies	Bouquet of Roses	You Can't Buy Happiness
1071	Smoothies	It's a Small World	Searching for a Rainbow
1072	unknown		
1073	Slim Coates	Hollywood Bowl and Spoon	January in June
1074–1075	unknown		
1076	Helen Lee with Dick Style and His Orchestra	Red Head	Don't Have to Tell Nobody
1077	Helen Lee with Dick Style and His Orchestra	Cabaret	Gotta Love You Till I Die
1078	The Wagners	I'm a Rollin'	Lili Marlene
1079	unknown		
1080	Francis Craig	By the Bend of the River	Comin' In on the C. N. R.
1081	Don Grimes	It Had to Be You	When an Old Flame Dies
1082	Dean Hudson and His Orchestra	Waiting for the Robert E. Lee	Snap Your Fingers
1083	Cecil Bailey and the Dixie Dons	Jealous Heart	Fairy Tales
1084	Cecil Bailey	You Sold Your Heart for a Holiday	Have a Heart
1085	Dean Hudson and His Orchestra	Regardless	Why Fall in Love with a Stranger
1086	Cecil Bailey	The Popcorn Song	Sunday Down South

Label	Artist	Side A	Side B
1087	Cecil Bailey	Dance at Your Wedding (Yes I Will)	Heart of the West
1088	Madge Suttee and Her Swing Quartet	Avalon	Angry
1089	Dean Hudson and His Orchestra	Yearning (Just for You)	Rose Room
1090–1091	unknown		
1092	Ethel Shutta	How Would You Feel	All for You
1093	Smith Brothers	Cry Baby Cry	You Ought to Be Ashamed
1094–1095	unknown		
1096	Daryl Harpa and His Orchestra	Tennessee Rumba	Waiting for the Robert E. Lee
1097	John Gordy	Salty Dog Rag	Over the Waves
1098	John Gordy	Ma (He's Making Eyes At Me)	Goodbye Waltz
1099	John Gordy Sextette	Slow Poke (vocal by Jack Shook)	I Still Love to Kiss You Goodnight (vocal by Jack Shook)
1100	unknown		
1101	John Gordy	Steamboat (Blow Your Whistle Again)	Way Down South (vocal by Hots Jackson and the Old Timers)
1102–1104	unknown		
1105	John Gordy	New Frankie and Johnny (vocal by Hots Jackson)	Me in "C"
1106	Charles Drake	Carolina in the Morning	Lonesome Now
1107	John Gordy and His Brush Hill Five	My Little Girl	Raggin' the Blues
1108	John Gordy and His Dixie Rhythm Gang	Honolulu Lulu	Tinkling on the Keys

Bullet (2000 series) (Mexican)
First issue: May 1947
Last known: 1947

2000	Los Cinco Troubadores	Las Altenitas	Ven Linda Morena
2001	unknown		
2002	Los Cinco Troubadores	El Mescal	Arminda Valse

Cheker (100 series) (Mainly Country)
First issue: possibly 1947
Last known: 1948

100	Jack Henderson accompanied by the Radio Playboys	The Tramp on the Street	Gonna Give You Back to the Indians
101–102	unknown		
103	Big Jeff and the Radio Playboys	Poppin' Bubble Gum	A Kiss and a Memory
104	Richard Armstrong	Gene Nobles Boogie	Gene Nobles Blues
300/301	Bob Jennings accompanied by the Eagle Rangers	Be My Darlin'	That Old Moon Seems to Know

Collegiate (2950 series) (Popular)
First issue: October 1948
Last known: October 1949

2950	Rufus Long Orchestra	Cheri	Would You Know
2951	unknown		
2952	The Dream Dusters	Give Me This Night	You Can Die from a Broken Heart

Label	Artist	Side A	Side B
2953	Ken Carroll	On New Year's Eve	You Darling
2954	unknown		
2955	same as 2952		
2956	Danny Cassella Orchestra	April May	Heart of My Heart
2957	Alan Foster and Bill Chester Orchestra	I Couldn't Stay Away from You	Jeanine, I Dream of Lilac Time
2958	Les Elgart and His Orchestra	Rockefeller Center	Sleepy Town
2959–2964	unknown		
2965	Bob Johnstone and the Owen Bradley Orchestra	Three Wishing Wells	I Couldn't Believe My Eyes
2966	Harrison Cooper and His Orchestra	It's a Small World	Have You Ever Been Told
2967	Bill Lockwood with Hawes Coleman and His Orchestra	Zingarella	
	Nina Claire and Bill Lockwood with Hawes Coleman and His Orchestra		Sandman Lullaby

Delta (100 series) (Country Gospel)
First issue: 1949
Last known: 1949

100	Stone Mountain Quartette	The Lords Prayer	Satan You Don't Hinder Me
101	Golden West Quartet	A Little While Longer	Savior Devine

Delta (200 series) (mainly R&B and Gospel)
First issued: March 1949
Last known: December 1949

200	Fairfield Four	Dear Lord, Look Down Upon Me	Soon as the General Say the War Is Over
201	Fairfield Four	Saviour, Don't Pass Me By	Dig a Little Deeper in God's Love
202	Big Three Trio	Don't Let That Music Die	Till the Day I Die
203	Fred Waller with Owen Bradley (organ)	Do You Still Love Me	Laurel Waltz
204	unknown		
205	Big Three Trio	Why Do You Love Me Like You Do	Goodbye Mr. Blues
206	Ernestine Woodard with Frank and his 4 Beats	How Can I Make You Mine	Why Can't a Dream Come True
207	Fairfield Four	Dig a Little Deeper in God's Love	In the Wilderness
208	Big Three Trio	Cigareets, Whiskey and Wild, Wild Women	Appetite Blues
209	Rhythm Rockers	Honey, I'm Falling for You	You Tell Me Your Dream
210	Fairfield Four	Tree of Level	Jesus Met the Woman at the Well
211	Fairfield Four	Lift Him Up	Just a Little Walk with Jesus
212	Fairfield Four	Ezekiel	Roll All the Burdens Away
213	Tom Douglas (test copies)	Raid on Cedar Street	I Should Have Known

Delta (600 series) (Country)
First issue: 1949
Last known: 1949

600	Slim Lay and The Crossroads Follies Gang	Talkin' About Susie (vocal by R.C. Johnson)	I'll Never Find Another You (vocal by R.C. Johnson)

Label	Artist	Side A	Side B

Delta (1500 series) (Country)
First issue: November 1955
Last known: 1956

Note: Delta 100, 200, and 600 series were Jim Bulleit's labels; the 1500 series that follows was run by Red Wortham with Bulleit's agreement.

1500	Tommy Smith	I'm a Fool	Tortured Man
1501–1502	unknown		
1503	Whitey Pullen	Broke Waiting for a Break	I'm Begging Your Pardon

Dot (200 series) (Country)
First issue: 1951
Last known: 1951/1952

201	Gabe Tucker and His Musical Ramblers	It'd Surprise You	Cracker Barrel Farmer
202	Cliff Butler	I Love You So Much It Hurts	Lucky Me
203	Lou Millet	That's You Without Me	Heart of Stone
204	Gabe Tucker and His Musical Ramblers	You Better Do Better Baby	Rainy Day Sweetheart

Dot (1000 series) (Popular, R&B, Gospel, and Country)
First issue: January 1950
Last known: 1957

1000	The Blue Jacks	Blue Jack Boogie	Late Hour Blues
1001	George Toon and the Tennessee Drifters	Boogie Beat Rag	Honest Heart
1002	George Toon and the Tennessee Drifters	Mean Ole Boogie	Drifter Special
1003	Fairfield Four	Tree of Level	Jesus Met the Woman At the Well
1004	Big Jeff and the Radio Playboys	Juke Box Boogie	You Talk in Your Sleep
1005	Johnny Maddox and the Rhythmasters	Crazy Bone Rag	St Louis Tickle
1006	Fairfield Four	Savior Don't Pass Me By	Dear Lord Look Down Upon Me
1007	Cuzzin Clem and the Country Cousins	Love or Indigestion	Chattanooga Stomp
1008	George Toon and the Tennessee Drifters	That There Gal o' Mine	Old Mellow Moon
1009	Cap-Tans	I'm So Crazy for Love	My Honey Dip
1010	Margie Day with the Griffin Brothers	Street Walkin' Daddy	Riffin' with Griffin
1011	Fairfield Four	In the Wilderness	O Let Me Tell You about Jesus
1012	Johnny Maddox and the Rhythmasters	I Get the Blues When It Rains	Hula Blues
1013	unknown		
1014	Billy Scott	Dear Daddy Uncle Sam	When I Was Just Thirteen
1015	Fairfield Four	I'll Tell the World	In the Upper Room
1016	Cecil Gant	Crying to Myself	Nobody Wants You
1017	Bob Lamm	No Tears for You	I'm Gonna Lock My Heart to Love
1018	Cap-Tans	With All My Heart	Chief, Turn the Hose on Me
1019	Margie Day with the Griffin Brothers	Little Red Rooster	Blues All Alone
1020	Griffin Brothers	Blues with a Beat	Griff's Boogie
1021	Andy Wilson and Judy Derryberry	This Side of Heaven	Faded Love
1022	Fairfield Four	I Don't Know Why I Have to Cry	When I Move in the Room

Label	Artist	Side A	Side B
1023	Johnny Maddox and the Rhythmasters	Memphis Blues	Alabama Jubilee
1024	Margie Day with the Griffin Brothers	Bonaparte's Retreat	Hot Pepper
1025	Jim Wilson with Ann Carr	If I Should Need You	Old Home Town
1026–1027	unknown		
1028	Bob Lamm	Corns a Poppin'	I Hope I Don't Live Long Enough
1029	Andy Wilson	You Count All My Mistakes	Don't Ever Say You Love Me
1030	Cecil Gant	Waiting for a Train	Cindy Lou
1031	Joe Liggins	The Honey Dripper Part 1	The Honey Dripper Part 2
1032	Joe Liggins	I've Got a Right to Cry	Last Night Blues
1033	Joe Liggins	Tanya	Down Home Blues
1034	Dixie Aires	My Trouble Is Hard	Elijah
1035	unknown		
1036	Ivory Joe Hunter	Blues at Sunrise	You Taught Me to Love
1037	unknown		
1038	Wes Britt with the Rhythmasters	Easy Melody	Red Sails in the Sunset
1039	Dink Embry and the Kentucky Lads	Mason Dixon Boogie	Please Stay Out of My Dreams
1040	Fairfield Four	Does Jesus Care	Don't Drive Your Children Away
1041	Margie Day with the Griffin Brothers	Sadie Green	One Steady Daddy
1042	Griffin Brothers featuring Margie Day	If You Want Some Lovin'	Your Best Friend
1043	Four Dots	My Dear	You Won't Let Me Go
1044	Billy Stickland	Queen of All Queens	Cry All Your Tears (On My Shoulder)
1045	Fairfield Four	Nobody to Depend Upon	Old Time Religion
1046	Fairfield Four	No Room at the Inn	Talking about Jesus
1047	Fairfield Four	I Love the Name Jesus	Leave Them There
1048	Fairfield Four	Love Like a River	Oh My Journey Now
1049	unknown		
1050	Bob Lamm	I'm Only a Friend	That's When Your Heartaches Begin
1051	Little Son Jackson	Homeless Blues	Gambling Blues
1052	L C Williams	You Never Miss the Water	Trying, Trying
1053	Cecil Gant	Alma	I'm Still in Love with You
1054–1056	unknown		
1057	Johnny Maddox	Sweet Georgia Brown	Dill Pickles
1058	Big Jeff and the Radio Playboys	Step It Up and Go	After We Are Through
1059	unknown		
1060	Griffin Brothers	Tra La La	Hoppin'
1061	Andy Wilson	Let's Live a Little	I Want to Be with You Always
1062	Mac Wiseman	Tis Sweet to Be Remembered	Are You Coming Back to Me
1063	unknown		
1064	Big Jeff and the Radio Playboys	Lifetime to Regret	Fast Women Slow Horses and Wine
1065–1066	unknown		
1067	Andy Wilson	Thank You	Please Send Me Someone to Love
1068	unknown		
1069	Cecil Gant	Raining Blues	Goodbye Baby

Label	Artist	Side A	Side B
1070	Griffin Brothers featuring Margie Day	Stubborn as a Mule	Pretty Baby
1071	Griffin Brothers featuring Tommy Brown	Weeping and Crying	Shuffle Bug
1072	unknown		
1073	Fairfield Four	Poor Pilgrim of Sorrow	Don't Drive Her Away
1074	Dink Embry	Doll Baby	Lay Your Head Upon My Shoulder
1075	Mac Wiseman	Little White Church	I'm a Stranger
1076–1079	unknown		
1080	Fairfield Four	Packing Every Burden	Don't Leave Me
1081	Fairfield Four	My Prayer	Come On to This Altar
1082	Fairfield Four	Waiting for Me	Angels Watching Over You
1083	Fairfield Four	I'm in Your Care	I Can't Tell You the Time
1084	unknown		
1085	Tommy Jackson	Arkansas Traveler	Soldiers Joy
1086	Tommy Jackson	Boil Them Cabbage Down	Mississippi Sawyer
1087	unknown		
1088	Big Jeff the the Radio Playboys	Move On Baby	I'm in Love Dear with Thee
1089	Jam Up and Honey	Wild Honey Rag	Slew Foot Mama
1090	unknown		
1091	Mac Wiseman	I Still Write Your Name in the Sand	Four Walls around Me
1092	Mac Wiseman	Georgia Waltz	Dreaming of a Little Cabin
1093	unknown		
1094	Griffin Brothers featuring Margie Day	It'd Surprise You	I'll Get a Deal
1095	Griffin Brothers	The Teaser	I've Got a New Love
1096	Big Jeff and the Radio Playboys	Counted on an Angel	Don't Talk to Strangers
1097	Gabe Tucker	Streamline Country Girl	Jive Around Old Joe Clark
1098	Tennessee Drifters	Mean Ole Boogie	Boogie Beat Rag
1099	Wally Mercer	Rock Around the Clock	Don't Wait Till Tomorrow
1100	Sister Rosa Shaw	My Mother Part 1	My Mother Part 2
1101	Sam McCrary	Maybe It's You, Maybe It's Me	If Jesus Had to Pray
1102	Andy Wilson	Step by Step	Great Speckled Bird
1103	L C Green	When the Sun Is Shining	Hold Me in Your Arms
1104	Griffin Brothers	I'm Gonna Jump in the River	Stormy Night
1105	Griffin Brothers	Comin' Home	Stay Away from the Horses
1106–1107	unknown		
1108	Margie Day	Ace in the Hole	Clock Song (Let Your Pendulum Swing)
1109	Fairfield Four	When We Bow	Let's Go
1110	Fairfield Four	Hope to Shout in Glory	All the Way
1111	Fairfield Four	I'll Be Satisfied	I've Got Good Religion
1112	Cecil Gant	All by Myself	It Hurts Me Too
1113	unknown		
1114	Jam Up and Honey	12th Street Rag	Holding the Sack
1115	Mac Wiseman	I Wonder How the Old Folks are at Home	You're the Girl of My Dreams
1116	Sister Rosa Shaw	Stop Playing the Numbers	House of the Lord

Label	Artist	Side A	Side B
1117	Griffin Bothers	I Wanna Go Back	Slow and Mellow
1118	Joe Warren	Nearer My God to Thee	Precious Memories
1119	Tommy Jackson	Texas Schottische	Put Your Little Foot Right Out
1120	Wally Mercer	Looped	Yellow Hornet
1121	Cecil Gant	Sloppy Joes	Train Time Blues
1122	Fairfield Four	Where Shall I Go	Don't You Want to Join That Number
1123	Fairfield Four	Standing in the Safety Zone	Don't Let Nobody Turn You Round
1124	Big Three Trio	You Sure Look Good to Me	Signifying Monkey
1125	Fairfield Four	When I Get Up in Heaven	Amazing Grace
1126	Mac Wiseman	Fire in My Heart	Going to See My Baby
1127	Andy Wilson	Hillbilly Boogie	Lonesome for My Baby
1128	L C Green	Little School Girl	Remember the Way Back
1129	Joe Claire	Blue Tennessee Rain	Going Home and Behave Myself
1130	Cliff Butler	Boogie with Lou	Can't Get Her Off My Mind
1131	Mac Wiseman	By the Side of the Road	Waiting for the Boys
1132	The Brewsteraires	Hold On	That's Enough
1133	The Brewsteraires	Jasper Walls	More of Jesus Less of Me
1134	Sister Rosa Shaw	He Rolled the Stone Away	On the Highway
1135	Sam McCrary	I'll Spend My Vacation	I'll Take My Rest
1136	Wally Mercer	Early One Morning	Motherless Child Blues
1137	Tommy Jackson	Leather Britches	Ragtime Annie
1138	Tommy Jackson	Cripple Creek	Uncle Joe
1139	Tommy Jackson	Sally Ann	Whistling Rufus
1140	Tommy Jackson	Fiddlin' Rag	Tennessee Wagoner
1141	Joe Warren	Rock of Ages	In the Sweet By and By
1142	Joe Warren	Amazing Grace	Softly and Tenderly
1143	Joe Warren	Now a Firm Foundation	Sweet Hour of Prayer
1144	Margie Day	Midnight	My Story
1145	Griffin Brothers	Black Bread	My Baby's Done Me Wrong
1146	Mac Wiseman	Six More Miles	It's Goodbye and So Long to You
1147	L C Green	Little Machine	Come Back Sugar Mama
1148	Tommy Jackson	Fishers Hornpipe	Jackson's Hornpipe
1149	Mac Wiseman	I Haven't Got the Right to Love You	My Little Home in Tennessee
1150	Mac Wiseman	Shackles and Chains	Going Like Wildfire
1151	Burl Lynn	Tear Drops	Is It Love or Is It Lies
1152	Griffin Brothers	Fare Thee Well Pretty Baby	Griff's Mambo
1153	Margie Day	Must I	I'm Gonna Raise a Ruckus
1154	Shorty Long	Crying Street Guitar Waltz	Pretend
1155	Fairfield Four	Gospel Train	God's Got His Eyes on You
1156	unknown		
1157	Tennessee Drifters	Boogie Woogie Baby	Gonna Drive Those Blues Away
1158	Mac Wiseman	You're Sweeter Than the Honey	Don't Let Your Sweet Love Die
1159	Fairfield Four	Come Over Here	Who Is That Knocking

Label	Artist	Side A	Side B
1160	Fairfield Four	Every Day	His Eye Is on the Sparrow
1161	Fairfield Four	How I Got Over	This Evening Our Father
1162	Fairfield Four	Stand by Me	Hear Me When I Pray
1163	Fairfield Four	When the Battle Is Over	Standing on the Rock
1164	Fairfield Four	Somebody Touched Me	Mother Don't Worry
1165	Dolly Long	Don't Play That Song	The Cat-Latin Song
1166	Tennessee Drifters	Boogie Woogie Baby	Drive Those Blues Away
1167	Jimmy Wilson	Big Fat Mama	Unwanted Love
1168	Mac Wiseman	Crazy Blues	Rainbow in the Valley
1169	Tommy Jackson	Draggin' the Bow	Orange Blossom Special
1170	Sister Rosa Shaw	I Need Jesus	Who Will Be Saved
1171	Griffin Brothers	Move It On Over	Bouncing Home
1172	Margie Day	String Bean	Don't Talk to Me about Men
1173	Mac Wiseman	You'd Better Wake Up	I'd Rather Die Young
1174	Gateway Quintet	Sampson and Delilah	Save Me Lord
1175	Gateway Quintet	Go Down to the River	I Wanna Go to Heaven
1176	Gateway Quintet	4 and 20 Elders	Sun Didn't Shine
1177	Gateway Quintet	Look Away	Steal Away
1178	Gateway Quintet	I'll Shake Mother's Hand	You Can't Do Wrong
1179	Golden Voice Trio	Jesus Is Real	Sweeter as the Days Go By
1180	Golden Voice Trio	Go Ahead	Job Saved
1181	Singing Stars	Only a Look	What I Would Do
1182	Mac Wiseman	Remembering	Let Me Borrow Your Heart
1183	Jimmy Binkley	The Judge	Blue Blue Night
1184	Brownie McGhee	Need Someone to Love	Cheatin' and Loyin'
1185	Doctor Gaddy	Honey Stealin' Blues	Hold That Train, Conductor
1186	Tommy Jackson	Katy Hill	Wake Up Susan
1187	Tennessee Drifters	Somebody Loves You	Corrine Corrina
1188	The Counts	Darling Dear	I Need You Always
1189	Griffin Brothers	Little Red Hen	Sittin' On It
1190	Margie Day	Don't Leave Me	The Price I Pay
1191	Mac Wiseman	Waltz You Saved for Me	Love Letters in the Sand
1192	Mac Wiseman	Dreams of Mother and Home	Reveille in Heaven
1193	Buddy Griffin with Claudia Swann	Fare Well Handsome Daddy	Oh, What a Smile Can Do
1194	Mac Wiseman	My Little Home in Tennessee	I Haven't Got the Right to Love You
1195	Jimmy Newman	Cry Cry Darling	You Didn't Have to Go
1196	Lonzo and Oscar	Let Me Be the One No. 2	Wild Oats
1197–1198	unknown		
1199	The Counts	Hot Tamales	Baby Don't You Know
1200	Wally Fowler	In My Father's House Are Many Mansions	I Wanna Go There
1201	Wally Fowler	Supper-Time	Walk in the Light
1202	Mac Wiseman	I Saw Your Face in the Moon	You Can't Judge a Book
1203	Bobby Marchan	You Made a Fool of Me	Just a Little Ol Wine

Label	Artist	Side A	Side B
1204	The Five Dots	The Other Night	Each Night
1205	Mr. Percy	Full of Misery	Somebody Help Me Out
1206	Lorry Raine	Laugh Laugh Laugh	Si Si Sira Con Me
1207	Jimmy Work	Don't Knock Just Come On In	Let 'em Talk
1208	Tommy Jackson	Lead Out	Chinese Breakdown
1209	Tommy Jackson	Bill Cheatham	Sugar in the Gourd
1210	The Counts	My Dear My Darling	She Won't Say Yes
1211–1214	unknown		
1215	Jimmy Newman	Night Time Is Cry Time	Diggy Liggy Lo
1216	Lonzo and Oscar	Crazy 'bout You Baby	Got It On My Mind
1217	Tommy Jackson	Flop Eared Mule	Liberty
1218	Tommy Jackson	Eighth of January	Golden Slippers
1219	unknown		
1220	Henry Smith	Good Rocking Mama	Lonesome Blues
1221	Jimmy Work	Making Believe	Just Like Downtown
1222	Singing Stars	Angels Angels	I'll Be Singing There
1223	unknown		
1224	Mac Wiseman	Keep on the Sunny Side	I Love You Best of All
1225	Bobby Young	Wailin' Mama	I Want You to Love Me
1226	The Counts	Baby I Want You	Waitin' Around for You
1227	Chanteclairs	Baby Please	Someday Love Will Come My Way
1228	Fairfield Four	We Never Grow Old	Jesus in Heaven
1229	Jane Turner	Danger Blues	
	Rusty Bryant		House Rocker
1230	Mac Wiseman	I Didn't Know	Don't Blame It All on Me
1231	Jimmy Newman	Your True and Faithful One	Can It Be Right
1232	Tommy Jackson	East Tennessee Blues	Sally Goodin'
1233	Tommy Jackson	Here and There	Rickets Hornpipe
1234	Tommy Jackson	Stones Rag	Rubber Dolly
1235	The Counts	Wailin' Little Mama	Let Me Go Lover
1236	Mac Wiseman	When I Get the Money Made	The Little Old Church in the Valley
1237	Jimmy Newman	Crying for a Pastime	Daydreamin'
1238	Uncle Bob Hardy	Little Cowboy Suit	There Ain't No Use in Dreamin'
1239	unknown		
1240	Mac Wiseman	Ballad of Davy Crockett	Danger Heartbreak Ahead
1241	The Allegro Singers	Show Me the Way	Jerusalem Morn
1242	The Allegro Singers	Ring Those Golden Bells	Live Humble
1243	The Counts	From This Day On	Love and Understanding
1244	unknown		
1245	Jimmy Work	That's What Makes the Juke Box Play	Don't Give Me a Reason to Wonder Why
1246	Kenny Roberts	Tennessee Spelling Bee	I'm Unwanted
1247	Tommy Jackson	Sugarfoot Rag	Buffalo Girl

Label	Artist	Side A	Side B
1248	Tommy Jackson	Stoney Point	Trouble among the Yearlings
1249	Tommy Jackson	Blackberry Blossom	Paddy on the Turnpike
1250	Tommy Jackson	Up Jumped Trouble	Gray Eagle
1251	Tommy Jackson	Hornpipe in A	Polk County Breakdown
1252	Tommy Jackson	Old Joe Clark	The Girl I Left Behind
1253	Tommy Jackson	Forked Deer	Tom and Jerry
1254	Tommy Jackson	Sally Johnson	When the Leaves Begin to Turn Brown
1255	Tommy Jackson	When My Cat Came Back	Dusty Miller
1256	Tommy Jackson	Rachel	Ricestrow
1257–1259	unknown		
1260	Jimmy Newman	Blue Darlin'	Let Me Stay in Your Arms
1261	unknown		
1262	Mac Wiseman	The Kentuckian Song	Wabash Cannonball
1263	Fairfield Four	God Knows I'm a Pilgrim	Heaven in My View
1264	Ray Parker	That's How I Feel	It's Not the Moon
1265	The Counts	I Need You Tonight	Sally Walker
1266	Mac Wiseman	Fire Ball Mail	When the Roses Bloom Again
1267	Jimmy Work	Don't Knock Just Come On In	Let 'em Talk
1268	Glenn Douglas	You Just Stood There	Standing at the End of the World
1269	unknown		
1270	Jimmy Newman	God Was So Good	I Thought I'd Never Fall in Love Again
1271	Sunbeams	I'm Gonna Go Home to Mama	Blue Mountain Waltz
1272	Jimmy Work	When She Said You All	There's Only One You
1273	Mac Wiseman	I Hear You Knockin'	Camptown Races
1274	Jimmy Logsdon	Cold Cold Rain	Midnight Blues
1275	The Counts	To Our Love	Heartbreaker
1276	Mac Wiseman	These Hands	I'm Eatin' High on the Hog
1277	Jimmy Work	My Old Stomping Ground	Hands Away from My Heart
1278	Jimmy Newman	Let's Stay Together	Seasons of My Heart
1279	Jimmy Work	Rock Island Line	That's the Way It's Gonna Be
1280	Sunbeams	Wrap It Up and Save It	How About It
1281	Kirk Hanserd	One Night	My Heart's Broke Baby
1282	Mac Wiseman	Meanest Blues in the World	Be Good Baby
1283	Jimmy Newman	I Wanta Tell All the World	Come Back to Me
1284	Jimmy Work	Blind Heart	You've Got a Heart Like a Merry Go Round
1285	Mac Wiseman	Smilin' Through	I'm Drifting Back to Dreamland
1286	Jimmy Newman	Honky Tonk Tears	Let the Whole World Talk
1287	Jimmy Work	Digging My Own Grave	That Cold Cold Look in Your Eyes
1288	Jimmy Newman	Way That You're Living	I've Got You On My Mind
1289	Jimmy Newman	Fallen Star	I Can't Go On This Way

Label	Artist	Side A	Side B

Dot (15001 series) (Popular)
First issue: September 1951
Last known: Post 1955
Note: The Dot 15000 series continued beyond 1955.

15001	John Maddox and the Rhythmasters	San Antonio Rose	Bully of the Town
15002	Beasley Smith Orchestra	My Wife and I	I'm Gonna Live and Die in Texas
15003	unknown		
15004	Johnny Maddox and the Rhythmasters	Under the Double Eagle	My Mary
15005	Beasley Smith	Lucky You	Darling Nellie Gray
15006	Johnny Maddox and the Rhythmasters	Star Dust	Piano Polka
15007	Johnny Maddox with Bob Lamm	Waiting for the Robert E Lee	That's My Weakness Now
15008	Johnny Maddox and the Rhythmasters	Johnny Maddox Boogie	Near You
15009	Jane Grant	Goody Goody	Just Believe in Me
15010	King Perry	Coquette	Sunny Side of the Street
15011–15013	unknown		
15014	Johnny Maddox and the Rhythmasters	Why Worry	Friday Night Stomp
15015	Johnny Maddox and the Rhythmasters	Listen to the Mocking Bird	Molly Darling
15016	Jane Grant	I'll Sail My Ship Alone	Double Dee Do
15017	unknown		
15018	The Hilltoppers	Trying	You Made Up My Mind
15019	unknown		
15020	Johnny Maddox	Coconut Grove	Little Grass Shack
15021	Johnny Maddox	Sioux City Sue	Johnny Maddox Special
15022	unknown		
15023	Jane Grant	Tomorrow Night	Is It True What They Say About Dixie
15024	Claude Sharp	Touch Me Lord Jesus	Through Your Sins Be Scarlet
15025	Bob Lamm	Lookin' Around	Rainbow at Midnight
15026	Johnny Maddox	At the Georgia Camp Meeting	Elite Syncopations
15027	Johnny Maddox	Porcupine Rag	Sunflower Slow Drag
15028	Johnny Maddox	Sleepy Sidney	African Pass
15029	Johnny Maddox	Smokey Mokes	Tickled to Death
15030–15033	unknown		
15034	The Hilltoppers	Must I Cry Again	I Keep Telling Myself
15035–15038	unknown		
15039	King Perry	Cocquette	unknown
15040–15044	unknown		
15045	Johnny Maddox	In the Mood	By the Light of the Silvery Moon
15046	Johnny Maddox	Twilight Time	Alice Blue Gown
15047	Billy Vaughn	Melody of Love	
15048	Dan Belloc Orchestra	You Are Ecstacy	Pretend
15049	Bobby Colton	If You Say Goodbye	Somewhere
15050	Hank Garland	Guitar Polka	Tea for Two

Label	Artist	Side A	Side B
15051	Jane Grant	I Ain't Got Nobody	You Loved Me Too Little
15052	Dan Belloc Orchestra	Ding! Ding! Ding!	I Was a Fool
15053	Roy Wiggins	It's a Sin	Cimarron
15054	unknown		
15055	The Hilltoppers	If I Were King	I Can't Lie to Myself
15056	Johnny Maddox	Johnny's Boogie Blues	Blue Danube
15057	Johnny Maddox	12th Street Rag	Little Girl
15058	Johnny Maddox	Goodbye Girls I'm Through	Sweet Lei Lani
15059	Johnny Maddox	Honey Song	Alice Blue Gown
15060	Al Lombardy Orchestra	New Summit Ridge Drive	Choppin'
15061	unknown		
15062	Johnny Maddox	Twilight Time	Alice Blue Gown
15063	Leon Berry	Miserlou	The Sorcerer Tango
15064	unknown		
15065	Frankie Taylor	Pig Ankle Rag	Crazy Piano Rag
15066	Johnny Maddox	Ida	School Days
15067	Johnny Maddox	Margie	Swanee River
15068	Johnny Maddox	Me and My Shadow	Peggy O'Neil
15069	Johnny Maddox	Angry	Shine
15070	Johnny Maddox	Blue Room	Shanty in Old Shanty Town
15071	Johnny Maddox	Should I	You Were Meant for Me
15072	Johnny Maddox	Baby Face	Moonlight and Roses
15073	Johnny Maddox	Jealous	Tea for Two
15074	Johnny Maddox	Hindustan	Carolina in the Morning
15075	Johnny Maddox	Avalon	Tip Toe through the Tulips
15076	Johnny Maddox	Bye Bye Black Bird	Shiek of Araby
15077	Johnny Maddox	Ain't She Sweet	Do You Ever Think of Me
15078	Tony Almerico All Stars Dixieland Band	I'm Saving Tonight for You	Farewell Blues
15079	Tony Almerico All Stars Dixieland Band	Big Boy Blues	Shiek of Araby
15080	Tony Almerico All Stars Dixieland Band	Hadacol Boogie	I'll Be Glad When You're Dead
15081	Tony Almerico All Stars Dixieland Band	You Cooked Your Goose with Me	Ding Dong Daddy
15082	Tony Almerico All Stars Dixieland Band	Basin Street Blues	I Want to Be Happy
15083	Tony Almerico All Stars Dixieland Band	Tail Gate Rumble	How Many Hearts Have You Broken
15084	unknown		
15085	The Hilltoppers	I'd Rather Die Young	P.S. I Love You
15086	Elmo Tanner	The Whistler and His Dog	Whispering
15087	Frank Amato	Beautiful Dreamer	Dearest One of Mine
15088	Marvin Hughes	By the Fireside	You Can't Be True Dear
15089	Hank Garland	Steel Guitar Rag	Moonlight on the Colorado
15090	Johnny Maddox	Eight Beat Boogie	Learnin'
15091	Don Estes	Cryin' Cryin' Cryin'	The Kumquat Song
15092	Roy Wiggins	Bouquet of Roses	Wiggle Waggle
15093	Leon Berry	La Borrachita	Blacksmith Blues

Label	Artist	Side A	Side B
15094	Terry Ryan	Funny Thing	Limehouse Blues
15095	Jane Kelly	Love Me Now	Truly Yours
15096	unknown		
15097	Dan Belloc	I'll Dream Tonight	Shortnin' Bread
15098	Eddie Peabody	St. Louis Blues-Baby Face	I'm Looking Over a Four Leaf Clover
15099	Eddie Peabody	Sing Song Girl Chinatown	Stars and Stripes
15100	Eddie Peabody	Sleep (I'll See You in My Dreams)	Sweet Sue Just You
15101	Eddie Peabody	La Golandrina	Tea for Two
15102	Johnny Maddox	Alexander's Ragtime Band	Dipsy Doodle
15103–15104	unknown		
15105	The Hilltoppers	Love Walked In	To Be Alone
15106	Del Courtney	Blue Mist Part 1	Blue Mist Part 2
15107	Bunny Paul	Magic Guitar	Never Let Me Go
15108	Claude Sharp	Lord Send an Angel	When They Ring the Golden Bells
15109	Gospel Trio	I'm Feeling Fine	Gonna Walk with You Lord
15110	Peggy Taylor	If You Wuz a Bird	When I Dance with You
15111	Al Lombardy Orchestra	Blue Jeans	Creole Love Call
15112	Elmo Tanner	Heartaches	Nola
15113	Jimmy Kellis	Only the Broken Hearted	Farewell to Spring
15114	Cap-Tans	With All My Love	I'm So Crazy for Love
15115	Dan Belloc Orchestra	It's Anybody's Hearts	I've Got a Right to Cry
11516	Marvin Hughes	Ain't She Sweet	Five Foot Two, Eyes of Blue
15117	Hank Garland	Brazil	Make Believe
15118–15119	unknown		
15120	Johnny Maddox	I Saw Mommy Kissing Santa Claus	Rudolph the Red Nosed Reindeer
15121–15125	unknown		
15126	Johnny Maddox	I Don't Love Nobody	There's a Star Spangled Banner
15127	The Hilltoppers	Time Will Tell	From the Vine Came the Grape
15128	Johnny Maddox	There's a Star Spangled Banner Waving Somewhere	I Don't Love Nobody
15129	unknown		
15130	Jimmy Sacca	You're All That I Need	Alone
15131	unknown		
15132	The Hilltoppers	Till Then	I Found Your Letter
15133	unknown		
15134	Rusty Bryant	Castle Rock	All Nite Long
15135	Del Courtney	The Basketball Game	Parts 1 and 2
15136	Marvin Hughes	Ain't She Sweet	Five Foot Two Eyes of Blue
15137	Hank Garland	Brazil	Make Believe
15138	Dottie Dillard	Treasure Island	I Don't Want to Set the World on Fire
15139	Bobby Colton	These Foolish Things	
15140	Kenny Roberts	Wagon Wheels	Smoke Gets in Your Eyes
15141	Leo Pepper	Life's What You Make It	It's Easy
15142	Johnny Maddox	Josephine	Johnny's Boogie Blues

Label	Artist	Side A	Side B
15143	Al Lombardy Orchestra	The Blues	The Boogie
15144–15149	unknown		
15150	Dan Belloc Orchestra	It's Anybody's Heart	I've Got a Right to Cry
15151–15155	unknown		
15156	The Hilltoppers	Wrapped in a Dream	Poor Butterfly
15157	Buddy Lee	Two Roads	Breakin' in a Brand New Pair of Shoes
15158	Jimmy James	After the Laughter and Wine	Challo Mio Ra
15159	Francis Craig	Near You	Beg Your Pardon
15160	Leon Berry	Sophisticated Swing	My Adobe Hacienda
15161	Jane Kelly	You're Out of My Sight	Now That I Know
15162	Claude Sharp	Take an Inventory of Your Soul	Will the Gate Open Wide for Me
15163	Jimmy Sacca	Alone with My Heart	Mansion on the Hill
15164	Rusty Bryant	Pink Champagne	Slow Drag
15165–15168	unknown		
15169	Johnny Maddox	Peg o' My Heart	Teddy Bear
16170	unknown		
15171	Fontane Sisters	If I Didn't Have You	Happy Days and Lonely Nights
15172	Bob Eberly	I'm a Sentimental Fool	You're the Only Star in My Blue Heaven
15173	Lorry Raine	I'm Only Human	I'll Tell the World I Love You
15174–15200	unknown		
15201	The Hilltoppers	Sweetheart	The Old Cabaret
15202	Jan Garber	Doll Dance	Love Tales
15203	Dottie Dillard	Oh Johnny Oh Johnny	Cow Cow Boogie
15204	Boddy Colton	Supper Time	Remembering
15205	Jim Hall	I Love You Truly	Parakeet
15206	unknown		
15207	Al Lombardy Orchestra	Cross Your Heart	Cozy Corner
15208	Jan Garber	How Long	I Love You Because
15209	Dick Duane	What More Can I Say	Gunga Din
15210–15219	unknown		
15220	The Hilltoppers	If I Didn't Care	Bettina
15221	Rusty Bryant	Merry Go Round	Blow Rusty Blow
15222	Jean Strange	If You See Me Crying	Speak with Your Heart
15223	Jimmy Griffin	A Love Like You	You Took My Loving
15224	Lorry Raine	Love Me Tonight	What Would I Do
15225	Keynotes	They Say	Who
15226	Johnny Maddox	Pattona Rag	Blue Hawaii
15227	Al Lombardy Orchestra	Flying Home	In a Little Spanish Town
15228	Monarchs	Gravy	Caravan Mambo
15229	Louise Barber	Tear Stains	Keep a Light Shining Bright
15230–15242	unknown		
15243	Fontane Sisters	Willow Weep for Me	A Love Like You
15244–15246	unknown		

Label	Artist	Side A	Side B
15247	Billy Vaughn Orchestra	Joy Ride	Melody of Love
15248	Fontane Sisters	A Love Like You	Willow Weep for Me
15249	The Hilltoppers	You Try Somebody Else	Time Waits for No One
15250	Karl Garvin and the Karltones	Paper Doll	I'm Sorry I Made You Cry
15251–15252	unknown		
15253	Louise Barber	Tear Stains	Keep a Light Shining Bright
15254	Lew Douglas	Green Eyes	I Wanna Be There
15255	unknown		
15256	Jan Garber	Wishing	P'Flugerville Flip
15257	unknown		
15258	Teddy Phillips	Daniel the Cocker Spaniel	How Much I Love You
15259	Judy Valentine	Mission of San Michel	Have Fun Baby
15260–15264	unknown		
15265	Fontane Sisters	Hearts of Stone	Bless Your Heart
15266	Hank Garland	Boo-Hoo	Have You Ever Been Lonely
15267	unknown		
15268	The Lorelis	Have Fun Baby	Now I'm Broken Hearted
15269	unknown		
15270	Johnny Maddox	Lady in Red	Blue Blue Night
15271–15279	unknown		
15280	Johnny Maddox	Oh Lady Be Good	Oh You Beautiful Doll
15281	Johnny Maddox	Camptown Races	I'm Looking Over a Four Leaf Clover
15282	Johnny Maddox	Pretty Baby	Shine On Harvest Moon
15283	Johnny Maddox	Smiles	Over the Waves
15284	Johnny Maddox	Humoresque	Stars and Stripes Forever
15285	Johnny Maddox	Dixie–Yankee Doodle	Whispering
15286	Johnny Maddox	After the Ball	Bye Bye Blues
15287	Johnny Maddox	Golden Slippers	Washington and Lee Swing
15288	Johnny Maddox	Sidewalks of New York	Chinatown My Chinatown
15289	Johnny Maddox	Glow Worm	Chicken Reel
15290–15317	unknown		
15318	The Hilltoppers	D-A-R-L-I-N	Privolette
15319	Elmo Tanner	Begin the Beguine	Remembering
15320	Marveleers	These Are the Things We'll Share	Marlina, Marlina
15321	Francis Craig	My Blue Heaven	When Your Lips Touch Mine
15322	Jean Martin	Sneakin' Around	Farewell to Arms
15323	Tony Almerico All Stars Dixieland Band	Tennessee Waltz	Woodchopper's Ball
15324	Rusty Bryant	Back Street	Record Delivery Blues
15325	Johnny Maddox	The Crazy Otto	Humoresque
15326	Hank Barnett	At Once	Only in Heaven
15327	Jane Grant	Goody Goody	Doodle Dee Do
15328	Jane Grant	Goody, Goody	Doodle Dee Do

Label	Artist	Side A	Side B
15329–15332	unknown		
15333	Fontane Sisters	Rock Love	You're Mine
15334–15336	unknown		
15337	The Hilltoppers	Marianne	You're Wasting Your Time
15338	Pat Boone	Two Hearts	Tra La La
15339	Gale Storm	On Treasure Island	Lucky Lips
15340	Jim Forrest	Night Train Mambo	Londonderry Air
15341–15344	unknown		
15345	Starliters	Theme from Parkwood	Part Two
15346	unknown		
15347	Billy Vaughn Orchestra	Silver Moon	Baby o' Mine
15348–15349	unknown		
15350	Ray McKinley Orchestra	Hoodle Addle	Down the Road Apiece
15351	Hilltoppers	The Door Is Still Open	Teardrops from My Eyes
15352	Fontane Sisters	Most of All	Put Me in the Mood
15353	Carol Woodward	Sweet Georgia Brown	Mary Had a Lover Man
15354	Alan Martin	Twilight Time	What a Sweetheart
15355–15363	unknown		
15365	Johnny Maddox	Johnny's Medley	The Whistlin' Piano Man
15366	Lew Douglas	With Love	I'm Getting Sentimental Over You
15367–15369	unknown		
15370	Fontane Sisters	Rollin' Stone	Playmates
15371	Joy Brinkley	Forces of Evil	Crazy Crazy Heart
15372	Commodores	Uranium	Riding on a Train
15373	unknown		
15374	Bill Vaughn Orchestra	The Waltz You Saved for Me	Billy Vaughn's Boogie
15375	Hilltoppers	The Kentuckian Song	I Must Be Dreaming
15376	Rusty Bryant	Hot Fudge	Ridin' with Rusty
15377	Pat Boone	Ain't That a Shame	Tennessee Saturday Night
15378–15379	unknown		
15380	Esquire Boys	Dark Eyes	Guitar Mambo
15381	Jim Lowe	Close the Door	Nuevo Loredo
15382–15384	unknown		
15385	Snooky Lanson	Why Don't You Write Me	Last Minute Love
15386	Fontane Sisters	Seventeen	If I Could Be with You
15387–15399	unknown		
15400	Francis Craig	In the Shade of the Moonlight	If You Care at All
15401	Tony Almerico All Stars Dixieland Band	Near You	Bourbon Street Parade
15402	Karl Garvin	I Wish	Somebody Else Is Taking My Place
15403	Al Lombardy Orchestra	Tuxedo Junction	Indian Love Call
15404	Chanteclairs	Believe Me Beloved	I've Never Been There
15405	Jan Garber	You Too, You Too?	Pretty Patricia

Label	Artist	Side A	Side B
15406	Tony Dino	I Stand Accused	To Have and to Hold
15407	Jim Lowe	Maybellene	Rene La Rue
15408	Johnny Maddox	Do It Again	When You Wore a Tulip
15409	Billy Vaughn Orchestra	Shifting, Whispering Sands Part 1	Shifting, Whispering Sands Part 2
15410	Beasley Smith Orchestra	Goodnight Sweet Dream	Parisian Rag
15411	Elmo Tanner	Nightingale	Avalon
15412	Gale Storm	I Hear You Knocking	Never Leave Me
15413	Ray McKinley Orchestra	Crazy Boogie	Wanderlust Blues
15414	Billy Vaughn Orchestra	Shifting Whispering Sands	Moody Trudy
15415	The Hilltoppers	Searching	All I Need Is You
15416	Melody Maids	I Could Dream Forever	Almost Everything
15417	unknown		
15418	Norman Leyden Orchestra	Promise Me	Down in the Meadow
15419	Jean Strange	Charm Bracelet	When I was Your Age
15420	Rusty Bryant	Moonlight Garden Stomp	The Honeydripper
15421	unknown		
15422	Pat Boone	At My Front Door	No Other Arms
15423	The Hilltoppers	Only You	Until the Real Thing Comes Along
15424	Snooky Lanson	It's Almost Tomorrow	Stop! Let Me Off the Bus
15425	Commodores	Cream Puff	Close to My Heart
15426	Jan Garber	Micky's Melody	Corpus Christi
15427	Johnny Maddox	Chicken Reel	I Never Knew
15428	Fontane Sisters	Adorable	Daddy-O
15429	Jim Lowe	John Jacob Jingleheimer Smith	St James Avenue
15430	Billy Vaughn Orchestra	Calico Cathy	I'd Give a Million Tomorrows
15431	Ray McKinley Orchestra	You Remind Me of Someone	Celery Stalks at Midnight
15432	Johnny Maddox	Hands Off	Hop Scotch Boogie
15433	Esquire Boys	At the Balalaika	Dance with a Rock
15434	Fontane Sisters	Silver Bells	Nuttin' for Christmas
15435	Pat Boone	Gee Whitakers	Take the Time
15436	Gale Storm	Memories Are Made of This	Teen-age Prayer
15437	The Hilltoppers	My Treasure	The Last Word in Love
15438	Teddy Phillips	Pochahontes	My Love for You
15439	Commodores	Speedo	Whole Lotta Shakin' Goin' On
15440	Zeke Clements	Blue Mexico Sky	You're Free Again
15441	Jan Garber	My Dear	Japanese Farewell Song
15442	Bob London	Lola	Reckless
15443	Pat Boone	Tutti Frutti	I'll Be Home
15444	Billy Vaughn Orchestra	Little Boy Blue	Theme from "Three Penny Opera" (Moritat)
15445	Snooky Lanson	Seven Days	Tippity Top

Label	Artist	Side A	Side B

Excello (2000 series) (Blues, R&B, and Gospel)
First issue: August 1952
Last known: Post 1955
Note: The Excello 2000 series continued beyond 1955.

2000	Boyer Brothers	Step by Step	Oh Lord Stand by Me
2001	Hendrix Singers	Away in the Manger	Oh Come All Ye Faithful
2002	Boyer Brothers	Nothing Can Change Me	Jesus, Saviour, Pilot Me
2003	Hendrix Singers	In the End	On the Beautiful Shore
2004	Silvertone Singers of Cincinnati	Jesus Be My Keeper	Since Jesus Came into My Heart
2005	Charlie Dowell and Orchestra	Allotment Blues (featuring Willie Lee Patton)	Wail Daddy (featuring Willie Lee Patton)
2006	Del Thorne and Her Trio	I Let Him Move Me	Down South in Birmingham
2007	"Little Maxie" Bailey	Brownskin Woman Blues	Tear Drops Are Falling
2008	Shy Guy Douglas	Detroit Arrow	New Memphis Blues
2009	Kid King's Combo	Skip's Boogie	Banana Split
2010	Boyer Brothers	He Delivered Me	He's Got the World in His Hands
2011	"Good Rockin" Beasley	Long Goody	Happy Go Lucky
2012	Young Gospel Singers	Glory to His Name	I Can Call Jesus Anytime
2013	Silvertone Singers of Cincinnati	I Got a Home in That Rock	In My Heart
2014	The Leap Frogs	Dirty Britches (Harmonica–Jimmy Johnson)	Things Gonna Change (vocal by Louis Campbell)
2015	The Sermonairs	Sweet Bye and Bye	Have Faith and Believe
2016	"Little Maxie"	Drive Soldiers Drive	My Baby's Blues
2017	Del Thorne and Her Trio	Fly Chick Blues	Goof Train
2018	Kid King's Combo	The Brass Rail	Gimmick
2019	Bro. Henry Edwards	Is There Anybody Else Like Jesus	Nothing Too Hard for Thee
2020	Bernie Hardison	Love Me Baby	Yeah It's True
2021	Waldo Singers	Jesus Brought Me Over	Jesus Paid It All
2022	Roosevelt Lee	Lazy Pete	I'm So Glad
2023	The Dixie Doodlers	She Was All I Had (vocal by Sam McNeese)	Best of Friends (vocal by James Campbell)
2024	Shy Guy Douglas	I'm Your Country Man	Wasted Time
2025	Kid King's Combo	Chocolate Sundae	Greasy Feet
2026	The Blue Flamers	Driving Down the Highway (vocal by Bob Elliott)	Watch On (vocal by Bob Elliott)
2027	Tommy McGhee	Late Every Evenin'	Poppin'
2028	Ray Batts	Stealin' Sugar	Maybe It's You, Sweetheart, Maybe It's Me
2029	Boyer Brothers	When Life Is Done	unknown title
2030	Louis Brooks and His Pine-Toppers	Bus Station Blues	Waddle Trot
2031	John Christmon	My Baby's Gone	Come with Me My Love
2032	Shy Guy Douglas	She's My Kinda Girl	No Place Like Home
2033	Jack Toombs	You're the Only Good Thing	Two Cheaters in Love
2034	Silvertone Singers of Cincinnati	Run On to the End	Way Bye and Bye
2035	Louis Campbell	Gotta Love You Baby	The Natural Facts
2036	Waldo Singers	Trust Him Today	Just Tell Jesus

Label	Artist	Side A	Side B
2037	Kid King's Combo	Dreamy Moods	Memories in Melody
2038	Castaways	Teasin'	I Wish
2039	Bobby Prince	Too Many Keys	Please Give Me Your Love
2040	Sons of the South	In My Saviour's Care	Didn't It Rain
2041	Jack Toombs	Foolish Jealousy	My Imagination
2042	Louis Brooks and His Hi-Toppers	Double Shot	Time Out
2043	Silvertone Singers of Cincinnati	Jesus My Saviour	Rescue the Perishing
2044	Peacheroos	Be Bop Baby	Every Day My Love Is True
2045	Sons of the South	I'm Waiting and Watching	One Day
2046	Kid King's Combo	Mambino	Strollin' Time
2047	Arthur Gunter	Baby Let's Play House	Blues After Hours
2048	Jack Toombs	Still I'm Yours (vocal By Jack Toombs and Lucinda Lee)	If You Want Me, Catch Me
2049	Beulah Bryant	What Am I Gonna Do	Prize Fighting Papa
2050	Sons of the South	God Is Alright	Travelin' Down This Road
2051	Kid King's Combo	Now Listen Baby (vocal by Good Rockin' Sam)	The Sneak
2052	Don Haggard and Judie Bess with the Sunset Drifters	Somebody Clipped Your Wings	Unloved, Unwed, Unwanted
2053	Arthur Gunter	She's Mine All Mine	You Are Doin' Me Wrong
2054	Jewel-Gospel-Aires	Oh Lord Guide the Way	After Awhile with Jesus
2055	Slim Hunt	Welcome Home Baby	Lonesome for My Baby
2056	Louis Brooks and His Hi-Toppers	It's Love Baby (24 Hours a Day) (vocal by Earl Gaines)	Chicken Shuffle
2057	Marigolds	Rollin' Stone	Why Don't You
2058	Arthur Gunter	Honey Babe	No Happy Home
2059	Kid King's Combo	Baby I'm Fool Proof	
	Good Rockin' Sam		Thing-A-Ma Jig
2060	Solotones	Front Page Blues	Pork and Beans
2061	Marigolds	Two Strangers	Love You Love You
2062	Blues Rockers	Calling All Cows	Johnnie Mae
2063	Earl Gaines with Louis Brooks and His Hi-Toppers	Can't Keep from Cryin'	Baby, Baby, What's Wrong
2064	Larry Birdsong	It Won't Be This Way Always	You Won't Be Needing
2065	Crown Prince Waterford	Driftwood Blues	I'm Gonna Do Right
2066	Lightnin' Slim	Lightnin' Blues	I Can't Be Successful
2067	Rainbow Valley Boys	Broken Hearted Means Nothing to You (vocal duet Billy and Joe)	Culleoka (featuring Hubert Binkley)
2068	Jerry McCain and His Upstarts	That's What They Want	Courtin' in a Cadillac
2069	Ted Jarrett	Love Love Love	Goofin' Off
2070	Good Rockin' Sam with Kid King's Combo	Funny Funny Feelin'	Don't Let Daddy Slow Walk You Down
2071	Lindsey Brothers	Big Hearted Joe	Let's Get Down to Business
2072	Earl Gaines	A Long Time Ago	It's Drivin' Me Mad
2073	Arthur Gunter	Trouble with My Baby	Baby You Better Listen
2074	Rudy Green	Cool Lovin' Mama	My Mumblin' Baby
2075	Lightnin´ Slim	Sugar Plum	Just Made Twenty One
2076	Larry Birdsong	Pleading for Love	You´11 Never Never Know

Gold (700 series) (Country)
First issue: 1953
Last known: 1953

Label	Artist	Side A	Side B
700	unknown		
701	Chickie King and Her Harvesters	I Need Your Lovin'	Love-You, Love-You, Love-You
702	Billy Wilson	I Can't Stop Loving You	Hen-Pecked Boogie
703	Chickie King and Her Harvesters	Just Walking in the Rain	Chapel Bells

Hickory (1000 series) (Country)
First issue: January 1954
Last known: Post 1955
Note: The Hickory label continued after 1955.

Label	Artist	Side A	Side B
1001	Bobby Dick	The Lord's Last Supper	Thank God I Came Out Alive
1002	Tommy Hill	The Life That I'm Living	Love Me Baby
1003	Al Terry	Good Deal Lucille	Say a Prayer for Me
1004	Jimmy Sweeney and the Varieteers	I've Got a Woman's Love	Deep Blues
1005	Danny Davis	Second Hand Dreams for Sale	Can't You Feel It in My Heart
1006	Rod Brasfield	Rod's Trip to Chicago (Part 1)	Rod's Trip to Chicago (Part 2)
1007	Bood Bryant	My Baby's Gone	I Wanta Go Fast
1008	Howard White	The Steel Guitar Dove	Ensonata
1009	Jimmy Collie	Why Can't You Love Me	My Heart and I
1010	Tommy Hill	Bright Lights Is Over Heaven	Say It Now
1011	Bobby Dick	A Prisoner of a Broken Heart	I Feel Lucky (Yes, I Do)
1012	Al Terry	Show Me That You Love Me	House of Glass
1013	McCormick Bros.	Red Hen Boogie	Banjo Twist
1014	The Varieteers	If You and I Could Be Sweethearts	I Pay with Every Breath
1015	Opal Jean	Tennessee Courtin' Time	That Done It
1016	Ernie Chaffin	I'm Gonna Salt My Sugar Away	Lonely Wind
1017	Al Terry	Let's Postpone Our Wedding	Hey Whatta Y'Say
1018	Jimmy Collie	Along the Way	Cajun Lingo
1019	Jimmy Collie	Conscience (Set Me Free)	Cry Like a Baby
1020	Tommy Hill	Honky Tonk Romance	Collision with Love
1021	McCormick Bros.	The Billy Goat Boogie	C.N.R. Special
1022	Al Terry	The Wall around Your Heart	Hate Me Not
1023	Opal Jean	You Gave Me Your Name	Part of Your Heart
1024	Ernie Chaffin	I Can't Lose the Blues	Get Me on Your Mind
1025	The Varieteers	Minnie, Go Home	Call My Gal, Miss Jones
1026	Jimmy Collie	My Fairyland Dreams	I'm Not Giving Up That Easy
1027	Rusty and Doug	So Lovely, Baby	Why Cry for You
1028	Wilma Lee and Stoney Cooper	Just for a While	How It Hurts to Cry Alone
1029	Al Terry	No, No, John	Gone Again
1030	McCormick Bros.	The Mad Banjo	Cross My Heart

Label	Artist	Side A	Side B
1031	Tommy Hill	Six Foot on Earth	Diddle, Diddle Dumpling
1032	Howard White	Rosette	Steel Guitar Swallow
1033	Jimmy Collie	Sinner's Angel	She Will Get Lonesome
1034	Wiley Barkdull	Pencil and Paper Love	I'll Give My Heart You (In Exchange for Yours)
1035	Wilma Lee and Stoney Cooper	Each Season Changes You	Please Help Me to Be Wrong
1036	Rusty and Doug	Look Around (Take a Look At Me)	Can I Be Dreaming
1037	Al Terry	(Dear God) I Love Her So	Goodbye Mr. Sunshine
1038	McCormick Bros.	Bugle Call Rag	Are You Feeling Blue
1039	Tommy Hill	Mr. Juke Box	Sugar Nanner
1040	Jimmy Collie	Nero Played His Fiddle	Except
1041	Wilma Lee and Al Terry	Not Anymore	We Make a Lovely Couple
1042	Rusty and Doug	Let's Stay Together	Honey Honey
1043	Wilma Lee and Stoney Cooper	I Want to Be Loved	Row Number Two, Seat Number Three
1044	Wiley Barkdull	Cause You're Always on My Mind	Me, You and My Heart
1045	Al Terry	Follow Me	The Lesson of Love
1046	McCormick Bros.	Pins and Needles	Shuffle, and Deal

Hillbilly All Star (5000 series) (Country)
First issue: c. 1952
Last known: c. 1952

5000–5001	unknown		
5002	Vernon Way and His Carolina Swing Band	Chili Dippin' Mama (vocal by Vernon Way)	I'll Mow You Down (vocal by Way and Hale)
5003	Rod Taylor and His Blue Valley Boys	The Night's So Long	Too Wet to Plow

J-B (200 series) (Country Gospel)
First issue: 1952
Last known: 1952
Note: J-B 200 (and possibly 201) was also issued by Jim Bulleit on the Webb City label

200	Rebels Quartet	Peace Like a River	Gospel Boogie
201	Rebels Quartet	If You Believe	I'll Leave It All Behind

J-B (600 series) (R&B)
First issue: October 1952
Last known: September 1953

600	unknown		
601	Jack Dixon with Red Calhoun and His Orchestra	My Blues and Me (vocal by Jimmy Smith)	Move Over Baby (vocal by Jimmy Smith)
602	Vivian Verson and Jimmy Smith with Red Calhoun and His Orchestra	Payday Lover	
	Vivian Verson with Red Calhoun and His Orchestra		I Want to Know
603	Eddie (Guitar Slim) Jones	Feelin' Sad	Certainly All
604	The Propheteers	I'm So Glad	Up Above My Head
605	Tasso Zachary	Louisville, Kentucky	Tasso's Blues

Label	Artist	Side A	Side B
606	Walter 'Tang' Smith	High Tone Mama	Every Sunday Morning
607	Red Calhoun and His Orchestra	Love Is the Thing (vocal by Jimmy Smith)	Miserable Man (vocal by Jimmy Smith)

J-B (1500 series) (Country)
First issue: October 1952
Last known: September 1953

1500	Johnny Mathis	Contented	Me for You and You for Me
1501	Bob West	Weeds of Hate	Tennessee Girl
1502	Johnny Mathis	Dream World	My Heart Lights Up
1503	Rocky Kirkland	Candy Baby	I Don't Care

J-B (5000 series) (Popular)
First issue: October 1952
Last known: September 1953

5000	Carole Wilson	Contented	When the Snowflakes Fall Again
5001	Monte Floyd	Beyond the Blue	Unwanted by You
5002	Buddy Cunningham	I Believe in You	Sentimental Souvenirs
5003	Buddy Cunningham	How Long Will It Be	Jealous Stars

Jamboree (500 series) (Country)
First issue: June 1950
Last known: July 1951
Note: Label also named Dixie Jamboree on some issues.

500	unknown		
501	Dick Stratton with the Nite Owls	Slippin' Around with Jole Blon'	Fat Gal Boogie
502	Roy Justice	Bonaparte's Retreat	Like Sand through My Fingers
503	Dick Stratton with the Nite Owls	Rainbow	Whistlin' Rufus
504	Ray Anderson	You're the Two Timing Kind	You'd Better Hold Your Tongue
505–507	unknown		
508	Alan Flatt	It's All Over Now	Watching My Past Go By
509	John Talley	Hillbilly Sweetheart	Tears Falling from Your Eyes
510	Dick Stratton and the Nite Owls	Music City, U.S.A.	It'll Be a Cold Day in July
511	Alan Flatt	I'm Movin' On	Steppin' Out
512	Hugh Cherry and the Nite Owls and the Dixielanders	Rockin' Horse	Walk, Chicken, Walk
513	Ray Anderson and the Tennessee Mountaineers	Draft Board Blues	I'm Lonely Because
514	John Talley	If You've Got the Money I've Got the Time	The Price of a Broken Heart
515	Alan Flatt and the Nite Owls	Scrapbook of Dreams	A Broken Heart and a Glass of Beer
516	Shorty Ashburn	You're Under Arrest	My Last Farewell
517	Dick Stratton and His Nite Owls	I Wouldn't Have You on a Christmas Tree	Poison Love

Ma an Pa Say (1 series) (Country)
First issue: circa 1950
Last known: circa 1950

1/2	Big Jeff	Ten-E-Cee Hom-Bru	Hom-Bru Boogie

Label	Artist	Side A	Side B

Mecca (100 series) (Popular and R&B)
First issue: 1949
Last known: 1951

Label	Artist	Side A	Side B
100/101	Buddy Estes with Del Shoemake and the Sunsetters	Take Your Finger Out of Your Mouth	Tears
102	Buddy Estes	I Remember	With All Your Heart
103	Tommy Brooks	Steam Pressing Woman	If You Love Me Baby

Nash Records (Details unknown)

Nashboro (500 series) (Gospel, R&B)
First issue: June 1951
Last known: Post 1955
Note: The Nashboro 500 series continued beyond 1955.

Label	Artist	Side A	Side B
500	Silvertone Jubilee Singers	I'm Looking for My Jesus	I Met My Mother This Morning
501	Zachary's Heavenly Gospelaires	Blessed Saviour	The Lord Came to Save Me
502	Silvertone Jubilee Singers	Prayer Changes Things	Just Can't Help from Crying
503	Skylarks	Stand by Me	Something about My Lord Mighty Sweet
504	Skylarks	My Rock	Four and Twenty Elders
505	Skylarks	Life's Burdens (Part 1)	Life's Burdens (Part 2)
506	Fireside Gospel Singers	Gabriel Sound Your Trumpet	Tell Jesus I'm Coming Home
507	Sherman Johnson	Back Alley Boogie	Nashville after Midnight
508	Skylarks	The Holy Father	Cheer the Weary Traveler
509	Skylarks	There Must Be a City	This Heart of Mine
510	Cross-Road Singers	Where Shall I Be	Sing Till the Power of the Lord Comes Down
511	Cross-Road Singers	Leave It There	Roll the Stone Away
512	Reverend W.M. Anderson and the Jordan River Singers	Jesus on the Main Line	Won't We Have a Time
513	Skylarks	Farther Along	I'm Satisfied
514	Swanee Quintet	Jesus on My Hand	Walk in the Light
515	Fireside Gospel Singers	What Did Jesus Say	God Leads His Dear Children Along
516	The Fat Man with the Sunnyland Slim Trio	You've Gotta Stop This Mess	Glad I Don't Worry No More
517	Jordan River Singers	I'm a Soldier	My Life in His Hands
518	Skylarks	What a Glorious Day	Jesus Won't Deny Me
519	Jack Cooley	It's So Fine	Tom Tom Boogie
520	Blair Gospel Singers	Forgive Me Lord	Standing at the Station
521	Swanee Quintet	The Old Time Religion	In My Saviour's Care
522	Fireside Gospel Singers	In the Garden	Two Little Fishes and Five Loaves of Bread
523	Skylarks	New Jerusalem	What Manner of Man Is This
524	Swanee Quintet	Come On to This Altar	My Lord Is Coming Back
525	Silvertown Singers of Cincinnati	Walk thru the Valley	When We Bow in the Evening At the Altar
526	unknown		
527	Jack Cooley	Hear My Story	Dyna-Flow
528	Jordan River Singers	Precious Lord	Seek and Ye Shall Find

Label	Artist	Side A	Side B
529	Flying Cloud Quintet	I'm Going Through	Jezebel
530	Blair Gospel Singers	In This World Today	Lord You Know My Mind
531	Skylarks	Come Over Here	I Want to Walk with Jesus
532	Blair Gospel Singers	I'm Striving Hard Each Day	I Want to Be More Like Jesus
533	Swanee Quintet	Let Us Stretch Out	Wasn't It a Pity
534	Silvertone Jubilee Singers	I've Got a Mother Gone On	What Are They Doing in Heaven
535	Skylarks	This May Be the Last Time	Jesus Prayed Every Step of the Way
536	Fireside Gospel Singers	When the Roll Is Called	Better Stop and Get Religion
537	Flying Clouds of Detroit	When Jesus Came	I, John, Saw a Mighty Number
538	Swanee Quintet	Sit Down Servant	Well Done
539	Fireside Gospel Singers	Get Your Soul Right	When They Ring Them Golden Bells
540	Skylarks	I Want to Know Will He Welcome Me There	Heavenly Light
541	Swanee Quintet	Long as Jesus Loves	Joy in Beulah Land
542	Blair Gospel Singers	Anyhow	I've Got Heaven on My Mind
543	unknown		
544	Skylarks	Lord Have Mercy	No Discharge in God's Army
545	Skylarks	Baptism of Jesus	I Stepped in the Water One Day
546	Swanee Quintet	Cry Sometimes	In My Heart
547	Swanee Quintet	On My Knees	Remember Me
548	Skylarks	Call You in the Morning	Letter from Jesus
549	Edna Gallmon Cooke	Nobody but You Lord	Somebody Help Me
550	Jewell Gospel Trio	Take My Hand, Precious Lord	Gonna Wake Up in Glory
551	Swanee Quintet	It's Hard to Get Along	Judgement
552	Spiritual Five	Heavenly Father	I've Been Born Again
553	Edna Gallmon Cooke	Who'll Be a Witness	My Joy
554	Skylarks	I Love the Lord	Gonna Wake Up in Glory
555	Blair Gospel Singers	Waiting for the Lord	I've Been Moaning So Long
556	Christland Singers	Where Could I Go	Nothing Will Move Me
557	Golden Trumpets	Down at the Cross	Just Like Jesus Did
558	Angelic Gospel Singers	Jesus Never Fails Me	I'll Be Alright
559	Trumpets of Joy	Last Mile of the Way	Sweeter Than the Day Before
560	Prof. Harold Boggs	Help Me Jesus	When the Spirit of the Lord Comes
561	Edna Gallmon Cooke	Said I Wouldn't Tell It	Hide Me
562	Swanee Quintet	I'm Alright Now	Low Down Chariot
563	Geneva White and Marie Strange (organ)	Just as I Am without One Plea	Blessed Assurance
564	Consolers	Nobody Knows	Give Me My Flowers
565	Skylarks	He's My All and All	God Is Able
566	Radio Four	An Earnest Prayer	How Much I Owe
567	Chosen Gospel Singers	It's Alright	When the Saints Go Marching In
568	Radio Four	Sending Up a Prayer (Part 1)	Sending Up a Prayer (Part 2)
569	Christland Singers	All the Way Lord	Sell Out to the Master
570	Jewell Gospel Singers	I Looked Down the Line	Somebody's Knocking at Your Door

Label	Artist	Side A	Side B

Nashboro (1000 series) (Country)
First issue: June 1951
Last known: February 1952

1000	unknown		
1001	Vance Morris and His Alabama Playboys	Sweet Georgia Brown	Goodbye Little Blue Eyes
1002–1004	unknown		
1005	Vance Morris and His Alabama Playboys	Rainy Weather (vocal by "Dub" Williams)	Crazy 'bout the Boogie (vocal by Vance Morris)
1006	Vance Morris and His Alabama Playboys	Boot Hill Drag	Some of These Days
1007	Vance Morris and His Alabama Playboys	You Won't Be Satisfied That Way	Blues on the Down Beat
1008	Joe Williams and His Rhythmaires	Smiles	Those Naughty Blues
1009	Vance Morris and His Alabama Playboys	Slap Happy Baby	I'll Get By, Don't You Cry
1010	Woody and Lena with the Dixie Ramblers	I Keep On Forgetting	She's Got Her Eye on Some Other Guy
1011	Joe Williams and His Rhythm Ensemble	Wabash Blues	In the Shade of the Old Apple Tree
1012–1014	unknown		
1015	Dixie Ramblers	I Saw You Turn and Walk Away (vocal by Woody and Lena)	If I Could Hear Your Name Once More (vocal by Woody and Lena)
1016	Joe Williams and His Rhythm Ensemble	Cotton Picker's Ball	Yes Sir, That's My Baby
1017	Dixie Ramblers	Lonely for You (vocal by Woody and Lena)	I'll Be Glad When It's Over (Over There) (vocal by Woody and Lena)

Raba Records (Details unknown)
Note: Bill Allen recalled issuing records on a Raba label in the later 1940s. Artists included the Tennessee State Collegians, but no discs have been collected from this label.

Randy's (1 series) (Gospel)
First issue: 1949
Last known: 1949

1	United Spiritual Singers featuring the Davenport Singers	In the Tabernacle	God Answers Prayer
2	The Sincere Singers	I'll Stand My Test	There Must Be a Mansion
3	United Spiritual Singers featuring the Capitol City Quartette	Home on High	I'm Not Ashamed to Be a Witness for the Lord
4	United Spiritual Singers	When I Join That Jubilee	Trusting in My Jesus
5	The Five Blind Boys	By and By	An Interest Over There

Randy's (100 series) (Blues)
First issue: 1949
Last known: 1949

100–103	unknown		
104	Richard Armstrong	Gene Noble's Boogie	Gene Noble's Blues

Label	Artist	Side A	Side B

Randy's (200 series) (Gospel)
First issue: 1949
Last known: 1949

200	Sister Alexie Barney	Strange Things Are Happening	When They Ring Those Bells

Reavis (150 series) (Popular)
First issue: 1953
Last known: 1953

150	unknown		
151	Becker Sisters	Campfire Capers	Two-Three-Four

Red Robin (500 series) (Country)
First issue: 1952
Last known: 1952
Note: This label was organized by Jim Bulleit but possibly not based in Nashville.

500	unknown		
501	Hank and Slim's Georgia Crackers	I Love My Neighbour	I Dreamed about Mom
502	unknown		
503	Uncle Si	Eleven More Months	Country Boy

Red Robin (600 series) (R&B)
First issue: 1952
Last known: 1952

600	unknown		
601	Jack Dixon with Red Calhoun and His Orchestra	Move Over Baby	My Blues and Me

Republic (100 series) + (700 series) (Blues and Country)
Republic (500 series) (Popular)
First issue: 1954
Last known: 1954
Note: Several Tennessee label 100 series and 700 series were re-pressed with a Republic 100 or 700 number in the latter part of 1952 and in 1953.

500	Chucky from Kentucky	What It Was, Was Football (Part 1)	What It Was, Was Football (Part 2)

Republic (7000 series) (Popular, Country, R&B, and Gospel)
First issue: August 1952
Last known: 1956

7000	Snooky Lanson	Roll On Mississippi, Roll On	Fool in Love
7001	Johnny Rowland	Sign on the Dotted Line	Don't Break the Laws of Man
7002	Sonny Sims	Tattle-Tale Eyes	Tears Falling Hearts Breaking
7003	Radio Four	Blood Done Signed My Name	Why Not Tonight
7004	Helen Carter and Grant Turner	I'll Keep On Loving You	My Dearest and Best
7005	J.T. Adams and the Men of Texas	Dear Lord Remember Me	My God Is Real

Label	Artist	Side A	Side B
7006	Sonny Sims with Harris Martin Band	Indian Love Call	
	Harris Martin		On Moonlight Bay
7007	Lee Bonds and Band	How About a Date	I've Just Got Your Heart Breaking Letter
7008	Gay Crosse and the Good Humor Six	No Better for You	Tired of Being Shoved Around
7009	Allen Flatt	I'm Lonely Tonight for You	I've Lost You
7010	unknown		
7011	Ted West and Band	She Bent My Pole	She's My Gal
7012	unknown		
7013	Helen Foster and Band	You Belong to Me (vocal by Helen Foster and the Rovers)	Oop-De-Doo
7014	Gwen Dalton and Band	The Honey Song	South
7015	Martin and Brown	Caravan	I'm Confessin'
7016	Connie and Babe	unknown title	unknown title
7017	J.T. Adams	Your God Is Near	Faith Is the Key
7018	Radio Four	Never Too Late	Help Me Run This Race
7019	Edna Gallmon Cooke	Nobody to Depend On	Walk Through the Valley
7020	J.T. Adams and the Men of Texas	Christmas Time Is the Best Time	It's Christmas Time
7021	unknown		
7022	Floyd Huffman	You Ain't Foolin' Me	My Heart Slowly Died
7023	Johnny Rowland	Ohio Baby	Memories of When You Were Mine
7024	Mr. Goon	My Blue Heaven	
	Martin and Brown		You Were Meant for Me
7025	Gwen Dalton and the Rag Time Five	I'm Looking for a Four Leaf Clover	Washington and Lee Swing
7026	Christine Kittrell and Gay Crosse with the Good Humor Six	Slave to Love	Gotta Stop Loving You
7027	Gay Crosse and the Good Humor Six	Easy Rockin'	G.C. Rock
7028	J.T. Adams	Love of God	His Tender Love
7029	Allen Flatt	I'll Go Where You Guide Me	Close Your Eyes
7030	Bob Harman	Bob's Boogie	Boogie Woogie Jubilee
7031	Snooky Lanson	I'm Alone Because I Love You	Don't Come Cryin' on My Shoulder
7032	Trenton Singers	Take Me Jesus	In Secret Prayer
7033	Smiley Wilson and Kitty Carson	I've Found My Own	Barn Yard Blues
7034	Lucile Barbee	I Just Can't Keep It to Myself	Where Could I Go
7035	Sonny Sims	Two Kinds of Women	Walk Off and Leave It
7036	Del Wood	12th Street Rag	Pickin' and Grinnin'
7037	Helen Foster and the Chapters	Somebody Somewhere	They Tell Me
7038	Chapters	Love You, Love You, Love You	Goodbye My Love
7039	Bob Hayes	Starving to Death for Your Kisses	Snow Flake Waltz
7040	Edna Gallmon Cooke	Amen (with the Radio Four)	He's So Good
7041	Lee Bonds	Give My Broken Heart a Break	
	Lee Bonds and Sonny Sims		I'm Glad That I Love You
7042	Radio Four	I've Been Saved	What More Can Jesus Do
7043	Del Wood	Elmer's Tone	Jersey Bounce
7044	Christine Kittrell	I'll Help You Baby	L & N Special

Label	Artist	Side A	Side B
7045	Don Windle	I Want You Too	Iron Curtain Has Parted
7046	Martin and Brown	Somebody Else Is Takin' My Place	Pagan Love Song
7047	Carl Sauceman and the Green Valley Boys	A White Cross Marks the Grave	I'll Be an Angel Too
7048	Edna Gallmon Cooke	I've Got Religion	Build Me a Cabin
7049	Pat Boone	Until You Tell Me So	For My Heart Belongs to You
7050	Jimmy (J.D.) Simpson	Ramblin' Blues	I Watched the Sun Go Down
7051	Del Wood	Ricky-Tic-Piano	Moonlight Cocktail
7052	J.T. Adams and the Men from Texas	Crying in the Chapel	Rock-a-My-Soul
7053	Joyce Paul with the Hal Brady Orchestra	Caribbean	I Forgot More Than You'll Ever Know
7054	Jimmy Sweeney	Believe in Me	Desire
7055	Christine Kittrell	Every Night in the Week	Evil Eyed Woman
7056	Trenton Singers	I Shall Know Him (Part 1)	I Shall Know Him (Part 2)
7057	Del Wood	Back Room Polka	Rag Time Annie
7058	Smith and Gaston Singers	Every Day of My Life	Tired Lord
7059	Allen Flatt	Get In or Get Out of My Life	All These Little Things
7060	Don Windle with String Band	The Girl Just Down the Street	When My Baby Gets Home
7061	J.T. Adams and the Men from Texas	Rock-a-My-Soul	Take Up Thy Cross
7062	Pat Boone with James Hall and his Orchestra	Half Way Chance with You	Remember to Be Mine
7063	Edna Gallmon Cooke	Evening Son	Higher Ground
7064	Jimmy (J.D.) Simpson with s-String Band	Oilfield Blues	I Hope Some Day You'll Think of Me
7065	Danny Cassella	April May	The Gang That Sang Heart of My Heart
7066	Andy Wilson	How Can I Ever Lose Something (That Never Belonged to Me)	God Was So Good
7067	Radio Four	God Don't Ever Change	Watcha Gonna Do
7068	Allen Flatt	That's What She Wrote	I Wouldn't Even Tell You Goodbye
7069	Edna Gallmon Cooke	Here Is One	Somebody Touched Me
7070	Del Wood	Columbus Stockade Blues	Bye Bye Blackbird
7071	Harris Martin	Love Rhapsody	Laura
7072	J.T. Adams	Hand of God	Precious Lord
7073	Christine Kittrell	The Price You Pay for Love	Snake in the Grass
7074	Mr. Goon	Honeysuckle Rose	Marie
7075	J.T. Adams and J. Ward	Pine Tree Pine over Me	Waltzing Melody
7076	Robert Gill	I Gave All I Had (I Only Had a Little)	Let's Have Some Fun
7077	Clay Eager	Bobaloo (Also issued as Bobbie Lou)	Don't Come Crying on My Shoulder
7078	Bob Hayes	Lonesome Call	I Wanted You Then
7079	Larry Dexter	Throwing Kisses (And Making Eyes at You)	Please Come Back to Me
7080	Jimmy Simpson	Did We Overlook Each Other	Sittin' on the Doorstep
7081	Lucile Barbee	Call Him by His Name	Beautiful Tomorrow
7082	Speer Family	Born Again	Supper Time
7083	Israelite Travelers	It's Alright	Send My Child Home
7084	Pat Boone	I Need Someone	Loving You Madly
7085	Del Wood	It's a Grand Old Flag	When I Lost You
7086	Edna Gallmon Cooke	Jesus Came by Here	Child of the King
7087	Del Wood	I Like Mountain Music	It's a Sin

Label	Artist	Side A	Side B
7088	J.T. Adams	Little Mustard Seed	Taller Than Trees
7089	Bob Harmon	Sad Blues Boogie (vocal by Johnny Viney)	Bye Bye Blues Boogie
7090	Connie and Babe - The Black Mountain Boys	Roll On Blues	Lonely Waltz
7091	Kavaliers	Get That Communist Joe	Good Bye Don't Ever Cry
7092	unknown		
7093	Larry and Jerry	It's Wonderful When You're in Love	Just You and I
7094	Larry Dexter	Skokiaan	Huggin' and Kissin'
7095	Buddy Killen with Band	What'cha Think about It Buddy	Big Jim
7096	Christine Kittrell	Lord Have Mercy	Sittin' Here Drinkin' Again
7097	Gwen Dalton	Notre Dame Victory March	Ragtime Careless Love
7098	Ted West	Parking Worries	If You'll Only Smile
7099	Lee Bonds and His Dixieland Quartet	Jesus Is My Leader	There Is a Crown
7100	Harris Martin	Over the Rainbow	September Song
7101	Four Bars	Memories of You	When Did You Leave Heaven
7102	The Clips with Band	Wish I Didn't Love You So	Your Lovin' Moves Me
7103	Tommy Smith	Magic Girl	Tinkerbell
7104	J.T. Adams and the Men of Texas	In That Great Gettin' Up	Heavenly Love
7105	Del Wood	Are You from Dixie	There Is a Tavern in the Town
7106	Connie and Babe - The Black Mountain Boys	How Well the Flowers Bloom	Last Love Letter
7107	Larry Dexter	Cause I Love You (and Betty Jo Foster)	Mambo Reminds Me of You
7108	Lucile Barbee	My Love Ones Are Waiting	Little More Faith and Grace
7109	Christine Kittrell	Leave My Man Alone	Call His Name
7110	Ruby Lee	The Day Before the Night That I Cried	The Mambo Reminds Me of You
7111	Bernard Hardison	Too Much	Come to Me Baby
7112	Sandra Mead	Take a Look at Me	Confession of My Heart
7113	J.T. Adams	In the Garden	Wonderful
7114	Bob Harmon	Begin the Beguine Boogie	Snag Rag Shuffle
7115	unknown		
7116	Mr. Goon	Goon Bones Ditty	Sweet Sue
7117–7118	unknown		
7119	Pat Boone	My Heart Belongs to You	I Need Someone
7120	Red Kirk	Red Lipped Girl	Davy Crocket Blues
7121	Glenn Reeves	The Last Time	That'll Be Love
7122	The Kelleys	Leaving Tennessee	Devils Little Angel
7123	Jim Lucas	My Favorite Doll	Tutti Frutti
7124	Marshall Pack	Mail Order from Heaven	When I Sit Down with God
7125	Christine Kittrell	Black Cat Crossed My Trail	If You Ain't Sure
7126	Bill Carter	You Ain't Got My Address	By the Sweat of My Brow
7127	Billy Wallace	I Can't Run Away (From These Blues)	That Old Love of Yours
7128	unknown		
7129	Lloyd McCollough	Cause I Love You	Gonna Love My Baby
7130	Lou Millet	Slip Slippin' In	Shorty the Barber
7131–7133	unknown		
7134	Whitey Gallagher	Searching (I'm Always Looking)	Gotta Roam

Label	Artist	Side A	Side B

Select (250 series) (Popular)
First issue: 1948
Last known: 1950

250–253	unknown		
254	Dottie Dillard with Owen Bradley and His Orchestra	Save That Confederate Money Boys	Put Your Shoes On Lucy
255	Dottie Dillard with Owen Bradley and His Orchestra	I Didn't Know the Gun Was Loaded	Let the Good Things Happen
256	unknown		
257	Bob Johnstone (and His Dixie Doodlers)	Nashville's Such a Friendly Place	
	Dottie Dillard (and Her Dixie Doodlers)		Nashville's Such a Friendly Place

Speed (100 series) (Country)
First issue: March 1951
Last known: 1954

100	Georgia Jim	Jig Saw Puzzle Heart	Flyin' Saucer Baby
101	Lattie Moore	Juke Joint Johnny	It's Good Enough for You
102	Georgia Jim	Fryin' Pan Boogie	Three Angels
103	Tennessee Slim	Dog House Blues	It's Raining Tears
104	Joedy Lea	The Devil Paid Me (With a Mother in Law)	Sweet Little Baby
105	Lattie Moore	My First Love	Baby I'll Soon Be Gone
106	Tennessee Slim	It's Your Turn to Cry	I'm an Old Wolf
107	Shorty Sergent	Night Life and Wine	You'd Better Think Again
108	Chickie King	O-O-O-H	Lov-ie Lov-ie
109	Tex Cronas	A Diamond Ring	Patches on My Heart
110	Betty Jo	You'll Need My Help	Fairyland of Love
111	Jack Toombs	Pin Ball Fever	I Can't Stop Lovin' You
112	Little Bun Wilson	Confess That You're Mine	Indiana Girl
113	Tennessee Slim	One Sided Love Affair	Crazy Hazy Kisses
114	Bobby Helms	Yesterday's Lovin'	Hangin' Around
115	Bob Rogers	Little Bit Late for Lovin'	I Want to Be Babied (By a Gal Like You)
116	Little Bun Wilson	I Lost My Heart	This Lesson of Love
117	Bobby Helms	Freedom Lovin' Guy	I've Never Seen Anyone (Like You)

Speed (300 series) (R&B)
First issue: 1952
Last known: 1952

300	Charles Ruckles and His Orchestra	Pitch a Boogie Woogie	I Got a Feelin'

Tennessee (100 series) (Gospel, Blues, and R&B)
First issue: December 1950
Last known: November 1952

100	Wings Over Dixie	Christ Is All	Uncloudy Day
101	Wings Over Dixie	Ride On King Jesus	What a Blessing

Label	Artist	Side A	Side B
102	Wings Over Dixie	Working on the Building	Freedom After Awhile
103	Wings Over Dixie	I'm Coming Home	Just a Closer Walk
104	Wings Over Dixie	In the Upper Room	I Must Tell Jesus
105	Radio Four	On My Journey Now	Get Back Jordan
106	Derrick Singers	Do You Know Him	He Delivered Me
107	Derrick Singers	Stand by Me	Go Ahead
108	Louis Brooks and the Downbeats	Almost Boogie	Wine Hangover
109–110	unknown		
111	Bernard Hardison	Hey Little Girl	Love You Baby
112	Billie McAllister with the Bernard Hardison Band	Walking in a Daze	I Go for That
113	Helen Foster with Louis Brooks and Band	I Got a Big Fat Daddy	Blues after Sunset
114	Bernard Hardison	Pretty Eyed Baby Blues	I Want
115	Radio Four	I'll Meet Mother	Leave It There
116	Gospel Five	Elijah	My Trouble Is Hard
117	Christine Kittrell with Louis Brooks and Band	Don't Do It	Old Man You're Slipping
118	Radio Four	Sending Up This Prayer (Part 1)	Sending Up This Prayer (Part 2)
119	Lucile Barbee	Rock Me in His Bosom	Gonna Wait Right Here
120	Bernard Hardison	Goodby Blues	Now or Never Blues
121	George White	My Gals Got Gold	If I'm Lying I'm Crying
122	Billie McAllister	Well Alright Baby	31 E. Blues
123	Julius King	I Want a Slice of Your Puddin'	If You See My Lover
124	Robert Tucker	Changeable Woman	It Sure Costs Money to Live
125	Radio Four	Somewhere	Seek Seek Seek
126	Louie Brooks	Keep Pushing	One Slow Rock
127	Julius King	Mississippi Boogie	One O'Clock Boogie
128	Christine Kittrell	Sittin' Here Drinkin'	I Ain't Nothing but a Fool
129–132	unknown		
133	Christine Kittrell	Heartache Blues	You Ain't Nothin' but Trouble

Tennessee (711 series) (Country)
First issue: January 1950
Last known: November 1952

711	Ricky Riddle with Hal Bradley and His Band	Second Hand Heart	Somebody's Stealin' My Baby's Sugar
712	Harry Meade	Lonesome Road Blues	Yellow Dog Blues
713	Ricky Riddle with Hal Bradley and His Band	Ain't You Ashamed	Smoke Comes Out My Chimney Just the Same
714	Jimmy Sweeney with rhythm accompaniment	I Gotta Leave This Town	Boogie Woogie Jockey
715	Jimmy Sweeney with string accompaniment	The Song of the Wind	Tobacco Road
716	Wes Holly with string accompaniment	How I Cried	Shadows 'round My Heart
717	Ricky Riddle with Hal Bradley and His Band	Boogie Woogie Tennessee	Price of Love (and Anita Kerr)
718	Randy Hughes with Hal Bradley and His Band	When Elephants Start to Roost in Trees	I'd Rather Be a Rooster
719	Billy Wallace	You Got Some Explaining to Do	Dog Hauled Around
720	Randy Hughes	If I Loved a Liar I'd Hug Your Neck	Guilty Conscience
721	Bob Jennings	Locked Inside My Heart	My Little Blue Eyes

Label	Artist	Side A	Side B
722	Wes Holly	Heavens Are Crying	
	Wes and Joy Holly with Hal Bradley' s Band		Teardrops from My Eyes
723	Jim Wilson and Peggy Carroll	Remember Me (I'm the One Who Loves You)	
	Jim Wilson with Music City Sextet		I've Found My Own
724	Randy Hughes	God Please Protect America	It May Be
725	Doy Hill and Don Williams with Band	I Didn't Mean to Cry	Feeling Sorry
726	Harry Meade	Harry's Blues	I Ain't Got Nobody
727	Carl Tipton	You'd Better Kneel and Pray	Going Home
728	Jack Hardy and the Ranch Boys	I Don't Have Time for You	Oh! Babe
729	Kirk McGee and the Tennessee Volunteers	A Soldier's Last Letter to Joan and Marie	She'll Be Sitting by Jesus Tonight
730–731	unknown		
732	Ricky Riddle with Hal Bradley and His Band	I Got Other Fish to Fry	Take Care
733	Del Wood and Sextet	Nagasagi Boogie	Dreamy Eyes (vocal by Jack Irwin)
734	unknown		
735	Bob Williams and His Band	Hot Rod Race	Morning After Blues
736	Randy Hughes	Tattooed Lady	It'll Feel So Good (When It Quits Hurtin')
737	Sandy Wilson	Whiskey Blues	Please Take My Heart
738	Mississippi Slim	Memorie of You	You're Gona Be Sorry
739	Randy Hughes	Let the Lower Lights Be Burning	Wrap My Body in Old Glory
740	Doy Hill and Bill Russell with Band	My Heart Cries for You	Beautiful Brown Eyes
741	Bob Williams	Waiting for the Tide to Change	Hillbilly Samba
742	Wes Holly	(My Heart Is Like) the Clock	Shufflin' Shoes Boogie
743	Bob Sweeney	With the Wind and the Rain in Your Hair (vocal by Johnnie Harris)	Tennessee Waltz (vocal by Johnnie Harris)
744	Alan Flatt and the Nite Owls	Those Things Money Can't Buy	Cheat, Cheat, Cheatin'
745	Mississippi Slim and the Nite Owls	Beer Drinkin' Blues	I'm Through Crying over You
746	Bob Williams and Del Wood, Bill Russell, Dick Stratton	What Am I Doing Down Here	
	Bob Williams		Crackers, Cheese and Beer
747	Billy Wallace	Reservations for Your Soul	There's a Hand Reaching Out from the Cross
748	Buddy Allen and the Nite Owls	Shine, Shave, Shower	Look What Thoughts Will Do
749	Don Davis and the Nite Owls	If You Did Half as Much Flirtin'	My Life with You
750	Dick Stratton and the Nite Owls	If You Want Some Lovin'	Somebody Robbed My Beehive
751	Harry Meade	Lula's Back in Town	Frankie and Johnny
752	John Talley and the Nite Owls	Look What Thoughts Will Do	Shine, Shave, Shower
753–754	unknown		
755	Peggy Carroll and Billy Wilson	Forever and Always	Love Is Just a Sometimes Thing
756	Bob Williams and the Nite Owls	Hot Rod Race No. 2	So Don't You Weep
757	Carl Cheek	You Can't Hide Your Love	You'll Always Be Brand New
758	Ricky Riddle	Cold Icy Feet	Lost
759	Ricky Riddle	The Old Rugged Cross	He Bought My Soul
760	Bob Williams	Pabst Blue Ribbon Beer	Pabst Blue Ribbon Beer (same both sides)
761	Helen Carter and Don Davis	Sparrow in the Treetop	Counterfeit Kisses
762	unknown		

Label	Artist	Side A	Side B
763	Del Wood	Wabash Blues	Please Don't Talk about Me
764	Kenny Martin and the Nite Owls	My Heart Is in Your Hands	I Want to Be with You Always
765	Babe Neely with the Nite Owls	Bab's Boogie	Turkey in the Straw
766	Carl Tipton	Pray, Pray, Pray	We Will Rise and Shine
767	Joy and Wes Holly	Oh My Darlin' How I Love You	Truly I Love You
768	Ricky Riddle	I Wish I May, I Wish I Might	Does Your Heart Have a Guarantee
769	unknown		
770	Bob Williams	Our Last Goodby	Pickup Truck
771	Bob Williams	I've Lived My Life Alone	Hot Rod Race No. 3
772	Bob Williams and His Band	Rhumba Boogie	
	Carl Cheek with the Nite Owls		Kentucky Waltz
773	Rebe and Rabe and the Happy Valley Boys	That Gloryland Mansion in the Sky	My Ship Will Sail
774	Helen Carter	I'm All Broke Out with Love	There's a Right Way, a Wrong Way
775	Del Wood	Down Yonder	Mine, All Mine
775	(later pressings) Del Wood	Down Yonder	Dreamy Eyes
776	Dick Stratton and the Nite Owls	Love, Love, Love	Sugar-Coated Love
777	Dick Stratton and the Nite Owls	I Ain't Cryin' over You	
	Randy Hughes and the Nite Owls		Roll On Freight Train
778	Randy Hughes and His Band	Easy Monthly Payment Blues	No Trespassing
779	Helen Carter and Bob Eaton		As Long as You Believe in Me Little Darling
	Bob Eaton with Band	I'm Crying at the Moon Tonight	
780–781	unknown		
782	Carl Runner	I've Got Time on My Hands	Intoxicated Harmony
783	Allen Flatt	No Darlin'	All I Lack Being a Monkey
784–785	unknown		
786	Ricky Riddle	Sun Kissed Cutie	Heartsick
787	Randy Hughes	Birthday Cake	Sweetly, Neatly and So Completely
788	Rebe and Rabe	Weapon of Prayer	Lord, You've Heard a New Voice Now
789	Helen Carter and Grant Turner	Heaven's Decision (featuring Del Wood at piano)	You Can't Stop Me from Dreaming
790	Fred Henderson and the Valley Troubadores	I'm in the Doghouse Now	Yellow Moon in the Sky
791	Tiny Bennett and Blackie Bennett and His Band	Boogie Woogie Plowboy	Every Time I See a Rose
792	Bob Pettus and Blackie Bennett and Band	I've Shed a Million Tears	Don't Leave Me Alone
793	Martin and Brown (The Harmonica Duo)	Darktown Strutters Ball	I'll See You in My Dreams
794	Mississippi Slim and the Nite Owls	I'm a Long Gone Doggie	I Know You Can't Be True
795	Dick Stratton and the Nite Owls	Pistol Boogie	Just Wait and See
796	Toby Dowdy	Cheatin' On Your Baby	I'd Cut Your Water Off
797	Bill Russell and the Nite Owls	I Don't Want You Anymore	Let's Start All Over Again
798	Kirk McGee and His Band	Ramblers Blues	It's Too Late to Change Your Mind
799	"Mr. Goon"	Bile Dem Cabbage Down	Just Because
800	Del Wood	Rainbow	Ragtime Melody
801	Ricky Riddle	I'm So Lonesome	If Tears Were Music
802	Randy Hughes	Talking in Your Sleep	My Little Country Rose
803	unknown		

Label	Artist	Side A	Side B
804	Lee Bond	Uh Huh Honey	You've Been Cryin,' Sweetheart
805	Del Wood	Jingle Bells	Here Comes Santa Claus
806	Sonny Sims	Down at the Old Square Dance	Bouncing Baby Boy
807	Dinning Brothers	Winter Wonderland	Give Me You for Christmas
808	Kirk McGee	Don't Fool around My Baby	Missing in Action
809	Jim Sweeney and the Dinning Brothers	It's Goodbye Again	It's Needless
810	Dinning Brothers	The Senator from Tennessee	Time
811	Helen Carter	Fiddlin' Around	I'm Thinking Tonight of My Blue Eyes
812	Johnny Rowland	Where the Bright Lights Glow	With a Heart Full of Misery
813	Roy Hall	Golden Slippers	Back Up and Push
814	Del Wood	Give My Regards to Broadway	Beer Barrel Polka
815	Del Wood	Peter Cottontail	Easter Parade
816	Snooky Lanson	Stay Away from Dixieland	Time
817	unknown		
818	Allen Flatt	There's Romance in My Heart	I'll Have the Last Laugh Yet
819	Vaughn Brothers	I've Gone and Done It Again	Was It Worth It
820	unknown		
821	Jimmy Richardson	Chinese Breakdown	Alexander's Ragtime Band
822	Randy Hughes	Not Big Enough	Tapping That Thing
823	Martin and Brown (The Harmonica Duo)	Sweet Georgia Brown	Don't Blame Me
824	unknown		
825	Jimmy Combs	I Left My Lord at Calvary	Unseen Hand
826	Lee Bonds	For Sale - One Broken Heart	Wild Cattin' Woman
827	Mississippi Slim	Queen for a Day	Tired of Your Lies
828	Carl Runner	You'll Never Think of Me	No Money
829	Billy Wallace and the Nite Owls	Southwind	I'm Gona Turn You a'Loose
830	Edgar Clayton	Just Have Your Way	Our Love's Not What It Used to Be
831	Rebe and Rabe with Band	Helen	You Didn't Say Goodbye
832	Dinning Brothers	unknown title	unknown title
833	Del Wood and "Mr. Goon"	Shanty Town	
	Del Wood		Nobody's Sweetheart Now
834	Bob Williams	We're Steppin' Out Tonight	Be Mine
835	Roy Hall	John Henry	Put on Your Old Grey Bonnet
836	Rebe and Rabe	Mother Sweet Mother	Land of Eternal Peace
837	Floyd Huffman	What Would I Do without You	Twice the Loving
838	Bob Eaton	I Love You	Don't You Know Me Anyhow
839–840	unknown		
841	Rebe and Rabe and the Sunny Valley Boys	I Couldn't Stand to Hear You Say 'I Do'	My Empty Arms
842–843	unknown		
844	Harry Meade	Sittin' on Top of the World	White House Blues
845	Del Wood	Listen to That Band	
	Del Wood and "Mr. Goon"		Waiting for the Robert E. Lee
846–847	unknown		
848	Del Wood	Waiting for the Robert E. Lee	Listen to the Band

Label	Artist	Side A	Side B

Tennessee (1000 series) (Country)
First issue: 1951
Last known: 1952

1000	John Daniel Quartet	Just a Rose Will Do	A Song in My Heart
1001	Bobby Joe and Joyce	Ain't Got Time	Reaping Heartaches
1002	unknown		
1003	Carter Sisters	No No It's Not You	Sweet Talking Man

Tennessee Jamboree (3000 series) (Country)
First issue: 1954
Last known: 1954

3000	Tommy Smith	Mexico	Melody of Love

Village (500 series) (Country Gospel)
First issue: March 1949
Last known: 1950

500	The Sunshine Boys	Lord Build Me a Cabin in Glory	When God Dips His Love in My Heart
501	The Sunshine Boys	Lead Me to That Rock	Danger Zone
502	The Sunshine Boys	Glory Train	He´11 Understand and Say Well Done
503	The Sunshine Boys	Sinners Plea	The Lord Is Coming By and By
504	Goodwill Carter Family	Closer Walk with Thee	When We Walk the Stairs of Gold
505	John Daniel Quartet	Thy Will Be Done	Gonna Coast to Gloryland
506	John Daniel Quartet	Little Boy Blue	Just a Closer Walk with Thee
507	Rev. A. D. Barrett and Miss Margie Barrett (piano)	Let Not Your Heart Be Troubled	
	Edie Palmer		My Sins Are Gone
508	Goodwill Carter Family	When I Make My Last Move	This World Is Not My Home

Wally Fowler (1000 series) (Country Gospel)
First issue: circa 1951
Last known: circa 1952
Note: Fowler issued further discs including 1052, 1064, 1066, 1068, but probably after 1955.

1000	Happy Goodman Family	Lead Me to That Rock	Just a Closer Walk with Thee
1001	Happy Goodman Family	When God's Chariot Comes Home	Telling My Blues Goodbye
1002	Oak Ridge Quartet	Whispering Hope	You Ain't Got Faith
1003	Happy Goodman Family	I Don't Mind	He'll Understand and Say Well Done
1004	Happy Goodman Family	Looking for a City	I'm Free Again
1005	Happy Goodman Family	When God´s Chariot Comes Home	Telling My Blues Goodbye
1006	Wally Fowler	I'll Be No Stranger There	The Funeral
1007	unknown		
1008	Wally Fowler	When They Ring the Golden Bells	unknown title
1009	Wally Fowler and the Oak Ridge Quartet	Hold to God's Unchanging Hand	unknown title
1010	Wally Fowler and the Oak Ridge Quartet	No Pass to Heaven	Perfect Joy

World (1500 series) (Country)
First issue: August 1948
Last known: December 1949

Label	Artist	Side A	Side B
1500	unknown		
1501	Buck Buchanon and the Rhythm Rogues	You Call Everybody Darlin' (vocal by Jimmy Allen)	Buck's Boogie
1502	Red Gilliam and His Texas Pals	Hair of Gold	You'll Always Be My Sweetheart
1503	Bob Jennings and the Eagle Rangers	That Old Moon Seems to Know	Be My Darling
1504	Bob Jennings and the Eagle Rangers	Is It True	Say You'll Be Mine
1505	unknown		
1506	Buck Buchanon and the Rhythm Rogues	Cornbelt Symphony	Rogues Gallery
1507	Buck Buchanon and the Rhythm Rogues	Life Gets Tee-Jus, Don't It	Lover's Blues
1508	Harry Blair and the Eagle Rangers	Dear Okie	Too Many Lies
1509	unknown		
1510	Buddy Pelham	Shortenin' Bread Boogie	By Blue Eyed Baby
1511	unknown		
1512	Jim Haynes	Sometimes	I Don't Know Why I Have to Cry
1513	Rusty Gilbert and the Louisiana Swing Boys	Please Don't Let Me Love You	Lovesick Blues
1514	Rusty Gilbert and the Louisiana Swing Boys	New Orleans Stomp (vocal Jim Dunningham)	Up Jumped the Boogey Man (vocal Roy Heflin)
1515	unknown		
1516	Bob Jennings	You Sweet Little You	Memories Are My Souvenirs
1517	Bob Jennings and the Farm Hands	One Hundred Dreams	One Sweetheart Too Many
1518	Catawba Valley Boys	Why Don't You Weep	The Glory Road
1519	unknown		
1520	Big Jeff	After We Are Through	Poppin' Bubble Gum

World (2500 series) (R&B and Gospel)
First issue: August 1948
Last known: September 1949

2500	unknown		
2501	Don Q. and His Orchestra	Tom, Tom the Piper's Son (vocal by Jimmy Brown)	I Ain't Lookin' (vocal by Jimmy Brown)
2502–2503	unknown		
2504	Olive Brown	Just a Drag	I'm Lonesome Tonight
2505	Four Gabriels	Recess in Heaven	Gloria
2506	Four Gabriels	How Many Times	Every Year
2507–2508	unknown		
2509	P. Dawson	I Give Up All My Sins	I Have a Friend
2510	P. Dawson	On the Battlefield	I Have Tried
2511–2512	unknown		
2513	Reverend W.M. Anderson and the Jordan River Singers	Jesus on the Main Line	When We Get Over Yonder

Label	Artist	Side A	Side B

World (1650 series) (Jazz)
First issue: possibly 1949
Last known: possibly 1949

1650	unknown		
1651	Burt Henry and Septet	Blues Impromptu	Roll Ohio

World (1400 series) (Country and R&B)
First issue: 1953
Last known: 1953
Note: The following World 1400 series was a different label from the three series above.

1400	unknown		
1401	Bob White and the Folklanders	String Band Boogie	Time (Can Never Change My Love for You)
1402	Ted Jarrett with Daddy Dean Orchestra	Love Me a Long Long Time	The Road
1403	Bob White	Hide and Seek	My Heart Depends on You

WSM (100 series) (Country, and Country Gospel)
First issue: circa 1950
Last known: circa 1950

100	unknown		
101	Mary and Curly with Earl Ketchum's Circle A Ranch Gang	Yesterday's Memories	Saturday Nite Waltz
102–106	unknown		
107	Happy Goodman Family	I Don't Mind	unknown title

Index of Song Titles

Index of Names and Places

Page numbers in bold italic indicate photographs.

Nashville's Jukebox: 1945–1955

Twenty Shots in the Dark

Some of the people and places covered in this book are well known. Others are quite obscure. My words, and other people's photographs, have indicated in this book who was important, for what, and why. But there is nothing like hearing the music and putting it alongside the story and the images.

The enclosed CD represents your own little jukebox of Nashville music, twenty typical songs aimed by local record companies at the emerging music markets of the postwar United States. The discs' fates ranged from international acclaim to obscurity, but each had the same chance on the day they were released more than fifty years ago. They sit side by side here as equals, examples of the musical styles that once filled Nashville's jukeboxes and airwaves.

1. **Zeb's Mountain Boogie**
   Brad Brady and His Tennesseans
   Bullet 600
   Issued in early 1946 and re-launched in April 1946
   (Zeb Turner / Wally Fowler)
   Universal-Songs of Polygram Int., Inc. (BMI)
   Courtesy of Rachel Bulleit

The first record issued commercially by Bullet records, this is an entertainingly successful amalgamation of elements of Owen Bradley's swing-jazz band and the hot folk-music guitar of Zeb Turner. It wasn't pure jazz, and it certainly wasn't what people now call country. It was a fitting start to a period of eclectic recording in Nashville that simply doesn't bear out some of the myths about the town and its music.

2. **Nashville Jumps**
   Cecil Gant
   Bullet 250
   Issued April 1946
   (Cecil Gant)
   Courtesy of Rachel Bulleit

Kicking off Bullet's "sepia" music series, this disc was one of the first to put black Nashville on the musical map. Cecil Gant was a big name when he recorded this vocal-and-piano tour de force, extolling the virtues of Cedar Street (later renamed Charlotte Avenue) and its associated good times. There was no real tradition of old-time blues in Nashville, and this was city music for the moment.

3. **Jealous Hearted Me**
Minnie Pearl with Pee Wee King
and the Golden West Cowboys
Bullet 613
Issued August 1946
(A.P. Carter)
Peer International Corp. (BMI)
Courtesy of Rachel Bulleit

This was one example of Bullet's attempt to corner the market in stars from WSM's Grand Ole Opry. Minnie Pearl typified the variety show, family-oriented aspects of the Opry. She didn't sing much, but when she did it would likely be a traditional mountain song or a string of nonsense couplets like these collected by A. P. Carter back at the start of commercialized folk music. Pee Wee King's western swing band played a commercial blend of all country styles and wasn't atypical for the period, even in Nashville.

4. **Headin' for the Pearly Gates**
John Daniel Quartet
Bullet 102
Issued January 1947
(Roman Rand Self)
Roman Rand Music (BMI)
Courtesy of Rachel Bulleit

In their country-gospel series, Bullet Records sought to promote famous local radio performers, and their records were every bit as important at the time as the label's hillbilly and blues series. There were no sales charts for this music, but it sold hugely by mail order and at personal appearances. The John Daniel Quartet was about as tight, organized and in-demand as a gospel group could be at the time, selling the good word over the radio while retaining their genuine motivation and tradition.

5. **Near You**
Francis Craig and His Orchestra
(with vocal by Bob Lamm)
Bullet 1001
Issued March 1947
(Kermit Goell / Francis Craig)
Supreme Music Corp. (ASCAP)
Courtesy of Rachel Bulleit

Almost two discs in one, with its separate solo and full band portions, this record was one of those accidental hits that went regional, national, and then international. Nobody could say why, but everyone was singing it. Francis Craig's orchestra typified the strong tradition of sweet music in Nashville's dinner clubs and on its radio stations, operating in the space between jazz and popular ballads.

6. **Standing in the Safety Zone**
Fairfield Four
Bullet 284
Issued April 1948
Courtesy of Rachel Bulleit

Black gospel music sold almost as well as country gospel, and the Fairfield Four was one of the great singing groups at the heart of the evolution toward modern gospel music. Bullet captured the group at its best, with the stirring lead voice of Sam McCrary carrying their soulful message to an eager audience. The Fairfield Four has survived as a leading name in Nashville's music into the current century.

7. **Lost Highway**
Leon Payne
Bullet 670
Issued October 1948
(Leon Payne)

Courtesy of Rachel Bulleit

Leon Payne was one of the great early singer-songwriters in country music, back when it was still called folk or western music. This song—his song—became one of the classics of country music via Hank Williams, who followed Payne's arrangement and style to the letter. A fine vocalist, Payne carried an influential band of young Texan musicians at that time.

8. **Tom, Tom, the Piper's Son**
Don Q and his Orchestra
(with vocal by Jimmy Brown)
World 2501
Issued October 1948
Public Domain
Courtesy of Ogden and McNeill Stokes

This long-lost gem of early Nashville R&B survives in very few copies. It showcases the band of Don Q. Pullen, a linchpin of Nashville's black music scene. It's a jivey, jazzy blues with a number of classy brass solos and a fine vocal. Pullen rarely recorded, and World Records achieved quite a coup in capturing him on disc for the first time.

9. **Save That Confederate Money Boys**
Dottie Dillard with the
Owen Bradley Orchestra
Select 254
Issued 1948/49
(Eleanor Fort)
Mutual Music (BMI)
Courtesy of Dottie Dillard

Something of a quirky period piece, this disc was firmly in the mainstream of Nashville music. It showcases Owen Bradley's swinging band, heard on WSM almost daily, and features the period's outstanding local pop vocalist, Dottie Dillard. Written for a projected musical stage show, the retro lyric is a lot of fun in that context. "If at first you don't secede"—great line.

10. **After We Are Through**
    Big Jeff and the Radio Playboys
    World 1520
    Issued July 1949
    (G.F. Bess)
    Peer International Corp. (BMI)
    Courtesy of Ogden and McNeill Stokes

G. F. (Jeff) Bess was for years a fixture on Nashville's WLAC radio as a singer and announcer. His bands included everyone who wanted to be somebody in the emerging world of country music, and his records were almost always superb, if never hits. This distinguished midtempo ballad stands comparison with anything the major labels were recording.

11. **Rag Mop**
    Johnnie Lee Wills and His Boys
    Bullet 696
    Issued November 1949
    (Deacon Anderson / Johnnie Lee Wills)
    Unichappell Music, Inc. (BMI)
    Courtesy of Rachel Bulleit

Another one-off pop hit, this music was typical of Bullet Records in its heyday—a Nashville label, but eclectic in content. Swing jazz had its finest western music expression in Johnnie Lee Wills's band, and this catchy record has a stomping beat and swinging steel and string sections.

12. **Boogie Woogie Jockey**
    Jimmy Sweeney
    Tennessee 714
    Issued May 1950
    (Jimmy Sweeney)
    Shelby Singleton Music, Inc. (BMI)
    Courtesy of Kirk Beasley

Tennessee Records was a new label when this song came out, and how better to get airplay than with a song extolling the virtues of the top local radio DJ, Gene Nobles? This was at the smoother end of Nobles's programming, but he must have liked the song, for he provides the spoken vocal interjection. Jimmy Sweeney was perhaps the first black singer and songwriter to make a living at the heart of Nashville's commercial music scene, and he has an impressive group of pop and country players behind him here.

13. **Music City USA**
    Dick Stratton and the Nite Owls
    Jamboree 510
    Issued August 1950
    (Billy Beasley / Dick Stratton / Ray Anderson)
    Shelby Singleton Music, Inc. (BMI)
    Courtesy of Kirk Beasley

This could—maybe should—have been developed into Nashville's theme song. Bill Beasley recalled writing the song as a theme for Dick Stratton's part on the *Hayloft Jamboree* radio show on WKDA—maybe that's why the better-known shows and stations wouldn't pick up on the tune. Stratton kept a good group of country musicians, and they were responsible for scores of hillbilly discs made in this period.

14. **I'm a Bible Lovin' Man**
    Wally Fowler and His Oak Ridge Quartet
    Bullet 116
    Issued February 1951
    (Don McCrossan)
    Universal—Songs of Polygram, Inc. (BMI)
    Courtesy of Rachel Bulleit

Wally Fowler steered Bullet Records' gospel-music output for many years, promoting the songs on WSM radio and even running a Record of the Month Club for a time. His stage shows were entertaining affairs, with folksiness and humor set alongside the gospel fervor. With its slightly tongue-in-cheek style, this song was a stage-show favorite.

15. **Down Yonder**
    Del Wood
    Tennessee 775
    Issued June 1951
    (L. Wolfe Gilbert)
    La Salle Music Publishers Inc. (ASCAP)
    Courtesy of Kirk Beasley

A top-seller in 1951, this was probably the biggest independent Nashville disc since "Near You." It was the tip of an iceberg of honky-tonk piano solos that took hold of Nashville recording sessions in the wake of Dot's success on jukeboxes with Johnny Maddox. Del Wood's rinky-tink piano sound was de rigueur for several years behind any number of pop and country recordings.

16. Birthday Cake
Randy Hughes
Tennessee 787
Issued July 1951
Courtesy of Kirk Beasley

Tennessee Records aimed at jukebox sales as much as at home record buyers. Singer Randy Hughes dealt in being unusual, in being first, in cashing in on whatever angle presented itself. Risqué "party" records were no exception, and this is a prime example of the salacious style.

17. The Price You Pay for Love
Christine Kittrell
Republic 7073
Issued March 1954
(Ted Jarrett / Christine Kittrell)
Babb Publishing Company (BMI)
Courtesy of Kirk Beasley

Picking only one of Christine Kittrell's Tennessee / Republic recordings from the early 1950s is difficult, because together they covered the full range of blues and R&B styles, and all sold well and steadily over time. This song shows off Kittrell's intense vocal style and approach, with her spoken intro and outro, and it has an unusual and engaging arrangement by Ted Jarrett, Nashville's first black record producer.

18. That's What She Wrote
Allen Flatt with string band
Republic 7068
Issued February 1954
(Jesse Rogers)
Golden West Melodies, Inc. (BMI)
Courtesy of Kirk Beasley

Allen Flatt was part of the glue that held the early Nashville record business together, and he helped draw the blueprint for thousands of would-be hillbilly singers to follow. His skill was to sound, when he wanted to, exactly like the big star Ernest Tubb, and Tennessee Records often told him he wanted to. Tubb himself liked the appositely named Flatt so much that he put him on his weekly radio show.

19. Little More Faith and Grace
Lucile Barbee
Republic 7108
Issued May 1955
(Mertis John, Jr.)
Mertis Music Co. (BMI)
Courtesy of Kirk Beasley

This record was issued in the name of local gospel-radio personality Lucile Barbee, but it was actually a two for one—you got to hear the top-selling Radio Four and their influential lead singer/composer, Morgan Babb, as well. This is a stirring vocal performance by Sister Barbee with fully engaged vocal group interactions that elevated the disc far beyond much of the competition on independent labels.

20. Too Much
Bernard Hardison
Republic 7111
Issued April 1955
(Lee Rosenberg / Bernard Weinman)
© 1956 Elvis Presley Music (BMI) / Southern Belle Music (BMI). Worldwide rights for Elvis Presley Music administered by Cherry River Music Co. (BMI) and Chrysalis Standards, Inc. (BMI)
Courtesy of Kirk Beasley

This jukebox closes at the dawn of the rock & roll era with a song that, when covered by Elvis Presley, helped define the new style. Performed here as a standard R&B song by singer-pianist Bernard Hardison, the disc nevertheless contains all the stylistic elements Presley later copied. This music is as typical and atypical of 1955 as "Zeb's Mountain Boogie" was of 1946.

CREDITS

Thanks to LeAnn Bennett for her tenacity in making this disc a reality; to Alan Stoker for audio supervision, disc transfers, and restorations; to John Sparks, Hollis Flatt, and Alan Stoker at Custom Mastering; and to Michael Gray for pulling together all the recorded sources and loose ends.